Men make their own history, but they do not make it as they please; they do not make it under self-selected circumstances, but under circumstances existing already, given and transmitted from the past. The tradition of all the dead generations weighs like a nightmare on the brains of the living.

– Karl Marx

Germany is now a field of corpses, soon it will be a paradise.

– Georg Büchner

For Oma

CONTENTS

PREFACE

I first became interested in Germany's so-called 1968 generation when I was working as a correspondent for *The Observer* in Berlin in 1999. Gerhard Schröder had just come to power at the head of a "red-green" coalition that was frequently described as a government of *Achtundsechziger*. But what this meant, particularly for German foreign policy, was unclear. It was widely believed that the 1968 generation had forced West Germany to engage with the Nazi past for the first time. And yet some commentators also expected the "red-green" government—the first in the history of the Federal Republic to be led by a chancellor who had no personal memories of World War II—to pursue a foreign policy that was less encumbered by contrition for the Nazi past than that of its predecessors. Increasingly it seemed to me that the 1968 generation had a more ambivalent relationship with the Nazi past than was often assumed.

It is this ambivalent relationship between Germany's 1968 generation and the Nazi past that I seek to explore in this book. My aim, therefore, was not to produce a comprehensive study of the 1968 generation but rather to write a narrative history that focused specifically on the relationship of leading *Achtundsechziger* with the Nazi past. However, although the emphasis is on the relationship of the protagonists to the Nazi past, I do not mean to suggest that the West German student movement can be understood exclusively by reference to the Nazi past. There were clearly also other factors that contributed to the emergence of the student movement, many of which were common to other countries where young people protested in 1968, such as France and the United States, but they are not the primary focus of this book.

The book was written primarily for an English-speaking audience. Although the dramatic story of the Red Army Faction is well known around the world (not least through the 2008 film, *The Baader-Mein-hof Complex*, based on Stefan Aust's definitive book of the same name), the wider history of the movement out of which it emerged remains little known in the English-speaking world. There have been some academic studies in English of the West German student movement and its influence on German politics—notably Andrei S. Markovits and Philip S. Gorski's *The German Left: Red, Green and Beyond*—but they were written before the "red-green" government. More recently, there have also been two English-language political biographies of Joschka Fischer aimed at a wider audience, Paul Berman's *Power and the Idealists*, and Paul Hockenos's *Joschka Fischer and the Making of the Berlin Republic*, that cover some of the same ground as this volume.

However, while many of them are informative and interesting in their own right, most books in English on the 1968 generation have tended to ignore recent research in Germany that has shown the history of the student movement to be more complex and contradictory than had long been thought. Firstly, it has become clear that there was a nationalist current within the student movement, embodied above all by Rudi Dutschke, who, unlike many of his comrades, was preoccupied with the division of Germany. This challenges the assumption that the student movement was an anti-nationalist movement. Secondly, since the publication in 2005 of Wolfgang Kraushaar's very important book *Die Bombe im jüdischen Gemeindehaus*, it is now clear that Dieter Kunzelmann, a leading figure in the Extra Parliamentary Opposition, was behind a bomb placed in the Jewish Community Centre in West Berlin in November 1969. This further complicates our understanding of the 1968 generation's engagement with the Nazi past and, in particular, raises the difficult issue of left-wing anti-Semitism.

These new revelations about the events of the sixties and seventies, which were mostly made towards or after the end of the "red-green" government, have led to a series of heated and somewhat polarising historical debates in Germany in recent years, often involving historians who were also protagonists in the events themselves. But, even in Germany, few people have examined the implications of the new research for our understanding of the influence of the 1968 generation on the foreign policy of the "red-green" government. Part of the aim of this book is therefore to reassess the foreign policy of the Schröder government—and in particular its response to the Kosovo, Afghanistan and Iraq crises—in the light of the more nuanced understanding of the

West German student movement that we now have. I argue that the "red-green" government itself had an ambivalent relationship with the Nazi past that can be traced back to the student movement. This, in fact, was the real influence of 1968 on the "red-green" government.

I have structured this book around the individual biographies of leading members of the 1968 generation. I chose to approach the subject in this way partly because, as a journalist, I was used to exploring ideas through stories involving characters. But I did so also because it seemed to me that the best way to illustrate the competing, contradictory currents within the 1968 generation—and in particular its ambivalent relationship with the Nazi past—was through people. I am aware that the 1968 generation is a somewhat nebulous concept that is used to refer to both a generational cohort and a political movement. In this case, I use it simply as shorthand for the small group of characters about whom I write, all of whom can be connected through their biographies back to the student movement and, I argue, were influenced to a greater or lesser extent and in various different ways by the events and ideas of 1968. It is for the reader to judge whether this approach is successful.

Countless people have inspired, motivated and guided me through the process of writing this book. Duncan Bell and Gary Savage have been an immense help from beginning to end. Arun Kundnani, Helen Pidd, Brendan Simms and Peter Thompson read drafts and provided me with extremely useful suggestions. Stefan Aust, Ze'ev Avrahmi, Peter Barker, Ze'ev Emmerich, David Goodhart, Andrew Granath, Tanja Howarth, Tina Hüttl, Martin Kloke, Karen Leeder, Peter Littger, Philipp Oehmke, Sukhdev Sandhu, Natalie Watts and Naomi Wolf also encouraged and helped me in various ways and at various stages of the process. I am indebted to all the people I interviewed for giving me their time and sharing their experiences and views with me. In particular I would like to thank Ulrich Enzensberger and Tilman Fichter, who not only talked to me at great length, but also helped me get in touch with other former comrades of theirs. I would also like to thank everyone at Hurst who worked on the book, in particular Michael Dwyer, who was extremely supportive from the beginning; Daisy Leitch, who edited the text; and Fatima Jamadar, who designed the cover. I owe my parents a huge debt of gratitude. Finally I would like to thank Trudi Oliveiro and her family, without whom I would not have been to able to begin this project, let alone finish it.

PROLOGUE

WAR, AGAIN

It stank. A protester had let off a stink bomb inside the Seidensticker Arena in Bielefeld, and within minutes an acrid odour had filled the cavernous auditorium. The conference should have started an hour earlier, but the arena was still only half-full, mainly because outside a pitched battle was taking place between angry protesters and riot police, preventing many of the delegates from getting in. Those who had fought their way through and made it inside chatted excitedly among themselves. Others waved banners and blew loudly on whistles. Occasionally there would be sudden shouting in one corner as security staff ejected an intruder from the masses gathered outside. At one point, a dreadlocked streaker ran in front of the stage, stark naked.

On stage, seated at a table alongside other leading members of Germany's Green party waiting for the conference to begin, Joschka Fischer looked weary and resigned. These days, as Fischer travelled across the globe engaged in shuttle diplomacy as the foreign minister of Europe's largest and economically most powerful country, he usually wore a dark three-piece suit with a signet ring on his right index finger—fitting attire for a statesman. But this morning, back among his old friends—and enemies—in the Green party, Fischer had decided to dress down in a steel-grey suit and a black t-shirt—the way he had habitually dressed during his days as an opposition politician a few years earlier. To him, the conference hall in front of him resembled a "witch's cauldron".[1]

The German Greens had gathered in this nondescript industrial town in Westphalia on Ascension Day in April 1999 to discuss war and peace. Seven weeks earlier, NATO had begun bombing Serbia in response to President Slobodan Milosevic's policy of ethnic cleansing

1

in Kosovo, causing inevitable "collateral damage" in the process. Among the aircraft taking part in the NATO air strikes were German Tornado bombers—the first time since World War II that German troops had been sent into combat. On this morning, Fischer, who, like many among his generation, had once called for Germany to leave NATO, would make a plea to his party to approve German participation in the NATO air strikes. If it did so, the Greens, the once-pacifist "anti-party" that had grown out of the movement against nuclear power in the 1970s, would be supporting not only Germany's first military action since World War II, but also NATO's first "out of area" operation without a mandate from the United Nations. It seemed to go against everything they had once stood for. In fact, some Greens thought it would be the end of the party. If, on the other hand, they refused to back Fischer and the party leadership, Germany's first ever "red-green" coalition—often thought of as a government of "1968ers"— would collapse less than six months after it had come into power.

Outside the conference hall several hundred anti-war protesters, who like the politicians and media had converged on Bielefeld to take part in what was about to become a spectacular piece of political theatre, were throwing paint bombs, eggs, and—only in Germany—yoghurt pots at the massed ranks of riot police. The crowd was an unruly mixture of disillusioned former Green party members, hippies and anarchists, who held banners with slogans like "Never again war!" and cartoon drawings depicting Fischer with a Hitler moustache. "Fascists!" they shouted at the arriving Green delegates, who had to fight their way through the ranks of protesters to get in to the conference. One leading Green, Rezzo Schlauch, narrowly escaped being beaten up by a group of anarchists.[2] Fischer himself, meanwhile, had made his way into the arena through the back entrance, flanked by the four secret service men who accompanied him everywhere he went since he had become German foreign minister and vice-chancellor in the autumn of 1998.

At 10.30 am, over an hour later than scheduled, the conference finally began. Suddenly, ten minutes into the introductory speeches, just as the delegates seemed to be settling down, there was a commotion in front of the stage. A figure ran out from the left side of the auditorium towards the stage and hurled a paint bomb at the foreign minister. It was a perfect shot, hitting Fischer on the right side of his head. He reeled and held his head in pain, his jacket now covered in red paint. The man was tackled by Fischer's bodyguards. There were cheers and shouts from the audience. Fischer was obviously shocked but remained seated and grim-faced, clutching his right ear.

It was a shot that Fischer himself might have been proud of back in the early 1970s, when he was a member of Frankfurt's militant, anti-capitalist "Sponti" scene and liked to describe himself as a "professional revolutionary." At that time Fischer and his friend Daniel Cohn-Bendit, the star of the May 1968 *évènements* in Paris, were part of a group called Revolutionary Struggle that frequently clashed with the Frankfurt police. During those clashes—part of an all-out war against the so-called "Auschwitz generation" that had lasted a whole decade—not just paint bombs but also rocks and even Molotov cocktails had frequently flown through the air. Fischer's transformation from 1960s revolutionary to 1990s politician was not unique—in the 1990s, baby boomers with radical pasts were in power all over the West. But no western politician's metamorphosis had been quite so extreme—or loaded with irony—as Fischer's.

And of all the ironies of Fischer's story, the one thrown up by the situation he faced in May 1999 was one of the most dramatic and intriguing. For 30 years, Fischer's generation—the first to grow up after the end of World War II—had been haunted by Germany's Nazi past. They believed passionately that, after its disastrous twentieth-century history, only peace should emanate from German soil, as the Greens put it. "Never again war," in fact, was one of the party's most emotive slogans, going back to the peace movement of the 1980s, which had transformed the Greens into a powerful political force in West Germany. Moreover, Yugoslavia was a country that Germany had occupied in World War II and in which the Nazis had committed terrible atrocities. For many in the Greens, it was a no-go area for Germany's military.

But Fischer saw things differently. Like many of his generation, he had been politicised by his discovery as a teenager of what happened at Auschwitz, which had become a kind of negative reference point for his morality and politics. If Germany stood by and watched as the Serbs "ethnically cleansed" Kosovo of its ethnic Albanian population, did that not mean that it would bear responsibility—again—for genocide? Surely Germany's history gave it a special responsibility, beyond even that of other Western nations, to intervene to prevent another genocide—even if that meant using military force? Fischer was certain of the answer—even though it was very different from the answer he would have given just a few years earlier. Pacifism was no longer enough. "I didn't just learn 'Never again war'," he had said a week after the bombing campaign had started. "I also learned, 'Never again Auschwitz.'"[3]

Others, like the paint-bomb thrower in Bielefeld, saw in Fischer's about-face a metaphor for the betrayal of the entire generation of 1968, the year of political upheavals across the world. Once that generation had dreamed of a better world. Now, the critics believed, it had sold out for the sake of achieving political power, and, in the process turned into exactly what it had once struggled against. Worse still, by invoking what was a uniquely terrible historical event to justify military action, it was "instrumentalising" Auschwitz.

The moral and political dilemma that Fischer faced in the spring of 1999 and that, more broadly, Germany's post-war generation had faced since they had come of age in 1968, was an extreme version of the question that humanity as a whole has faced since first learning of the Nazi death camps. The Holocaust seemed to impose on mankind a moral responsibility to do everything in its power to prevent something similar ever occurring again anywhere in the world. But, how was it possible to do so without comparing Auschwitz with other terrible events taking place at other times and in other places around the world and therefore implicitly relativising it? To put it a different way, was it possible to "historicise" the Nazi past? As the children of those responsible for the Final Solution, Germany's generation of 1968 faced these questions in such an intensified form that they became, for many of them, an existential dilemma.

An hour later, Fischer returned to the stage. Even though he had been a member of the Green party for 17 years, he had never felt fully at home in it—and now less than ever. He was furious at the way that pacifists had turned the conference into an "infernal spectacle".[4] The paint bomb had struck him on the ear and he was later taken to hospital, where it was discovered that his eardrum had been perforated. He had not changed his suit, which was still covered in red paint. One German commentator would later say wore the stain "like the *Pour le Mérite*," Germany's highest military award in World War I.[5]

Fischer could barely hear himself speak as he delivered his speech over jeers and whistles from the back of the auditorium. Almost immediately he was heckled with shouts of "Warmonger!"

"Yes, I'm a warmonger, and next you're going to give Milosevic the Nobel Peace Prize," he fired back, his anger flashing. Fischer knew how to handle heckling. After all, it had once been his own speciality.

Fischer continued calmly and with conviction. He said that he too had wanted a diplomatic solution to the crisis in Kosovo, but despite all his efforts that had proved impossible. He had been to see Milosevic in Belgrade. He had spent two and a half hours talking to him. He had done everything he could do to avoid war. But he had failed.

"Now it's war," he said. "I would never have dreamed that a "red-green" government would be part of a war. But this is a war that has not just been going on for 51 days but since 1992. Peace pre-supposes that people are not being murdered and expelled and that women are not being raped."

Fischer said the unilateral, indefinite ceasefire the anti-war protesters were demanding would be disastrous. It would send the wrong signal to the Serbian president, who would be strengthened rather than weakened. "Where do you get your trust in Milosevic?" he asked the audience. "Where do you get your trust that without massive armed protection, the people [in Kosovo] won't suffer the same fate as the men in Srebrenica, who lie cold in mass graves to this day?" It was a simple choice, he said. "The crux of the issue is not whether we go home with clean consciences or whether we cover each other with paint, but whether we make political decisions that allow the refugees to return home—yes or no."

If the party refused to back him, the Greens would be out of government. Fischer would almost certainly have to choose between his party and his job as foreign minister. And in case there was any doubt about which of the two he considered more important, Fischer spelled out what would happen if the conference rejected the party leadership's motion.

"Just so it's clear," he said, "if that's what you decide, I won't implement it."

"Hypocrite!" came the shouts from the back of the auditorium.

Later that afternoon, the party voted by 444 votes to 318 to support Fischer and defeat the motion demanding an immediate and unconditional end to the bombing. The fragile coalition would remain intact to literally fight another day. Fischer would remain German foreign minister, and a member of the Green party. What, if anything, remained of the dreams of the 1968 generation was another question.

1

CHILDREN OF MURDERERS

At 2.30 in the afternoon on Friday, 2 June, 1967, the Shah of Iran, Mohammed Reza Pahlavi, and his wife Farah Diba appeared in front of West Berlin's City Hall. It was the same place where thousands of Berliners had cheered President John F. Kennedy when he had come to the city and delivered his historic "Ich bin ein Berliner" speech in June 1963. But four years later, attitudes to the United States and its client regimes around the world had dramatically changed. Paid pro-Shah demonstrators—*Jubelperser*—had cheered and waved Iranian flags at Tempelhof airport when the Shah had arrived on a state visit that morning. But outside the city hall, hundreds of protesters, mainly students, had gathered and shouted, "Murderer!"

Like the United States, West Germany had long maintained friendly relations with the Shah, not least because Iran was one of its main sources of oil. The Shah had deposed the nationalist prime minister Mohammed Mossadegh in a CIA-backed coup in 1953 and had instituted a regime of brutal political repression supported by the United States. In preparation for his visit to Berlin, the West German government had closed off roads and taken Iranian opposition figures living in West Germany into preventive custody without any basis in law. It had even allowed the Shah to bring with him agents of the Iranian secret police Savak, who mingled with the demonstrators in front of the City Hall. Some of the demonstrators threw eggs and paint bombs in the direction of the Shah, and were attacked by the Iranian secret service men, who struck them with wooden sticks. The West Berlin police stood by and in some cases even joined in using their own rubber nightsticks.

In the evening, the royal couple was to attend a performance of Mozart's *The Magic Flute* at the Deutsche Oper in the Charlottenburg district. Just before 8 pm, they arrived and entered the opera house. The demonstrators, confined behind a barrier on the other side of the street, threw eggs, tomatoes, paint bombs, and in some cases, rocks. Once the royal couple was safely inside the building and the demonstrators began to leave, fourteen ambulances suddenly appeared in the street. Then the police attacked. The Berlin chief of police Erich Duensing, a former *Wehrmacht* officer, who had been inside watching the opera with the Shah at the time, later described it as "Leberwurst tactics": "If we think of the demonstrators as a Leberwurst," he explained, "we have to stab in the middle so that it squirts out at the ends."[1]

It was the most brutal street battle in Berlin since the end of World War II. The police fired on the demonstrators with water cannon and then chased and hit them with their nightsticks, even those who fell injured to the ground. The ambulances quickly filled with blood-splattered demonstrators, many of them women. As they dispersed, groups of plainclothes officers identified ringleaders—in practice, anyone with a beard or long hair—and arrested them.

At around 8.30 pm, one team of officers confronted a group of demonstrators in a side street around the corner from the opera. Four of them moved into the crowd and wrestled one man to the ground. One of the officers, a 39 year-old policeman in plain clothes named Karl-Heinz Kurras, was holding his pistol with the safety catch off. Suddenly, Kurras fired, and the demonstrator slumped to the ground.

"Are you crazy, shooting here?" one of the other officers shouted at him.

"It just went off," Kurras replied.[2]

The bullet had entered the demonstrator's skull above his right ear, passed through his brain and exited through the top of his head. He was taken to Moabit hospital, where he was pronounced dead. His name was Benno Ohnesorg. He was a 26 year-old student of romance languages at the Free University of Berlin. It was the first time he had ever been on a demonstration. He had got married just six weeks earlier, and his wife, Christa, was pregnant.

However, the Berlin authorities felt they had little to apologise for. "The patience of the city is at an end," Social Democrat mayor Heinrich Albertz declared the next day. "A few dozen demonstrators, students among them, have not only rendered the unfortunate service of abusing and offending a guest of the Federal Republic of Germany, but are also responsible for a death and numerous casualties."[3]

CHILDREN OF MURDERERS

Ohnesorg's death, and the official reaction to it, sent shockwaves through West Berlin's student movement. Later that evening, as rumours began to circulate about what had happened at the opera house, some of the demonstrators gathered at the Ku'damm headquarters of the West Berlin branch of the *Sozialistischer Deutscher Studentenbund* (Socialist German Students League (SDS)), the leading left-wing student group, to discuss how to respond. Shock quickly gave way to rage. Tilman Fichter, a leading member of the West Berlin SDS, would later remember a slim, blonde woman—whom he claimed was Gudrun Ensslin, then a 26 year-old German literature student and later one of West Germany's most wanted terrorists—weeping loudly and shouting: "This fascist state is planning to kill us all. We have to organise resistance. Violence can only be answered with violence. This is the Auschwitz generation—you can't argue with them!"[4]

West Germany was not the only place where the post-war generation was in protest. In the late sixties, young people around the world were protesting against authority. In each location there was a different context: in countries like Czechoslovakia, where socialist governments were in power, the protesters' demands differed greatly from those in capitalist countries such as the United States. Nevertheless there were common themes. Everywhere it was a revolt of the young against the old.[5] And all over the West, at least, the young—led by the baby boomer generation—were protesting against authoritarianism and consumerism, capitalism and imperialism. For Tariq Ali, a leading figure in the campaign against the Vietnam war in Britain, a global movement was coalescing around the idea that "people should be measured not by success or material possessions but by the humanity of their aspirations, that the economy should be reorganised to serve the interests of the many, not the few, and that the destiny of socialism was inseparably intertwined with real freedom and meaningful democracy."[6]

But one thing above all separated the students demonstrating against the Shah in West Berlin in June 1967 from their counterparts in Berkeley, Paris or London. While in the United States the baby boomers had grown up in the shadow of what Tom Brokaw would later call the "greatest generation", Germany had what Gudrun Ensslin called the "Auschwitz generation."[7] And while the German student movement's counterparts in other countries also routinely described their opponents and in particular the establishment as "fascists", in West Germany they were deadly serious.[8] The knowledge of what their parents had done during the war—and what they had failed to do—gave the generational conflict a sharper edge than it had elsewhere. "You don't understand about our parents," Tariq Ali remembers Ulrike Meinhof, a columnist for *konkret*, a West German left-wing magazine, telling him.[9]

What became known as the "1968 generation" or just the "Achtund-sechziger" was actually a tiny group of people, mostly born in the decade between 1938 and 1948.[10] The oldest of them had childhood memories of the war—in some cases traumatic ones. Others had no memories of war at all. But even those who had no memory at all of the Nazi era had grown up knowing that their mothers and fathers were responsible, directly or indirectly, for the most horrific crimes of the twentieth century. This, perhaps, was the root of the strange mix-ture of guilt and moral superiority that was to characterise their gener-ation. Many of them would spend their lives struggling to break free from Nazism while all the time fearing that Nazism was, in fact, "in" them.

Like many of his generation, Rainer Langhans was deeply affected by this sense of being "the child of murderers."[11] Born in 1940, he grew up in Peenemünde on the Baltic coast, where his father, a Nazi party member, was an engineer in an aircraft factory.[12] He believed that post-war Germany was a society that was built "on top of a pile of corpses" and felt an overwhelming need to re-invent it from scratch.[13] After leaving school he briefly attended an elite academy for army officers—where he was taught by former *Wehrmacht* generals—then dropped out and went to West Berlin in 1962 to study psychology and joined the student movement. "We wanted to look deep into our-selves and see if another kind of life was possible because we didn't want to become murderers ourselves," he says. "Our parents had given us life and showed us how to live and love, so we had to assume we had the same murderousness inside us as they did—and we wanted to get it out of us."[14]

Some of the post-war generation challenged their own parents about their role in, and responsibility for, Nazism, but found them unwilling to talk about the past. "They did not speak," remembers Karl-Dietrich Wolff, a leading figure in the student movement whose father had been a judge and a member of the Nazi party.[15] For others, like Langhans himself, the rebellion against the entire "Auschwitz generation" was to become a substitute for a confrontation with their own parents that they were unwilling, or unable, to face. Some, including many of the leaders of the West German student movement, had lost their fathers in the war. But even those fathers who were still around had been completely de-legitimised and had lost any sense of moral authority. In that wider sense, the post-war generation in Germany was a "fatherless" one.[16] As the sociologist Norbert Elias put it, the "national habitus" that normally connected different generations within a country had, as a result of Nazism, been severely weakened.[17]

If what became known simply as "1968" was a "psychodrama" rather than a revolution based on real political grievances, as the French sociologist Raymond Aron has described it, then in West Germany it was largely one in which the trauma of being the children of the so-called "perpetrator generation" was played out.[18] It was a drama that would last for thirty-five years as the "generation of 1968" made their way through life and eventually became the establishment. Some of them would spend their entire lives attempting to escape their fathers' influence and to become the opposite of their fathers—and perhaps in doing so to atone for their fathers' sins. And paradoxically, others became their fathers in the end.

"1968" in Germany was therefore a moral movement before it was a political one. Many among the post-war generation in West Germany gravitated initially to the far left, and in particular to Marxism, as a reaction against the past. It was, as Norbert Elias puts it, a "contrary creed" to that of their fathers and grandfathers. This creed enabled the post-war generation to distance itself from the atrocities of the past, an "antitoxin to Hitler's teachings".[19] But as well as representing a radical rejection of Nazism, Marxism was also a uniquely liberating ideology for the post-war generation in Germany. By blaming capitalism for the emergence of Nazism, Marxism also exonerated the post-war generation—and its parents. As Elias says, it was "the only ideological framework that provided them with an explanation of fascism and at the same time gave them the feeling that they had nothing to do with the past and that they were free of all guilt."[20]

For the next thirty years, some members of Germany's post-war generation would continue to be haunted by the prospect of the genocide symbolised by Auschwitz repeating itself, both in Germany and in other far-flung corners of the world. Torn between the dream of a socialist Utopia and the nightmare of the Holocaust, it would go through a series of convulsions as it wrestled with what it meant to be German after Auschwitz. More than in any other country, therefore, the struggle of the post-war generation in West Germany was an existential one. The students coming of age in 1968 did not merely dream of a better world as some of their counterparts in other countries did; they felt compelled to act to save Germany from itself. It was an all-or-nothing choice: Utopia or Auschwitz.

Growing up, the post-war generation had been surrounded by silence about the Nazi past. After the end of the war, with the country in ruins, most Germans had simply wanted to forget. 1945 became "zero hour", a new beginning from which a democratic Germany would come into existence—at least in the zones of the country occupied by the British, Americans and French. In 1949, West Germany was created with Bonn as its capital, and the Christian Democrat former mayor of Cologne, Konrad Adenauer, who had been ousted in 1933 and imprisoned by the Nazis, was elected as its first chancellor. Adenauer, who was to remain in office for the next fourteen years, was spectacularly successful in reconstructing and rehabilitating West Germany. With the Cold War looming, West Germany was allowed to re-arm and join NATO in 1955, institutionalising what became known as the *Westbindung*—West Germany's integration into the West. Adenauer's economics minister, Ludwig Erhard, who was later to succeed him briefly as chancellor, helped to create the "economic miracle" that brought unprecedented affluence to West Germans. As prosperity replaced austerity, citizens became consumers.

But although the concept of a "zero hour" suggested a complete break with the past, beneath the democratic, affluent surface of West German society, disturbing traces of the Nazi regime had persisted. Under the pressure of reconstructing West Germany, Adenauer had, after 1949, effectively ended any real engagement with the past.[21] The war crimes trials begun by the Allies were largely dropped and convicted war criminals were released. Civil servants who had been dismissed in 1945 because of "post-war events", as one piece of legislation euphemistically put it, were reinstated or compensated. By the mid-1950s, many of those involved in the Nazi regime had been reintegrated into society; the elite in the civil service, the judiciary and in academia was largely the same as during the Third Reich. Former

Nazis even held some of the highest offices in post-war West Germany. For example, Heinrich Lübke, the German president from 1959, had built arms factories for Albert Speer's armaments ministry (including the underground complex where V-2 rockets were built) using slave labour during the war.[22] The most disturbing case of all was that of Hans Globke, one of Adenauer's closest advisers and the state secretary in the chancellor's office, who, as an official in the interior ministry, had written the official commentary to the 1935 Nuremberg laws and had come up with the idea of forcing all Jewish males to adopt the name "Israel" and all females to adopt the name "Sarah".[23]

The German mentality in the post-war period was described by two psychologists, Alexander and Margarete Mitscherlich, in *The Inability To Mourn*, a Freudian analysis of Germany's response to the end of Nazism published in 1967. The majority of Germans, they claimed, were in denial about the Nazi past and in particular the Holocaust. During the Nazi era, Germans had identified completely with Hitler, blindly followed him, committed crimes in his name, and were even prepared to die for him. In psychological terms, the *Führer* had become their collective Ego Ideal. After his death, Germans should therefore have mourned him. But this did not happen. Instead, they simply eliminated the Nazi past from their collective consciousness and focused instead on re-building Germany. "Industriousness and its success soon covered the open wounds left behind by the past," they said.[24] In other words, most Germans were pretending that Hitler and Nazism had never existed.

Gradually, however, the ghosts of the past became impossible to ignore. From the second half of the 1950s onwards, the German Democratic Republic (GDR), which regarded itself as "anti-fascist" and the Federal Republic as the successor state of the Third Reich, had begun exposing the Nazi pasts of leading figures in West German public life, especially in the judiciary. In 1959, partly with source material provided by the East Germans, a West Berlin student named Reinhard Strecker put on an exhibition that revealed the Nazi pasts of leading West German judges.[25] The exhibition was intended as a protest against the statute of limitations in West Germany, which would have made it impossible to continue to mount prosecutions for most crimes committed during the Nazi era after the end of 1959. The exhibition, which travelled to various German cities and later to Holland and the United Kingdom, caused a major controversy. As a result, the West German parliament agreed to extend the statute of limitations.

In 1960, the Israeli secret service Mossad captured Adolf Eichmann—the SS officer instrumental in planning and executing the Final Solution—in Buenos Aires where he had been living under a false identity since fleeing Germany after the end of the war. He was brought back to Israel, where he was put on trial for crimes against humanity and subsequently hanged. In 1963, seventeen former guards at Auschwitz were put on trial in Frankfurt—the first war crimes trial in Germany since the Nuremberg tribunal seventeen years earlier. They had been living quiet and successful lives in West Germany—one of the defendants, Victor Capesius, who had worked closely with Josef Mengele in Auschwitz, had been running a pharmacy near Stuttgart. They were all convicted.

The Auschwitz trial inevitably raised the question of how many had escaped justice and also of what the post-war generation's own apparently "normal" parents had done during the war. It was the first time Nazi war crimes had been widely discussed in West Germany since the end of the war and for many young people the first time they had heard them discussed at all. In particular, it was the first time the details of the genocide of Europe's Jews were presented in any real detail in West Germany. The term Holocaust was not yet in common use, but it was the first time the genocide had been presented as an entity in its own right, as distinct from the war crimes of the Nazis as a whole.[26]

The Auschwitz trial had a huge, but complex, effect on younger Germans such as the novelist Martin Walser, who was born in 1927 and belonged to the so-called *Flakhelfergeneration* (those who had been old enough to help man anti-aircraft batteries as teenagers at the end of war). In 1965 he wrote an essay entitled "Our Auschwitz", which was published in the first issue of *Kursbuch*, the literary journal set up by the poet Hans Magnus Enzensberger, that was to become the bible of the West German New Left. In it he described the powerful impact of the descriptions in the trial of the horrible reality of Auschwitz. "We know the faces of the accused, we remember individual witnesses and above all we remember the terrible details," he wrote.[27]

And yet, Walser said, the very extremity of these terrible details had, paradoxically, made Auschwitz seem alien and remote, as if it were something that had nothing to do with peaceful, affluent post-war Germany. "I think we will all soon forget Auschwitz again if we just know it as a collection of brutalities," he wrote.[28] Walser argued instead for a deeper confrontation with the phenomenon of Nazism that would answer the question of the responsibility of ordinary Germans for the Holocaust. "Each of us is in some way partly the cause of Auschwitz," he wrote. And yet, what part each individual had played, he said, was something only they themselves could answer. In other words, the engagement with the Nazi past he was calling for was both political and, at the same time, private.

As the silence about the past was being broken, the post-war generation was reaching adulthood. Germany's baby boomers had grown up in a society that was, despite the transition from dictatorship to democracy, deeply authoritarian. In the fifties and early sixties it remained strictly hierarchical, corporal punishment was still common in schools and it was still technically against the law to rent a room or apartment to an unmarried couple under the age of 21. The post-war generation already had a sense that Adenauer's post-war West Germany had been built on a lie. Many now began to discover that people around them— teachers, professors, even their own parents and grandparents—had supported Hitler. "We had the feeling that we were surrounded by Nazis," one student activist, Christian Semler, remembers.[29]

In May 1965, with West Germany entering its first recession since the end of World War II, the three main political parties in parliament reached an agreement to amend the Basic Law—the provisional West German constitution—in order to pass to the government the emergency powers for use in times of severe internal unrest which until then had been held by the Allies. In effect, the transfer of these emergency powers to the West German government was a step towards full sovereignty. Much of the left, including some of the most powerful trade unions such as the metalworkers' union IG Metall, vehemently opposed the "emergency laws", which they saw as a restriction of democratic rights. But to some among the post-war generation, the emergency laws were eerily reminiscent of the Enabling Law that Hitler had passed in 1933 to give the Nazis special powers. They referred to the emergency laws or *Notsstandsgesetze* as the "NS-Gesetze" ("NS" was also the abbreviation for *Nationalsozialismus*, or National Socialism). In other words, it was 1933 all over again.

In December 1966, Erhard's coalition of Christian Democrats and Free Democrats collapsed. The Social Democrats under Willy Brandt, who until then had been the mayor of West Berlin, agreed to form a grand coalition with the Christian Democrats, the first ever in the Federal Republic. The Christian Democrat Kurt-Georg Kiesinger—a member of the Nazi party from 1933 to 1945 and a senior official in Joseph Goebbels' propaganda ministry—became the new chancellor. If there was any further proof needed of the continuities between the Nazi regime and the Federal Republic, this was it. Brandt, meanwhile, became the foreign minister. By backing Kiesinger, the Social Democrats, who had already supported the emergency laws, now seemed even more complicit with the fascist tendencies of the Federal Republic.

The formation of the grand coalition left no parliamentary opposition except for the liberal Free Democrats, who held 49 out of 496 seats. In fact, since the West German Constitutional Court had banned the German Communist party (*Kommunistische Partei Deutschlands* (KPD)) in 1956 as a threat to the post-war democracy, there was no parliamentary alternative to the left of the SPD at all. In its place emerged what came to be known as the Extra Parliamentary Opposition (*Außerparlamentarische Opposition* (APO)). From then on, in other words, the real opposition would be on the streets. Meanwhile, the National Democrats (*Nationaldemokratische Partei Deutschlands* (NPD)), a far right party that had been formed in 1964 and, unlike the KPD, had not been banned, had also been gaining support.

During the summer of 1967—the "summer of love" in the United States—the mood of the post-war generation in West Germany took a dark, almost apocalyptic turn that diverged from that of its counterparts in other countries. Haunted by the spectre of Nazism, many of them saw in the death of the student Benno Ohnesorg on 2 June the beginning of a new wave of political terror. The SDS, which had become the hub of the student movement in West Berlin, called it "the first political murder of the post-war period."[30] The student leaders said there was now an "undeclared state of emergency" in West Germany.[31] In other words parliamentary democracy in West Germany was a mere façade: behind it was a system that was on the verge of becoming fascist. The continuities between the Federal Republic and Nazism were thus no longer simply a matter of the biographies of individuals: they were structural. "The post-fascist state in the Federal Republic of Germany has become a pre-fascist one," the SDS declared in a written statement a few days after Ohnesorg's death."[32]

The conspiracy of silence about the past, the continuities between the Nazi state and the Federal Republic, and finally the brutality of the state in its response to the protest movement all seemed to point in one direction: Nazism had not been defeated in 1945; rather, it had metamorphosed into a new, insidious form. Thus the Federal Republic was not a new beginning but a "restoration". Just as Nazism had grown out of the Weimar Republic after the depression of the 1930s, so now the Bonn Republic was transitioning into fascism, a fear exacerbated by the military coup that took place in Greece in April 1967.

The implication of the logic was clear. The students' parents had, with a few heroic exceptions, failed to resist the Nazis. It was now down to the post-war generation to organise resistance—as Ensslin urged—to the Federal Republic. As one of the students' leaflets put it:

Let us offer resistance against former Nazi judges, Nazi prosecutors, Nazi legislators of all stripes, Nazi police officers, Nazi officials, Nazi defenders of the constitution, Nazi teachers, Nazi professors, Nazi priests, Nazi journalists, Nazi propagandists, Nazi chancellors and last but not least against Nazi war profiteers, Nazi industrialists and Nazi financers. [...] Let us mobilise a permanent ANTI-NAZI CAMPAIGN. Let us prepare an uprising against the NAZI generation."[33]

The idea that the Federal Republic was in some sense a continuation of Nazism—what I will call the continuity thesis—was perhaps the central driving force of the West German student movement and one that would dominate the West German New Left for the next decade. It was above all this idea that differentiated the student rebellion in West Germany from its counterparts elsewhere, fuelled its intensity and gave it its urgency. Whereas young people in some other countries were driven by a dream of creating a better society, in West Germany they were driven by a nightmare that Nazism was about to recur. Their critique of the society they lived in was, in many ways, more fundamental than that of their counterparts in Britain, France or the United States. To put it another way, the student movement in West Germany was essentially a defensive movement that aimed above all to prevent a recurrence of Auschwitz.

It was, at first glance, a counter-intuitive, paradoxical idea. After all, the Federal Republic had been established by the western powers that had defeated Nazism in 1945 at a cost of hundreds of thousands of lives. But to the post-war generation in Germany, it seemed entirely possible that fascism could lay hidden inside a system that purported to be its opposite. It was a way of thinking that was facilitated by a dialectical logic that was rooted in German idealist philosophy and had been developed by Marx, whose writing was filled with images of inversions and illusions. And the student movement in Germany was nothing if not intellectual. In contrast to their counterparts elsewhere in the West, they were more interested in theory than music or fashion. Over the next decade, some leading members of the student movement would adapt theory in increasingly bizarre ways that took them further and further away from reality. Ultimately they would create an entirely enclosed, hermetic logic that could be used to justify almost anything while blinding them to the glaringly obvious.

The student movement's equation of the Federal Republic with the Third Reich was not simply hyperbole. Rather, it was based on a particular theoretical understanding of Nazism and its relationship with capitalism. The consensus of the Adenauer era had rested on the idea that Nazi Germany had been first and foremost a totalitarian state, and therefore had more in common with the Soviet Union than a liberal, capitalist democracy like West Germany. To the Marxist students of the SDS, on the other hand, Nazism was a form of fascism, which had grown directly, and perhaps even inevitably, out of liberal democracy and industrial capitalism.[34] This was also the official position of the GDR, which regarded itself as a socialist state and therefore by definition "anti-fascist".

However, this view of Nazism had some subtle and complex consequences. Firstly, by seeing the explanation for fascism principally in the dynamics and development of capitalism, it tended to downplay the collective responsibility of the German people for Nazism. This tendency contained within it the danger that, ultimately, the German people could themselves be seen as victims of Nazism—the direct opposite of the post-war generation's stated view of their parents as the "perpetrator generation". Secondly, the reduction of Nazism to fascism tended to sideline the specific character of National Socialism as it had developed in Germany as opposed to other countries where fascism had taken hold such as Italy. In particular, it marginalised the anti-Semitic nature of Nazism and with it the Holocaust. Thus, paradoxically, although the student movement spoke of Auschwitz in its rhetoric, at a deeper level it actually tended to marginalise the Holocaust.

As well as lending the West German student movement its particular intensity, the continuity thesis also led the students to see their own rebellion as "resistance". Other opposition movements around the world also thought of themselves as "resisting" state power. But to the West German student movement, that concept—*Widerstand* in German—had entirely different connotations drawn directly from the recent German past that led them to more extreme conclusions. If they really faced a fascist regime, surely that made it legitimate—perhaps even morally obligatory—for them to use any means necessary to overthrow it? In the years to come, the concept of "resistance" would justify methods that were more appropriate to fighting a totalitarian regime than reforming a fledgling democracy.

The description of the Federal Republic as a Nazi state had another paradoxical consequence. The more the student activists became interested in the apparent structural similarities between Nazism and the Federal Republic, the less interested they became in the details of the Nazi era itself. As Axel Schildt has put it, they "de-realised" the Third Reich.[35] In particular, their "resistance" was targeted increasingly against the post-war West German system as a whole rather than individual ex-Nazis within it. The West German authorities began investigations and prosecutions against many former Nazis in 1968, particularly those involved in the death camps.[36] But, as Götz Aly has argued, although they featured regularly in the West German press, these individual cases were of little interest to the student movement and rarely featured in any of its journals.[37] By 1968, Nazism had morphed in the minds of many of the activists in the student movement from a real, historical phenomenon to an abstract, omnipresent threat.

This idea of an *ex post facto* resistance to Nazism was embodied by Ulrike Meinhof, the columnist for *konkret*. The daughter of a Nazi party member, she was an intensely moral figure, driven by a sense of outrage at injustice in Germany and around the world and in particular at what she, like many in the student movement, saw as continuities between Nazism and the post-war Federal Republic. She even looked like a member of the resistance, styling herself after Sophie Scholl, the Munich student who, along with her brother Hans, was active in the resistance group "The White Rose" and was executed in 1943 after a show trial at the People's Court in Berlin.[38] While her crusading moralism inspired some, others found her intolerant. "She thought that what she believed was the truth," says Stefan Aust, who met her in the mid-sixties when he was young member of staff at *konkret*. "If you were of a different opinion, she considered you unpolitical."[39] When Joachim Fest, at the time a television journalist and later an historian of Nazism, met her in 1964, her "energetic self-assurance" and "cheerful fighting spirit" reminded him of the Nazi officers he had fought alongside during the war.[40]

Ulrike Marie Meinhof was born in 1934, which meant she was significantly older than most members of the student movement and, unlike most of them, was old enough to remember the war. Her father was the director of a museum in Oldenburg in northern Germany and had been involved in the exhibition of "Degenerate Art" the Nazis put on in 1937 in order to inflame German public opinion against the corrupting influence of modernism.[41] He died when she was six years-old so Ulrike was raised by her mother until 1949, when she too died, and thereafter by Renate Riemeck, her mother's lover. Riemeck would later claim to have been a member of the resistance, but in fact she had also been a Nazi party member and had worked as an assistant to Johann von Leers, a university professor and SS officer who had written an anti-Semitic tract called "Jews are watching you". He fled Germany after the war and ended up in Egypt producing anti-Israeli propaganda for President Gamal Abdel Nasser.[42]

By the 1950s, Riemeck had become a professor of education, a member of the Social Democrats (*Sozialdemokratische Partei Deutschlands* (SPD)) and an active figure in the movement against re-armament and nuclear weapons in West Germany. Ulrike Meinhof followed in her footsteps: she won a prestigious scholarship to study education and psychology in Marburg and then Münster, joined the SPD and began writing articles for student newspapers and organising lectures and petitions against nuclear weapons. At a meeting of anti-nuclear campaigners in 1958, she met Klaus Rainer Röhl, a member of the illegal KPD and the owner of *konkret*, the Hamburg-based left-wing magazine, which, it would later emerge, was financed predominantly by the East German state. Attracted above all by its anti-fascist history, Meinhof also joined the KPD, moved to Hamburg and began writing for *konkret*. In 1960 Röhl made Meinhof its editor and the following year they got married.[43]

Meinhof's columns for *konkret* were passionate and polemical and often used the Nazi past as a kind of negative moral reference point for her politics. For example, in May 1961, she wrote a column called "Hitler in you" in which she compared the Bavarian Christian Democrat leader Franz Josef Strauss to Hitler. "Just as we ask our parents about Hitler, so we will one day be asked about Herr Strauss."[44] Strauss sued her unsuccessfully for libel, turning her into a celebrity in West Germany and increasing *konkret*'s circulation. Meinhof's lawyer was Gustav Heinemann, a minister in Konrad Adenauer's government who had quit in protest against re-armament and later became a Social Democrat president of West Germany. After the trial, Meinhof, who in 1962 had given birth to twin girls, Bettina and Regine, became one of the most well-known and popular journalists in West Germany. She was invited to exclusive parties in Hamburg and Sylt, the North Sea resort where the Hamburg establishment vacationed in summer, and frequently appeared on the radio and the television.

But although Meinhof focused on the continuities between Nazism and the Federal Republic, she actually had a somewhat complicated attitude to the Nazi past. Mingling uneasily with her outrage at the crimes committed by the Nazis was also a sense of anger at perceived crimes committed against Germany by the Allies during World War II. In a column written in February 1965 to coincide with the twentieth anniversary of the British and American bombing of Dresden during World War II, Meinhof claimed that 200,000 people had died during the two nights of bombing in February 1945, a figure based on the work of the British historian David Irving, who was later to become known as a Holocaust denier (the real number was probably less than a fifth of this). "For the first time in the history of war, an air raid destroyed its target so devastatingly that there were not enough uninjured survivors to bury the dead," she wrote.[45] With the Dresden raid, Meinhof said, "the anti-Hitler war degenerated into what it was supposed to be fighting against and what it was actually fighting against—into barbarism and inhumanity for which there is no justification."[46]

These sentiments were taboo in West Germany in the early 1960s. If there had been a silence about Nazism in the Adenauer's Federal Republic, there was also a silence about the suffering of the German people during World War II at the hands of the countries that were now their Cold War allies. In its rejection of the consensus of the Adenauer era, the post-war generation would break both of these silences. On the one hand, it would seek to challenge the idea that the Federal Republic represented a break with Nazism. But on the other hand, it would also seek to challenge the idea that the Allies—who had created the Federal Republic—had liberated Germany in 1945. In other words, while it wanted to break the silence about the role of Germans as perpetrators, the post-war generation in West Germany also wanted to break the silence about the Germans as victims.

In 1964, the East German state withdrew funding from *konkret* after it refused to sack a writer who had supported the opposition in Czechoslovakia; Röhl responded by mixing soft porn with politics to raise the circulation of the magazine and bring in money. Meinhof became more and more disillusioned with the magazine and, although she continued to write columns, with her focus increasingly on the disadvantaged in West German society, she gradually withdrew from her role as editor. She spent less and less time in Hamburg and more and more time in West Berlin. There, radical students were beginning to revolt against Adenauer's Federal Republic and in particular against what they, like Meinhof, saw as a resurgence of Nazism within it.

Appropriately enough, given the dark history that overshadowed the post-war generation in West Germany, a huge Nazi eagle hung above the doorway of Kurfürstendamm 140, the epicentre of the student rebellion. The elegant, five-storey corner building, whose top floor had been damaged by wartime bombs, was where the West Berlin branch of the SDS had its headquarters—and where several of its members also lived in a makeshift commune. During the war it been the offices of the Reich Commissioner for the Strengthening of Germandom (*Reichskommissar für die Festigung deutschen Volkstums*) a department of the SS set up by Heinrich Himmler.[47] It was from here that the so-called *Generalplan Ost*—a plan to resettle the newly occupied terrorities in Poland and the Soviet Union, henceforth Nazi Germany's *Lebensraum*, with five million ethnic Germans—was devised between 1941 and 1942. It in effect complemented the policy of genocide being carried out in the East.[48]

The SDS had originally been the student organisation of the German Social Democrat party and students who joined the SPD, like Ulrike Meinhof, were automatically members of it. However, in the late 1950s, frustrated by over a decade of opposition, the Social Democrats began to move to the centre ground of West German politics. At their Bad Godesberg conference in 1959, the Social Democrats dropped their commitment to Marxism and reconciled themselves to re-armament and membership of NATO. Their leading Marxist theoretician, Wolfgang Abendroth, was expelled from the party. The student campaign against former Nazi judges—which the SDS supported and senior figures in the SPD opposed—worsened the rift. In 1961, the SDS disaffiliated from the SPD and the SPD responded by banning its members from joining the SDS. It was the beginning of a split between the SPD and the radical left—and between the wartime generation and the post-war generation—that was to become increasingly acrimonious.

The SDS would never again be a mass organisation and even at its peak would have only a few thousand members. But by the mid-sixties it was once again becoming an influential organisation within the universities, linked to the now illegal KPD and sympathetic to the GDR. It had intensified its Marxist critique of capitalism and in 1960 brought out a journal, *neue kritik*, in which it set out its radical new theoretical positions.[49] It was nothing if not serious-minded. The SDS's most famous poster, which would later become one of the enduring visual images of the West German student movement, depicted Marx, Engels and Lenin in profile against a red background, with the slogan: "Everyone is talking about the weather. We aren't." In essence, the SDS had redefined itself as the intellectual vanguard of Socialist revolution in West Germany. And the vanguard of the vanguard was the West Berlin branch of the SDS.

In the 1960s, West Berlin was the heart of the Cold War.[50] A claustrophobic capitalist enclave deep in communist central Europe, its inhabitants had lived in constant fear of being overrun by the Red Army since the end of the war. In 1948, when the Soviets had blockaded the city, it had survived only because of the Allied airlift, during which British and American C-47 aircraft—dubbed "Rosinenbomber", or "candy bombers", by the West Berliners—had dropped supplies into the city for 15 months until Stalin relented and re-opened road and rail routes from West Germany to the city. Then, in the summer of 1961, the Berlin Wall went up. Although in GDR terminology it was called the "anti-fascist protection barrier" and had been built to stop East Germans leaving, it was West Berlin that was actually encircled by it—a "surrealist cage", as one observer put it, in which those inside were free.[51] West Berlin became a *Frontstadt*, or "Front City", in which paranoia, fuelled by the city's virulently anti-communist press, was rife; the newspapers of Axel Springer, which included both broadsheets like *Die Welt* and tabloids like *Bild*, being very much at the forefront.

West Berlin had been in economic decline since the end of the war. It had been a thriving industrial hub until World War II, but nearly all of its factories, which had been built during Germany's rapid industrialisation in the nineteenth century, had been destroyed by bombing and, with the city's future uncertain after the war, would never return. In fact, West Berlin was in many ways the complete opposite of the rest of West Germany in the 1950s. Whereas the West German economy had boomed in the two decades after the end of the war, Berlin now survived only through the vast subsidies it received from the West German government. The ruins that had by the mid-sixties been cleared away in most West German cities remained in West Berlin. The city's population was shrinking and ageing and real estate became virtually worthless.

However that was the very aspect that made it attractive to young people, who could live in huge, grand apartments for much lower rents than in other West German cities. The city's febrile atmosphere also attracted anyone frustrated with the provincialism and conformism of Adenauer's West Germany.[52] West Berlin was a stronghold of the Social Democrats, who had run the city since the end of World War II. Since it was not technically a state of West Germany, its residents were exempt from military service, making it a magnet for conscientious objectors. By the mid-sixties it had become a city of students, radicals and dropouts. In short, if there was going to be "resistance" anywhere, it would be in West Berlin.

The Free University (*Freie Universität* (FU)) was to become the base of the student movement in West Berlin. Set up in 1948 after the Berlin airlift, it had been funded largely by American money and indeed its main building was named after Henry Ford. It had been conceived as an alternative to Berlin's original university, which was now in communist East Berlin and had re-opened in 1946 as a "people's university" under direct Soviet control.[53] Most German universities remained hierarchical and authoritarian, with a handful of *Ordinarien* (senior professors) determining virtually every aspect of university life. In comparison, the Free University was liberal and democratic, with student representation on all of the university's decision-making bodies—the so-called "Berlin model". And yet it was here that the student movement began, borrowing forms of protest—for example "sit-ins" and "teach-ins"—from American universities and in particular the Free Speech movement in Berkeley. Soon the Free University became the "Berkeley of the Federal Republic".[54]

Initially, the protests focused on conditions at the Free University, which had grown rapidly and, like many West German universities, struggled to accommodate the baby boomer generation and became overcrowded. But gradually the students broadened and radicalised their critique of the university. To the students it seemed that the Free University was only "free" in the sense of being anti-communist.[55] Anti-communism, in other words, masked a lack of real democracy. Increasingly the students began to see the Free University as a kind of microcosm of the state of West Berlin, which was in turn a microcosm of West Germany. "We should see the freedom of the university as a problem that reaches beyond the university," they said.[56] In other words, democratic reform of the university could be a model for democratic reform of West German society.

If Berlin was where the action was, Frankfurt was where the intellectual roots of the student movement lay. It was the philosophical school that bore that city's name that was to provide the theoretical framework for the student movement and in particular its analysis of postwar West German capitalism. In fact, nearly all the key themes of the student movement—the continuities between the Nazi past and the Federal Republic, the connection between capitalism and fascism, the role of the media in manipulating mass consciousness—were drawn from the writings of the "Frankfurt School". Above all, it was from the Frankfurt School that the student movement was to derive its sense of itself as an "anti-authoritarian" movement.

The Institute for Social Research (*Institut für Sozialforschung*) had been founded in Frankfurt in 1923. During the years of the Weimar Republic, its leading members, Theodor W. Adorno, Max Horkheimer and Herbert Marcuse—all of whom were Jewish or part-Jewish—began to create a so-called "Critical Theory" that developed the Hegelian Marxist critique of Georg Lukács and also incorporated the insights of psychoanalysis into Marxist thought. Critical Theory, largely an attempt to explain why the proletariat in the West had failed to fulfil its historical role as envisaged by Marx, was both utopian and pessimistic: it held out the possibility of a socialist dream without ever accepting that any existing socialist society came close to it.

After Hitler came to power in 1933, the Institute migrated to New York, where it was given a home in exile at Columbia University. From there, and from California, where Adorno and Horkheimer subsequently re-located, it developed the analysis of advanced capitalism and fascism, and the connection between the two, that was to make the Institute's name. For the Frankfurt School, fascism was an outgrowth of advanced capitalism and could not be understood without it, hence Horkheimer's dictum that "he who does not wish to speak of capitalism should also be silent about fascism."[57] Horkheimer's theory, outlined in an essay written during the war called "Authoritarian State", was that Nazism was a system of state capitalism, or "integral étatism", in which the state took on the functions of a monopoly capitalist and completely dominated society through a mixture of terror and manipulation by the mass media.[58] The rise of Nazism had been facilitated by certain specific "authoritarian" character traits among the German people such as a tendency towards conformity, which Adorno examined in a series of studies entitled *The Authoritarian Character*, and through manipulation by the mass media.

Adorno and Horkheimer radicalised their critique yet further in *The Dialectic of Enlightenment*, a spectacularly gloomy critique of western rationality written during the war and published in 1947. In the book, which owed as much to Nietzsche as it did to Marx, Adorno and Horkheimer extended their pessimism from capitalism to the entire history of the western Enlightenment. They argued that in the supposedly democratic countries of the West, mass culture and the mass media had now so completely manipulated and distorted consciousness that critical thinking was no longer even possible. It was what they called the "administered world".[59]

After the war, Adorno and Horkheimer returned to Germany and in 1951 the Institute re-opened as part of Frankfurt University, while Marcuse stayed in the United States, where he worked for the State Department and later became a professor at various American universities. Adorno in particular became a vocal critic of post-war West Germany, which—as he argued in a famous essay published in 1959 that prefigured the work of the Mitscherlichs—had not yet "worked through" its Nazi past.[60] Authoritarian attitudes prevailed among Germans, whose acceptance of post-war democratization, he argued, was fragile and superficial. Until the end of his life, in fact, Adorno feared a resurgence of anti-Semitism and worried that an economic crisis could revive Nazism in Germany.

Adorno, more than any other member of the Frankfurt School, was also to become increasingly preoccupied with Auschwitz, which he came to regard not merely as an historical catastrophe but as a metaphysical break. In 1966 he published what was to be his magnum opus, *Negative Dialectics*, which challenged the notion of progress implicit in Hegel's logic. For Adorno, Auschwitz had shattered the idea that history was moving inevitably towards a predestined end point or *telos*. Haunted by the guilt of the survivor, he said the central question facing philosophy was now simply:

whether after Auschwitz you can go on living—especially whether one who escaped by accident, one who by rights should have been killed, may go on living. His mere survival calls for the coldness, the basic principle of bourgeois subjectivity, without which there could have been no Auschwitz; this is the drastic guilt of him who was spared.[61]

Auschwitz, Adorno said, had created "a new categorical imperative": Man now had an obligation "to arrange one's thoughts and actions so that it will not be repeated, so that nothing similar will happen."[62]

The Frankfurt School had a massive but also complex and contradictory influence on the West German student movement. Unsurprisingly, its influence would be greatest in Frankfurt itself, where the SDS had its national headquarters and which, after West Berlin, would become the major centre of the student rebellion. In fact, many of the students in Frankfurt had come there specifically to study under professors like Adorno, who became a kind of pop star for the West German student movement. "We loved him," says Arno Widmann, a philosophy student and member of the SDS in Frankfurt.[63] The Frankfurt students, who daubed Horkheimer's early aphorisms on the walls of university buildings, considered themselves theoretically more sophisticated than the West Berliners, who in turn thought the Frankfurters were too theoretical.[64] "We thought they weren't revolutionary enough," says Tilman Fichter, a leading figure in the West Berlin SDS, "and they thought we weren't intellectually avant-garde enough."[65]

It was from the Frankfurt School, and in particular from Adorno and Horkheimer, that the student movement got its analysis of Nazism. "They gave us the language to analyse the Nazis," Fichter says.[66] In particular, "anti-authoritarianism", which became the central idea around which the student movement mobilised, was derived from Adorno and Horkheimer's work on the authoritarian state and the authoritarian personality. However, the radical students of the SDS wanted not just to borrow but also to develop the insights of their intellectual mentors. "Our idea was to attempt to develop the *Dialectic of Enlightenment* further," says Detlev Claussen, a philosophy student at Frankfurt University, who had come to Frankfurt specifically to study under Adorno. "That is to say, we wanted to find a theoretical basis for a world beyond capitalism and also beyond socialism as it existed in the GDR."[67]

This ambitious theoretical project would be overtaken by events and as such never be completed. But in the meantime, many of the students came to adopt a simplified, distorted version of the work of Adorno and Horkheimer as a basis for their actions. Although Adorno and Horkheimer had posited a connection between capitalism and fascism, they had never simply equated the two. The students, on the other hand, thought that Horkheimer's theory of the authoritarian state, which had been written with Nazism and the Soviet Union in mind, could also be directly applied to the Federal Republic. "Our idea was that the Federal Republic had never freed itself from the model of the authoritarian state," says Claussen.[68] They believed not just that, as Adorno had argued, authoritarian attitudes had persisted in post-war Germany, but that the Federal Republic was also, like the Third Reich itself, an authoritarian state.[69] This leap was to provide the theoretical background for the student movement's continuity thesis, which would be used to justify increasingly radical forms of "resistance".

2

REVOLUTIONARY OPTIMISM

While the Frankfurt School gave the students a theoretical framework with which to articulate their growing sense of alienation their parents' generation, it was the Vietnam war that would galvanise from them into action and bring them into conflict with the authorities beyond the university itself for the first time. "No political event played so decisive a role in the discussion and in the politicization of the students as the Vietnam war," the leaders of the West German student movement would write in the summer of 1967 shortly after the death of Benno Ohnesorg.[1] Through the Vietnam war, the post-war generation's attitude to the United States would also be transformed.

When President Kennedy had begun the United States' involvement in Vietnam in the early 1960s, there had been almost no opposition in West Germany. But as the war escalated after 1965, when President Lyndon B. Johnson began the bombing of North Vietnam and sent the first US troops to South Vietnam, perceptions of the war in West Germany changed. Some of the students began to see in the conflict in south-east Asia "the Spain of their generation."[2] Opposition to the Vietnam war was one of the factors that united the protests across the West in the mid-sixties. And yet, as with the concept of "resistance", the specific history of West Germany gave it a particular resonance that differentiated it from similar protests elsewhere.

In particular, beneath the students' growing anger about the Vietnam war lay West Germany's deeply ambivalent, perhaps even schizophrenic, relationship with the United States. The United States had liberated Germany from Nazism and yet now also occupied it. Many Germans, therefore, felt resentment as well as gratitude towards the Americans. Nowhere was this ambivalent relationship with the United States more tangible than in West Berlin. Since the end of the war, the city, which depended even more heavily on US protection than the rest of West Germany, had been the most pro-American city in West Germany, particularly after the Berlin airlift. And yet it was West Berlin that was to become the centre of anti-American protest in West Germany.

When President Kennedy had given his "Ich bin ein Berliner" speech in 1963, he had turned West Berlin into a symbol of the free world. Given West Berlin's special place in the geopolitics of the Cold War, the American argument that the war in Vietnam was being fought in support of a free people under communist oppression had a special resonance there. The Americans and the Berlin authorities had explicitly claimed that West Berlin's freedom was being defended in Vietnam. This was not mere propaganda: fear of Soviet retaliation against West Berlin, which Nikita Khrushchev called "the testicles of the West", had, for example, been a key factor in President Kennedy's decision to limit US support for the Bay of Pigs invasion in April 1961.[3] The vulnerability of West Berlin to Soviet invasion also played a major role in determining US policy elsewhere in the world during the Cold War, including South-East Asia.[4]

But as the war in Vietnam escalated, perceptions of the United States and its role in the world changed, particularly among the generation that had grown up after the war. Many felt as if their illusions about America had been shattered at the same time as their illusions about their parents' generation.[5] Hans-Christian Ströbele, a young left-wing lawyer in the mid-sixties, remembers having had tears in his eyes as he took part in a vigil in front of the West Berlin City Hall after the assassination of Kennedy. "The USA and Kennedy were the embodiment of freedom to me," he recalls, "and then in the middle of the sixties everything was turned upside down.[6] With the Vietnam war, the B-52 replaced the C-47 as the defining symbol of the United States. The presence of American troops in West Berlin, which had until then been a reminder of how much the city relied on the United States to protect it from a possible Soviet invasion, now became a symbol of oppression. "They became a target of our aversion, our struggle against US imperialism in Vietnam," Ströbele recalls.[7]

Nowhere was this shift clearer than at the "half-American" Free University.[8] In 1966, two students there, Peter Gäng and Jürgen Horlemann, produced an exhibition and book, entitled *Vietnam—The Genesis of a Conflict*, that played a major role in changing the students' perception of the war.[9] It was, the authors argued, not a war for freedom at all, as the Americans and the West German establishment had argued, but an imperialist war waged by the United States against an exploited Third World colony. By extension, the Vietnamese National Liberation Front (NLF)—the Vietcong—was not a communist threat, as it had been portayed in the "bourgeois press", but a heroic anti-colonial movement.

The Vietnam war, and in particular the area bombing of North Vietnam, evoked complex collective memories in Germany in which Germans were both perpetrators and victims.[10] On the one hand, it suggested parallels to the bombing of German cities in World War II. "Many of us who had experienced the war recognised ourselves in the pictures of children burned with napalm," one member of the student movement old enough to remember the wartime bombing recalled.[11] At the same time, however, some saw parallels with the Holocaust. The American war in Vietnam was, in the words of the SDS in 1966, "genocide emanating from imperialist political and economic interests."[12] An article in konkret at the beginning of 1967 directly compared American soldiers in Vietnam to the Einsatzgruppen, the SS killing squads which operated behind the lines on the Eastern Front, targeting Jews in particular.[13]

The description of Vietnam as genocide was the first time, but not the last, that the post-war generation in Germany would look at a conflict in a distant part of the world through the prism of their own history and see in it a repetition of Auschwitz. It was the beginning of a loose and inflationary use of the concept of genocide by the post-war generation in Germany that would have complicated consequences. Protesters in other parts of the world, including the United States itself, also described the Vietnam war as genocide. But in Germany, in the context of the West German students' obsession with their parents' guilt for Nazism, it was a deeply significant and complex parallel to draw. On the one hand, it was an expression of their desperation to avoid a repetition of their parents' crimes and, perhaps, to atone for the sins of their fathers—the kind of political engagement with Auschwitz, in fact, that Martin Walser had called for in his essay in Kursbuch in 1965. At the same time, though, it had another, more subtle implication. If the United States—one of the countries that had liberated Germany from Nazism—was responsible for a genocide in Vietnam, it paradoxically also meant that Auschwitz was no longer unique or a specifically German phenomenon. Dan Diner would later call this use of images and metaphors connected with Nazism to describe events in other countries, thus relativizing Nazism and in particular the Holocaust, "exonerating projection".[14]

The students also believed that, although the Vietnam war was being fought by the United States, the Federal Republic was deeply implicated. Although as chancellor in 1965 Ludwig Erhard had turned down President Johnson's request to send a battalion of West German troops to Vietnam—much to Johnson's annoyance—the Federal Republic did provide financial and logistical support and thus to the students it seemed that it was tacitly supporting the war. The students' banners accused the West German and West Berlin political leadership of supporting "the genocide in Vietnam."[15] Anyone in West Germany who understood what was happening in Vietnam, Ulrike Meinhof wrote in a column for *konkret* in 1967 entitled "Vietnam and the Germans", would "begin to understand that their inability to stop the war becomes complicity with those who are waging it."[16] Conversely, the supposed loyalty of the West German government seemed to the students to implicate the United States in the fascist tendencies of the Federal Republic. "Our view of America was not just that they liberated us from fascism but also that they had allowed the post-war fascist development of West Germany," Hans-Christian Ströbele says.[17] This continuity between Nazi Germany, the Federal Republic and the United States was captured in the slogan that began to appear on banners and graffiti: "USA—SA—SS."

The first protest against the Vietnam war in West Berlin took place in February 1966. On the evening of 3 February, posters appeared all over West Berlin that were signed "International Liberation Front" and read:

Erhard and the parties in Bonn are supporting MURDER. Murder by napalm!
Murder by poison gas!
Murder by atomic bombs? [...]
How long are we going to allow murder to be committed in our name?
Americans out of Vietnam![18]

The following day, 2,500 students blocked the Ku'Damm for 20 minutes and then moved on to the Amerika-Haus, the American cultural institute, for a sit-in. The police tried to forcibly disperse the demonstrators. Some of them managed to pull down the US flag and one demonstrator threw eggs at the building. The following morning the West Berlin media, led by Axel Springer's pro-American newspapers, was outraged: *Bild*, West Germany's biggest-selling tabloid, called it "shameful"; *B.Z.*, the Berlin tabloid, called it "a disgrace." The following day, the rector of the Free University and Willy Brandt, then the mayor of Berlin, felt obliged to apologise to the US authorities. The response of the university, the city government and the press, who were apparently more concerned with law and order on the streets of West Berlin than murder in Vietnam, seemed to prove to the students that the people running West Germany and West Berlin, even the Social Democrats among them, were authoritarian.

The man behind the "International Liberation Front" was Rudi Dutschke, a short, stocky figure with a saturnine stare and a shock of dishevelled black hair. Although he talked in sentences crammed with long-winded Marxist jargon that seemed to go on forever, he nevertheless spoke with a passion and an intensity that was unlike any of the other West German student leaders. Whereas others seemed to theorise about revolution, Dutschke seemed to live it. When he talked about Marxist icons like Rosa Luxemburg, it sounded "as if he'd just met them at the bus stop," as Tilman Fichter puts it.[19] Dutschke's passion and charisma became a major factor in attracting young people to the student movement first in West Berlin and then throughout West Germany.

Dutschke, perpetually dressed in tatty, knitted sweaters and a beat-up black leather jacket, cut a quite different figure from most of the buttoned-down, suit-wearing members of the SDS. When he spoke in public, his rhetoric was so powerful that some of his comrades advised him to tone it down in case it evoked memories of Hitler. But they also knew he was able to appeal to a completely new audience that the student movement had until then not been able to reach. "His speeches were so abstract that no-one understood them, or at least I didn't," Michael "Bommi" Baumann, a high school dropout who was to become a key figure in the Berlin political scene, later wrote. "But when you just talked to him he was totally cool. He was a totally normal person just like anyone else."[20] Although he never held a formal post within the SDS, Dutschke became the *de facto* leader of the West German student movement.

However, although Dutschke became the public face of the student movement, he was in many ways untypical of it. Unlike most of his comrades, Dutschke had grown up not in the Adenauer's Federal Republic but within the Soviet-occupied zone, which subsequently became the GDR. He was born in Luckenwalde, 30 miles south-east of Berlin, in 1940. At the time of his birth, his father Alfred, who had been a postal worker before the war, was a soldier on the Eastern Front. Dutschke met him for the first time seven years later when he finally returned from a Soviet prisoner of war camp. Until then, Dutschke was brought up by his mother Elsbeth, a devout Lutheran Protestant. He would remain deeply religious for his entire life—another thing that distinguished him from most of his comrades in the student movement. He was horrified when Soviet troops crushed the uprisings in East Berlin on 17 June, 1953, and in Budapest in 1956, experiences that would influence his view of communism. Whereas many young left-wing people in West Germany tended to romanticise the GDR and see it as the "better Germany", Dutschke had no such illusions.

As a teenager, Dutschke's real passion had been sports. He excelled as a track athlete, specialising in the decathlon, and, after his lack of height prevented him going further, dreamed of becoming a sports reporter. At home he emulated the commentators he had heard on the radio—something those close to him would later say influenced his urgent rhetorical style. But as an 18 year-old he had refused to volunteer for military service in the *Nationale Volksarmee* (NVA), the East German army, because, as he announced in a speech to his class, he would not serve in an army in which he might be called on to shoot on fellow Germans. As a result of his "anti-social behaviour", Dutschke was unable to study sports journalism in Leipzig as he had hoped.[21] Instead he began an apprenticeship in a textile factory in Luckenwalde.[22]

A year later, Dutschke discovered there was one place he still could study: at the Free University in West Berlin. He got an apartment in West Berlin and took evening classes to re-take his *Abitur* (high school diploma), as his East German version was not recognised in the West. He also got a job working as a sports reporter for *B.Z.*, the downmarket, anti-communist Berlin tabloid owned by Axel Springer—something he would later keep a secret. Then, on the morning of Sunday, 13 August, 1961, Dutschke awoke to find the Berlin Wall bisecting the city from north to south. He was enraged. He now had to choose, once and for all, between East and West and between university and his family. Later that day, he registered as a political refugee in West Berlin. He would not see his mother for another four years. This was the real beginning of Dutschke's political career.

That autumn, Dutschke began studying sociology at the Free University and started to work his way through the entire canon of Marxist political thinkers. Some—Marx himself, Lenin, Rosa Luxemburg and Lukács—he was familiar with from his school days. Others—such as the theorists of the Frankfurt School—were unknown in East Germany. Bernd Rabehl, another exile from the east, remembers meeting Dutschke at the Café am Steinplatz, a student hangout, where he was sitting with a pile of Lenin books in front of him. "I said to him, 'You don't need all that anymore. The time for that is over.' He replied, 'No, now is exactly the time we need to study it all over again.'"[23] The two men became best friends and together joined a group called "Subversive Action," an offshoot of the French situationists led by a Munich-based artist named Dieter Kunzelmann. In December 1963 it had published an unsigned manifesto entitled "You killed Kennedy too!" which claimed that West German society had secretly "longed" for the American president to be killed.[24] The group had originally planned to establish "microcells" across West Germany. But in January 1965 its members decided to join the SDS and, by establishing "actionist factions", radicalise it from within.[25]

Unlike many of his comrades who tended to be pessimistic about Germany, Dutschke was an optimist. He was drawn to Ernst Bloch, a somewhat mystical German Marxist thinker who had developed the concept of "concrete Utopia"—essentially an attempt to rehabilitate Utopian Socialism, which Engels had criticised. He later said that "a Marxist does not have the right to be a pessimist."[26] Dutschke's optimism may have been at least in part due to the fact that he had few of the hang-ups about the Nazi past that his West German comrades did. Whereas most of the students had grown up haunted by the continuities between the Nazi era and the Federal Republic, the Nazi past cast much less of a shadow over those like Dutschke who had grown up in the "anti-fascist" GDR. He "looked more to the future than the past," Bahman Nirumand, one of his colleagues from the student movement, remembers.[27]

In fact, unlike many in the student movement who were almost obsessed with the Nazi past, Dutschke rarely mentioned it. In a remarkable passage written late in his life, he explained why:

I asked myself about the responsibility for the Second World War. My Christian shame about what had happened was so great that I declined to read further evidence and satisfied myself with a general insight: the victory and power of the Nazi party and the origins of the Second World War cannot be separated from the alliance between the Nazis and the rich (monopoly capital). That gave me the space to make the first decision: to make a fundamental distinction between capitalism and socialism and at the same time not give up my Christianity.[28]

As this passage illustrates, Dutschke had a view of the Nazi past, connected to his religious faith, that set him apart from many of his comrades in the West German student movement. In ascribing Nazism to capitalism, he had in effect absolved Germany as a nation—and in particular his parents' generation—of any responsibility for the Third Reich. As a consequence, whereas many other members of the student movement would remain deeply suspicious of the West German masses because of their perceived complicity with Nazism, Dutschke would continue to have an almost naive faith in their revolutionary potential.

In particular, Dutschke was not interested in the Holocaust. There are no scathing references to the "Auschwitz generation" in his writings. Even in the passage quoted above, Dutschke does not mention the genocide specifically. Tilman Fichter, Dutschke's comrade in the West Berlin SDS, remembers asking him why he did not seem to be interested in the Holocaust. "He said, 'Tilman, it's all so hopeless. If you talk about it all the time, you won't have any energy left for the revolution.' The Holocaust didn't fit into his revolutionary optimism.'"[29] It was a remarkable lacuna in Dutschke's political thinking that would have far-reaching consequences for the West German student movement.

Karl Marx had always expected the revolution to begin in a highly industrialised western country like Germany. But not only had the expected revolution failed to materialise, Germany had embraced Nazism—an apparently retrograde political movement. Now, twenty years after the end of the war, the West German masses seemed to have no interest in revolution whatsoever—the proletariat least of all. Explaining this paradox was the central dilemma facing the Marxist students of the SDS in the mid-sixties. For Rudi Dutschke, Marx no longer had all the answers. "Marx analyses fantastically and clearly," he had written in his diary in 1963. "But today, as far as western

Europe is concerned, his analysis leads nowhere."[30] In the West, the proletariat now enjoyed an unprecedented standard of living and had become entirely de-politicised. "The western European worker today has more to lose than his chains," Dutschke noted.[31] In Marxist terms, it meant the proletariat was objectively, but not subjectively, the revolutionary subject. Put simply, it had been bought off.

Like many other young students, Dutschke looked to the Frankfurt School for answers. But he was drawn less to Adorno and Horkeimer than to Herbert Marcuse, whom the students in Frankfurt did not consider intellectually serious.[32] Marcuse had remained in California after the end of the war and in 1964 published *One-Dimensional Man*, a critique of post-war capitalist society that built on the ideas that Adorno and Horkheimer had developed during the war and became one of the most influential texts for the New Left around the world. Capitalism's growth in productivity, Marcuse argued, should have liberated the proletariat but in fact had further enslaved it. Increased affluence and new techniques of manipulation, particularly through the mass media, had created societies with totalitarian tendencies and without opposition—which was precisely how West Germany looked to the students after the formation of the grand coalition. "The scope of society's domination over the individual is immeasurably greater than ever before," he wrote.[33]

Despite this near-complete domination over the individual, Marcuse suggested tantalisingly that there remained a small hope for revolutionary change. Capitalism could yet be transformed, he said, not by the workers as classical Marxism had taught, but by a new revolutionary vanguard of "outcasts and outsiders, the exploited and persecuted of other races and other colours, the unemployed and the unemployable."[34] Marcuse was thinking in particular of the college students in the United States who had stood shoulder to shoulder with African-Americans in the civil rights struggle. But to the West German students it was a *raison d'être* for their own movement, which, if Marcuse was right, no longer had to defer to the proletariat as the revolutionary subject.

These marginalised groups, Marcuse suggested, offered new ways of challenging capitalism from the outside:

Their opposition hits the system from without and is therefore not deflected by the system; it is an elementary force that violates the rules of the game and, in doing so, reveals it as a rigged game. When they get together and go out into the streets, without arms, without protection, in order to ask for the most primitive civil rights, they know that they face dogs, stones, and bombs, jail, concentration camps, even death. Their force is behind every political demonstration for the victims of law and order. The fact that they start refusing to play the game may be the fact that marks the beginning of the end of a period.[35]

Such opposition was radically different from traditional forms of protest, which the totalitarian tendencies of advanced industrial society had rendered ineffective and perhaps even dangerous because they created an illusion of real democracy. In other words, even protest could now be tolerated, recuperated and turned into a repressive force. It was what Marcuse, in an essay that was written in English the following year, termed "repressive tolerance."

In his conclusion to the essay, Marcuse wrote that it was absurd to demand that marginalised groups in society protest lawfully. There was, he wrote:

a natural right of resistance for oppressed and overpowered minorities to use extralegal means if the legal ones have proved to be inadequate. Law and order are always and everywhere the law and order that protect the established hierarchy; it is nonsensical to invoke the absolute authority of this law and this order against those who suffer from it and struggle against it—not for personal advantages and revenge, but for their share of humanity. There is no judge over them other than the constituted authorities, the police and their own conscience. If they use violence, they do not start a new chain of violence but try to break an established one. Since they will be punished, they know the risk, and when they are willing to take it, no third person, and least of all the educator and intellectual, has the right to preach them abstention.[36]

Marcuse's essay was published in Germany in 1966 and instantly became essential reading among left-wing students in West Germany. In fact, the conclusion to "Repressive Tolerance", and in particular Marcuse's claim that minorities had a "natural right of resistance" would become a kind of manifesto for the student movement. It seemed to justify extralegal means in the students' struggle. If they used violence, it would be, in Marxist terms, not reactionary violence but progressive violence. The essay was a key catalyst in the student movement's transition from discussion to action. As Dutschke explained that summer in an essay that was to become another key text for the student movement, it had:

clarified our feeling of uneasiness about the fact that our constant discussions had no practical consequences. We realised that the bourgeoisie, the ruling class in every country of the "free world", can afford to have critical minorities discussing the problems in their own and in foreign societies, and that they are prepared to allow any discussion as long as it remains theoretical.[37]

To the optimistic Dutschke, the recession that hit in 1966 showed that West Germany's post-war economic miracle was coming to an end and that capitalist society was on the verge of imminent collapse. In fact, he said, the grand coalition was "the last desperate attempt of the ruling oligarchies to resolve the structural difficulties of the system."[38] West Germany was now in the middle of a transitional phase of "cultural revolution" that would precede the actual revolution. It was therefore time for the vanguard of the revolution to take the initiative, to move beyond mere protest to the resistance Marcuse talked about.

The question of what form such resistance should take, and in particular what role violence should play in it, would be the single biggest question for the West German left over the next decade. The classical Marxist-Leninist answer was that violence was to be used only during a revolutionary situation, but Marx and Lenin were not writing about a "one-dimensional society." In any case, some of the students also had another way of looking at the question. If the Federal Republic was a fascist state, and another Holocaust was taking place in Vietnam, was it not one's moral duty to use violence if necessary to prevent it?

Dutschke advocated what he called a "strategy of escalation".[39] The crucial thing, he said, was that resistance should "violate the rules of game", thus setting up what he hoped would be an "ever more effective dialectic between enlightenment and mass action"—a kind of virtuous circle of theory and practice.[40] Through "systematic, controlled, and limited confrontation" with the West German state, Dutschke thought the APO could provoke the state's latent violence and thus expose its real character as a "dictatorship of violence".[41] That, in turn, would create a new revolutionary consciousness among an ever-greater number of students, and, ultimately, the proletariat itself—at least in theory. This idea, which I will call the "provocation thesis", would become, alongside the "continuity thesis", the central idea that would animate the radical left in West Germany for the next decade.

For inspiration, Dutschke looked to the Third World, which, largely through his influence, would come to take on a pivotal role for the

West German student movement. Even before the Vietnam war had escalated, Dutschke, who had by now married Gretchen Klotz, an American theology student living in Berlin, had been already interested in revolutionary movements in the Third World, particularly in Africa and Latin America, which were struggling against repressive regimes supported by the United States in the name of anti-communism. While they were still members of Subversive Action, Dutschke and Rabehl had organised a spontaneous demonstration against the visit to Berlin in December 1964 of the Congolese prime minister Moise Tshombe, who was believed to be responsible, with CIA help, for the murder of his predecessor, the African nationalist Patrice Lumumba. The group around Dutschke was sometimes called the "Viva Maria Group" after the Louis Malle movie starring Brigitte Bardot and Jeanne Moreau as Latin American revolutionaries, which was released in 1965. Increasingly, the group came to see the national liberation movements of the Third World not merely as heroic but also as a model for their own form of "resistance" in West Germany.

In August 1965, the *Kursbuch* published an extract from the radical French-Caribbean psychologist Frantz Fanon's anti-colonial manifesto *The Wretched of the Earth*, which had been published in France a few years earlier with a foreword by Jean-Paul Sartre. The book, whose title was taken from the first line of the original French version of the Internationale, was published in full in West Germany the following year, translated by another member of the West Berlin SDS, and quickly became a key text for the "Dutschkists".[42] Fanon argued that it was the dispossessed of the shantytowns of Third World cities that were now the true agent of revolutionary change. He also argued that violence was not only justified as part of the anti-colonial struggle but also had a cathartic effect for colonised peoples, helping them to overcome the inferiority complex that inevitably arose from their colonisation. Decolonisation, Fanon said, "is always a violent phenomenon".[43]

Influenced by Fanon, the "Dutschkists" began to see the national liberation movements in the Third World as the vanguard of a global revolution. Marx, it seemed to them, had got it wrong. The revolution would not begin in the centre of the West but in the periphery of the Third World. The anti-colonial movements in Africa, Asia and Latin America—led by the Vietcong—would overthrow the undemocratic regimes in their countries and, in doing so, undermine the prosperity of the developed world, which was built on the exploitation of the developing world. Then, and only then, would the proletariat in the West be roused from its false consciousness and come to realise its own revolutionary role. It was a kind of domino theory—except, of course, that Dutschke wanted the dominoes to fall.

By the summer of 1967, identification with the national liberation movements of the Third World had become central to the student movement's ideology. It provided, for example, the theoretical background for the protests against the visit of the Shah of Iran to West Germany in June 1967 that led to the death of Benno Ohnsesorg.[44] A few weeks after the Shah's visit, Herbert Marcuse visited West Berlin for a four-day discussion with students at the Free University. The professor was received by the students almost as a guru, although, to their frustration, he refused to give them concrete advice for their struggle. In his contribution to the debate, Dutschke said that:

The complete identification with the necessity of revolutionary terrorism and of the revolutionary struggle in the Third World is the essential pre-condition for the liberation of the struggle of the struggling peoples of the world and the development of our own new forms of resistance.[45]

For Dutschke, the West German student movement was thus part of a global struggle against American imperialism. Although his wife was American, he referred in letters to the "Dreckamis", the "shitty Yanks".[46] His goal was, as he put it, to open up a "second front" in the Vietnam war.[47]

But at the heart of this anti-imperialist struggle was a deep ambiguity. For although nationalism was taboo on the West German left, the "Dutschkists" were prepared to identify with and support nationalist movements in other parts of the world—in fact, the student movement's "internationalism" consisted of little more than doing precisely this.[48] Thus the idea that intellectuals in West Germany should complement the struggle of national liberation movements in the Third World—in other words, that the APO, or Extra-Parliamentary Opposition, should see itself as part of the anti-imperialist struggle—raised as many questions as it answered. In the Third World, national liberation movements were fighting a guerrilla war against imperialist oppressors. But where did a movement of metropolitan intellectuals like the West German student movement fit into this struggle? Were they simply to wait until the time when the West German proletariat, inspired by the uprisings in the Third World, developed a revolutionary consciousness and joined the students? Or should they themselves in the meantime emulate guerrilla movements like the Vietcong?

Dutschke never gave a clear answer. In 1967 he and his friend Gaston Salvatore, a Chilean studying in Berlin, wrote an introduction to a German edition of Che Guevara's "Message to the Tricontinental", published as "Create two, three, many Vietnams", which Salvatore had translated. They said the role of revolutionaries in the metropolis was twofold: firstly, to "help to globalise the revolutionary opposition through direct participation in the current struggle in the Third World", and secondly, to "develop specific forms of struggle that are appropriate to the stage of historical development in the metropolis."[49] In another article that summer Dutschke went on:

> The question is: how and under what conditions can the subjective factor enter as an objective factor into the historical process? Guevara's answer for Latin America was that the revolutionaries do not always have to wait for the objective conditions for revolution, but through the focus, an armed vanguard of the people, can create the objective conditions for the revolution through subjective activity. [...] Do we have to assume in all our actions the permanent impotence of our political work, or have we reached an historical point in which the subjective creative activity of individuals co-operating politically will determine reality and whether it can be changed?[50]

Guevara was referring to Regis Debray's "foco" theory—the idea that a small group of revolutionaries could become a "foco", or "focus"—a motor that could set the masses in motion independently of social conditions at the time. In classical Marxist terms, it could create the objective conditions for revolution through subjective action. In fact, Dutschke, who like many in the West Berlin SDS had a tendency to think they were at a kind of Archimedean point at the centre of the world, thought that the student movement in West Berlin could be a "focus" too. In the summer of 1967, just after the death of Ohnesorg, he developed a bizarre plan to create a kind of Berlin Soviet—what he called a "free city of Berlin"—independent of the two superpowers. Dutschke not only believed the United States and the Soviet Union would allow this to happen. He also thought it could be, as he wrote under the pseudonym "R.S." in an article in the West Berlin magazine *Oberbaumblatt*, "a strategic transmission belt for a future reunification of Germany."[51] In private, he called the plan for a Berlin Soviet his *Machtergreifungsplan*—a term closely associated with the Nazi seizure of power in 1933.[52]

The article, whose authorship would become known only years later, was remarkable in several respects. Firstly, it showed that Dutschke believed that the student movement could, as it were, force history's hand. Secondly, he thought that the "foco" theory could be applied to western Europe. In other words, he was applying theories developed for the Third World to a first world country like West Germany. Thirdly, and even more surprisingly, the article in the *Oberbaumblatt* suggested that his ultimate goal was German reunification.[53] To most of the West German student movement, German reunification was a nationalist taboo associated with far right parties like the NPD. Many of them laughed at those who still believed reunification was possible.[54] But to Dutschke, having grown up in the GDR and been separated from his family by the Wall, it was part of the revolution.

This conflation of Germany with the Third World was typical of Dutschke. Again and again in his writing, he sought to apply lessons from the Third World and in particular Vietnam—a country that was also divided by the Cold War—to Germany. He seemed to see not just a connection but a parallel between the struggle of the national liberation movements in the Third World—and in particular the Vietcong—and the student movement in West Germany. The distinctions between Germany and the Third World dissolved. The implication, though Dutschke would never spell this out, was that the Germans were themselves a colonised people. As Dan Diner has shown, this was an idea that went back to the twenties, when many on the German left and right identified with Central and South American victims of American imperialism and thought Germany was itself becoming a colony of the United States.[55] This was very different from much of the student movement's rhetoric about West Germany. There were, in other words, two competing conceptions of the Federal Republic within the student movement's thinking. On one side was the idea of West Germany as a fascist state—Germany as perpetrator. On the other was the idea of West Germany as a colony—Germany as victim. For Dutschke, the Germans were not Nazis. They were the wretched of the earth.

The days after Benno Ohnesorg's death were ones in which, according to the SDS member Tilman Fichter, there was a "civil war-like atmosphere" in West Berlin.[56] After the events of 2 June, the West Berlin authorities immediately banned all further demonstrations and the

Free University brought disciplinary proceedings against the students who had participated in the "riot" at the opera house. (The proceedings were led, incidentally, by Roman Herzog, at the time a law professor at the Free University and the chair of the university's disciplinary committee and later the president of Germany.) The students, meanwhile, set up their own investigation into the night's events. The generational conflict was loaded with historical associations. The press compared the students' methods to those of the SA, Hitler's brown shirts. The students, on the other hand, saw themselves as, Ulrich Enzensberger later put it, as the "new Jews."[57]

The SDS also immediately organised a conference to debate how to respond to the escalation of violence between the state and the protest movement. The conference took place on 9 June, 1967, directly after the burial of Ohnesorg in Hanover, his hometown. It would become the high point of what Detlev Claussen has called the West German student movement's "summer of theory".[58] Around 7,000 students from around West Germany attended the conference, along with the former Marxist theoretician of the SPD, Wolfgang Abendroth, and the young Frankfurt school philosopher and professor at Frankfurt University, Jürgen Habermas. A protégé of Adorno's born in 1929, he had completed his *Habilitation* under Abendroth. Habermas had initially been sympathetic to the students and had repeatedly met with them to discuss the political situation in West Germany. He had been one of the most outspoken supporters of university reform among German professors and also shared the students' anxiety about the direction in which West German democracy was heading, especially after the formation of the Grand Coalition and what he called the "legal terror" in West Berlin. Under these circumstances, he said the student movement temporarily provided a much-needed opposition.

However, Habermas was also troubled by the kind of direct action that Dutschke, inspired by Marcuse, wanted the student movement to use to create a revolutionary situation. Habermas saw no signs that there was any objective prospect of a revolution in West Germany, however much the students wished it. Therefore, he told the conference, there was a danger that in the long-term the students could regress into "actionism"—in other words, action for action's sake. The students, Habermas said, were making the mistake of thinking that the revolution depended on their will alone. In Marxist terms, this was "voluntarism"—what Marx had once accused the anarchist Bakunin of. In these circumstances, to systematically provoke violence by the state as Dutschke seemed to be suggesting was to "play a game with terror that has fascistic implications."[59]

Dutschke, who had been in Hamburg on 2 June when Ohnesorg had been killed and returned to Berlin the following morning, passionately defended the student movement's use of provocation, which he said was not irrational at all. In advanced capitalist societies such as the Federal Republic, he argued, the forces of production had advanced to such a point that emancipation did, in fact, depend only on the will of the vanguard. "History has always been made by men," he said. "It all depends on the conscious will of the people to finally consciously make it, to control it, to subject it to their will."[60] Habermas, he said, had made the classic philosopher's mistake of merely interpreting the world and not changing it—in Marxist terms, "objectivism." Dutschke called for students across West Germany to organise demonstrations, in particular against German membership of NATO, which he regarded as "an instrument for suppressing revolutions in Europe".[61] If the authorities would not permit them, they should undertake "Kampfaktionen"—a vague term that, intentionally or not, echoed the language of the Nazis (*Kampf* and *Aktion* were both terms central to Nazi ideology).[62] Dutschke received rapturous applause.

Habermas left. But, as he drove home after midnight and turned over Dutschke's comments in his head, he became anxious at the reaction of the audience to Dutschke's speech, and particularly his use of the word *Kampf*, which seemed to confirm exactly what he feared might happen to the student movement. He returned to the conference, hoping to force Dutschke to explain his position on the use of violence, but arrived just as the congress was finishing. The hall was half-empty and Dutschke had already left. To boos and whistles from what remained of the audience, Habermas attempted to clarify what he had said earlier. He said Dutschke's calls for the systematic, deliberate provocation of state violence represented a "voluntarist ideology" that during the revolutions of 1848 would have been called "utopian socialism" and now could be described as "left-wing fascism."[63] Given the students' view of what their struggle was about and their rhetoric about the "Auschwitz generation", it was an astonishing reproach. And yet, it was one that, years later, would seem remarkably prophetic.

In Dutschke's absence, it was left to other leaders of the student movement to respond to Habermas's accusation. One—who turned out to be the last to speak at the conference in Hanover—was Horst Mahler, a 31 year-old lawyer who had represented members of the APO, including Dutschke himself, and who was leading the students' own investigation into the events of 2 June. Mahler said there was "a right to resistance in a democracy" and that "we have to ask ourselves whether we are now in a situation in which the question of resistance seriously arises."[64] He went on:

After 1945, people often asked what kind of accusations we could make of our parents' generation. Was it right to hold it against them that they did not resist the fascist dictatorship? Very quickly they raised the objection that it was a dictatorship of absolute terror in which control was all encompassing, and no one could be expected to commit suicide. But perhaps we can hold it against them that they did not resist at a time when resistance was still possible and had a point.[65]

Mahler said his generation was determined to act differently from the "Auschwitz generation" and not wait until it was too late. "And that means," he concluded, "that in this situation we are prepared to take risks and offer resistance."[66] A few days later in West Berlin, Dutschke heard an audio tape of Habermas's criticism of him. He said he was "honoured" to have been accused of "voluntarism". "Habermas does not want to grasp that it is only carefully-planned action that can prevent deaths, not only in the present but even more so in the future," he wrote in his diary. "Organised counter-violence is the best way for us to protect ourselves."[67]

At almost exactly the same time during those frenetic days at the beginning of June 1967 when students in West Germany were coming to the conclusion that they now lived in a fascist state and that it was time to begin offering "resistance", another event took place thousands of miles away that would have almost as big an impact on the West German student movement as the death of Benno Ohnesorg. At the time, it was unsurprisingly overshadowed by the events taking place in West Berlin itself. It was only years later that the effect it had had at such a crucial moment in the development of the German New Left would become apparent.

Three days after the death of Ohnesorg in West Berlin, with the West German student movement still in tumult, the world learned that Israel had invaded its Arab neighbours.[68] War clouds had been gathering for some time as the Soviet-supplied armies of Egypt, Syria and Jordan, which had pledged to liberate Palestine and had created a joint military command, mobilised on Israel's frontiers.[69] Egypt's President Nasser had spoken of "total war" and said its goal was the "annihilation" of Israel.[70] On 5 June, after Egypt had ejected a United Nations peace-keeping force from the Sinai desert and closed the Straits of Tiran to Israeli shipping, Israel launched a pre-emptive attack. Militarily, it was a stunning victory: the Israeli Defence Forces destroyed the Arab air forces on the ground, advanced rapidly through the Sinai desert and reached the Suez canal in two days, occupied the West Bank, East Jerusalem and the Golan Heights and penetrated thirty miles into Syria. By 10 June, the war was over.

There was an explosion of sympathy for Israel in West Germany when war broke out as the nascent Jewish state's existence appeared to be threatened. West Germany remained officially neutral but politicians of all parties, including the Social Democrats, expressed sympathy for Israel and there were spontaneous demonstrations in support of Israel.[71] This sympathy for Israel was typical of the mainstream consensus that had developed in West Germany since the end of the war. Under Konrad Adenauer, the Federal Republic had gradually normalised its relations with Israel.[72] In 1951, Adenauer had publicly indicated that the Federal Republic would be prepared to pay reparations to the Jewish people. The following year, he signed the Luxemburg Agreement, under which West Germany paid DM 3.5 billion to Israel and, through the Jewish Claims Conference, to Jews living outside Israel. In 1957 West Germany also began supplying arms to Israel—initially covertly—and in 1965 the two states formally established diplomatic relations, a move that prompted an Arab boycott of West Germany.

The West German media, once again led by Axel Springer's anti-communist newspapers, gleefully celebrated Israel's "Blitzkrieg" and compared the Israeli defence minister, Moshe Dayan, to Field Marshall Rommel.[73] Springer, a deeply religious man born in 1912 who had lived through the war, was in fact as haunted by the Holocaust as anyone among the post-war generation and for the remainder of his life felt a "cloud of death" hung over Germany.[74] But he drew different lessons from the Nazi past than the students. To him, the only way to respond to the Nazi past was to fight against communism—which he saw as indistinguishable from Nazism—and to unconditionally support the state of Israel. In fact, journalists who worked for him had to sign a statement committing them to a set of corporate principles that included support for Israel.[75] Springer would later quip that for six days he had published Israeli newspapers in German.[76]

Until the Six-Day War, the West German student left had tended to follow the pro-Israeli consensus of the Federal Republic's establishment. In fact, until then, younger and better-educated people tended to be more pro-Israeli than older and less educated people in West Germany.[77] The SDS, which had generally seen itself as "linkszionistisch", or "left-wing Zionist", had been at the forefront of support for Israel in West Germany and had played a key role in promoting reconciliation with Israel. But in the run-up to the war that support began to weaken. When, at a demonstration in Frankfurt against the Shah's visit to West Germany on 2 June, 1967, a student suggested holding another demonstration in support of Israel, he was told flatly by Peter Gäng, one of the West Berlin SDS's Vietnam experts, that Israel was now an imperialist country—exactly the way that the Soviet Union and the Arab states described the "Zionist entity".[78]

In the week between the death of Benno Ohnesorg on 2 June and his burial in Hanover on 9 June, the students sporadically discussed the situation in the Middle East. The day after Ohnesorg's death, the writer Günter Grass tried unsuccessfully to persuade students at the Free University to pass a motion in support of Israel.[79] Tilman Fichter would later remember the discussion as a turning point in the student left's attitude towards Israel.[80] A few days later one student activist, who said that as a member of the post-war generation he felt "no special moral obligation towards Israel", accused Grass of attempting to transfer his generation's "own guilt onto us young people".[81] While the war was still going on, the SDS declared that socialists in the Federal Republic "should not confuse their feelings for the Israeli people with the rational, economic and political analysis of the state of Israel in the international conflict between highly industrialised countries and the countries of the Third World."[82]

Like many of the students, Ulrike Meinhof was also deeply sceptical about the establishment's pro-Israeli position. In a column in *konkret* in July 1967 she distinguished between three kinds of sympathy for Israel: firstly, that of the left which had fought and continued to fight against the "the spirit and practice of the SS, whose latest victim's name is Benno Ohnesorg"; secondly, that of the United States, which was motivated by economic and strategic interests; and thirdly, that of the right-wing press in West Germany, which was motivated by anti-communism. She wrote sarcastically that "in the Sinai desert 25 years later, *Bild* won the battle of Stalingrad after all."[83] Others suggested the wartime generation's pro-Israeli position was a kind of compensation for its earlier anti-Semitism. The post-war generation, as the SDS chairman, Reimut Reiche, wrote in a letter to the weekly news magazine *Spiegel* a few days after the war, did not need to be pro-Israeli "because we don't have any problems with racism and we don't have any anti-Semitism to overcome."[84] (One critic responded that "there is a certain type of intellectual on the German left that takes dialectics out of its human context and degrades it into an immoral intellectual game."[85])

Very quickly, what was essentially a neutral position turned into hostility towards the state of Israel. In fact, within a remarkably short space of time and at precisely the point that the post-war generation was beginning to organise "resistance", its view of the Arab-Israeli conflict would be virtually turned on its head. Just as the Vietnam war had transformed the student left's view of the United States, so the Six-Day War provided the impetus for a sudden and complete transformation in its view of the Middle East. Just as the United States went from being the liberator of Germany from Nazism to an imperialist power, so Israel went from being the refuge of the victims of the Holocaust to being the "bridgehead of American imperialism in the Middle East". What had previously been seen as a nation of Holocaust survivors that the children of the "Auschwitz generation" had a special responsibility to support was now seen as a racist state that they had a special responsibility to fight against. In short, Israel went from being a "victim" to a "perpetrator" in the post-war generation's black-and-white political worldview.

Conversely, the students quickly began to voice almost unqualified support for the Palestinians. Just as they had identified with the Vietcong, so they quickly began to identify with the Palestine Liberation Organisation (PLO), which had been formed in 1964, as another "national liberation movement". In fact, such was the solidarity of the West German student movement with the Palestinian struggle that, over the next few years, it would replace the war in Vietnam as its *cause célèbre* and become an obsession for some of its members. This radical swing to the Palestinian cause, which came at precisely the moment when the Palestinians were themselves turning increasingly towards armed resistance, would have fateful consequences for the New Left in West Germany.

3

FROM PROTEST TO RESISTANCE

The death of Benno Ohnesorg on 2 June, 1967, transformed the West German student movement. Suddenly there were young people all over the Federal Republic who sympathised with the "anti-authoritarian" students' view of the society they lived in. Until then, the West Berlin SDS had had only around 30 or 40 active members. Now there were suddenly several hundred, and thousands at its teach-ins. "We were completely unprepared," Bernd Rabehl remembers.[1] The SDS, which before the summer of 1967 had effectively existed only in West Berlin and Frankfurt, also now began to spread to universities across West Germany. By the end of the year it had 2,000 members.[2] Exhilarated by the explosion of support, they began to think seriously about the "question of power"—in other words, how they might overthrow the state.

The reality, however, was the student movement remained a tiny minority in West Germany as a whole, even among university students. Gerd Koenen, a member of the SDS in Tübingen, estimates that at its height, the movement had only 20,000 active participants, 4–5,000 of them in West Berlin.[3] But although their numbers meant their dreams of a full-scale revolution were completely unrealistic, their ideas had, in fact, started to resonate beyond that tiny minority. Over the next 35 years they would exert an enormous influence, first on the West German left and then on Germany as a whole. However, at the very moment the APO appeared to be becoming a coherent national organisation, it was in fact already beginning to fall apart.

The man who was perhaps more responsible than anyone else for the fragmentation of the student movement in West Germany was Dieter

Kunzelmann, the founder of Subversive Action, who had followed Dutschke and Rabehl to Berlin at the end of 1966. Kunzelmann and his friends Rainer Langhans and Fritz Teufel were what in America were called "freaks". They had outlandish mop-headed hair and beards, wore long leather trench coats, scarves and beads, and smoked marijuana. They believed in free love and were opposed to all forms of private property. Unlike the austere theorists of the SDS, they thought the revolution should be fun. To a lot of young people in West Germany like Bommi Baumann, who would later join them, they were just much cooler than the "book worms" of the SDS.[4] While the SDS was trying to build a mass movement against the Vietnam war, Kunzelmann and his friends began to experiment with new forms of protest.

Kunzelmann was born in 1939 in Bamberg, a town in Franconia, the deeply conservative region in southern Germany then run by Julius Streicher, the publisher of the anti-Semitic Nazi newspaper *Der Stürmer*. The son of a bank manager, Kunzelmann had never been a student and considered himself an artist like the Dadaists of the 1920s. In his early twenties he had lived in Paris and then moved to Schwabing, Munich's Bohemian quarter, where he became a key figure in SPUR, the German section of the Situationist International. The situationists argued that in advanced capitalist society, man was alienated not just in his work but also in his leisure. But although they believed that there was no longer any refuge from the commodification of everyday life, they also thought the revolution was about to happen—as countless acts of rebellion, from an egg lobbed at a professor to a riot, showed. "Under the pavement the beach!" as one situationist slogan, which was to be taken up by students in Paris in May 1968, had it.

After falling out with the situationists, Kunzelmann had formed Subversive Action, the group that Rudi Dutschke subsequently joined in West Berlin. Kunzelmann, however, had a different take on the Nazi past than Dutschke. Dutschke took the traditional Marxist view that Nazism had been caused by monopoly capitalism—in other words, that it was in the system. Kunzelmann, on the other hand, was haunted by the idea that it went deeper—that it was in them. Unlike Dutschke, he turned to psychoanalysis and in particular the work of Wilhelm Reich, who argued there was a connection between capitalism and sexual repression. Kunzelmann believed that in order to liberate society one first had to liberate the individual by breaking out of the bourgeois nuclear family and conventional sexual relationships, which in his view were the real cause of fascism. Marx had famously said the philosophers had interpreted the world, whereas the point was to change it. For Kunzelmann, the point was to change yourself.[5]

But although Kunzelmann and Dutschke could not have been more different, the two men were drawn to each other. In 1966, after breaking away from Subversive Action, they began to discuss creating a "revolutionary commune" in West Berlin. Inevitably, however, Dutschke and Kunzelmann meant very different things by "commune". Kunzelmann had in mind an experimental commune along the lines of the Provos, an anarchist collective formed in Amsterdam the previous year, in which there would be no boundaries between the public and private. The somewhat puritanical, almost ascetic Dutschke, on the other hand, was thinking more of a Berlin Soviet along the lines of the Paris Commune of 1871—which he would later develop into his plan for a "free city".[6] He had little time for theories of alternative living or experiments with free love, which he considered a distraction from the revolution. Besides, he was now married.

In February 1967, just after the formation of the grand coalition, nine members of Kunzelmann's group created "Kommune 1".[7] Apart from Kunzelmann, the undisputed patriarch of the commune, the group included Fritz Teufel; Hans Magnus Enzensberger's Norwegian ex-wife Dagrun Kristensen; their nine year-old daughter Tanaquil; his youngest brother Ulrich; and Kunzelmann's two year-old daughter Grischa and her mother Marion Stergar. They moved into two apartments in the district of Friedenau, one belonging to the writer Uwe Johnson, who was living in New York at the time.[8] Hans Magnus Enzensberger himself was more than a decade older than most of the members of the student movement but shared much of their politics, in particular Dutschke's fascination with Latin America. The following year, he would quit a fellowship at Wesleyan University in Connecticut to go and live in Cuba, declaring in an open letter that the political situation in the United States reminded him "of the situation in Germany in the thirties."[9]

The commune had no television or hi-fi and there was to be no private property or monogamous relationships. The more straight-laced members of SDS called it the "horror commune."[10] For the first few months, living from money they made selling a pirate edition of Reich's *The Function of the Orgasm* to students at the Free University, the communards relentlessly psychoanalysed each other in order to reach a point where they could begin to re-create their personalities.[11] Rainer Langhans, who had become a leading figure in the SDS after moving to West Berlin in 1962 to study at the Free University and joined Kommune 1 a couple of months after it was created, says the ultimate motivation behind it was to confront their "inner fascism". "We wanted to overcome and root out this fascism, this murderousness and this influence of our parents that existed within us, not just externally by addressing the symptoms but by going deep into ourselves."[12]

Soon, however, Kunzelmann became dissatisfied with introspection—he wanted action. "He said, 'If we just sit around thinking, nothing will change," Langhans recalls. "We didn't want to end up totally resigned like the Frankfurt School."[13] Kunzelmann, who had been convicted for blasphemy in 1961 and given a suspended jail sentence, believed, like Dutschke, in the "provocation thesis". By shocking bourgeois West German society, he believed, they could shatter the conspiracy of silence and unmask the real, in other words fascist, nature of the Federal Republic that lurked beneath its democratic surface. "We will provoke massive trials and use them to publicise our ideas," Kunzelmann had written to another member of Subversive Action in 1964.[14] West Berlin, with its paranoia about communism, was what he called a "provocateur's paradise."[15]

The communards began to plan semi-political pranks deliberately designed to outrage bourgeois society, and, if possible, to break the law. They gauged the success of their actions largely by the response they got from the media and every day would trawl the West Berlin newspapers—in particular the Springer press—for articles about themselves. For Kunzelmann, any publicity was good publicity. The more pictures there were of them in the newspapers and the more vitriolic the editorials, the more effective their actions seemed to be. The media's outraged response appeared to confirm to them that West Germany was a fascist state. And they, as the communard Ulrich Enzensberger would later write, were the "new Jews."[16]

In April 1967, Kommune 1 prepared what was to be its most spectacular prank yet for the visit of US Vice-President Hubert Humphrey. While the SDS planned a conventional demonstration, the communards were busy filling balloons with custard and paint that they planned to throw at Humphrey. A few days before Humphrey's arrival, as they practised in the woods in the leafy West Berlin suburb of Grunewald, they were arrested by the police. "Planned: Berlin—bomb attack on US Vice President," headlined the outraged *Bild* the following day. Even the *New York Times* carried the story on its front page.[17]

It later transpired that the police had been informed about the commune's activities by Peter Urbach, an intelligence agent working for the West Berlin authorities. Urbach, who had worked as a plumber for the Berlin S-Bahn and hence became known as "S-Bahn Peter", had successfully infiltrated the West Berlin scene by offering to do odd jobs, and, although he never moved in to the commune, soon became an ubiquitous presence at demonstrations and meetings. When his cover was finally blown, he left the country and assumed a new identity. The West German state would never fully explain the role he played in an apparent attempt to radicalise and discredit the APO.

The communards, however, were exhilarated by the media's outraged response to their spectacularly failed stunt, which had turned them into celebrities in West Berlin. Writing in *konkret*, the columnist Ulrike Meinhof discerned in Kommune 1's stunt a "progressive moment" inspired by Marcuse.[18] It was, she wrote, "a brilliant means of irritating the police, press and politicians and provoking them into a knee-jerk reaction that exposes the moral and political insecurity of their position regarding the Vietnam war." The way the West German state had responded, she said, revealed the absurdities of its position on the war:

It is regarded as inappropriate to throw custard at politicians, but not to receive politicians who erase villages and bomb cities. [...] Napalm, yes, custard, no.[19]

Uwe Johnson, who had read about the planned attack on Humphrey in the *New York Times*, was less impressed and asked Günter Grass, who lived next door, to kick the communards out of his apartment.[20] He did so. However, the communards turned even their own eviction into a media event, with photographers taking pictures as they moved out.

The SDS, meanwhile, was growing increasingly irritated with the communards' tactics. Dutschke agreed that provocation was necessary to break the existing rules of political protest—such was the de-politicised state of the West German public that it had become anaesthetised to traditional forms of protest. But provocation, he believed, had to politicise the masses. The "pseudo-left-wing" Kommune 1 seemed to be becoming less and less interested in politics and more and more interested in themselves. They even seemed to be losing interest in the war in southeast Asia. On one occasion, Langhans had told a newspaper half-seriously, "What do I care about Vietnam? I have trouble having an orgasm!"[21] (The remark was later frequently incorrectly attributed to Kunzelmann.[22])

In May 1967, the West Berlin SDS voted to expel the communards, including Kunzelmann and Langhans—just as the members of the SDS had themselves once been expelled from the SPD. The SDS accused the commune of "existential voluntarism" and "political cynicism".[23] Dutschke, who abstained in the vote, would later say it was an "awkward attempt to maintain our political credibility as socialists."[24] In fact, it would turn out to be the beginning of the break-up of the West German student movement. It was also the end of the movement's peaceful phase. Instead of "bombs" filled with custard, soon the APO would be using real bombs to get its message across.

Two weeks later—and just a few days before the Shah of Iran arrived in West Germany—Kommune 1 distributed a series of leaflets to students at the Free University that celebrated a recent fire in the Brussels department store *A l'Innovation*, which had killed 300 people, as "a new kind of demonstration". One of the leaflets spelled out, in Kunzelmann's typically sarcastic style, what they meant:

When will the department stores of Berlin burn?

The Yanks have been dying in Vietnam for Berlin. We were sorry to see those poor pigs shed their Coca-Cola blood in the Vietnamese jungle. So we marched with placards through empty streets, occasionally threw an egg at the Amerika-Haus, and finally we would have liked to have seen HHH (Hubert Horatio Humphrey) die smothered in custard.

Now our Belgian friends have at last got the hang of really involving the whole population in the fun of Vietnam: they set a department store on fire, three hundred saturated citizens end their exciting lives, and Brussels becomes Hanoi. None of us need shed any tears over our morning newspapers about the poor Vietnamese people. From today we can just go into the ready-to-wear department of KaDaWe, Hertie, Woolworth, Bilka or Neckermann and discreetly light a cigarette in the changing rooms.

If there is a fire anywhere in the near future, if a barracks somewhere goes up in smoke, if in some stadium the terracing collapses, don't be surprised. Just as little as you were by the bombardment of the Hanoi city centre. Brussels has given us the only possible answer: Burn, ware-house [sic], burn![25]

– – – – – – – – – – – –

At the same time, the "anti-authoritarian" students were also starting to break with their intellectual fathers. As the students radicalised after 2 June, 1967, their relationship with the professors of the Frankfurt School had become increasingly difficult. Soon the students would come to perceive some of them simply as representatives of the generation they were struggling against. The split between the Frankfurt School and the student movement was epitomised by the relationship between Theodor Adorno and his doctoral student and teaching assistant, Hans-Jürgen Krahl. Krahl, a short, pale figure with a rasping voice, was never as well-known beyond the student movement as Rudi Dutschke. But within it he was an almost equally important influence and became, with Dutschke, the leader of the "anti-authoritarian" faction of the SDS. Unlike Dutschke, he was far from a gifted speaker, but was considered an even more brilliant theoretician. "He was the smartest of us all," Dutschke himself would later say.[26]

Krahl was born in Hanover in 1943. His father was an engineer who worked in the factory in Peenemünde on the Baltic coast where the V-2 rockets had been manufactured before they were moved to an underground factory to protect them from Allied air raids.[27] During one air raid in 1944, Krahl had lost his eye; since then he had worn a glass eye, which he liked to take out and show people. As a young man his inclinations were to the German romantic poets and to the political right. As a teenager he was a member of anti-Semitic organisations and in 1961 joined the *Junge Union*, the youth wing of the Christian Democrats, completing what he later called "an odyssey through the organisational forms of the ruling class."[28] As an undergraduate at Göttingen University he was influenced by Heidegger and was a member of a right-wing duelling fraternity. In 1964 he shifted to the left, joined the SDS, moved to Frankfurt and there began a PhD under Adorno. Like many others, Krahl was radicalised by the killing of Benno Ohnesorg and quickly became one of the leading figures in the student movement.

Adorno had initially been sympathetic to the student protests. He agreed with the students that the authoritarian and hierarchical structures that existed in Germany needed to be reformed, especially within the university system. He too saw the emergency laws as a threat to democracy and even helped to organise protests against them. He was disturbed by the press campaign against the protests and had even remarked during one of his sociology seminars that "the students have taken on something of the role of the Jews"—a confirmation, in effect, of the way many of the students liked to think of themselves.[29]

Adorno had been particularly disturbed by the killing of Benno Ohnesorg. He began his aesthetics lecture on 6 June, 1967, by asking his students to stand in memory of the dead student, "whose fate, whatever the reports, is so disproportionate to his participation in a political demonstration." (In the same lecture, however, he added that following the outbreak of the Six-Day War he was also worried about the "the terrible threat to Israel, the refuge of countless Jews who have fled a horrifying fate."[30]) In contrast to Horkheimer, who publicly criticised the protests against the Vietnam war, saying Germany should be grateful towards the United States because it had liberated Germany from the most terrible totalitarianism, Adorno even sympathised with the war movement. The war, he said, was proof of the persistence of the "world of torture" that had begun in Auschwitz.[31]

But like his colleague and former student Habermas, Adorno became increasingly disturbed by the students' use of direct action and especially at how they used the Frankfurt School's theories to justify it. He wrote to Marcuse in California that the students' leaders tended to "synthesise their practice with a non-existent theory, and this expresses a decisionism that evokes horrible memories."[32] The students had misunderstood Critical Theory if they thought they could make immediate practical use of it: he had never imagined, he would later say, that people might exploit his ideas to justify throwing Molotov cocktails. In any case, it was illusory to speak of a revolutionary situation in the Federal Republic.

Led by Krahl, the students in Frankfurt put increasing pressure on Adorno to publicly support them. Things came to a head during a lecture Adorno was due to give on Goethe at the Free University in Berlin in 1967. A group of students marched up to the lectern and unfurled a banner that, referring to Habermas's comments at the congress in Hanover, read: "Berlin's left-wing fascists greet Teddy the Classicist."[33] The students pressured Adorno to abandon his lecture and discuss the political situation in Berlin and in particular the impending trial of the Kommune 1 member Fritz Teufel, who had been arrested for allegedly throwing rocks at the police during the demonstrations of 2 June and was still in jail. Adorno refused. Krahl later wrote that Adorno's "progressive fear of a fascist stabilisation of restored monopoly capital had changed suddenly into regressive fear of the forms of practical resistance against this tendency of the system."[34]

Adorno remained supportive of the student movement's political demands and continued to meet with representatives of the SDS, but at the same time began to publicly distance himself from them, criticizing their use of direct action and the disruption of lectures. For him, the university was not part of the "administered world" but a refuge from it. Above all, he rejected the students' characterization of the Federal Republic as a fascist state. He warned them not to make the mistake of "attacking what was a democracy, however much in need of improvement, rather than tackling its enemy, which was already starting to stir ominously."[35]

The SDS's 22nd annual congress in September 1967 was the first at which the "anti-authoritarian" faction around Dutschke had a majority over the KPD-oriented "traditionalists" who had dominated it until then. It was also the biggest congress since 1958, with 70 representatives from 35 different universities across West Germany where the SDS was active, and hundreds more students attending to participate. There were also delegations from abroad, including one from the American group Students for a Democratic Society. The mainstream media—or "bourgeois media", as the students called it—was also present. Millions of West Germans saw television pictures of Dutschke speaking against the background of a Vietnamese NLF flag, a yellow star on a red and blue background. The five-day congress would represent the high point of the West German student movement's influence.

Until the 22nd annual congress, the West Berlin and Frankfurt branches of the SDS had been regarded as representing very different political approaches. It therefore came as a big surprise to most of the delegates when Dutschke and Krahl gave a joint paper on the *Organisationsfrage*—the "question of organisation". The paper focused on how to turn the thousands of students who had been outraged by the death of Ohnesorg and spontaneously joined the protest into a revolutionary movement. Explicitly applying Horkheimer's theory of "integral étatism"—intended to explain Nazi Germany—to post-war West Germany, they argued that in a repressive authoritarian state such as the Federal Republic in which the masses were manipulated, the opposition could no longer organise itself like a bourgeois political party. Instead they proposed that the APO transform itself into a de-centralised movement of "urban guerrillas."[36]

Dutschke and Krahl envisaged the urban guerrilla movement in industrial countries as a kind of complement to the guerrilla movements in South American countries inspired by Che Guevara (who would be killed in Bolivia the following month, and after whom, the following year, Dutschke would name his son, Hosea Che) and of course in Vietnam. From their base in the universities in West Germany, groups of *guerrilleros* would fight a campaign to undermine the institutions of the authoritarian state. Their first goals would be to prevent the emergency laws being enacted, to raise awareness about the role of the Springer press and to campaign for West Germany to unilaterally quit NATO.

The paper on the "question of organisation" became a key moment in the radicalisation of the West German student movement. At precisely the moment when the APO seemed to be on the verge of becoming a mass movement, its two most prominent leaders had suggested it start a guerrilla campaign against the West German state. In effect, it was a revival of Bakuninian anarchism, Marx's critique of which, Dutschke and Krahl said, was no longer valid. Taking the "provocation thesis" a stage further, they suggested the "propaganda by deed" of the urban guerrillas would enlighten the "passive and suffering masses" that were prevented by advanced capitalism's "massive system of manipulation" from "rising up."[37] The concept of the "urban guerrilla" would become the theoretical basis for what would become the left-wing terrorism of the 1970s. Unified by Dutschke and Krahl's joint paper, the "anti-authoritarian" faction was now able to wrest control of the SDS from the "traditionalists" and succeed in getting its candidate—Karl-Dietrich Wolff, a Freiburg law student who had been active in the campaign against the emergency laws—elected as the national chairman of the SDS.

At the same conference the SDS also passed a motion in which it unambiguously laid out its new view of the Middle East:

The war between Israel and its Arab neighbours can only be understood in the context of the anti-imperialist struggle of the Arab peoples against Anglo-American imperialist oppression. [...] The current annexation plans of Zionist capitalism have removed any remaining doubts about the reactionary character of Israel.[38]

The motion went on to reject the existence of Israel as a Jewish state, saying that its "recognition of the right of Jews to live in Palestine cannot be identical with the recognition of Israel as a bridgehead of imperialism and as a Zionist state entity.[39]

It was a crude form of guilt by association. US imperialism had already, in the minds of some of the students, become synonymous with fascism. Now, within a remarkably short space of time, Zionism had in turn become synonymous with both: in effect, Israel, too, was a fascist state. The Jewish state's policy in the Middle East was in their view a continuation of US policy in Vietnam, which in turn was a continuation of Nazi Germany's policy in Europe. To the West German students, Israel would become, as Paul Berman puts it, "the crypto-Nazi site par excellence, the purest of all examples of how Nazism had never been defeated but instead lingered into the present in ever more cagey forms."[40]

By the beginning of 1968, the atmosphere in West Berlin was becoming increasingly tense. Heinrich Albertz, the Social Democrat mayor at the time of Ohnesorg's death, had resigned and been replaced by Klaus Schütz, a close associate of Willy Brandt. Erich Duensing, the chief of police, had also quit. But a Berlin court had acquitted Karl-Heinz Kurras, the police officer who had shot Benno Ohnesorg, of manslaughter. Years later, it emerged that Kurras was in fact a Stasi agent, though there was no evidence that he shot Ohnesorg on orders from the Stasi.[41] Meanwhile Fritz Teufel had remained in jail and had started a hunger strike. The battles on the streets of West Berlin continued. The police had violently dispersed a crowd of demonstrators, led by Dutschke, who in November 1967 tried to forcibly enter the court in Moabit where the "terror trial" against Teufel was taking place. Teufel was finally acquitted in December and released.

The student movement now had huge support among young people in West Germany. According to an opinion survey carried out on behalf of the government at the beginning of 1968, more than two-thirds of students in the Federal Republic said they sympathised with the demonstrators.[42] But the protests against the Vietnam war and the emergency laws seemed to be having almost no effect on the mainstream of West German society, especially as the economy began to improve again and unemployment fell at the beginning of 1968. In frustration, the students began to turn their anger more and more on the anti-communist Springer press—Dutschke's former employer—which they regarded as responsible for manipulating the masses against the revolution and against them. The Springer press, which accounted for 70 per cent of the newspapers sold in West Berlin, had been running an increasingly aggressive campaign against the students and the man it referred to as "red ringleader Rudi" in particular. The students, who already saw themselves the "new Jews", felt there was now a "pogrom atmosphere" directed against them.[43] They likened *Die Welt* and *Bild* to Nazi newspapers like the *Völkischer Beobachter* and *Der Stürmer*.[44]

In fact, by the beginning of 1968 the campaign against the Springer press had become, alongside the Vietnam war and the emergency laws, one of the central focuses of the student movement. "Expropriate Springer!" would become one of the movement's key slogans. The SDS also talked about creating a *Gegenöffentlichkeit*, or "counter-public sphere", which in practice meant setting up a left-wing daily newspaper in West Berlin.[45] For obvious reasons, the liberal West German media was supportive of the anti-Springer campaign. In fact, several other leading German newspaper and magazine publishers, including Rudolf Augstein, the publisher of the *Spiegel*, and Gerd Bucerius, the publisher of the liberal Hamburg-based weekly newspaper *Die Zeit*, donated money to the SDS to organise a "hearing" into the role of the Springer press in West Berlin. The SDS, however, wanted to turn the "hearing" into a more radical "tribunal". Eventually, the plan broke down and neither a hearing nor a tribunal ever took place.

Dutschke, who had had a baby son (Hosea Che) in January 1968, was travelling almost non-stop to speak to young people around the country and abroad and had been appearing more and more in the mainstream media. With his own celebrity, Dutschke believed that "an authoritarian moment has entered our movement."[46] Others in the SDS had also become resentful of Dutschke's status and after he appeared on the cover of the April 1968 issue of the business magazine *Capital*, the "traditionalists", led by the Bonn student Hannes Heer, unsuccessfully attempted to kick him out of the SDS. Dutschke was also receiving an increasing number of death threats. Alain Krivine, the French student leader, remembers Dutschke showing him a pistol that his comrades had given him for protection when he met him in West Berlin in early 1968.[47] Dutschke's wife Gretchen persuaded him they should leave Germany that summer. Though Dutschke never made this public, he planned to travel with Gretchen and Hosea Che to the United States, and probably from there go on to South America to follow in the footsteps of his hero Che Guevara and join the guerrilla. Some, like his best friend Bernd Rabehl, were dismayed. "I told him, you can't just mobilise people and then say, 'Bye!'" Rabehl recalls. "'You have a responsibility.'"[48]

Meanwhile, some of the students were starting to look for more radical methods to continue their struggle. At a meeting at the Free University in February 1968 as part of preparations for the planned Springer hearing, a film student named Holger Meins had shown a short film entitled "How to Make a Molotov Cocktail," a step-by-step by guide to how to manufacture a home-made bomb. The film ended with a shot of the Springer office tower that stood next to the Berlin Wall. Dutschke was also talking more and more openly about the use of violence as part of the struggle in the Federal Republic. For him, the choice was a all-or-nothing one between, as he had put in the *Kursbuch* in October 1967, "two possibilities: to admit that there can be no peace on earth, or to take the step to resistance, to desertion, to illegal work, to sabotage on military centres."[49] By the beginning of 1968, Dutschke and his circle were, according to his wife, "feverishly thinking about what practical illegal steps they should take."[50] She says they were also making contacts with terrorist groups in other countries like ETA and the IRA.[51]

Years later, it would emerge that Dutschke had been planning to blow up an American cargo ship that was docked in a German port en route for Vietnam. The radical Italian publisher Giangiacomo Feltrinelli, who had become a kind of Godfather for the European New Left, had even supplied him with dynamite and fuses, which Dutschke took to a friend's house hidden underneath his baby son in a pram.[52] What eventually became of the dynamite remains a mystery. On another occasion Dutschke travelled to Frankfurt with a bomb provided by the intelligence agent Peter Urbach, planning to blow up an antenna used by AFN, the American armed forces radio station.[53] Technical problems stopped them following through with the plan, which Dutschke later said was supposed to be a "symbolic act" not intended to injure anyone.[54]

It was against this background that, in February 1968, the SDS staged its biggest event yet, an International Congress on Vietnam, at the Technical University (TU) just off the Ku'Damm. Two weeks earlier, the Vietcong had launched the Tet offensive, striking deep into US-controlled South Vietnam, capturing the ancient capital of Hué and even penetrating the US embassy in Saigon. Now the SDS aimed to strike a second symbolic blow against the United States by holding a massive anti-war summit in what had been the most pro-American city in Europe. The students' unannounced aim was to create a new International.[55] Dutschke also wanted to use the conference to transition into a "militant phase of the anti-Springer campaign".[56]

Five thousand people, including leaders of the anti-war movement from around the world, gathered for the conference in the University's Auditorium Maximum. Backed by a huge banner with the words "For the victory of the Vietnamese revolution" and Che Guevara's slogan "The duty of a revolutionary is to make a revolution," Dutschke now gave what was to become his most famous speech and attempted to turn the anti-war movement into a revolutionary force. He argued that it was time for the students to take the struggle against the war into the mainstream of German society, calling for a "Long March through the Institutions". It was, like the "urban guerrilla", a concept from the Third World applied to the metropolis. "The aim of the long march will be to build counter-institutions, liberated zones in bourgeois society, which will be the equivalent of the areas freed by Mao's partisans in China during the Long March of the Chinese Communists."[57] Dutschke recognised that it was a reformist proposal but saw it as one half of a "double strategy" that would be complimented by illegal actions.[58] The speech sent out ripples that would continue to be felt in Germany for the next thirty years.

The following day between 12,000 and 20,000 people, according to various estimates, gathered on the Ku'Damm and marched, chanting, "Ho, Ho, Ho Chi Minh!" and "Che, Che, Che Guevara!" to the spot in front of the opera house where Ohnesorg had been killed eight months earlier. Those who participated, especially those from abroad, left exhilarated. "We had raised our banners in the very heart of American-dominated Europe," Tariq Ali, who was there representing the British Vietnam Solidarity Campaign, later wrote.[59] The French representatives, who began their own rebellion a month later, were deeply impressed with how organised the West German students were and inspired by how radical they were. "It was in Berlin that we learned how to demonstrate in the streets," says Alain Krivine, one of the leaders of the protests that would bring France to a standstill three months later.[60]

Others, meanwhile, were already taking matters into their own hands. The highly-strung Gudrun Ensslin, who, according to a psychologist who later analysed her, suffered from a "heroic impatience," had become more and more restless since the events of the previous summer.[61] She and her boyfriend, Andreas Baader, decided it was now time to make the "resistance" to the "Auschwitz generation" that she had spoken of on the night of Benno Ohnesorg's death a reality.

Ensslin was born in 1940, the daughter of a Protestant minister from Baden-Württemberg who had been opposed to, but not resisted, the Nazis—a distinction that would become crucial for her own compulsion to act. "We have learned that it is wrong to talk without acting," she would later say.[62] As an undergraduate at Tübingen University she had met Bernward Vesper, the son of Will Vesper, a Nazi poet who had spoken at the infamous ceremonial burning of Jewish, communist and "degenerate" books in May 1933 and who celebrated Hitler as "sent by God" in a poem in 1939.[63] Vesper had grown up on his father's farm near Hanover, which had used eastern European slave labourers during the war. Vesper, who aspired to be a writer himself, had a deeply ambivalent relationship with his father, whom he hated but whom he, together with Ensslin, would also seek to re-habilitate.

For several years Ensslin and Vesper lived a bizarre double life.[64] They set up a small publishing house for radical contemporary literature and essays, calling it "neue literatur"—the same name as the anti-Semitic literary magazine that Will Vesper had edited in the thirties, which had called for a new Aryanised German literature to accompany the Nazis' racial policies.[65] They brought out books like *Gegen den Tod* (*Against Death*), an anthology of essays by leading left-wing German writers opposed to nuclear armament like Hans Magnus Enzensberger and Heinrich Böll.[66] At the same time, however, they attempted to sell privately printed volumes of Will Vesper's "Blut und Boden" poems to right-wing collectors. In 1964, after Will Vesper had died, Ensslin began a PhD at the Free University in West Berlin on the writer Hans Henny Jahnn. She and Vesper also volunteered for the SPD until the formation of the grand coalition, when they left the party. They were drawn to the student movement, and in 1966 Vesper launched a series of pamphlets by members of the APO as well as international figures from Stokely Carmichael to Isaac Deutscher. Along with the *Kursbuch*, the Voltaire pamphlets became essential reading for the student movement.

Ensslin and Vesper got engaged in 1965 and had a baby son, Felix, in May 1967—three weeks before the Shah's visit. But at a political meeting that summer Ensslin met Baader, a charismatic 24 year-old car thief who had a reputation in left-wing circles in Berlin as something of a lunatic. Baader was born in Munich in 1943 and grew up in what Dorothea Hauser has called a "community of grieving women".[67] His father, who had been an historian before the war, was killed in action on the Eastern Front. Baader was expelled from various exclusive schools he attended and, like Kunzelmann, claimed to be an artist, while making a living from theft and burglary.[68] Although he loved fast cars and motorcycles, he never tried to get a driver's license and picked up a series of convictions for driving without a licence.[69] He moved to Berlin in 1962 and two years later, like Dutschke, started an internship at the *B.Z.*[70] He was initially drawn to West Berlin's art scene rather than politics. But in the summer of 1967, he began attending demonstrations and spending time at Kommune 1, which had now moved into another apartment above a seedy bar on Stuttgarter Platz in Charlottenburg.

Whereas the communards spent most of their time sitting around, psychoanalysing each other and smoking grass or doing acid, Baader was, according to Bommi Baumann, "a Marlon Brando type" who was always getting into bar fights.[71] At a time when others still had only the vaguest idea of what "resistance" might mean, Baader had already made up his mind. Shortly after the death of Benno Ohnesorg, when a group of students suggested hanging a "Expropriate Springer" banner from the Kaiser-Wilhelm Memorial Church in West Berlin, Baader had suggested it would be better to just blow it up.[72] But despite his reputation for physical violence, he was also a dandy who tailored his own clothes and sometimes wore make-up.[73]

Baader and Ensslin became a couple and in January 1968 she left Vesper and her son, who would be raised by Vesper and Ensslin's families. Two months later, shortly after Fritz Teufel and Rainer Langhans had been acquitted of incitement to arson for publishing the "Burn, warehouse, Burn!" leaflet, they paid a visit to Kommune 1. They told the communards they planned to, as they put it, "play with fire" in a few West German department stores and asked if anyone wanted to join in.[74] No-one did. A few weeks later, Baader and Ensslin borrowed a Volkswagen and, together with two other friends of theirs, Thorwald Proll and Horst Söhnlein, set off for West Germany. They stopped off at Ensslin's parents' house in Stuttgart, and then drove on to Frankfurt.

At 6.30 p.m., on 2 April, 1968, Baader and Ensslin went into the Schneider department store in Frankfurt just before it was about to close. They put a homemade petrol bomb on a wall unit in the ladies' clothing department on the first floor and another in a wardrobe in the furniture department on the third floor. They set the timers, made using travel clocks, and left the store. At around midnight, the two petrol bombs ignited, along with others in the nearby Kaufhof department store. No one was hurt. Shortly before, a woman—presumably Ensslin—had telephoned the German Press Agency and told them about the bombs. "This is a political act of revenge," she declared.[75] It was the first action by the terrorist group that would become infamous worldwide as the Baader-Meinhof gang. The four arsonists were apprehended by the police two days later.

The reaction to the Frankfurt department store arson gave a hint of the split that was rapidly developing in the student movement. Kommune 1, which had provided the inspiration with its "Burn, warehouse, burn!" leaflet, was ambivalent, saying it did not approve of the action but "understood the psychological situation that led individuals to take such measures."[76] Ulrike Meinhof once again saw a "progressive moment" not so much in the action itself but in its criminality.[77] The SDS quickly distanced itself from the bomb attack, saying in a statement (written by the "traditionalist" former chairman Reimut Reiche) that it was "deeply disturbed that there are people in the Federal Republic who believe they can give expression to their opposition to the social and political situation in this country by such unwarranted acts of terror."[78]

But although the SDS was officially critical of the department store arson attack, Dutschke was moving slowly in much the same direction as Baader and Ensslin. In a television interview recorded in March 1968 and broadcast a month later, he suggested that he was himself prepared to use violence in the anti-imperialist struggle in West Germany:

Of course I am prepared to take up weapons as part of the struggle. And I think that there are thousands more who are prepared to fight if the Federal Republic, or to be more precise the ruling cliques and oligopolies in the Federal Republic, are not willing to go their own way outside of NATO and if they provide direct help, including in military terms, for American imperialism. In that case, we will have to defeat imperialism wherever it appears, and that means here in West Germany, using the same means that it uses itself.[79]

— — — — — — — — — —

At the same time, political violence was also breaking out elsewhere in the West. Just after 6 pm on 4 April, Martin Luther King, Jr., was shot dead as he stood on the balcony of the Lorraine motel in Memphis, Tennessee, where he had gone to campaign for union recognition for local garbage collectors. Over the next four days, there were riots in forty cities across the United States, including New York, Baltimore and Chicago. In Washington, D.C., smoke billowed up behind the Capitol. "Non-violence is a dead philosophy," declared Floyd McKissick, the director of the Congress of Racial Equality.[80] Rudi Dutschke was in Prague, where he had gone to meet with Czech student leaders, when he heard the news.

At 4.35 pm on Maundy Thursday, 11 April, 1968—exactly a week after King's death—Dutschke walked out of the SDS headquarters on the Ku'Damm, where he also lived, to go to the chemist to buy medicine for his three month-old son, Hosea Che. He was approached by a slim young man with short, carefully parted hair, wearing a light brown leather jacket.

"Are you Rudi Dutschke?" the man asked.

"Yes," Dutschke replied.

"You dirty communist pig," the man said, pulled out a pistol and shot Dutschke in the face. Dutschke fell to the ground. As he lay there, the man shot twice more, hitting Dutschke once in the head and once in the shoulder, before running away.

One of the first people on the scene was Albert Fichter, a 23 year-old architecture student at the Technical University, who, together with his older brother Tilman, a leading figure in the West Berlin student movement, also lived in the SDS building.[81] He had heard the shots and immediately rushed outside, where Dutschke fell into his arms, covered in blood and said, "They shot me."[82] As Dutschke lost consciousness, his last words were, "Soldiers, soldiers…"[83]

A few minutes later, Dutschke's assailant was found hiding in a basement by the police and arrested. His name was Josef Bachmann, a 24 year-old house painter from Munich. In his pocket he had a copy of a far-right newspaper, *Deutsche National- und Soldatenzeitung*, with the headline, "Stop Dutschke now!" along with six photos of Dutschke. He had arrived in West Berlin that morning and asked a taxi driver where Dutschke lived. The taxi driver took him to Kommune 1, where Rainer Langhans told him Dutschke did not live there and sent him to the SDS headquarters on the Ku'Damm. When Bachmann arrived there that afternoon, he recognised Dutschke from the pictures. Asked later why he shot Dutschke, Bachmann said, "I heard of the death of Martin Luther King and since I hate communists I felt I must kill Dutschke."[84] It was horribly ironic. Dutschke, an exile from communist East Germany, had been shot by an anti-communist. Dutschke, a man who had refused to do military service because he would not fire upon fellow Germans and wanted to reunify Germany, had been attacked by a German nationalist.

People soon gathered at the SDS building as they heard the news. Dutschke's shoes still lay on the street outside the building, circled by chalk, and his blood dotted the pavement. It was, however, a different atmosphere than the scene after the death of Benno Ohnesorg. There were no loud discussions or inspiring speeches. This time, there was only silent rage. The students quickly began to point fingers at the Springer press that had demonised them. They hurriedly put together a flyer that read:

Regardless of whether Rudi was the victim of a political conspiracy: we can already say that this crime is merely the consequence of the systematic incitement against the democratic forces of this city that the Springer corporation and the Berlin Senate has increasingly pursued.[85]

In the next few hours, as news emerged from the hospital that Dutschke's chances of survival were slim, around 3,000 students crowded into the Technical University's Auditorium Maximum—where Dutschke had addressed the Vietnam Congress just two months before—to plan what to do next. They passed a resolution demanding the resignation of the Berlin Senate, the expropriation of the Springer corporation, and immediate plans to democratise publicly owned radio stations in Berlin.

The students then moved to the Springer headquarters in Kreuzberg, smashing the windows of the Amerika-Haus on the way there. When they reached the office tower that stood looking over the Berlin Wall on Kochstraße, they shouted "Murderers!" smashed the windows and set delivery trucks on fire. They also threw Molotov cocktails provided by Peter Urbach, the intelligence agent who had informed the police about Kommune 1's "bomb plot". Bommi Baumann, who took part, said it was a liberating feeling to be able to fight back. "Before they transport me to Auschwitz again, I'd rather shoot back first," he said. "That's obvious."[86]

Over the Easter weekend, violence swept across West Germany as students tried to forcibly block the distribution of Springer newspapers. On Easter Monday alone, an estimated 45,000 people in more than twenty cities across West Germany—West Berlin, Frankfurt, Hamburg, Munich, Essen, and Hanover among them—took to the streets, leading to clashes with police on a scale that had not been seen since the street battles of the Weimar Republic. At the end of the weekend, a 27 year-old student and a 32 year-old press photographer had been killed, 400 people had been injured and 1,000 students had been arrested. Horst Mahler, the APO lawyer, who along with several others had managed to break into the Springer building on the night of the shooting, was relaxed about the two deaths. "We knew from the beginning that such accidents might happen," he said. "It's exactly the same as I when I get behind the wheel of a car knowing that a tyre might burst."[87]

For the columnist Ulrike Meinhof, who had herself joined the students at the SDS building immediately after she heard the news of the attack on Dutschke, it was a turning point. In a column for *konkret* entitled "From protest to resistance," she argued that a crucial boundary had now been crossed. Until now, the students had been merely protesting; now they were resisting. Paraphrasing a Black Power activist who had spoken at the Vietnam congress in Berlin, she wrote: "Protest is when I say something doesn't suit me. Resistance is when I make sure that something that doesn't suit me doesn't happen anymore."[88]

The students, Meinhof said, had now become more radical in their demands and their methods. After the death of Benno Ohnesorg, they had burned Springer newspapers; now they were attempting to blockade their distribution. After 2 June, they had thrown eggs and tomatoes; now they were throwing rocks. The violence demonstrated that there were political methods other than the peaceful protests, which, she said, "have failed because they were not able to prevent the attack on Rudi Dutschke."[89] But, Meinhof admitted, the students and the state were now locked in an essentially unpredictable spiral of violence:

Counter-violence, as it has been practised over Easter, is not designed to awaken sympathy or to get shocked liberals on the side of the Extra-Parliamentary Opposition. Counter-violence runs the risk of becoming violence, where police brutality determines the course of action, where powerless rage replaces considered rationality, where the paramilitary deployment of the police is met with paramilitary means."[90]

At the end of the Easter Weekend the students had little to show for their "counter-violence". The following Tuesday, *Bild* was still being distributed, sold and read across West Germany as if nothing had happened. The APO was left with a feeling of utter powerlessness. To many of them, it seemed that yet more radical strategies were now called for. "The fun is over," Meinhof concluded darkly.[91]

4

AN ABOMINABLE IRRATIONALISM

Rudi Dutschke survived the assassination attempt but was initially unable to speak or write and left Germany soon afterwards with Gretchen and their baby. First they went to Switzerland, where Dutschke underwent two operations to remove a bullet from his brain and then replace skull tissue. He checked into a sanatorium under the pseudonym "Mr. Klein" and was told by doctors that the gunshot wound had left him prone to epilepsy. His recovery would be long and difficult. He would also remain traumatised by the attack and would not move back to Germany for another decade. His absence left a gaping hole on the West German New Left at a crucial time.

The Dutschkes spent the summer of 1968 in Italy, where they stayed with the composer Hans Werner Henze; they then went to Ireland, where Conor Cruise O'Brien had given them the use of his house. Dutschke wanted to move to San Diego to work on his PhD under Herbert Marcuse, but was unable to get a visa for the United States. Instead they went to England and moved in with Erich Fried, the Austrian poet who had fled Vienna after the *Anschluß* in 1938 and settled in London. Later that year they had a daughter, Polly. Dutschke was given a temporary residence permit on condition that he remain politically inactive, and was accepted at Cambridge University. Meanwhile he also began to write to his assailant Josef Bachmann. "Don't shoot at us, fight for yourself and your class," Dutschke told him in one letter.[1] In March 1969 Bachmann was convicted and sentenced to seven years in prison. The following February, he killed himself. Among the five people present at his funeral was Dutschke's lawyer Horst Mahler.

While Dutschke was still recuperating, the West German masses seemed for a brief, tantalizing moment to be on the verge of developing the revolutionary consciousness he had always hoped for. On 1 May, 30,000 people—including Vice-Chancellor Willy Brandt's own son Peter—attended the Berlin SDS's alternative May Day rally. In West Berlin, members of the SDS were busy setting up grassroots groups in places like Wedding—a working-class area—in an attempt to gain support beyond the university. The campaign against the emergency laws was now coming to a head as the *Bundestag* debated the bill, and the unions now also mobilised against it. On 11 May around 50,000 students, trade unionists and workers, including 3,000 auto workers from a Ford plant in Cologne, marched on Bonn to protest.[2]

Meanwhile, in Paris, matters had already come to a head the night before. After a week of clashes with the university authorities and the notorious CRS riot police, 30,000 students—themselves inspired by their West German counterparts—had set up barricades in the Latin Quarter. All night, the *enragés*, as they became known, fought pitched battles with the police. The following day, the main trade unions, the communist-backed *Confédération Générale du Travail* (CGT) and the moderate *Confédération Française Democratique du Travail* (CFDT), called for a demonstration to show solidarity with the students. Nearly a million people took part in the demonstration on 13 May and called for General de Gaulle's resignation. Over the next ten days, as ten million workers all over the country went on strike, France stood on the brink of revolution.

Inspired by the *évènements* in Paris, the student movement in West Germany hoped it too could bring the country to a halt. On 27 May, students at universities all over West Germany went on strike. In West Berlin, German literature students at the Free University decided to seize the "means of production" and occupied the department and re-named it the "Rosa Luxemburg Institute". They locked out the professors and set up an impromptu pirate radio station, with Dieter Kunzelmann and Fritz Teufel as DJs. The aim was to "organise academia as permanent resistance to the 'emergency society.'"[3] Frankfurt University was also occupied and re-named "Karl Marx University". The students created their own "political university", with seminars on subjects like "revolutionary theory" and "the history of the right to resistance".[4]

But unlike in France, the students received only sporadic support from the proletariat. The SDS, together with trade unions, had called for a general strike to begin on 27 May. But the unions had mobilised primarily against the emergency laws. When these were finally passed on 30 May, the battle was over and the common ground they shared with the student movement was gone. The West German unions had little time for Marxist ideas that were so favourably viewed in France. So with the end of the campaign against the emergency laws, the chance of a mass movement of students and workers disappeared—and with it the possibility of revolution in West Germany. "Democracy in Germany is at an end," Hans-Jürgen Krahl declared apocalyptically in a speech in Frankfurt.[5] He said that the West German state was "prepared to turn itself into a fascist *Führer*" and warned that if the students and workers did not now begin a "new phase" of resistance, a development would ensue that "could end in war and concentration camps."[6]

It was now that the West German student movement diverged from many of its counterparts elsewhere in the West. In most other countries, the utopian movement that had gathered pace in the mid-sixties and culminated in the protests of 1968 now fizzled out. In West Germany, on the other hand, it radicalised even further as a section of the post-war generation turned to ever more desperate measures to overthrow what it saw as the fascist Federal Republic.[7] Even the convalescent Dutschke urged the movement towards greater violence. In a foreword to an anthology of *Letters to Rudi D* published as one of Bernward Vesper's series of Voltaire Pamphlets, he suggested that the West German proletariat would be disappointed that the APO had not reacted more radically towards the assassination attempt on him: "You let your guy get shot and then you go on messing around."[8] The movement's response to increasing state violence, he said, should be "increasing counter-violence".[9]

On both sides of the Iron Curtain, 1968 ended in disappointment. In France, Charles de Gaulle won the election held at the end of May and reached a compromise with the trade unions. By the end of the summer, he had regained control. In the United States, the radical hopes that were embodied by the anti-war candidacy of Eugene McCarthy in the spring of 1968 ended in November with the election of the Republican Richard M. Nixon as president. In Czechoslovakia, meanwhile, the Prague Spring had come to an end in August when Soviet troops, assisted by the East German NVA, invaded the country. "What dogs, what barbarians, what traitors," Dutschke wrote in his diary after he heard the news from Czechoslovakia.[10] Everywhere those who had led the protest movements retreated.

The West German students, however, understood their struggle as "resistance" against Nazism and could therefore not simply give up. Some did now move towards the mainstream, hoping that change could be achieved through the system. But many among the post-war generation in West Germany, including some of the leading figures in the student movement, now became even more radical. After the assassination attempt on Rudi Dutschke, a small number of them decided to wage an all-out war on the West German state. They were a tiny minority within a tiny minority, but for the next decade they would exert a huge influence on the West German left.

Horst Mahler, the APO lawyer, was in a sense the elder statesman of the West German student movement. Born in 1936, he was, like Ulrike Meinhof, slightly but significantly older and more experienced than most of the students, and by the time the rebellion started, he was already practising as a lawyer. Complete with raincoat, suit and tie, and umbrella, he was a ubiquitous figure at demonstrations in West Berlin in the late 1960s.[11] He had defended nearly everyone who was anyone in the student movement, including Dutschke himself, and also held seminars on Marxist theory for young members of the APO.

When Horst Mahler talked about the "perpetrator generation" he was, like Bernward Vesper, talking not just about his parents' generation in general but about his own parents in particular, both of whom had been, as he later put it, "convinced Nazis."[12] His father, a Silesian dentist, had been a party member and was devastated by the defeat of Nazism and the death of the Führer. Four years after the end of the war, he committed suicide. His mother had won the *Mutterkreuz*, the medal given to Aryan women who had had given birth to at least four children. After his father's death, his family moved to West Berlin, where Mahler studied law.

As a student, Mahler was, like Krahl, a member of a right-wing duelling fraternity. But after graduating, he moved from right to left and in the 1950s, like Meinhof, became active in the movement against nuclear weapons. He joined the SDS in 1959, but was forced to leave the SPD in 1961 when it banned SDS members.[13] After qualifying as a lawyer in 1963, he started a commercial law practice while at the same time becoming increasingly involved with the embryonic student movement. In 1967, he was one of the founding members of the Republican

Club, a kind of debating society for the APO, and led the students' own investigation into the death of Benno Ohnesorg. He represented many of the students who were arrested that night, including Fritz Teufel, who had remained in jail for six months.

In October 1968, Mahler represented Andreas Baader in his trial for the Frankfurt department store arson attack in April. The trial, in Frankfurt, was a media event that turned Mahler into a celebrity in West Germany along with Baader and Ensslin, who laughed, kissed and smoked cigars as the proceedings began. Mahler told the court that the attack was not primarily a protest against the Vietnam war, as Ensslin had claimed in her defence, but was in fact an act of "rebellion against a generation that during the Nazi era had tolerated millions of crimes and in doing so was itself responsible for them."[14] In other words, the arson attack had been "resistance". Mahler admitted that the judge was unlikely to understand this reasoning. If he did, Mahler said, he would have to take off his robes and join the protest movement himself. He added that if the defendants were sent to prison, it would mean that prison was the only place in this society for a decent human being.[15] The judge was unimpressed and sentenced both Baader and Ensslin to three years in prison. There were shouts of "Fascist!" from the gallery.[16]

By the time of the trial, Mahler had become not just the student movement's lawyer but one of its leaders. The night that Rudi Dutschke was shot in April 1968, Mahler had joined the students to protest at the Springer building. The following morning, *Bild* accused him of instigating the violence that had ensued and Axel Springer sued him for damages totalling DM 500,000. In November 1968—the month after the Baader trial—the West Berlin authorities called Mahler to appear in front of a disciplinary panel. On 4 November, around 1,000 students gathered outside the court on the Tegeler Weg in West Berlin, where the hearing was due to take place, with placards that read "Hands off Mahler". This time the police were hopelessly outnumbered. The students—joined, for the first time, by gangs of leather-jacketed kids from housing projects in West Berlin, so-called "rockers"—attacked them with paving stones and even captured a water cannon and turned it on them. 130 police officers as well as 21 demonstrators were injured during a riot that became known as the "Battle of Tegeler Weg."

The riot, which came just as 1968 was drawing to a close—Nixon was elected president the following day—marked, in a sense, the end of the West German student movement as a political force and the beginnig of a more militant phase of the post-war generation's struggle against the West German establishment. The violence that broke out on the Tegeler Weg was the students' revenge for the events of 2 June, 1967, when they had been helpless as they were attacked by the West Berlin police. But it also marked a turning point for the 1968 generation, especially in its attitude to the "question of violence". It was the first time the student movement had gone on the offensive. "Our resistance against the police has liberated us from our position as passive victims," proclaimed an anonymous leaflet two days later.[17] If they were just sufficiently well organised and well armed, it seemed to some in the APO, they could take on—and defeat—the state.

Meanwhile, the break between the student movement and the Frankfurt School was about to become complete. In California, Herbert Marcuse, who had visited West Germany several times during the rebellion, remained sympathetic to the students. He regarded the idea of "left-wing fascism"—Habermas's criticism of the student movement—as a "contradiction in terms".[18] The student movement, he had written in 1968, could function as a "catalyst of rebellion" within the population as a whole.[19] But while Marcuse remained optimistic, Adorno and Horkheimer were increasingly distressed by the increasing aggression of the student movement.

After the disappointments of 1968, the Frankfurt SDS was at a loss about what to do next and feared losing the support it had gained the year before. "We had mobilised people by saying that if the emergency laws were passed, it meant fascism," remembers Detlev Claussen, at the time a close friend of Hans-Jürgen Krahl. "But the emergency laws were passed and the next day the sun shone."[20] In an attempt to keep the momentum going, the Frankfurt SDS decided to try to stimulate the revolt within the university once again. It was a desperate strategy but one that Krahl believed was necessary in order to save the student movement.[21] During the winter semester of 1968–9, the Frankfurt SDS organised an "active strike", which meant disrupting lectures and preventing the university from functioning. The main building of the Johann Wolfgang Goethe University—now re-named "Karl Marx University"—was blockaded and the rector's office was violently occupied. For most of the next year, the university was in chaos, with student-led teach-ins replacing professor-led seminars. The students gave little thought to the consequences. "We considered mobilizing people more important than achieving anything politically," Claussen says.[22]

At the Frankfurt Book Fair in September 1968, Krahl and Adorno shared the podium for a panel discussion on "Authority and Revolution." Krahl accused his intellectual mentor of having deserted the student movement and the revolution. "On the threshold of praxis," Krahl declared, "he retreated into theory."[23] Günter Grass, who was a member of the SPD and would campaign for Willy Brandt during the following year's election, also shared the podium with Adorno and Krahl and admonished Adorno, who he said was afraid of his own students. Adorno replied privately to Grass that he had "nothing in common with the students' narrow-minded direct action strategies which are already degenerating into an abominable irrationalism" but did not wish to join "the platform of the German reactionaries in their witch-hunt of the New Left."[24]

For their part, the students now became yet more aggressive towards Adorno and the Frankfurt School. In December they decided it was time to "re-function" the Institute for Social Research itself. "Critical theory," the students' strike committee wrote in a leaflet:

has been organised in such an authoritarian manner that its approach to sociology allows no space for the students to organise their own studies. We are fed up with letting ourselves be trained in Frankfurt to become dubious members of the political left who, once their studies are finished, can serve as the integrated alibis of the authoritarian state.[25]

The student movement's critique of its intellectual ancestors had come full circle: those who had developed the critique of the authoritarianism were themselves now dismissed as authoritarian.

A few days later Adorno and Habermas took part in an open discussion with a group of students in an attempt to find common ground. The more militant among the Frankfurt students had started wearing leather motorcycle jackets and became known as the "leather jacket faction." The strike leaders called on the students to "smash the bourgeois academic machine". Adorno and Habermas left and the dialogue between the student movement and the Frankfurt School was over.[26] Adorno told his friend Samuel Beckett in a letter about the way the students in Frankfurt had turned on him. "Was ever such rightness joined to such foolishness?" Beckett asked rhetorically in reply.[27] Horkheimer, who was the most critical of the student movement of all the leading figures in the Frankfurt School, noted among the radical students an "affinity to the mindset of the Nazis" and thought many of the radicals would be at home in a far-right government.[28]

In January 1969, following a further occupation of the Institute led by Krahl, its directors, Adorno among them, called in the police and the students were arrested and charged with trespass. Marcuse criticised Adorno privately, writing to him that "if the alternative is the police or left-wing students, then I am with the students."[29] On the other hand, the student Detlev Claussen, who was among those who occupied the Institute, would later admit that "we gave Adorno no alternative but to call the police".[30] Adorno, who had been on sabbatical during the winter semester, resumed teaching in April 1969. His first lecture was immediately disrupted: students stormed the podium, shouted "Down with the informer!" and wrote on the blackboard, "If Adorno is left in peace, capitalism will never cease!"[31] Meanwhile a group of female hippies came onstage, scattered rose petals on him and bared their breasts in front of him. Adorno left embarrassed and humiliated and, after further disruption, cancelled his lectures for the remainder of the semester.

In the summer, the 65–year-old professor, exhausted from his struggles with the students and facing the prospect of testifying at Krahl's trial, wrote to Marcuse that he was now "in a phase of extreme depression."[32] The student movement, Adorno said, had become increasingly irrational and did not have "even the slightest chance of having any impact on society." Because of this, there was a chance that authoritarian attitudes could come to prevail within it. "I take the risk that the student movement may turn to fascism much more to heart than you," he told his former colleague.[33] At the end of July, Adorno and his wife Gretel travelled to Switzerland in the hopes of recovering his equanimity. There, on 6 August, he had a heart attack and died.

Among those who experienced first hand the tumult at Frankfurt University in 1968 was a dropout named Joschka Fischer, who was not enrolled as a student but hung around the university and got to know the key figures in the student movement. But just as Fischer was getting involved with the student movement, it was falling apart as different factions within it argued about the reasons for its failure in 1968. Fischer would be influenced not so much by the rebellion of 1968 itself as by its aftershocks. Nevertheless, he, perhaps more than any other member of his generation, would bring the ideas of the West German student movement into the mainstream and ultimately into government itself.

Joseph Martin Fischer, the youngest of three children, was born in 1948, in a small town, not far from where Gudrun Ensslin had been raised, in Baden-Württemberg, south-western Germany. Fischer's parents were ethnic Germans who had lived near Budapest, Hungary, until they were expelled in 1946. Although Fischer's father Joszef spoke German, he was a "cultural Hungarian" who had fought in the Hungarian army rather than the *Wehrmacht* in World War II and cried when West Germany defeated Hungary in the 1954 World Cup final.[34] In Budapest, he had been a self-employed butcher, but after the family's move to Germany worked in a slaughterhouse. Baden-Württemberg was one of the most affluent and conservative states in West Germany—in 1968, the far-right NPD had won 9.8 per cent of the vote in regional elections, its highest percentage of the vote ever.[35] But it was also part of the American zone, which meant Fischer grew up around American soldiers. "In comparison to our fathers, they were of course cool guys," he says.[36]

Fischer's parents had never been Nazis. As devout Catholics, they followed the Pope rather than Hitler.[37] Nevertheless, as a child in the fifties, Fischer was, like many of his generation, surrounded by silence about the Nazi past. "During that time, I only got to know German victims and heroes," he says.[38] The Eichmann trial, which began the day after Fischer's thirteenth birthday, was a "wake-up call" for him.[39] When Fischer was 14 years-old, one of his teachers showed his class a film that included footage of *Kristallnacht* and the liberation of concentration camps. "I was totally shocked," he remembers. "I wondered how it was possible that this could have happened in my country. That was when I started to confront my parents' generation and ask them how they allowed this to happen."[40]

As a teenager, Fischer started listening to Bob Dylan and dropped out of both high school and an apprenticeship with a local photographer.[41] In the summer of 1966, aged 17, he hitchhiked to London and then decided to follow the hippy trail to India but had only got as far as Kuwait when the news reached him that his sister Irma was dying of kidney failure. Soon after he returned to Germany, his father had a sudden heart attack while at work and died. Five days later, Irma also died. Fischer moved to Stuttgart, where he got a job working in a toy store. One night at the Club Voltaire, an alternative café in the city's red light district, he met a girl named Edeltraud Fischer and in April

1967—shortly before Benno Ohnesorg was killed in West Berlin—they travelled to Gretna Green and got married.

Back in Stuttgart, the newly-married couple began to attend demonstrations against the Vietnam war and in October 1967 were arrested for the first time. Fischer joined the SDS and in January 1968 even demonstrated alongside Rudi Dutschke in Baden-Baden.[42] In April 1968, he took part in the anti-Springer protests that followed the assassination attempt on Dutschke. On Good Friday—his twentieth[43] birthday—he took part in a blockade of the Springer press in Esslingen, near Stuttgart, to prevent the delivery of the regional edition of *Bild*.[43] By Easter Monday, he and Ede, as she was known, had relocated to Frankfurt and taken part in another anti-Springer demonstration there that ended in violent clashes with the police. To the young man from the provinces, the Frankfurt scene was exhilarating. He was just "a little foot soldier," as he would later put it.[44] But he had seen action.

In Frankfurt, which he would later describe as the place where he "breathed fresh air for the first time", Fischer began to work his way through Hegel, Marx and Lenin.[45] Although never officially enrolled as a student, he attended Adorno and Habermas's seminars in the famous Lecture Hall VI and also listened to Hans-Jürgen Krahl expound on critical theory over copious amounts of *Doppelkorn* in a pub near the university. In Frankfurt, Fischer also met Daniel Cohn-Bendit, one of the key figures in the *évènements* in Paris in May 1968, who was to become the decisive influence on his political development for the next thirty years. Cohn-Bendit had arrived in Frankfurt in the summer of 1968 after being expelled from France. The redheaded Cohn-Bendit (hence his nickname, "Dany le rouge", or "Dany the red") was less theoretically minded than the austere West Germans. Like many of the student leaders in Paris in 1968, but unlike those in West Germany, he was Jewish. And unlike most of the West German students who had grown up in the shadow of the Nazi past—but like Dutschke—he was an optimist.

Cohn-Bendit was born in southern France in April 1945, while his parents, Jewish-German intellectuals, were on the run from the Nazis. He would later describe himself a "child of freedom."[46] Erich Cohn-Bendit, who had been active in the Trotskyist left in Berlin before the Nazis came to power, had fled for Paris with his family in 1933. There he became part of a Marxist discussion group that met at the home of Walter Benjamin, the Jewish-German philosopher who had been close to the Frankfurt School. Hannah Arendt also sometimes attended. After his father moved back to Germany, Cohn-Bendit attended a German high school and chose West German citizenship, albeit only because, as a Jew, he was exempt from military service. As a sociology student at Nanterre University in the suburbs of Paris, an overcrowded new campus much like the Free University in West Berlin, he was influenced by the situationists. He attended the Vietnam Congress in February 1968 in West Berlin, where he met Rudi Dutschke, and left impressed by the militancy and dynamism of the SDS. He also visited Kommune 1, where, according to Bommi Baumann, Dieter Kunzelmann called him a *Saujude*—a "Jewish pig".[47]

The following month, after a group of students had been arrested for smashing the windows of an American Express office in Paris, around 150 students at Nanterre led by Cohn-Bendit started the "March 22 Movement"—a reference to Fidel Castro's "26 July Movement" in Cuba—which, along with the Trotsykist *Jeunesse Communiste Révolutionnaire* (JCR), was to become the motor of the *évènements* of May 1968. Like the student movement in West Germany, it started by demanding reform of the university but quickly broadened into a radical critique of the authoritarianism of de Gaulle's Fifth Republic. The March 22 Movement also opposed the sectarianism of the Marxist left in France and argued that the ideological positions of the various groups were of secondary importance; political positions would emerge from the struggle itself.

Within just a few months, Cohn-Bendit became as much of a celebrity in France as Dutschke was in West Germany. Jean-Paul Sartre interviewed him for *Le Nouvel Observateur* and ended by telling him, "What is interesting about your action is that it is putting imagination in power. You have a limited imagination, just like everyone else, but you have a lot more ideas than your fathers."[48] Then, towards the end of May, Cohn-Bendit travelled to speak in West Germany and, when he tried to return to France, was refused entry. On the night of 22 May, 4,000 students marched through the Latin Quarter in Paris in solidarity with him, chanting "Nous sommes tous des juifs allemands"—"We are all German Jews." It was a slogan that expressed the French students' solidarity with Cohn-Bendit but also, like the West German students' perception of themselves as the "new Jews", a desire to see themselves as victims. As Alain Finkielkraut later put it, it suggested that "every child of the post-war era could change places with the outsider and wear the yellow star."[49]

Unable to return to France, Cohn-Bendit decided to stay in Frankfurt, where the SDS had its headquarters. Although he was treated as a celebrity, he felt homesick—"without theoretical orientation and emotional roots" was how he put it—and found it difficult to integrate himself into the West German student movement.[50] It was only after the dissolution of the SDS that Cohn-Bendit found his feet in West Germany.

To the "traditionalists" in the SDS, who had close links to the illegal KPD and were implicitly loyal to the Soviet Union, the events of 1968 had proven that the "anti-authoritarian" Dutschkists had been wrong all along. History had shown that the key ideas that had defined the APO, many of which had come from Marcuse—that a revolutionary intellectual group like the student movement could align itself with national liberation movements in the Third World and become a new revolutionary subject and create the conditions for revolution—were incorrect. It had turned out that proletariat was, after all, the only revolutionary subject. In essence they rejected the ideas of the New Left and returned to orthodox Marxism-Leninism.

The "traditionalists" said the "petit-bourgeois" students needed to re-connect with the proletariat. They pointed to the series of wildcat strikes in West Germany during 1969, which seemed to suggest that the proletariat's consciousness was becoming more revolutionary and could become, in Marxist terms, a "class for itself".[51] The students therefore needed to leave the ivory tower and "establish" themselves in the factories. They set up grass roots groups in working-class neighbourhoods and factories and study groups to pore over Marx's *Das Kapital* and Lenin's *What is to be Done?*[52] The "traditionalists" were also given a boost by the legalisation of a communist party in West Germany that was directly aligned to the GDR. Given the government's tolerance of the far-right NPD, it could no longer justify the ban on the German Communist party, which had been illegal since 1956. In October 1968, around 7,000 members of the old KPD had formed a new party, the *Deutsche Kommunistische Partei* (DKP). The DKP viewed West Germany as a system of state monopoly capitalism—"Stamokap" for short—and set up cells in the factories, in particular in the metal industry, which was centred in the Ruhr.[53]

While the "traditionalists" joined groups that were aligned to the GDR and the Soviet Union, such as the DKP, many of the former "anti-authoritarian" students set up their own sub-groups—known as "K-Groups"—that tended to regard the GDR and the Soviet Union as retrograde and instead allied themselves with China or other non-aligned communist regimes such as Enver Hoxha's Albania. They were essentially sects, distinguished from each other only by single initials, obscure points of Marxist ideology and the different communist states to which they pledged allegiance and from which many of them drew financial support. Most were rigidly hierarchical and enforced strict, almost military discipline, suggesting that authoritarian tendencies still existed within the post-war generation.

Two leading figures from the West Berlin SDS—Jürgen Horlemann, who had been one of the SDS's two Vietnam experts, and Christian Semler, a close associate of Dutschke and the organiser of the "Battle of Tegeler Weg"—set up a new Berlin-based group called the KPD/AO (*Kommunistische Partei Deutschlands—Aufbauorganisation*).[54] Although it shared its initials with the old German Communist Party, it was Maoist in outlook and therefore critical of the GDR and the Soviet Union as well as the United States. Another former SDS activist from Heidelberg, Joscha Schmierer, formed another pro-Beijing party, the Communist League of West Germany (*Kommunistischer Bund Westdeutschland* (KBW)), which later became the West German Communist Party (*Kommunistische Partei Westdeutschland* (KPW)). The KBW had an especially high opinion of the Khmer Rouge in Cambodia, which it considered, along with Robert Mugabe's Zanu PF party in Zimbabwe, one of its "peer groups". Members of the group referred to Pol Pot as "brother number one".[55] One of the most successful groups, in terms of numbers, was the Communist League (*Kommunistischer Bund* (KB)), a Hamburg-based group that argued, in the spirit of the student movement, that West Germany was tending towards a fascist state.

Despite their ideological differences, the "K-Groups" all believed the priority for the vanguard was to develop closer links with the proletariat. They sent their cadres—mostly intellectual university graduates—to "serve the people" by working in factories. However, they usually found little prospect of building support for the revolution. Instead they often found apathy at best and at worst anti-communism, racism and even nostalgia for Nazism. Some of them found the dull monotony of factory work unbearable and quickly quit. Others were surprised to discover that the day-to-day life of a West German worker was relatively tolerable and began to wonder whether the West German proletariat was really as oppressed as they had always assumed.

The student movement was also fragmenting along other lines. The SDS had been almost entirely dominated by men, while female students had tended to be relegated to the sidelines. But from January 1968, a group of female SDS members led by Helke Sander, a film student who was making an agitprop film about the Springer corporation called *Break the Power of the Manipulators*, created the Action Committee for the Liberation of Women within the SDS. They refused the traditional socialist idea that sexism was a "secondary contradiction" within capitalism and organised separate campaigns around issues like the need for childcare for students with children.[56] They received a lukewarm response from the SDS leadership, however, and at the SDS conference in Frankfurt in September 1968, they staged an internal rebellion within the student movement and threw tomatoes at Hans-Jürgen Krahl.[57] It was from this group within the SDS that the West German women's movement, focused largely around the issue of abortion rights, grew. Like the student movement in general, it saw itself as being in radical opposition to Nazism and in particular rejected the traditional roles assigned to women under Nazism. In fact, so extreme was the rejection of Nazism that some of the women in the student movement regarded simply wanting to be a mother as "fascist".[58]

The influence of the intellectuals of the SDS on the APO was in any case declining, especially in West Berlin. There, what had been the student movement was by 1969 turning into something more amorphous and unpredictable. The tone of the movement was increasingly being set by people in the communes who had nothing to do with the university. Dropouts like Andreas Baader and Dieter Kunzelmann, who had only a limited grasp of classical Marxist theory and for whom action was more important than analysis, were moving into the centre of the APO, or perhaps the APO was shifting to their idea of what "resistance" was. There was also an implicit competition in which each faction tried to outdo each other in terms of radicalism. As Bommi Baumman put it, "the vanguard creates itself (Che Guevara). Whoever carries out the toughest actions sets the trend."[59]

Kommune 1 had moved, yet again, to a disused factory in Moabit that it had hoped to turn into a kind of cultural centre, complete with a disco. Fritz Teufel had left and moved in to another commune in Munich. Rainer Langhans was sick of the revolution and wanted to put on rock concerts and produce records. He and Uschi Obermaier, a model from Munich who had arrived in Berlin in 1968, had become an exclusive couple—West Germany's equivalent of John and Yoko.[60] Meanwhile, Holger Meins, the student who had made the film "How to Make a Molotov Cocktail" in 1968, had moved in. While some members of the commune, like Langhans, were becoming more introspective, others, like Kunzelmann, who had apparently been more excited than upset by the shooting of Dutschke, were becoming more aggressive.[61] When President Nixon visited West Berlin in February 1969, some members of another commune in Wielandstraße where Bommi Baumann now lived planted a bomb on his route, though it didn't explode.[62] Baumann later said it couldn't have caused any damage and had been intended "just to send a message."[63] The police subsequently searched Kommune 1 and found more bombs, and Dieter Kunzelmann and Rainer Langhans were arrested. In both cases, the bombs had been supplied by Peter Urbach, the *agent provocateur*. Demonstrations against the arrests were organised, and, like the one on Tegeler Weg in November 1968, turned into riots.

Drug use was also becoming heavier in the APO, and, as Bommi Baumann put it, "integrated into our [political] praxis."[64] The communards had started experimenting with acid and speed and Kunzelmann had even started using heroin. Finally Kunzelmann was kicked out of the commune and began hanging out with members of the "Wieland commune." It leaned more towards anarchism than psychoanalysis: while Kommune 1 sold pirate editions of Wilhelm Reich, it sold pirate editions of Bakunin.[65] Kunzelmann, his girlfriend Ina Siepmann and several members of the commune started calling themselves the "Central Council of Roving Hash Rebels" (*Zentralrat der Umherschweifenden Haschrebellen*)—an ironic reference to Mao's essay *On the Ideology of Roving Rebel Bands*.[66] They went around Berlin selling drugs, holding "smoke-ins" and throwing Molotov cocktails at the police.

Meanwhile, with court cases for criminal offences hanging over them, a growing number of young people in West Berlin were also beginning to think about going underground and beginning an all-out "armed struggle" against the West German state. In other words, the urban guerrilla strategy that Dutschke and Krahl had outlined at the SDS Congress in 1967 was about to become a reality in West Germany. In October 1969, an article about the Tupamaros, a Uruguayan urban guerrilla group, was published in the *Kursbogen*, a supplement to the *Kursbuch*. The Tupamaros became the model for a series of underground groups that formed in West Berlin. The groups would continue the struggle against imperialism in the metropolis, but no longer would they attempt to persuade the masses through teach-ins. From now on, they would speak with actions, not words—"propaganda by deed". With Dutschke gone, no one was looking to the SDS for leadership anymore. The confrontation between the APO and the state was spiralling in a direction over which the students who had started it no longer had any control.

9 November was the anniversary of *Kristallnacht*, the infamous Nazi pogrom in 1938 during which Jewish synagogues, shops and homes were destroyed and Jews attacked—the prelude to the Holocaust. On 9 November, 1969, West Berlin's tiny Jewish community (of Berlin's prewar Jewish community of 173,000, only 1,400 had survived) gathered to commemorate the anniversary at the Jewish community centre on Fasanenstraße, just off the Ku'Damm. The 250 guests in attendance at the ceremony included politicians and children from a nearby school. The centre was itself a symbol of the tentative re-birth of Jewish life in Berlin. Built in 1957 on the site of the biggest synagogue in Germany, which had been burned down by the Nazis during *Kristallnacht*, it included a library, school and kosher restaurant.

The following morning, a cleaning lady at the centre heard a ticking noise and discovered it was coming from an object wrapped in red paper hidden inside a drinks machine on the first floor of the building. It turned out to be a homemade bomb, left there the previous day. When the police forensics team examined it, it was found to be similar in construction to another that had been discovered in the police search of Kommune 1 earlier in the year—in fact, it was one of Peter Urbach's. Only a loose connection had prevented it from exploding (it remains unclear whether this was deliberate or not). Dieter Kunzelmann—who was due to begin a nine-month jail sentence for various offences and whose whereabouts were unknown—immediately came under suspicion.

The remarkable thing about the bomb in the Jewish community centre—if indeed Kunzelmann or another member of the APO was responsible—was the choice of target. It was not a symbol of the mass media such as the Springer building, nor a symbol of capitalism such as the department stores Baader and Ensslin had set on fire, nor was it even a symbol of the United States or the state of Israel. Rather, it was the Jewish community itself. Until then in the Federal Republic, such anti-Semitic attacks had been carried out only by far right or neo-Nazi organisations. The idea that a left-wing group might carry out such an attack was so shocking that most on the left simply refused to believe it. In fact, Adorno's fears about the student movement were becoming reality.

Since the Six-Day War, the Middle East had gradually replaced south-east Asia as the APO's primary focus beyond the Federal Republic. The Israeli ambassador Asher Ben-Natan—who happened to be a close friend of Axel Springer—had been shouted down at a series of discussions with students at universities in West Germany in June 1969.[68] Meanwhile, as attitudes to Israel hardened, contacts between the SDS and Palestinian groups had been quietly developing. In July 1969, a group of around twenty SDS members had flown to Amman and visited various training camps in Jordan run by Fatah and the Democratic Front for the Liberation of Palestine (DFLP), two factions within the PLO. The trip was meant to be a secret, but news leaked out and it was reported in the West German press. The SDS insisted it had been merely a fact-finding mission. But when asked if they also intended to visit Israel, Hans-Jürgen Krahl quipped, "We'll go there when it becomes a socialist country."[68]

The night before the anniversary of *Kristallnacht*, Jewish cemeteries in Berlin had been desecrated with the words "Shalom and Napalm" and "Al Fatah". The following night—hours after the commemoration ceremony at the Jewish community centre, a public meeting entitled "Palestine—a New Vietnam?" took place at the Republican Club, the debating club in West Berlin with close links to the APO. There, a leaflet was handed out, entitled "Shalom + Napalm" and signed by an unknown group called "Black Rats TW". Its text described the Israeli conflict with the Palestinians as a continuation of the imperialist war in Vietnam, and implicated West Germany, which, "using its guilty conscience about fascist atrocities against the Jews as cover, helps Israel to carry out fascist atrocities against the Palestinians."[69] It also referred to the bomb in the Jewish Community Centre—twelve hours before it had been discovered.

The leaflet went on to justify the attempted bombing, as well as the desecration of Jewish cemeteries the night before. Such actions, it said:

can no longer be defamed as far right excesses, but rather are a crucial part of international socialist solidarity. The way the left remains stuck in theoretical paralysis in dealing with the Middle East conflict is a product of a German guilty conscience: "We gassed the Jews and must protect the Jews from a new genocide." Neurotically reassessing the historic illegitimacy of the Israeli state does not overcome this helpless anti-fascism. Real anti-fascism consists of clear and simple solidarity with the fighting *fedayeen*. Our solidarity will not be restricted to verbal-abstract awareness-raising à la Vietnam. Instead we will ruthlessly combat, through concrete action, the seamless integration of Zionist Israel and the fascist Federal Republic. Every commemoration in West Berlin and West Germany reminds us that the *Kristallnacht* of 1938 is being repeated daily in the occupied territories, in the refugee camps and in Israeli prisons. The Jews driven out of Germany by fascism have themselves become fascists who, in collaboration with American Capital, want to exterminate the Palestinian people.[70]

A few weeks after the bombing, *Agit 883*, an alternative Berlin newspaper that had also run the "Shalom + Napalm" leaflet in full and without commentary, published a "Letter from Amman" by Dieter Kunzelmann, dated "mid-November 1969." *Agit 883*, whose name referred to the first three digits of its telephone number, had been started in January 1969 by Dirk Schneider, a former journalism student at the Free University, and quickly became the cult newspaper of the embyronic urban guerrilla movement. In the letter, Kunzelmann said he was now in Jordan, where he had had a revolutionary epiphany and joined Fatah. The West German left was "still in the refugee camp". He, on the other hand, had identified the enemy and joined the armed struggle—*Kampf*—against it. "What makes everything so simple here," he wrote, "is the struggle. If we don't take up the struggle, we are lost."[71]

Kunzelmann went on to explain his view of the relationship between the struggle of the post-war generation in West Germany and the Palestinian struggle:

I'm not saying that we should simply identify with the struggle of the Palestinians. The Israelis haven't blown up my house. I wasn't born in a refugee camp. But one thing is for sure: Palestine is for West Germany what Vietnam is for the Americans. The left just hasn't realised it yet. Why? Our *Judenknax* (hang-ups about the Jews). We think, 'We gassed six million Jews. The Jews are called Israelis now. So if you are anti-fascist you are pro-Israel.' It seems so simple and yet it's not true. When we finally learn to understand the fascist ideology of "Zionism", we will no longer hesitate to replace our simple philo-Semitism with clear solidarity with Fatah, which has taken up the struggle against the Third Reich of the past and the present and its consequences in the Middle East.[72]

The "Letter from Jordan" strengthened suspicions about Kunzelmann's involvement in the bomb attack on the Jewish community centre yet also gave him an alibi. In fact, it was a hoax. Kunzelmann had indeed been to Jordan, but by November he was back in Berlin. A large group of "Hash Rebels" had left Berlin in July 1969 in a Ford Transit van borrowed from the student union of the Technical University in Berlin and driven south. They stopped off in Munich, where they threw a petrol bomb through a judge's window, then drove to Italy, where they picked up money from Giangiacomo Feltrinelli and were also briefly joined by the filmmaker Wim Wenders and his girlfriend in a VW bus.[73] From there, Kunzelmann, together with his girlfriend Ina Siepmann and three others, drove through to the Balkans, Turkey, Syria and finally into Jordan just over two months later. They were taken to a Palestinian training camp near Amman, where they were shown how to fire Kalashnikovs and to make primitive bombs; they also met leading figures in Fatah, including Yasser Arafat and Abu Jihad. In October they returned to Berlin, with the exception of Ina Siepmann, who decided to remain with the Palestinians.

After their return from the Middle East, Kunzelmann's group—now known as the "Palestine Faction"—had decided, exactly as he wrote in his "Letter from Amman", to join the armed struggle. Abandoning the countercultural model of Kommune 1, they formed an underground urban guerrilla cell and called themselves the "Tupamaros West Berlin", or "TW" for short. With their hair cut short to make themselves less conspicuous, they were suddenly unrecognizable to even their closest friends. "They looked totally straight," Bommi Baumann would later write.[74] They embarked on a series of bomb and arson attacks on symbols of capitalism and imperialism in Berlin. And as their first target, they chose, of all things, the Jewish community centre.

The idea that the APO might have anti-Semitic tendencies was so astonishing that for years many on the German left would simply refuse to consider the possibility and, in fact, some still do. It was not just that anti-Semitism had been associated with the right—though many on the left took it for granted that, as socialists, they could not be anti-Semitic. What made the possibility of anti-Semitism within the APO even more astonishing was that it was a movement that had originated in the idea of "resistance" against the "Auschwitz generation". However that was part of the problem. The APO had focused so much on the continuities between Nazism and the Federal Republic and was so convinced that it had made a decisive break with the past that it simply did not consider the possibility that continuities might also exist between the ideology of the "Auschwitz generation" and its own thinking. In fact, it was not so simple. The attack on the Jewish community centre was a logical development, albeit in extreme form, of ideas that had been at the centre of the student movement since its beginnings.

Firstly, the student movement's engagement with the Nazi past had been flawed. The use of the concept of "fascism" to describe Nazism meant that although the student movement had attacked their parents' generation, they were in another sense absolving them of responsibility for Nazism and in particular for the Holocaust. By describing other states like the United States as "fascist", they had taken this tendency a step further. In doing so, they universalised the specifically German phenomenon of National Socialism and "normalised" Germany. Similarly, the application of the term "genocide" to the Vietnam war meant Auschwitz was no longer a specifically German phenomenon—what Dan Diner later called "exonerating projection".[75] The description of Israel as a fascist state was the most extreme form of "exonerating projection". Adorno had identified a similar phenomenon himself in the fifties. He called it *Schuldabwehrantisemitismus*—a new kind of secondary anti-Semitism that functioned as a psychological defence mechanism against feelings of guilt.[76]

Secondly, from its origins in a struggle against the "Auschwitz generation", the APO had developed a black-and-white worldview in which everyone was either friend or enemy; this owed as much to the right-wing decisionism of Carl Schmitt as it did to the Marxist Critical Theory of Theodor Adorno. In fact, some of its language—particularly the word *Kampf*, which, from Dutschke to Kunzelmann, it had used almost fetishistically—was strikingly reminiscent of Nazism itself. Since the Six-Day War in 1967, Israel had within a remarkably short space of time gone from friend to enemy. Although some in the student movement, like Dutschke, had defended Israel's right to exist, with the ascendancy of the "anti-authoritarian" students around him, the student movement had become increasingly obsessed with Israel.

By 1969, some members of the student movement had come to regard Zionism as a conspiracy—one of the key features of modern anti-Semitism. It took on in their minds "the stature of a invisible, gigantic force operating worldwide," as Gerd Koenen, a member of the SDS in Tübingen, later put it.[77] This was strikingly similar to earlier anti-Semitic conspiracy theories such as those that referred to the "Protocols of the Elders of Zion", the faked document published in 1905 that purported to be the minutes of a meeting of a secret council of Jews plotting world domination. At the heart of this view of Zionism was an ambiguity. "It was not always clear whether it was merely an instrument of imperialism or in fact its actual power centre and secret *spiritus rector*," Koenen wrote.[78] It was as if, with the Six-Day War in 1967, the post-war generation's anti-Semitism had found its object.[79]

Thirdly and finally, the APO's experiments with revolutionary tactics were now coming back to haunt it. Going all the way back to Subversive Action's surrealist pranks, provocation had been central to the anti-authoritarian students' methods. They thought provocation could be used to trick the media—as Kommune 1 believed it had done during the "custard attack" on Hubert Humphrey—and force the state to expose its real, fascist character. That, in turn, seemed to confirm to the students that they were the "new Jews". Given that anti-Semitism was the greatest taboo in post-war West Germany, it stood to reason that breaking it would therefore have the greatest shock effect—the student movement's "provocation thesis" taken to its logical conclusion.

Despite various leads pointing to known members of the West Berlin student scene around Kunzelmann, the police never conclusively established who was behind the attack on 9 November and no one was ever charged. It was only in 2005 that an academic, Wolfgang Kraushaar, would solve the mystery. The man who planted the bomb turned out to be Albert Fichter, the architecture student into whose arms Rudi Dutschke had fallen after being shot in April 1968. The son of a Stuttgart doctor born during a bombing raid in 1944, he had been traumatised by the experience of seeing Dutschke shot and become more militant. He had been present at the violent demonstrations at the Springer building the weekend afterwards and in the "Battle of Tegeler

Weg" in November 1968. He joined Kommune 1 and, under pressure from Kunzelmann, was soon taking two or three acid trips a day.[80] He was one of the group that travelled with Kunzelmann to Jordan in the summer of 1969. He claimed that after they returned, Kunzelmann had become more and more openly anti-Semitic, frequently using racial epithets like *Saujude*.[81] Although the bomb had been supplied by Peter Urbach, Fichter said it was Kunzelmann who came up with the idea of planting it in the Jewish community centre during the *Kristallnacht* commemoration, at which he said that "the most prominent Zionists in Europe" would be present.[82]

Fichter said Kunzelmann had repeatedly told him he wasn't militant enough and decided he should be the one to plant the bomb. "Dieter wanted to give me an anti-Semitic action to carry out as a test," he said.[83] It was also apparently part of his own personal battle with Albert's brother Tilman Fichter, who had been a critic of Kunzelmann's "Letter from Amman". Albert Fichter claimed he had not known that 9 November was the anniversary of *Kristallnacht*, and had in any case wired the bomb so that it would not go off. To what extent, if at all, Palestinian groups in West Berlin were involved in the attack remains unclear. After the bomb attack, Tilman Fichter, who had been increasingly disturbed by his younger brother's growing militancy and drug use, helped him escape to Latin America, where he remained for years.

By the end of 1969, just eighteen months after the death of Benno Ohnesorg, the student movement had virtually ceased to exist. Different factions within the SDS were pulling in different directions based on their different analyses of what had gone wrong in 1968. Some of the students, for example those that had occupied the German literature department at Frankfurt University, thought the movement had been insufficiently organised and now wanted to organise highly disciplined cadres. Some felt that the movement had failed because at the decisive moment, it had failed to mobilise the masses: they now moved from the university to the factories, focusing on creating new links with the proletariat. Others had given up on the proletariat altogether and wanted to form underground cells and wage a guerrilla campaign against the West German state. Some of the "traditionalists" within the SDS wanted the APO to try to enter parliament or even join the

SPD and its youth organisation, the Young Socialists, and "radically reform" it from within. Others still had simply become apathetic.

In October 1969, Willy Brandt, who had led the Social Democrats into the grand coalition with the Christian Democrats and helped pass the emergency laws, took over as chancellor at the head of a new coalition of Social Democrats and Free Democrats—the first Social Democrat-led government in the history of the Federal Republic. Brandt promised a continuation of the Christian Democrats' economic policy but also a raft of liberalizing social reforms. "We do not stand at the end of our democracy but at the beginning," he declared, directly contradicting the student movement's leaders' view that the Federal Republic was transitioning from democracy to fascism.[84] While 1968 had ended with a swing to the right in France and the United States, in West Germany it would lead to the most liberal government since the war. And yet, paradoxically, in West Germany, the rebellion of 1968 would radicalise even further and produce an explosion of left-wing terrorism that was more aggressive and larger in scale than anything in France or the United States.

On 14 February, 1970, Hans-Jürgen Krahl was killed in a car accident on an icy road near Marburg. He was 26 years-old. With Dutschke out of the country and no longer involved in West German politics and Krahl dead, the student movement had lost its two most brilliant leaders. A week afterwards Krahl was buried in Hanover, a funeral reminiscent of that of Benno Ohnesorg in the same city less than three years earlier. After the burial, around eighty SDS delegates from around West Germany met in the café in the architecture faculty at Hanover's Technical University and agreed to dissolve the SDS. A month later in Frankfurt, the decision was formalised at the last general meeting of probably the most politically important student organisation in German history. No one from West Berlin—where the student movement had begun—even bothered to make the trip.[85]

5

THE STRUGGLE CONTINUES

As the sixties came to an end, the remaining members of the APO in West Berlin were in a melancholy mood. Kommune 1 had continued for a few months after Kunzelmann was kicked out, but was finally abandoned after it was trashed by a group of "rockers". The commune's life had almost exactly coincided with that of the grand coalition from 1966 to 1969.[1] Fritz Teufel had gone to Munich and formed the "Tupamaros Munich", a counterpart to Kunzelmann's group in Berlin. Several months later, he was arrested and sentenced to two years in prison. Rainer Langhans and Uschi Obermaier had also moved to Munich. Soon afterwards, however, Obermaier, who had had an affair with Jimi Hendrix when he visited Berlin in January 1969, left him. Many members of the APO who remained in Berlin had a series of pending court cases or convictions against them and knew they were likely to face prison time. Some began to think about going underground and continuing the struggle from there. Their main target was the judicial system, which, more than any other part of the West German establishment, they saw as being run by old Nazis.

Following the 9 November attack on the Jewish community centre, the "Tupamaros West Berlin" had gone on a bombing spree. During November and December 1969, there were a series of twelve bomb and arson attacks on judges and the police and on American and Israeli targets such as the Amerika-Haus and the offices of the Israeli airline El Al. The campaign culminated in a bomb in KaDaWe, West Berlin's top department store, just before Christmas 1969. In an attempt to give the impression there were now numerous functioning urban guerrilla cells in West Berlin, they claimed responsibility in the name of a different group each time—the "Black Rats", "Palestine Faction",

"Amnesty International", "Red Christmas Commando"—basically, whatever occurred to them on the spur of the moment. From the beginning, however, it was clear to the Berlin police that Kunzelmann and his associates were responsible for all of the attacks. The first "Wanted" posters, which would become a ubiquitous feature of West Germany in the 1970s, went up.

Kunzelmann and his group were now almost completely isolated from what was left of the APO in West Berlin. It had not reacted to the attack on the Jewish community centre in the way Kunzelmann had hoped. In fact, instead of inspiring others to take up the armed struggle against Israeli imperialism, even the more radical members of the movement had reacted to the attack either with indifference or with antipathy. In the middle of their bombing campaign in December 1969 the Tupamaros distributed a flyer, signed by a long list of imaginary guerrilla groups, entitled, "An Explanation of why we no longer want anything to do with the bunch of layabouts called the 'APO.'" It read:

The APO is dead. We've known it for a long time, but in the past few weeks it has been proved to us in black and white just how irrevocably broken the scene really is. The front ranks are shirkers, blowhards and cowards. Those who can see through it pretend to be blind while they almost piss their pants in fear. Promises are made and not kept. It's just words, words and more words, but behind them a reality so repulsive and narrow-minded it makes you sick. We now only believe those who can guarantee that they can back up their words with actions.[2]

Kunzelmann's group had also completely abandoned Marxism. Their philosophy, in so far as they had one, consisted of an unsophisticated version of anarchism allied to a celebration of narcotics. One of their slogans ran:

Hash, opium, heroin
For a black West Berlin![3]

Their fantasies were becoming increasingly violent as a degree of cynicism that had not existed until then crept into the movement, along with a blithe romanticisation of crime for its own sake. Initially, the model for the armed groups in West Berlin had been the Black Panthers. Increasingly, however, they emulated gangsters and even Charles Manson, the cult leader who in August 1969 had gone on a killing spree in Los Angeles. Fuelled by ever-larger amounts of acid, their actions were becoming less about political goals than personal gratification: acts of terror were just another way to get their kicks. For the first time, the embryonic guerrilla groups were beginning to openly use the term "terror", which until then had been associated predominantly with the practices of the Nazi state. In the commune in the Wielandstraße where Bommi Baumann lived—officially rented by Otto Schily, a left-wing lawyer who worked with Horst Mahler and had been part of the legal team that defended the Frankfurt department store arsonists in October 1968—were posters of both Bakunin and Stalin. Its inhabitants got a kick out of explaining the apparent contradiction to confused visitors: what the two had in common was "terror, revolutionary terror."[4]

Kunzelmann, meanwhile, continued his struggle against the post-war generation's *Judenknax*. In February 1970, Palestinian terrorists failed in an attempt to hijack an El Al airliner at Munich airport, killing a Holocaust survivor in the process. In another mysterious letter to *Agit 883*, Kunzelmann suggested that "better-organised, more targeted terrorist squads organised by ourselves" would be more effective than desperate groups of Palestinians.[5] The day after the failed hijacking, a Jewish old people's home in Munich was set on fire. Seven people died from suffocation and burns as a result of the arson attack, which inevitably recalled the bomb in the Jewish community centre in West Berlin on 9 November, 1969. However, the crime was never solved.

In July 1970, Kunzelmann was finally arrested at Tempelhof airport, where he had gone to meet his girlfriend Ina Siepmann, who was on her way back from the Middle East. Unable to find him, Siepmann left the airport and drove to a four-bedroom apartment in the Schöneberg district of West Berlin. Later that day when the police opened the door with a key found on Kunzelmann and searched it, they found a vast array of incriminating evidence, including bomb-making equipment; 28 different passport photos of Kunzelmann in various outfits and disguises; Kunzelmann's diary for 1969, in which he had marked with a cross each day when a bombing or arson attack had taken place; details of his contacts with Palestinian organisations; a 36–page handwritten plan for a terrorist attack on the 1972 Olympic Games in Munich, written by Georg von Rauch, one of the group that had travelled with Kunzelmann to the Middle East in 1969; and two lemurs in a cage.[6] He was subsequently sentenced to nine years in prison. With Kunzelmann's arrest, the first half-serious attempt at armed struggle in West Germany had come to an end. Other more professional attempts, however, would soon follow.

— — — — — — — — — —

Such was the pull of the underground, with its echoes of the wartime resistance against the Nazis, that even Horst Mahler, the APO lawyer, was feeling it. At the beginning of 1969, he had given up his commercial law practice, which had in any case collapsed since he had become involved with the APO, and, together with two other young lawyers, Hans-Christian Ströbele and Klaus Essen, formed the Socialist Lawyers Collective. Mahler grew a Fidel Castro-style beard and began to see himself as a fully-fledged member of the "struggle" rather than just its legal representative. As members of the APO like Dieter Kunzelmann began to go underground, Mahler would become their link with the outside world. He had also become the political spokesperson as well as legal representative for young West Germans who had deserted from the *Bundeswehr* and had gone into hiding.[7]

Mahler had already helped Kunzelmann in his bomb campaign, for example by providing him with tickets to a lawyers' ball in January 1970 where Kunzelmann planned to plant a bomb.[8] Mahler later claimed he had been vehemently opposed to the bomb in the Jewish community centre but was told by Kunzelmann he had no right to interfere unless he himself joined the armed struggle. He now took the plunge. He got together a group of people that included Jan-Carl Raspe, a member of Kommune 2 (a spin-off of Kommune 1), Manfred Grashof, one of the *Bundeswehr* deserters, and Grashof's girlfriend Petra Schelm, a pretty teenage hairdresser.[9] After a short-lived attempt to join forces with Kunzelmann failed, Mahler's group decided to go their own way. They would be completely underground, they would be more professional and they would have guns.

In June 1969, after serving 14 months of their sentence for the Frankfurt department store arson in April 1968, Gudrun Ensslin, Andreas Baader, Thorwald Proll and Horst Söhnlein were released while they awaited the outcome of an appeal against the judgment. Baader and Ensslin, now celebrities in their own right, spent a few months in Frankfurt, where Ensslin hung around the university and began doing social work with young offenders. Then, in November, after their appeal was rejected, the four of them decided to leave the country, although Söhnlein and Proll eventually turned themselves in and completed their sentences. Together with Thorwald Proll's younger sister Astrid, Baader and Ensslin drove to Paris, where they stayed in Regis Debray's apartment for several weeks, and then on to Milan, where, like Kunzelmann, they visited Giangiacomo Feltrinelli, who was himself about to go underground and start the terrorist Partisan Action Group (*Gruppi d'Azione Partigiana* (GAP)). In Rome, they received a visit from Mahler, who was still Baader's lawyer. Mahler, who had also been to see Dutschke in London, brought them money and encouraged them to join the armed struggle. They agreed.

In February 1970, Baader and Ensslin returned to Berlin and stayed with Ulrike Meinhof, who was now living in West Berlin with her new boyfriend, Peter Homann. Meinhof had started visiting Ensslin during her time in prison and had become enamoured with Ensslin's absolute commitment to revolutionary action and disillusioned with her own life as a journalist. In April 1969 she had left *konkret*, the magazine owned by her former husband Klaus Rainer Röhl, which she said had become "an instrument of counter-revolution."[10] Since then she had agonised over whether to join the armed struggle herself. She had twins, Bettina and Regine, who were now seven years-old. But Ensslin had left her own son, Felix, with her ex-fiancé Bernward Vesper and her family. In fact, after being released from prison in 1969, Ensslin probably never even saw Felix, who was now two years-old.[11]

In West Berlin, the new terrorist cell began preparing for life on the run. Baader was sceptical of Mahler's aptitude for the armed struggle and gave him little tests—throwing a Molotov cocktail here, stealing an American tourist's handbag there—to see if he was up to it. He wasn't. In April 1970, in the course of a bungled attempt to procure guns from Peter Urbach, the intelligence agent who once again tipped off the authorities, Baader was arrested and taken to Tegel prison to finish his sentence. Many in the APO had long suspected Urbach of being an informer. It was Mahler, more than anyone, who had vouched for him.

It is not clear exactly when Meinhof decided to commit to the armed struggle. But together with Ensslin, she now hatched a plan to help Baader escape from prison. They told the prison authorities Meinhof was writing a book with Baader that would require him to visit libraries outside the prison, and acquired pistols in a neo-Nazi hangout called the "Wolf's Lair"—the name of Hitler's wartime headquarters in East Prussia.[12] One morning in May 1970, Baader was taken to a research institute in Dahlem, a quiet, leafy neighbourhood near the Free University, to meet with Meinhof. Armed with their pistols, one man and three women including Ensslin stormed the institute and helped Baader escape. In the process, Georg Linke, a 62 year-old librarian, was shot in the liver and nearly died.

The group had already made contact with the PLO through Said Dudin, a Palestinian student who had organised Dieter Kunzelmann's trip to Jordan the year before. The month after the "liberation" of Baader, the whole twenty–strong group, including Mahler, flew via East Germany to Jordan to go to a Fatah training camp. There, Baader and Mahler struggled for the leadership of the embryonic terrorist cell. Mahler, who had now exchanged his coat and tie for fatigues and a Fidel Castro-style cap, considered himself the natural leader of the cell: he had, after all, recruited Baader and Ensslin. But Baader, who refused to wear fatigues and kept on his favourite skin-tight red velvet trousers in the camp, seemed to have a hold over the other members of the group, particularly the women.[13] With Ensslin at his side, he attacked Mahler in front of the others and within days had established himself as the de facto leader of the group. Baader and Ensslin also threatened to kill Ulrike Meinhof's boyfriend, Peter Homann, who they declared was an "Israeli spy".[14] Mahler later described it as the first "outbreak of fascism" within the group.[15] Homann subsequently left and returned to West Germany.

The reality of life in the camp came as something of a shock to the anti-authoritarian West Germans, who soon clashed with the Palestinians running it. As if it were a West German university, they went on strike, during which time, much to the horror of the Algerian camp commandant, some of the female members of the group sunbathed naked on the roof of one of the huts in the camp. "The anti-imperialist struggle and sexual liberation go hand in hand," they declared.[16] After a disastrous meeting with Ali Hassan Salameh aka Abu Hassan, a senior PLO leader who was later to become notorious as the chief of operations of Black September, the terrorist group which kidnapped Israeli athletes at the 1972 Olympics, Fatah disarmed the young West Germans, stopped their military training, and politely sent them back home. Meinhof, who was now completely committed to the armed struggle, had meanwhile decided to send her twin daughters to be raised in a Palestinian orphanage. However, Stefan Aust, who had been a colleague of Meinhof's at *konkret* and was now a television journalist, got wind of Meinhof's plans through Peter Homann. Aust travelled to Sicily, where the twins were waiting to be picked up and brought to the Middle East, and reunited them with their father, Klaus Rainer Röhl.

On their return to Berlin, Baader and Ensslin began stealing cars and robbing banks to raise money for the armed struggle, while Meinhof contacted old friends and sympathisers from Hamburg and West Berlin who she thought might be prepared to help them. They gave themselves code names: Baader was "Hansel" and Ensslin was "Gretel"; Meinhof was "Anna"; and Mahler was "James".[17] They also tried to recruit new members. Tilman Fichter remembers Mahler trying to convince him to join the armed struggle and even lifting up his shirt to show him the pistol that "Comrade Urbach" had given him. "It was amazing," Fichter says. "They were a group of 30 people and they wanted to take on a functioning democracy."[18]

For Mahler, however, the adventure was soon over. In October 1970—just a couple of months after returning from the Middle East—the Berlin police received an anonymous tip-off, raided an apartment near the Ku'damm, and found him and four other members of the group. In his back pocket, Mahler had a loaded Spanish-made Llama 9mm pistol with two spare clips. He was wearing a wig and had grown a bushy beard to disguise his appearance, but the police recognised him immediately.[19] He would spend the next decade in prison.

The anarchist-influenced Daniel Cohn-Bendit was instinctively opposed to the "K-Groups" that began to form soon after he had arrived in Frankfurt in the summer of 1968. Through the influence of his father, he had always been fiercely anti-communist—his first demonstration, in fact, had been against the Soviet invasion of Hungary in 1956.[20] To Cohn-Bendit, Stalinism was a totalitarian system that represented a continuation of bourgeois thinking—it was, in a word, authoritarian. "For a young person of 1968," he wrote, "to be a revolutionary means to be against the Communist party."[21] To Cohn-Bendit, the revolution should have a light touch. At the centre of his political thinking was the idea of "spontaneism", which in classical Marxist theory was an insult. Cohn-Bendit believed that the French student movement's lack of organisation had been its strength. "Our ideology was absolute spontaneity," he would later write in his account of the évènements in Paris.[22] Even the "night of the barricades" in May 1968 had been organised spontaneously. "Everyone did something, without knowing what," he remembered.[23] That experience had given him a faith in the possibility of impromptu revolution that distinguished him from most of his West German comrades. "That night I became optimistic about history," he said. "Having experienced those hours, I can never say, "It is impossible!"[24]

Joschka Fischer was in awe of the celebrity from France who he saw as "a cross between Charles de Gaulle and Che Guevara."[25] Fischer had become a leading figure in the SDS in its dying days, so much so that his name—still written as Jòska, the Hungarian spelling—appeared on the masthead of the last ever issue of *neue kritik*, the SDS journal, in 1970.[26] In December 1969, he was also selected, along with the SDS chairman Udo Knapp, as one of five members of a delegation to attend a Fatah conference in Algiers—the first SDS trip to the Middle East since the fiasco earlier that year.[27] The West German students sat in the front row of the conference hall as the new PLO chairman Yasser Arafat spoke and Fatah passed a resolution calling for support for the Palestinians' armed struggle against Israel.[28]

In September 1970, after making a "Marxist Western" called *Le vent d'est* (*The Wind from the East*) with Jean-Luc Godard, Cohn-Bendit formed a "project group" in Frankfurt. After a year of theoretical discussion, the group became *Revolutionärer Kampf* (RK), or "Revolutionary Struggle." It never had a formal membership: it simply consisted of those who turned up to its weekly plenary sessions, which could be anything from 30 to 120 people, including several people who had been leading figures in the SDS.[29] The core of the group, however, was four men who lived in a four-story all-male commune in Bornheimer Landstraße: a German literature student named Thomas Schmid, a law student named Matthias Beltz, Fischer and Cohn-Bendit. It also included Tom Koenigs, the son of the CEO of the Frankfurt stock exchange, who in 1973 gave his inheritance to the Vietcong.[30]

As "spontaneists", or "Spontis", they agreed with the "K-groups" that it was necessary to create closer links with the proletariat but they differed about how it should be done. Unlike their communist counterparts, the "Spontis" did not spell out the relationship between the intelligentsia and the proletariat—it would be defined during the course of the struggle. They too set up "project groups" in the factories, but they were envisaged as "exploratory" groups with a dual purpose: not just to intervene in but also to investigate the realm of production. In other words, it was a learning process in which the intellectuals would learn as much as the workers.

Inspired by the militancy of auto workers in France and Italy in 1968 and 1969, Revolutionary Struggle decided to start with the massive Opel plant in Rüsselsheim 20 miles outside Frankfurt, where 35,000 people, many of them so-called "guest workers" from southern

Europe and Turkey, were employed.[31] Fischer and several other members of the group got themselves hired to work on the production line at Opel (Cohn-Bendit was already too well-known), set up a newspaper called *Wir wollen alles*, or "We want everything", and attempted to agitate and organise the workers. Fischer was fired after six months in the autumn of 1971 when he called for a strike, while most of the others couldn't cope with the hard work on the production line and quit. After the fiasco at Opel, Revolutionary Struggle looked for another focus. But unlike the "K-Groups", they were not exclusively focused on the means of production. Ultimately, it was the issue of housing in Frankfurt that became the focal point for Revolutionary Struggle and would bring it into a conflict with the Social Democrat-led city government that was reminiscent of that between the students and the West Berlin authorities a few years earlier. It was in that conflict that Joschka Fischer was to come into his own—as a street fighter.

While the remnants of the SDS tried, through a mixture of toil and terrorism, to create the revolutionary consciousness that seemed to have receded since 1968, the mood in the rest of West Germany was upbeat. In fact, beyond the universities, the communes and the embryonic terrorist cells, there was a mood of unprecedented optimism. Willy Brandt's "social-liberal" coalition ushered in the most significant period of reform since the founding of the Federal Republic. Brandt urged West Germany to "dare to be more democratic"—an implicit recognition of Adorno's criticism that democratic attitudes in West Germany were superficial and needed to be deepened, even if that meant more dissent. The grand coalition, in other words, would turn out not to be the beginning of a new era of fascism in Germany, as the student movement had feared, but rather the prelude to a period of liberal reform.

The student movement had always had an ambivalent attitude to Brandt—the "German Kennedy". Born Herbert Frahm in Lübeck, he had fled Germany in 1933 and spent most of the Nazi era in exile in Norway, where he assumed the pseudonym Willy Brandt and worked with the resistance. He returned to West Germany after the war, joined the SPD and became mayor of West Berlin in 1957. The students however disregarded his anti-Nazi past. They were more interested in the fact that he had become foreign minister in Kurt-Georg Kiesinger's government, had welcomed the Shah of Iran to West Berlin on 2 June, 1967 and had even sent Albert Speer's daughter a bunch of flowers after her father was released from Spandau prison in 1966.[32] The students were also suspicious of Brandt because Axel Springer had supported him. In October 1967, when Brandt had spoken at the Free University in West Berlin, with Springer in the audience, students including Dutschke had protested outside and Kunzelmann had distributed a sarcastic leaflet entitled "Our Willy" that compared Brandt to Hitler.[33]

But with the election of Brandt as chancellor, many young people who had been politicised by the events of 1968 began to feel that radical change was now possible within the democratic system. Although almost none of the leading figures in the West German student movement joined the SPD, thousands of young people who had sympathised with the students did. "We had the feeling that Brandt understood us," says Ottmar Schreiner, a law student at the Free University in West Berlin in 1968, who had never been a member of the SDS but had participated in demonstrations and even tried to help Daniel Cohn-Bendit return to France.[34] Turned off by the "blind dogmatism" of the "K-Groups" that had emerged out of the SDS, he instead joined the SPD in 1969 and later became a leading figure within it.[35]

The Young Socialists or *Jusos*, the youth wing of the Social Democrats, now became the leading left-wing student organisation in West Germany. In 1969, it had 190,000 members; by 1973, it had 250,000.[36] The influx meant that the conflict between the wartime generation and the post-war generation would now be continued within the democratic system and in particular within the SPD. In fact, the early 1970s were halcyon days for West German democracy. In the 1972 election, 91 per cent of the electorate voted—the highest percentage ever.[37] Moreover, while under the grand coalition political opinion had moved to the extremes, both left and right, it was now concentrated in the four main parties. In 1972 (and again in 1976) 99 per cent of votes cast were for the four main parties: the Christian Democrats and their Bavarian sister party, the CSU, the SPD and the FDP.[38]

The greatest achievement of the Brandt government was probably its *Ostpolitik*. Brandt's foreign minister, the Free Democrat Walter Scheel, began negotiations with the Soviet Union and in 1972, for the first time, the Federal Republic recognised the GDR and signed a treaty with East Germany that also guaranteed the security of West Berlin. A similar treaty with Poland followed, which finally accepted the Oder-Neisse line as the eastern border of Germany. One of the effects of the treaties was to lessen the anti-communist hysteria that had dominated the Adenauer era and that, as far as the student movement was concerned, was a major indicator of continuities between Nazism and the Federal Republic. It particularly lessened the tension in West Berlin, where the student movement had begun. In the election of 1972, the Social Democrats gained nearly 46 per cent of the vote—the first time they had ever received a higher share than the Christian Democrats and a resounding endorsement of the new direction.[39]

The Brandt government also made education reform one of its major priorities. This, however, was frustrated by the *Bundesrat*, the upper house of the West German parliament, which was controlled by the Christian Democrats, and by the Supreme Court, which overturned a proposal to give students equal voting rights on university governing bodies. Nevertheless, it made significant progress in increasing funding for education and also lowered the voting age from 21 to 18 to bring more young people into the democratic process. Soon after taking office, the Brandt government also created an amnesty for crimes committed in connection with the APO resulting in prison sentences of up to nine months. That meant that nearly all of those around Kommune 1 who were tempted to go underground because they were facing prison terms were now free. The only exceptions were Baader and Ensslin, whose sentences were too long to qualify for the amnesty.

Brandt did however soon come under pressure to crack down on the radical left. Against the background of the *Ostpolitik*, the opposition had attempted to portray Brandt as soft on communism and, in a kind of West German version of McCarthyism in the United States, fuelled fears that West German democracy might be undermined by communist sympathisers. In particular, referring to Dutschke's call at the 1968 Vietnam congress for a "long march through the institutions," the Christian Democrats raised the spectre of "extremists" infiltrating the civil service. In 1972, in response to this pressure, Brandt passed a law requiring members of the civil service to declare their allegiance to the West German constitution. The so-called *Radikalenerlaß*, or Decree on Radicals, largely re-stated existing law and was designed to exclude only members of the DKP, the pro-Soviet Communist party, but it was later interpreted more widely by the West German Supreme Court, most of whose members had been appointed during the Adenauer era.

The effect was to start a witch-hunt that lasted for most of the 1970s and which ended up excluding thousands of left-wing activists from such professions as teaching. The New Left called it a *Berufsverbot*, a "ban on careers"—a term that recalled the Nazis' banning of Jews from many professions. Many in the APO, including Joschka Fischer, saw it as a legitimisation of their fundamental opposition to the Federal Republic.[40]

To the outside world, the symbolism of Brandt's government seemed as important as the practical measures it had taken. In particular, Brandt addressed the Nazi past directly in a way no previous West German chancellor had. In December 1970, he visited Warsaw and kneeled down at a memorial to the Warsaw ghetto uprising in 1944. It was, as Jeffrey Herf puts it, "the first time that a West German chancellor had so publicly acknowledged and expressed remorse and atonement for what the Germans had done to the peoples of Eastern Europe and the Soviet Union during World War II."[41] It was an unprecedented public display of precisely the kind of engagement with the Nazi past that the West German student movement had demanded. Brandt was awarded the Nobel Peace Prize the following year.

Such gestures, however, were of little consequence to what had become known as the Baader-Meinhof group. On the run, their "struggle" had become increasingly detached from the reality of West German politics. Since the arrest of Mahler, along with four other members of the terrorist cell, they had shelved plans for "actions" as they focused more and more on simply surviving. Cut off from the outside world, the political origins and goals of the student movement, which had led to the formation of the urban guerrillas, receded into the background. Whether or not they had started off as a criminal "gang," as the West German media described them and they vehemently denied, they very quickly became one.

The group's members were now all armed with guns and permanently in disguise: Baader had dyed his hair blonde while Ensslin had cut hers short and dyed it brown. They spent most of their time and energy planning and carrying out bank robberies, stealing cars (preferably BMWs, which became known in West Germany as "Baader-Meinhof-Wagen") and blank passports, which became increasingly important as police spot checks became more frequent. Meinhof, meanwhile, was responsible for contacting sympathisers—professors, writers and journalists, many of whom she knew from her *konkret* days—who might be prepared to let "people from left-wing circles", as she put it when she knocked on doors, stay with them for a few days. At the end of 1970, the group decided to leave West Berlin as it had become too dangerous. From now on, they would criss-cross West Germany in small groups in an attempt to stay one step ahead of the police.

Tensions within the group had also worsened. Baader and Ensslin were increasingly suspicious that there was an informer in their midst and became more and more aggressive towards the others, especially Meinhof. She, meanwhile, had become more and more anxious. Old friends were encouraging her to give up the armed struggle, and she was feeling increasingly guilty about having abandoned her children. Baader had little sympathy and called her a "bourgeois cunt."[42] The group also had some new members. One was Holger Meins, the film student who had made the short film "How to make a Molotov Cocktail" that was shown in West Berlin in February 1968. A shy, slightly neurotic young man from Hamburg, Meins, who had lived for a time in Kommune 1, had wanted to use the camera as a political weapon, and had made a documentary about the visit of the Shah of Iran in June 1967. After Baader was sprung from prison, the police raided Meins' apartment and held a gun to his head. Shortly afterwards, he decided to join the armed struggle.

Apart from a short message that was published in *Agit 883* shortly after the Baader jailbreak, the Baader-Meinhof group had made little attempt to communicate with the outside world. From his prison cell, Horst Mahler had made an attempt to articulate the theory of the urban guerrilla, entitled "On the armed struggle in Western Europe", but this was rejected by Baader in what was the beginning of Mahler's estrangement from the group. Instead Baader designated Ulrike Meinhof as the official "voice" of the cell. At the beginning of 1971, she wrote a manifesto, "The Concept of the Urban Guerrilla," which gave the terrorist cell a new, official name: the Red Army Faction (*Rote Armee Faktion* (RAF)). By describing themselves as a "faction," they wanted to suggest they were part of a broader international movement. They also created a kind of logo: a Heckler & Koch machine gun against the background of a five-pronged star, with the letters "RAF."

The pamphlet expanded and developed the theory of the urban guerrilla outlined by Dutschke and Krahl in 1967. It began by attacking the group's critics, especially those on the left who had rejected their methods, and then went on to define the RAF's political position. Unlike the "K-Groups", the RAF did not think the APO had been wrong. The student movement's analysis had been correct, Meinhof said. In particular, by making a connection between the privilege of the West and the exploitation of the Third World, it had brought the West German left out of its "theoretical isolation". But it had not success-fully made the transition from theory to praxis:

The contribution of the student movement in West Germany and West Berlin—its street fights, its arson attacks, its use of counter-violence, its pathos, its exaggerations and its ignorance, in short, its praxis—has been to have recon-structed Marxism-Leninism, albeit it only in the consciousness of intellectuals, as the political theory without which political, economic and ideological facts and their manifestations cannot be grasped, and without which their inner and outer context cannot be described.[43]

As a movement of bourgeois intellectuals, Meinhof said, the APO had had unrealistic expectations and had underestimated the strength of the system it was fighting against. The student movement collapsed, according to Meinhof, when its

specifically petit-bourgeois student form of organisation proved itself unsuit-able to develop a form of praxis appropriate to its aims, when its spontaneity could not be continued either simply in the factories or in a workable urban guerrilla movement or mass organisation.[44]

Put simply, the APO had not been organised enough. Unlike Cohn-Bendit, who argued the spontaneity of the student movement had been its strength, the RAF argued it had been too spontaneous. Meinhof now called for "practical revolutionary intervention by the vanguard". It was what she called the "primacy of praxis."

The state, however, was now closing in on the terrorist cells. The *Bundeskriminalamt* (BKA), West Germany's criminal investigative agency, had formed a specialist unit to deal with what it called the "Baader-Meinhof complex" and was becoming more and more sophis-ticated in its methods. In 1971, several members of the group were arrested. In July, Petra Schelm, one of the original members of the group that had gone to Jordan, was shot dead by the police after they tried to arrest her in Hamburg. She was just 20 years-old. In March 1972, another member of the group, Thomas Weisbecker, was shot dead in Augsburg.

Soon afterwards, the RAF struck back. During May 1972, they set off pipe bombs in an officers' mess in the US Army headquarters located in the IG Farben building in Frankfurt, killing a 39–year-old officer, and at a US base in Heidelberg, killing two soldiers. They also, in the space of a few days, blew up a car belonging to a federal judge in Karlsruhe and set off three bombs inside the head office of the Springer Corporation in Hamburg. They claimed that the motivation for the "May offensive" was political. They said the Frankfurt bombing, for example, had been carried out to demonstrate that that the "crimes against the Vietnamese people have created new, embittered enemies, and that there will no longer be any place in the world where they are safe from the attacks of revolutionary guerrilla units."[45] The RAF's targets—the United States, the West German justice system and the Springer press—were indeed the same as those of the APO's leaflets and banners. However, as the timing of the attacks and the name they used in their claim of responsibility—"Petra Schelm Commando"— suggested, it was the deaths of several of their own members, rather than the political situation in Germany or elsewhere, that had prompted them into action.

Their logic was also becoming more and more bizarre and torturous. The RAF's communiqué about the Heidelberg bombing declared:

The people of West Germany are not assisting the security forces in their search for the bombers, because they want nothing to do with the crimes of American imperialism and the tacit approval of them by the ruling class here; because they haven't forgotten Auschwitz, Dresden and Hamburg; because they know that bomb attacks against the mass murderers of Vietnam are justified; and because they have learned that demonstrations are useless against imperialist criminals.[46]

Strikingly, the communiqué drew a parallel between Auschwitz and the Allied bombing of Dresden and Hamburg, echoing Meinhof's 1965 column about the bombing of Dresden and implicitly relativising the Holocaust. But despite the RAF's insistence that the West German population was behind them, the police were in fact now receiving an increasing number of tip-offs about the group's activities.

On 1 June, 1972, following one tip-off, the police identified Baader, Holger Meins and Jan-Carl Raspe entering a parking garage in the West End of Frankfurt. 150 police officers supported by armoured cars surrounded the garage and used tear gas grenades to force the three men out. Raspe and Meins gave themselves up, and several hours later, after a police sniper shot him in the thigh, they were also able to arrest Baader. Exactly a week later, a sales assistant in a clothes store in Hamburg noticed a female customer had a pistol in her handbag and called the police, who arrested Gudrun Ensslin. A week after that, after receiving another tip-off, the police raided a flat in Hamburg and arrested Ulrike Meinhof. All the founding members of the Red Army Faction—the so-called "first generation" that had grown out of the West German student movement—were now in custody. However, it was only the beginning of the spiral of violence that would emerge from the radicalised remnants of the West German student movement.

A few months later, the 1972 Olympic Games took place in Munich, the first time they had been held on German soil since Hitler's 1936 Olympics. In the early hours of 5 September, just as the games were getting started, a group of Palestinian terrorists from a group calling itself Black September—named in memory of the expulsion of Palestinian refugees from Jordan during the civil war in September 1970—broke into the Olympic village, killed two Israeli athletes, and took the remaining nine members of the Israeli team hostage. They demanded the release of 234 Palestinian prisoners held in Israeli prisons—and Baader and Meinhof.[47] The organiser of the terrorist action was Ali Hassan Salameh aka Abu Hassan, the PLO leader whom the Baader-Meinhof gang had met in Jordan in 1970. By the end of the day, all the Israeli athletes were dead.

From her cell in Ossendorf prison in Cologne, Meinhof offered a macabre defence of the terrorist attack. It was, she said, "anti-imperialist, anti-fascist and internationalist"—in fact, a model for the West German left.[48] She said it was particularly appropriate that an attack on Israelis should have taken place in Germany:

Our comrades in Black September have taken their own Black September of 1970, when the Jordanian army slaughtered more than 200 Palestinians, back to the place where the massacre was originally concocted: West Germany, previously Nazi Germany and now an imperialist centre, from where the Jews were forced to migrate from western and eastern Europe to Israel, from where Israel got its reparations and until 1965 its weapons, and where the Springer corporation celebrated Israel's *Blitzkrieg* of June 1967 as an anti-communist orgy."[49]

In Meinhof's bizarre, inverted logic, which echoed that of Dieter Kunzelmann's "Letter from Amman", Israel had become so synonymous with Nazism that the attack made brilliant sense. According to her, the fascist West German government had intended for the 1972

Olympics to wipe out the memory of "1936, Auschwitz and *Kristall-nacht*". The Arab terrorists, "displaying a sensibility for historical and political connections that only the people have", therefore decided to use it as the stage for their attack on "Israel's Nazi fascism".[50] And it was Israel, not the terrorists, which had "incinerated its athletes like the Nazis incinerated the Jews—fuel for its imperialist policy of extermination."[51]

Ulrike Meinhof had started out as the embodiment of the idea of "resistance" against the "Auschwitz generation". It was she, perhaps more than anyone else in West Germany, who had drawn attention to the continuities between Nazi Germany and the Federal Republic. But in her desperation to create, by force if necessary, a different world in which a repetition of Auschwitz would not be possible, she had embraced a radical ideology that itself had continuities with Nazism. She was not openly anti-Semitic like Dieter Kunzelmann, but under the cover of anti-imperialism and anti-fascism, she was defending the kill-ing of Jews. Like many others on the West German New Left, she had moved into a grey area between anti-Zionism and anti-Semitism.

In the process, she had also relativised Auschwitz and in doing so exonerated the German people. Later that year, she made this exonera-tion explicit in a statement that echoed Rudi Dutschke's view of the Nazi past. Testifying as a witness at Horst Mahler's trial, she declared "unless we acquit the German people for fascism—because people really didn't know what was going on in the concentration camps—we will never be able to mobilise them for our revolutionary struggle."[52]

Although the key members of the Baader-Meinhof group were now in custody, others around West Germany were also taking up the armed struggle. In West Berlin, what remained of the "Hash Rebels"—minus Dieter Kunzelmann—had coalesced into a group calling itself the 2 June Movement. The name—referring to the date of the killing of Benno Ohnesorg in 1967—emphasised the roots of the group in the West German student movement and also implicitly credited Fidel Cas-tro's "26 July Movement". Initially the 2 June Movement and the Baader-Meinhof gang had attempted to co-operate. But whereas the Baader-Meinhof gang had operated completely underground, the 2 June Movement wanted to remain part of the broader left-wing scene in West Berlin, both as a means of broadening its support and as a cover.

They had started as what might be called "armed Spontaneists".[53] In practice this meant they did "grass roots work" and also held up banks. Unsurprisingly, the quasi-military Baader-Meinhof gang considered them to be lacking in revolutionary seriousness.[54] After one of its leading members, Georg von Rauch, was killed by the police in West Berlin in a shootout in December 1971, some of its members, like Bommi Baumann, gave up the armed struggle, while others vowed to get revenge and became more professional—and more extreme.

Meanwhile, in Frankfurt, other groups were forming out of the fragments of the SDS. Karl-Dietrich Wolff, whom the "anti-authoritarian" faction of the student movement had succeeded in getting elected as the national chairman of the SDS back in 1967, had gone to the United States in 1969, where he spoke out against the Vietnam war and visited the Black Panthers in Oakland. He was subsequently called before the US Senate security committee, where he took on Senator Strom Thurmond, a member of the committee, calling him a "bandit".[55] On his return to Germany, Wolff set up a West German Black Panther solidarity committee, which was involved in helping African-American GIs stationed in West Germany to desert.[56] He also set up a publishing collective called Roter Stern (Red Star), which brought out left-wing pamphlets and, after he visited Pyongyang in 1970 at the invitation of the North Korean government, writings by Kim Il Sung.

In the early 1970s, two members of the collective, Johannes Weinrich and Winfried Böse, formed a new terrorist group called Revolutionary Cells (*Revolutionäre Zellen* (RZ)). Böse, who was known as "Boni" because his middle name was Bonifatius, was a former sociology student who was well known in the Frankfurt scene. Wolff remembers him returning from a visit to Paris in 1972, where he had met Palestinian terrorists who had asked him to investigate several premises belonging to businessmen who imported oranges from Israel.[57] Böse also recruited Hans-Joachim Klein, a mechanic whose mother had been imprisoned in Ravensbrück concentration camp during the war for *Rassenschande*, or sexual relations with a non-Aryan. "Klein-Klein", as everyone called him, had for a time been a Sponti and even lived with Cohn-Bendit and Fischer in the Revolutionary Struggle commune on Bornheimer Landstraße.[58]

For a long time, the West German police underestimated the Revolutionary Cells, whose members had continued to be involved with a plethora of legitimate left-wing political groups and initiatives. In fact, the group had at the same time become a well organised, albeit informal, network of terrorist cells, with extensive international connections, in particular to Arab groups and to the Paris-based Venezuelan terrorist Ilyich Ramirez Sanchez aka "Carlos". Hans-Joachim Klein would later claim that Böse and his girlfriend, Brigitte Kuhlmann, had provided Black September with logistical support for its attack on the Israeli athletes at the 1972 Olympics.[59]

The dividing lines between all these groups, and the other left-wing groups that had grown out of the West German student movement, including the "Spontis", were fluid. Not only did everyone know each other, especially in West Berlin and Frankfurt, but also they essentially shared the same politics and considered themselves "comrades" in the same struggle. Thus the Frankfurt "Spontis" felt they owed "solidarity" to their "comrades" in the armed struggle. In October 1968, for example, when Baader and Ensslin were on trial in Frankfurt for the department store arson attack, Cohn-Bendit sat in the public gallery and shouted at the judge, "They are with us!"[60]

Conversely, the RAF also thought they could work with Revolutionary Struggle, and other groups that had grown out of the student movement like Proletarian Front (*Proletarische Front*), a Hamburg-based group led by Karl-Heinz Roth, another former student leader. In the summer of 1973, Margrit Schiller, a member of the RAF who had just been released from prison, stayed with Cohn-Bendit and Fischer for several nights at their commune in Frankfurt and tried to persuade them to join the armed struggle. Cohn-Bendit later remembered that she always referred to the United States as "USA-SS".[61]

Schiller later said that Cohn-Bendit was not against the armed struggle in principle but wanted to talk about the "when and where", while Fischer was "absolutely against it."[62] This, however, was a discussion about tactics, not principles. The question was not whether violence was morally justified. It was merely about which particular form of violence was the most effective way to overthrow the West German state. To the "Spontis", the RAF were fighting the same struggle by different means.[63] Or, as Fischer would later put it, the differences between them were tactical and strategic, but not ethical.[64] In fact, with the exception of the "K-Groups", which had essentially rejected the ideas of the student movement and reverted to orthodox Marxism-Leninism, the post-1968 left remained, in theoretical terms, in the same place it had been in 1967. Above all, it still believed in the "continuity thesis". Its main enemy was still imperialism, which was considered synonymous with fascism, and which was represented by the West German state, the United States and Israel. Its actions had become increasingly extreme. But it still understood its struggle as "resistance" in the same way as the student movement had.

From the "Spontis" to the RAF, the West German New Left also still believed in the provocation thesis. The concept of violence against the state as "provocation" had originated in the student movement, influenced by Marcuse's theory of "repressive tolerance" and anarchist-influenced theories of "propaganda by deed". Violence against the state, so the theory went, would expose the fascism hidden beneath the surface of capitalism. The RAF conceived of the whole enterprise, in fact, as a kind of Brechtian *Lehrstück* (Brecht's *Die Maßnahme*, or *The Measures Taken*, was required reading for members of the RAF) through which the audience—the West German proletariat—would come to understand the true fascist nature of the Federal Republic.[65] The provocation thesis was, as Gerd Koenen later wrote, "the central *idée fixe* that united the core political personnel of the 68er movement and the terrorist groups."[66] They would now test its limits.

Meanwhile for other members of West Germany's post-war generation, the burden of being the children of Nazis was already too much to bear. After Gudrun Ensslin had left him, Bernward Vesper had remained obsessed with her and unsuccessfully attempted to seduce her 14 year-old sister Ruth. Over the next two years, as Ensslin went underground, Vesper sunk deeper into despair and experimented with drugs, particularly LSD, as a way of finding what he called his "centre", where, according to Wilhelm Reich, the "natural, the normal, the healthy" self resided.[67] Still struggling with his own identity as the son of Will Vesper—his friends in Berlin complained that he would constantly talk about the "Hitler in me"—he returned to the manor house in Triangel near Hanover where he grew up.[68]

There, influenced by acid and by Jack Kerouac's idea of "spontaneous prose", Vesper began to write a psychedelic "novel-essay" that he originally planned to call *Hate* and eventually entitled *The Trip* (*Die Reise*). The semi-autobiographical book combined a bitter account of the "subtle fascism" of his childhood with a stream-of-consciousness description of his experiences during an acid trip with a Jewish-American alter ego named "Burton". In it the narrator alternated between bitter tirades against the Germans, whom he referred to as "vegetables", and visions that he, the narrator, was Hitler.[69] Before it was completed, however, Vesper was admitted to a mental hospital in Hamburg, where in May 1971 he killed himself with an overdose of sleeping pills.[70]

The West End was an affluent, middle-class residential area of Frankfurt between the city centre and the university, consisting of ornate, turn-of-the century villas that had escaped extensive damage from wartime bombing raids. Among its inhabitants were a number of academics—Theodor Adorno, for example, had lived there until his death in 1969. In the summer of 1968, to the horror of local residents, the city—which had become West Germany's financial capital after the war and had expanded rapidly—agreed to a developer's plan to build a 20–storey tower block on the site of the Rothschild park nearby, which seemed to indicate that the West End was about to be transformed into an area of office blocks.[71]

The re-development of the West End was symptomatic of a broader problem in Frankfurt. Rents in the city, where West Germany's central bank, the *Bundesbank*, was located, had been rising, driven partly by real estate speculators. By 1970, many of the buildings in the West End were empty, while affordable housing was scarce. The issue had particularly affected the families of "guest workers"—immigrants from southern Europe and Turkey who had come to West Germany in the 1950s and 1960s—who had organised protests and rent strikes. In September 1970, a group of twenty students barricaded themselves inside a large, empty five-storey corner building in the West End and handed out a leaflet in which they said they were prepared to negotiate a "reasonable" rent with the owner.[72] The owners of the building took legal action to remove the squatters but were unsuccessful.

For many of the revolutionary left-wing groups in Frankfurt like the "K-Groups", housing was a non-issue or, in Marxist terminology, a "secondary contradiction." But for the "Spontis", it was an opportunity to make a radical critique of capitalist ideas about property (profit was more important than human needs), while also being practical (it opened up living space for those in need) and experimental (it created an alternative commune-like living arrangement). One Saturday in September 1971, they occupied Bockenheimer Landstraße 111, a large stucco house near the university that belonged to the real estate developer Ignatz Bubis. In the months that followed, they took over two adjoining buildings, turning them into what became known as the "Block," an elaborately fortified headquarters. It was from here that the "Spontis" co-ordinated what they called the *Häuserkampf*—a term that literally meant "house-to-house-fighting" and that conjured up images of the battle of Stalingrad.

The first confrontation took place on a Wednesday in March 1973, when the police attempted to clear Kettenhofweg 51, another occupied building that was coincidentally located on the same street where Baader, Meins and Raspe had been captured the previous summer. Revolutionary Struggle had transformed the building into a fortress surrounded by large pieces of furniture to hinder the police's advance. From speakers inside the house, the squatters played the Rolling Stones' "Street Fighting Man" and shouted "Hands off Ketten-hofweg." For two and a half hours, in scenes reminiscent of Paris in May 1968, hundreds of police officers fought running battles with demonstrators who threw rocks and paving stones from outside the building, inside neighbouring buildings that had also been occupied, and in the side streets. Despite using water cannon and tear gas, the police were unable to break through. "Bloody Wednesday", as it became known, was a huge success for Revolutionary Struggle. Between 3,000 and 5,000 people took part in the usual Saturday demonstration three days later, bringing the centre of Frankfurt to a standstill and leading to further clashes between demonstrators and the police. The level of violence, and the organisation of the demonstrators, was a shock to the Frankfurt authorities and the city's Social Democrat mayor, Rudi Arndt.

With the outbreak of the *Häuserkampf* in Frankfurt, a new group emerged within Revolutionary Struggle. They were known as the *Putzgruppe* or, literally, the "cleaners": a group of around 20 men, mostly the more athletic members of Revolutionary Struggle and often also the most proletarian, who specialised in defending the houses against the police.[73] Their leader was Joschka Fischer, whom some even started to call the "defence minister." Although Fischer had avoided military service because of his poor eyesight, other people in Revolutionary Struggle thought physical combat seemed to come naturally to him.[74] Under his leadership, the *Putzgruppe* practised hand-to-hand combat with police equipment near the Taunus river on Sundays. They were almost medieval in style and tactics: wearing thick leather jackets and motorcycle helmets and armed with sticks and shields, they specialised in hit-and-run attacks and in isolating small groups or individual police officers and surrounding them.[75] During one clash between the *Putzgruppe* and the police in April 1973, a group wearing motorcycle helmets surrounded a police officer, Rainer Marx, and repeatedly punched and kicked him. Several photographers captured the scene and it was shown on German TV later that night, but the identity of the men was not known. In fact, Fischer was one of them.

The police finally moved in against the "Block" with military precision in the early hours of 21 February 1974. They surrounded the building, lit it with floodlights, then at 4.20 a.m., took apart the barricades outside the building with chain saws and heavy equipment. They entered the three occupied houses and cleared them before reinforcements arrived. Within hours they had pulled the building down. The owner of the building, Ignatz Bubis, who happened to be a leader of the Jewish community in Frankfurt and later the chairman of the Council of German Jews, told the press that within two weeks work would begin on a 28–storey office tower.[76] In fact, it remained as rubble for more than a decade.

The Saturday after the "Block" was demolished, 6,000 people marched in silence through the centre of Frankfurt in protest against the city's policy, as if mourning the end of the West End as a residential district. After the demonstration had ended, a riot started that eclipsed even the previous clashes with the police. Plain clothes officers mixed in with the demonstrators were particularly aggressive, shattering the shins of a 25 year-old demonstrator. By the end of the day, 200 demonstrators and 77 policemen had been injured and 192 arrests had been made. The police also forced their way into Frankfurt University's student union building, where many of the demonstrators had taken refuge. Some of those arrested would later claim they were tortured in police custody and one 18 year-old claimed that he had been forced to lick his own blood. Fischer, comparing the authorities to the regime of General Pinochet in Chile, described it as "Santiago in Frankfurt."[77]

From the moment of Baader, Ensslin and Meinhof's arrest, the RAF ceased to be a political movement in any meaningful sense. Where the original rationale for its violence had been to expose the fascism hidden within capitalism, the terrorist cell now turned inwards and focused solely on changing the conditions of its leaders' imprisonment with their freedom the ultimate goal—Baader's freedom above all. Though they took many of their sympathisers with them, they lost any connection with the wider political struggle on the outside and they, along with most of the other West German terrorist groups, became, as Rainer Langhans later put it, nothing more than a "free the guerrilla guerrilla".[78]

The members of the RAF were scattered around various maximum security prisons across West Germany—Baader in Schwalmstadt, north of Frankfurt; Ensslin in Essen; Meinhof in Cologne—and they were kept in almost complete isolation from each other and from other prisoners. Mostly confined to their cells, they were allowed visitors only rarely, and then only with a guard present. The authorities insisted that it was normal procedure to keep those awaiting trial in solitary confinement. However, the RAF had to wait much longer for their trial to commence than regular prisoners. They complained that the state was trying to destroy their "revolutionary identity", which in turn, of course, consisted of using any means necessary to destroy the state.

At the same time, however, some leading members of the RAF seemed almost pleased that the conditions they were being held in confirmed their accusations that the West German state was fascist in nature and their claims that they were the "new Jews". As they awaited trial, the RAF imagined they were in a concentration camp or even a death camp. In other words, the provocation had worked, and the hidden brutality of the state had been revealed in all its horror. In a solipsistic twist of logic, the West German state's treatment of them proved it was a fascist state. The main focus of their anger was solitary confinement, which they called "isolation torture." They also referred to the conditions they were held in as *Sonderbehandlung*, or "special treatment"—the euphemism used by the Nazis to describe the mass killing of the Jews—and as *Vernichtungshaft*, or "extermination incarceration".

Meinhof was kept for a year in a cell in a wing of the Essendorf prison in Cologne that was completely empty apart from her. She called it the *Toter Trakt*—the "dead wing". In her cell, which was neon-lit 24 hours a day, she could not hear any sounds except those she made herself. Suffering from extreme mood swings and visual and acoustic hallucinations, she wrote at one point that she had a "clear consciousness that there is no chance of survival."[79] Finally she compared the conditions of her captivity to a Nazi death camp:

The correct political concept for the dead wing, Cologne—I say it quite clearly—is: Gas. It turns out that my Auschwitz fantasies were realistic.[80]

Ensslin made the comparison even more precise. She wrote that the difference between solitary confinement and the dead wing was analogous to the difference between a death camp and a concentration camp: "Auschwitz versus Buchenwald."[81]

In order to maintain their "political identity" and "revolutionary consciousness" in what Gerd Koenen has called their "imaginary gas chamber", the RAF prisoners set up a system of communicating with each other through secret notes carried out of their prisons by their lawyers. Ensslin created new code names for them taken from characters in *Moby Dick*, one of the group's favourite texts: Baader was Ahab, the ship's captain; Ensslin was Fleece, the cook; Meins was Starbuck, the first mate; and Mahler was Bildad, one of the ship's owners. Only Meinhof was not given a name. The equivalent of the white whale that the crew of the *Pequod* hunted in Melville's novel was, of course, the West German state.

In protest against the conditions of their imprisonment and in particular their solitary confinement, they also began a hunger strike. Only Mahler, who was becoming increasingly cut off from the RAF, refused to participate. In October 1974, the core members of the group were moved to a newly built maximum-security wing of the Stammheim prison near Stuttgart, the most modern in Europe. Ensslin and Meinhof were put in cells next to each other in a separate wing on the seventh floor and allowed to spend several hours a day together. Holger Meins, however, was too ill and remained in Wittlich prison in the Rhineland. After six weeks, Manfred Grashof, the *Bundeswehr* deserter, who had been arrested in 1972, temporarily stopped his hunger strike. Meins, aka Starbuck, whose flesh Melville had described as being "hard as twice-baked biscuit", wrote to him furiously, accusing him of betrayal:

Either a pig or a man
Either survival at any cost
Or struggle unto death
Either problem or solution
There is nothing in between.[82]

In fact, things were not so black and white. As even the group's supporters on the outside knew, the RAF had a "death list" that predetermined the order in which its members were supposed to die, based on the unofficial hierarchy of the group. While the group's peripheral figures were expendable, the leaders—above all Baader and Ensslin—were supposed to survive, and ate secretly to make sure they did.[83] After two months, Meins was reduced to a skeleton. Six feet tall, he weighed only 85 pounds, could no longer get out of bed and could barely move his arms. When, on the morning of 9 November, 1974—the anniversary of *Kristallnacht* and exactly five years after the bombing of the Jewish community centre in 1969—Meins' lawyer, Siegfried Haag, visited him, he realised it would be for the last time. He spent two hours with him, with his ear close to Meins' mouth so as to be able to hear him speak. Before leaving, he put a cigarette in his mouth and lit it as Meins had asked him to. Haag demanded that a doctor be sent to Meins. When the doctor arrived at 5.15 pm, Meins was already dead.

Long before beginning the hunger strike, Meins had written a testament, in which he had said: "In case I pass from life to death in prison, it was murder. Whatever the pigs claim... Don't believe the murderers' lies."[84] When the news of Meins' death was broadcast on the radio, spontaneous protest marches took place in Berlin, Cologne, Frankfurt, Hamburg and Stuttgart. Immediately graffiti appeared promising "Revenge for Holger Meins". The next day, the 2 June Movement shot dead Günter von Drenkmann, the 64–year-old chief justice of the West Berlin supreme court, at his home. Drenkmann, a Social Democrat, was a liberal judge who had never been involved in trying terrorists. He was simply picked as a symbol of the judicial system as a whole. It was not clear whether his cold-blooded killing was carried out as revenge for the death of Meins or not. But the remaining members of the Red Army Faction declared that they welcomed his "execution."[85]

Thousands of people turned up for Meins' funeral, which took place at a small cemetery in Hamburg a few days later. Among them was Rudi Dutschke, who, together with Hans-Jürgen Krahl, had introduced the concept of the "urban guerrilla" to West Germany back in September 1967 and had known Meins in West Berlin before he was shot in April 1968. In 1971, the British authorities had refused Dutschke a long-term residence permit, despite a massive campaign led by the Labour MP Michael Foot, and the Dutschkes had been forced to move yet again, this time to Aarhus, Denmark. Since then, Dutschke had been visiting West Germany with increasing frequency, both to receive medical treatment and to work on his PhD, and had begun to re-establish contact with the West German left. In January 1973 he had addressed 20,000 people at a Vietnam rally in Bonn—the first time he had spoken in public in West Germany since the assassination attempt. Dutschke had been persuaded to come to Hamburg by Otto Schily, the left-wing lawyer who had been part of Baader and Ensslin's legal team in 1968 and had also represented Horst Mahler at his trial in 1971. Now wearing a bushy moustache, Dutschke stood alongside Schily at the side of Meins' grave. After throwing a handful of soil onto the coffin, he raised a clenched fist, and, in full view of the cameras, declared, "Holger, the struggle continues!"

To many it looked as if the icon of the West German New Left was condoning terrorism. He later sent a letter to the *Spiegel* that was meant to clarify his position but in fact made it even more opaque. What he had meant, he said, was that "the struggle of the exploited and the oppressed for social liberation is the sole foundation of our political action as revolutionary socialists and communists." He condemned the killing of Drenkmann as "murder in the reactionary German tradition" but pledged solidarity with the RAF prisoners in their struggle against the conditions of their imprisonment.[86] A few days later Dutschke sent out more mixed signals by visiting Jan-Carl Raspe—another old friend from West Berlin—at Ossenheim prison. The reality was that, like many on the West German left, Dutschke disagreed with the RAF's methods but agreed with much of their politics. In his diary he described Meins' death as a "half murder" by the "pigs".[87] He rejected "individual terrorism" for tactical reasons and thought the RAF "fetishised illegality".[88] But whatever the excesses of terrorists like the RAF, ultimately he saw them—and almost all of the sub-groups that had grown out of the student movement—as "comrades" who were on the same side of the ongoing "struggle"[89]. And, however violent that struggle was now becoming, it needed to be continued—to the bitter end if necessary.

6

DEATH TRIP

By the end of 1974, the economic and political situation in West Germany and the world as a whole had changed dramatically. After the Yom Kippur war in October 1973, the Arab oil-producing states had cut supplies of oil to the West, sending the price of crude oil spiralling by 172 per cent between 1973 and 1974 alone.[1] In 1974, the West German economy grew by only 0.4 per cent and would shrink by 3.4 per cent the following year. As a result, unemployment rose from 600,000 in 1974 to 1.1 million in 1975.[2] The pressures on the West German economy put an abrupt end to Willy Brandt's expensive social reforms. In May 1974, Brandt was forced to resign after it emerged that one of his leading aides, Günter Guillaume, was an East German agent—precisely the kind of communist infiltration of which the Christian Democrats had always warned. It was an ignominious end to the most socially liberal government in the Federal Republic's history.

Brandt was succeeded by his finance minister, Helmut Schmidt, a technocratic figure who had a reputation for economic conservatism. Schmidt was born in 1918 and was thus a member of the so-called "sceptical generation" that had experienced both Nazism and the disaster of 1945.[3] He had been a *Wehrmacht* officer on the Eastern Front during the war and, as a student after the war, the chairman of the SDS before its split with the SPD. In his first speech as chancellor, Schmidt spoke of the need for "continuity and concentration"—very different from the grand visions of Brandt in 1969.[4] His assumption of the chancellorship represented a shift from idealism to pragmatism, and from a politics of symbols to one of results. From now on, the priority would be economic stability, not social reform, which in the new climate had become a political liability. The terrorists of the left had, in fact, themselves played no small part in this shift. The fear caused by the series of bomb attacks beginning with the Baader-Meinhof gang's "May offensive" in 1972 had made many West Germans more cautious about Brandt's reforms.[5] Now, as the "urban guerrillas" stepped up their war with the West German state, Schmidt was to prove an unyielding adversary. During his chancellorship, the conflict between the wartime and the post-war generation would once again sharpen, with dramatic consequences.

A few weeks after Holger Meins' death, Ulrike Meinhof was sentenced to eight years imprisonment for her part in the Baader jailbreak in 1970 and joined Baader, Ensslin and Raspe on the seventh floor of Stammheim prison. Although they were completely cut off from the general population of the prison, the two men and two women were allowed to spend increasing amounts of time together. But that, if anything, worsened tensions within the group. Baader and Ensslin increasingly blamed Meinhof for the failures of their strategy, telling her she was a "knife in the back of the RAF".[6] In fact, although it was in theory a collective, the RAF was run along increasingly authoritarian lines. Baader was the undisputed leader and gave orders that the others, both inside and outside Stammheim, followed without question. In February 1975, he officially called off the hunger strike. When the doctors told Meinhof she could start eating again, she refused to believe them and told them she wanted to see it in writing from Baader. Baader wrote the word "eat" on a piece of paper and signed it "a". The doctors showed Meinhof the note and she immediately started to eat.[7]

Meanwhile the legal proceedings against the first generation of the RAF continued. The defendants were allowed to spend a remarkable amount of time with their lawyers, many of whom saw themselves as part of the same political struggle as the RAF. Among them were Otto Schily, who became Ensslin's lawyer, and Hans-Christian Ströbele, the co-founder, along with Horst Mahler, of the Socialist Lawyers' Collective, who became Baader's lawyer. Some of the lawyers helped to pass secret notes between the RAF members and to and from the outside world as part of what they called their "info system". Ströbele addressed his clients as "comrade" and was later convicted of smuggling a note from Ensslin out of Stammheim and given a ten-month suspended jail sentence. While in Stammheim, Baader even fathered a child by one of the female members of his legal team. However, the lawyers were still not radical and committed enough for the RAF, who fired several of them, including Klaus Croissant and Ströbele.

On the outside, the RAF had become more influential than ever. Although it remained a tiny group consisting of only a handful of people, it now set the agenda for much of the West German New Left. "Torture committees" sprang up all over West Germany to organise protests against the conditions in which the "political prisoners" of the RAF were being held. Even Jean-Paul Sartre came to visit the RAF during the hunger strike in 1974 after Meinhof wrote to him. He was driven to Stammheim by Hans-Joachim Klein, the mechanic and former member of Revolutionary Struggle who had joined the Revolutionary Cells. In 1972, the West German police estimated they were looking for 40 people; by the end of 1974, they were looking for 300 and estimated the Red Army Faction had 10,000 "sympathisers."[8] "At no time during the 'underground struggle' did the RAF exert such magnetic power of attraction as they did when they were in custody," wrote the journalist Stefan Aust, who had worked with Meinhof at *konkret* and later became the editor of *Spiegel*.[9]

In particular, it was the sheer rage at the death of Holger Meins—which was routinely described as murder by many on the West German left—that prompted some young people into action. "The death of Holger Meins and the decision to pick up a weapon were one and the same thing," said Volker Speitel, a young graphic artist from Stuttgart who later joined the RAF. "It was no longer possible to think."[10] The widely circulated photos of the dead Meins provided a powerful visual image that fitted in with the narrative the RAF had constructed and fuelled young people's anger. If the Federal Republic was a Nazi state, as the RAF had always claimed, then Meins was the equivalent of a Holocaust victim. Birgit Hogefeld, who later joined the RAF, said the pictures of Meins's emaciated corpse seemed to her "so similar to the concentration camp inmates, to the dead of Auschwitz". After seeing them, she felt compelled to act. If she did not, she believed, she would be "just as ignorant and cowardly" as the generation before hers.[11]

Thus the imprisonment of the leaders of the RAF and in particular the death of Meins now created a "second generation" of terrorists in West Germany who were even more violent than the first. Some of the "second generation" of the RAF, such as Margrit Schiller, came from the so-called "Socialist Patients Collective", a bizarre Heidelberg-based group founded by a psychiatrist, Dr. Wolfgang Huber, who believed that mental illness had social and political causes and that the cure was to destroy the "system". Others were simply young people who had little interest in politics or German history but were simply turned on by the RAF's violence. What had begun as an attempt to expose the latent fascism of the system hidden beneath its democratic surface had now become an all-out war between a small number of terrorists and the West German state—"six against sixty million," as the writer Heinrich Böll famously put it. The terrorists' choice of targets were now almost arbitrary. Any representative of the state was now fair game. Insofar as they had a purpose at all, their actions were aimed at freeing terrorists already in custody.

The West German state responded by making wide-ranging changes to German law to deal with the new threat. It extended the powers of the *Bundesgrenzschutz* (the federal police) to carry out searches, which became increasingly common, especially at motorway junctions. The BKA, West Germany's criminal investigative agency, also expanded. Until the early 1970s, it had been an "insignificant agency" in a country where the police was de-centralised—a response to the centralisation of the Nazi era.[12] But the terrorist threat changed that. Horst Herold, a tank commander in World War II and the BKA president from 1971 onwards, became almost obsessed with the RAF and made it his personal mission to defeat it. He created a vast database of suspected terrorists and "sympathisers" as part of a system of computer profiling unlike anything previously seen in the Federal Republic. *Stern* magazine called him "Big Brother Herold."[13] But in fact, as Dorothea Hauser has shown, he was a more complex figure than this description suggested. A left-wing socialist, he believed the Federal Republic needed to be radically reformed. In fact, his commitment to expanding the use of information technology in law enforcement was rooted in a belief that it could be used to make the justice system less biased and repressive.[14]

In February 1975, Peter Lorenz, a 52 year-old Christian Democrat lawyer who was campaigning to become mayor of West Berlin, was kidnapped. The 2 June Movement, which was behind the kidnapping, released a photo showing Lorenz with a hand-written sign around his neck that read "Prisoner of the 2 June Movement," and demanded the release of six of their comrades who were in prison for various terrorist offences, including Horst Mahler. The West German authorities agreed to the demands. The following month, five of the terrorists were flown on a Lufthansa jet from Frankfurt to Aden in South Yemen, accompanied, at the terrorists' insistence, by Heinrich Albertz, the mayor of West Berlin at the time of Benno Ohnesorg's death in 1967 and now a Protestant pastor. Mahler declined to join them and remained in prison. The following day, after Albertz had returned to Germany safely, Lorenz was released in a West Berlin park. According to Fritz Teufel, who had become involved with the 2 June Movement after the collapse of Kommune 1 and would later be prosecuted for his alleged involvement in the kidnapping of Peter Lorenz, it showed that "armed actions are, in an ideal situation, possible without bloodshed."[15]

Inevitably, however, situations were not always ideal. In fact, after the Lorenz kidnapping, the actions of West German left-wing terrorist groups became increasingly brutal. Two months later on 25 April, six members of the "second generation" of the RAF stormed the West German embassy in Stockholm armed with pistols and explosives, and took eleven members of staff, including the ambassador, hostage. After shooting dead the West German military attaché, the terrorists, calling themselves the "Holger Meins Commando", demanded the release of 26 prisoners, including Baader, Ensslin, Meinhof and Raspe, whose trial was about to begin. This time, the West German state was not as accommodating. After all, unlike the terrorists released two months earlier, Baader, Ensslin, Meinhof and Raspe were charged with murder. "My entire instinct tells me that we cannot give in," Chancellor Schmidt told his advisers shortly after hearing the news.[16] The terrorists were told of the decision and offered the chance to release the remaining ten hostages in exchange for a free passage. They refused. Just before midnight, a huge explosion, accidentally set off by the terrorists, ripped through the third floor of the embassy building. Swedish police stormed the building. In the ensuing battle, two embassy employees and two of the terrorists were killed.

The following month, under massive security, the trial of Baader, Ensslin, Meinhof and Raspe began in a concrete and steel courtroom in Stammheim prison that had been specially built at a cost of DM 12 million.[17] They were tried on four counts of murder and at least 54 counts of attempted murder and from the beginning it was chaos. To the defendants, who saw themselves as "resisting" a fascist regime, the trial was as illegitimate as a show trial in the People's Court in the Third Reich.[18] Baader and the other three defendants heckled the judge, Theodor Prinzing—for them the reincarnation of the notorious Nazi judge Roland Freisler, who had ordered the execution of Sophie Scholl—until they were finally removed from the courtroom. They were in and out of the courtroom for the remainder of the trial.

The RAF's legal team, led by Otto Schily, argued that the defendants were unfit to stand trial, thus making the conditions of their imprisonment and in particular their "isolation torture" the subject of the trial. After weeks of delays and interruptions, they then attempted to put the trial "on a political footing" and asked the court to subpoena, among others, Richard Nixon and Willy Brandt, in order to show that "the US government had, through its military intervention in Vietnam and Cambodia, broken international law, that it had also operated from the soil of the Federal Republic" and that "the use of violence against certain US military installations within the territory of the Federal Republic, such as US bases in Frankfurt and Heidelberg, was justified."[19]

As the trial continued into the autumn of 1975, Baader, Ensslin, Meinhof and Raspe were allowed to see each other more frequently and even bathe together. But although they continued to present a united front to the outside world, the conflict within the group had in fact worsened after nearly four years in prison. Baader and Ensslin's bullying of Meinhof, to which she seemed to react almost masochistically, worsened. By the spring of 1976, she had become completely desperate. At 7.30 am on Sunday, 9 May—the day after the twenty-first anniversary of the liberation from Nazism—two guards opened cell 719 of Stammheim prison to find Meinhof hanging dead from one of the windows. Meinhof, aged 41, had left no note, but the authorities concluded it was suicide. Forensic investigators believed that she had torn towels into strips, knotted them together and tied them to the bars on the window. She then made a noose which she put around her neck, stood on a stool placed on top of her mattress, and kicked it away.

Many in the outside world, however, knew little of the dynamic within the "hard core" of the RAF. They claimed that, like Meins before her, Meinhof must have been murdered—a fiction encouraged by Raspe, Baader and Ensslin. "We believe Ulrike was executed," Raspe declared in court. "We don't know how, but we know by whom."[20] He went on: "If Ulrike had decided to die because she saw it as the last possibility of asserting her revolutionary identity against the slow destruction of the will in the agony of isolation, she would have told us, or at least Andreas."[21] Exactly a week later, Meinhof was buried in a West Berlin cemetery. 4,000 people followed her coffin, carrying banners with slogans such as: "Ulrike Meinhof, we will avenge you."[22]

While some on the left were vowing to continue their war against the West German state after the death of Ulrike Meinhof, others, like Joschka Fischer, were slowly beginning to realise that it led nowhere. The "armed struggle" had gradually been getting closer to home for Fischer. In December 1975, a six-man team led by Ilyich Ramirez Sanchez aka "Carlos" held up an OPEC oil ministers' meeting in Vienna and killed three people in the process. The aim had been to kidnap the ministers until each of the countries they represented issued a pro-Palestinian statement.[23] One of the terrorists turned out be Hans-Joachim Klein aka "Klein-Klein", who had lived in the commune on Bornheimer Landstraße in Frankfurt. He was shot in the stomach during the battle with the Austrian police but was able to escape with "Carlos" to Algeria. Johannes Weinrich, another member of Revolutionary Cells, had also joined Carlos's group.

At the same time, the battles between left-wing demonstrators and the police in Frankfurt had also been getting ever more violent. In protest against the execution by the Franco government in Spain of five opponents in September 1975, a group of 200 demonstrators, including members of Revolutionary Struggle's *Putzgruppe*, had attacked the Spanish consulate in a quasi-military operation. With the police numbers at the consulate reduced by several decoy operations, the demonstrators approached the embassy in waves, threw paint bombs at the building and the police, followed by stones and Molotov cocktails, before disappearing from the scene in an equally organised way.[24] The boundaries between "militancy" and terrorism were becoming ever more blurred.

On 10 May 1976, the Monday after Meinhof's death, around 1500 people took part in a spontaneous, illegal demonstration through the centre of Frankfurt. Once again, the demonstrators were well prepared for the inevitable confrontation with the police, who had sealed off the streets leading to the city centre. After the initial clashes, the demonstrators broke into smaller groups and attacked the police in hit-and-run operations with rocks and Molotov cocktails for the rest of the afternoon.[25] At around 5 pm, a police car parked away from the demonstration in Große Gallusstraße was set on fire. The driver, a 23 year-old police sergeant named Jürgen Weber, was unable to get out. By the time he was dragged from the car by other officers, he was, as the local newspapers put it, "a human torch".[26] He sustained severe burns and was taken to hospital, where he remained in critical condition for several days. Three days later at 5.30 in the morning, police raided fifteen Frankfurt apartments and communes and arrested twelve men and two women and held them for two days. Their photos were printed in *Bild* and other newspapers the next morning. Among them was Fischer, by now well known to the police in Frankfurt as the leader of Revolutionary Struggle's *Putzgruppe*.

Although no one would ever be charged for the attempted murder of Sergeant Weber, the events of 10 May prompted Fischer to re-think the strategy of confrontation with the West German state. Two weeks later on Whit Sunday, the *Sozialistisches Büro*, an umbrella organisation of left-wing groups, held a conference which was attended by 10,000 activists from around West Germany, including Rudi Dutschke. The speakers at the so-called "Anti-Repression Congress" were supposed to talk about the way the state had responded to the terrorist threat by taking repressive measures against the left in West Germany. But Joschka Fischer gave a speech on behalf of the "Spontis" in which he—to the surprise of most people in the audience—questioned the logic of the left's own strategy. It would later come to be seen as a turning point in the political journey of the 1968 generation in Germany.

Introduced simply as a "'Sponti' comrade" and joined at the podium by several other members of Revolutionary Struggle, Fischer began by defending the way the New Left had "resisted" the forces of reaction that had "destroyed" Meinhof. But in doing so, he went on, the "Spontis" had hit a wall and were on the way to making the same mistake as the urban guerrillas:

The more politically isolated we became, the more militaristic our resistance became, the easier it was to isolate us, and the easier it was for the cops to re-label us from "polit-rockers" to "terrorists" and to charge us for breach of the peace, criminal organisation and murder.[27]

Fischer concluded the speech by urging his terrorist "comrades" to give up the armed struggle:

Precisely because we are in solidarity with our comrades in the underground and because we feel so closely connected to them, we urge them here to end this death trip, to come out of their "armed isolation", to put down the bombs and pick up rocks, and to once again take up a different kind of resistance in the form of a different life.[28]

The speech at the "Whitsun congress", which Fischer would expand upon the following year in his "Sponti" comrade Thomas Schmid's magazine *Autonomie*, was significant for a number of reasons. Firstly, he had made explicit that the armed struggle of terrorist groups and the street battles of the Frankfurt "Spontis" were essentially parallel. "We militants in the "Sponti" movement (*Putzgruppe* etc.) have followed essentially a similar development as our urban guerrilla comrades," he wrote in the essay.[29] Secondly, he had admitted that the "strategy of escalation" that Dutschke had propounded was essentially futile. "This in essence parallel development, this experience of oppression and fear that was in essence the same for "Sponti" militants as for the urban guerrilla, has diverted us into a similar dead end." He added that although, unlike their urban guerrilla comrades, none of the "Spontis" were in prison, he was fully aware of how close they had come.[30]

This was, of course, not a critique of the armed struggle on principle—Fischer never once said it was morally wrong to kidnap judges or attempt to murder police officers—but merely a criticism of the tactical hopelessness of confrontation with the West German state. Nevertheless, Fischer's intervention included, as Gerd Koenen, a member of the Frankfurt scene, later put it, "an element of genuine horror at where you would or could be driven as soon as you succumbed to the logic of terror and anti-terror."[31] Ironically, Ulrike Meinhof had herself identified precisely this danger in her column in *konkret* after the shooting of Rudi Dutschke back in 1968. The "armed struggle" had turned out to be a Brechtian *Lehrstück* after all, but with a different message than the one the terrorists had hoped for. Instead of exposing the fascism hidden within capitalism as the strategy had intended, it had simply illustrated the futility of the strategy itself. However, although doubts had started to set in about the use of violence by groups that had grown out of the West German student movement, it was not yet the end of the story. Worse was still to come.

On 27 June, 1976—seven weeks after Meinhof's death—an Air France Airbus A300 flying from Tel Aviv to Paris took off after making a stop at Athens airport. Shortly afterwards, three men and a woman armed with automatic weapons and hand grenades seized control of the aircraft. Two of the terrorists were Arab members of the Popular Front for the Liberation of Palestine (PFLP). The other two were Germans—a man travelling with a Peruvian passport under the name "Garcia", and a woman with an Ecuadorian passport under the name "Ortega". In fact, the two Germans were Winfried Böse and his girlfriend Brigitte Kuhlmann, two members of the Revolutionary Cells. They were both familiar figures in left-wing circles in Frankfurt. After re-fuelling in Libya, the terrorists ordered the pilot to fly to Entebbe in Uganda, where they demanded the release of 53 Arab prisoners being held in prisons in Israel, West Germany and three other countries. In Entebbe, where three other terrorists were waiting for them, they separated 103 Jewish and Israeli passengers, who were taken to an airport building and held there, and released the remaining 100 non-Jewish passengers. The Ugandan president, Idi Amin, visited the airport and offered the terrorists his support.

At around 1 am on 4 July, an Israeli commando unit transported to Uganda in three C-130 Hercules aircraft made a surprise landing at Entebbe airport and stormed the airport building in what was code-named Operation Thunderbolt. In a battle that lasted 35 minutes, the 29 Israeli soldiers killed all seven hijackers and 20 Ugandan soldiers and destroyed 11 MiG fighters—a quarter of Uganda's air force. Three of the hostages and an Israeli officer, 30 year-old Lieutenant-Colonel Yonatan Netanyahu, were also killed. The remaining 100 hostages were flown to Israel. When news of the hijacking filtered back to Frankfurt, those who knew Böse and Kuhlman were shocked but not surprised. "It was like a nightmare come true," says Karl-Dietrich Wolff, who had worked with Böse at the Roter Stern publishing collective.[32]

The Entebbe hijacking was disturbing in a different way from the other increasingly violent terrorist actions carried out by the individuals and groups that had come out of the West German student movement. It was not just, as Fischer said in his speech at the Whitsun congress, that groups like the "Spontis" and the RAF were creating a spiral of violence that could only end in prison or death. This went beyond the "question of violence", about which Fischer and others had begun to change their minds. Rather it raised even deeper, more difficult questions not just about the tactics but also about the politics of the New Left that had grown out of the West German student movement.

To many of the students growing up in Adenauer's West Germany, the Federal Republic had represented a continuation of Nazism. But in the decade since the death of Benno Ohnesorg in the summer of 1967, an even more terrifying possibility had gradually emerged that had only now become fully apparent to them. The grotesque "selection" of Jewish passengers in Entebbe, with its echoes of the Nuremberg laws and the concentration camps, illustrated in extreme and graphic form that perhaps Nazism had lived on not just in the post-war Federal Republic and its establishment but within the post-war generation itself—in other words, that perhaps it was not just in the system, it was also in them. "It was the first time we noticed that in a sense we were not that far from the generation we had denounced," says Thomas Schmid, who also knew Böse.[33] Nor was it possible to claim that West Germans such as Böse and Kuhlmann had simply been led astray by Palestinian groups like the PFLP. That itself raised another difficult question: why had the radical left in West Germany, of all countries, aligned itself so closely with the Palestinian cause in the first place?

In retrospect, Entebbe was merely the culmination of an arc of anti-Semitic violence that had begun with the bomb in the Jewish community centre in West Berlin on 9 November 1969. The current of anti-Semitism within the West German New Left had begun as anti-Zionism at the zenith of the student rebellion in the summer of 1967, when students had begun to empathise with the Palestinian cause. But remarkably quickly, some young people who belonged to the first generation of Germans that did not bear any direct responsibility for the Nazi era had come to see Jews themselves as the enemy. Hans-Joachim Klein would later claim that the Revolutionary Cells had also planned to murder the leaders of the Jewish communities in Frankfurt and West Berlin and even to kidnap Simon Wiesenthal—a man who had dedicated his life to exposing former Nazis.[34] That also had once been the self-proclaimed driving force of the West German student movement.

Entebbe came as a particular shock to Joschka Fischer, not least because it was so close to home. Fischer had known Winfried Böse, though he later said that, even before Entebbe, he had never had a high opinion of him.[35] Revolutionary Struggle had never been anti-Semitic like some among the revolutionary left in West Germany. It did, however, share the New Left's critique of Israeli imperialism. After a trip to

Israel in the spring of 1969, Daniel Cohn-Bendit had rejected what he called his earlier "naïve Zionism" in favour of a more critical view of Israeli society, which he now saw as having "faschistoid tendencies".[36] Specifically, he adopted the anti-Zionist position of a tiny Israeli anti-capitalist group called Matzpen, which opposed the Israeli occupation of the West Bank and the Gaza strip and rejected the idea of Israel as a Jewish state. They proposed, in other words, a one-state solution to the conflict between Israelis and Palestinians.[37] Revolutionary Struggle subsequently took Cohn-Bendit's view of the Middle East as its own position. "We were anti-Zionist, not against Israel, but anti-Zionist," Fischer says.[38]

Following the Entebbe hijacking, however, Fischer would turn away from this anti-Zionism and return, in a sense, to the pro-Israeli position of the West German student left before 1967. In a heated debate with his comrades from the Frankfurt scene, Fischer defended the Israeli action in Entebbe and said Böse and Kuhlmann had deserved to be killed. "When Germans are once again involved in selecting Jews and non-Jews, they don't deserve anything else," he later claimed to have said in the days after the bloody end of the hijacking.[39] Fischer told his biographer Sibylle Krause-Burger that Entebbe illustrated "how those who emphatically set themselves apart from National Socialism and its crimes had almost compulsively repeated the crimes of the Nazis."[40]

Some who knew Fischer in those days in Frankfurt's alternative scene, like the journalist Michael Schwelien, did not immediately notice his change of heart.[41] But Entebbe would later become a key episode in the narrative on which Fischer's subsequent political career would be based. Years later Fischer said that Entebbe was an even important turning point in his life more than the death of Ulrike Meinhof. "Entebbe was Joschka Fischer's Damascus," Krause-Burger concluded."[42] By publicly describing his horror at the events in Entebbe in the years to come, it would come to stand for the shattering of the 1968 generation's illusions about its "struggle". In the process, Fischer would also turn himself into a kind of exemplary figure for the 1968 generation, presenting his biography as a kind of *Bildungsroman* whose narrative was driven by an ongoing re-engagement with Auschwitz that would continue for the next twenty-five years.

Joschka Fischer was not the only one having a crisis of faith. Still in prison, Horst Mahler was also doing some soul-searching. After being arrested in 1970, he had been moved from one prison to another. However, unlike the other members of the Baader-Meinhof group, he was not kept in strict solitary confinement.[43] He had spent most of the early 1970s in court as he sought get himself acquitted. In 1971 the case against him for his role in freeing Andreas Baader from prison collapsed after Peter Urbach, the intelligence agent who had provided the weapons, refused to answer questions in court. This was, according to Mahler, because he would in the process be forced to tell the truth about the origin of the bomb in the Jewish community centre in November 1969.[44] Urbach was subsequently provided with a new identity, left Germany and was never heard from again, leaving many unanswered questions about the role that he, and the West Berlin authorities, played in the APO.

Two years later, Mahler went on trial again, this time for conspiracy to commit aggravated robbery and establishing a criminal organisation. His lawyer, Otto Schily, was hopeful he might again be acquitted. But at the end of the trial, the judge had turned to Mahler and asked him if he had anything to add. "One doesn't speak to judges," Mahler said "One shoots them." He was sentenced to 12 years in prison and the following year debarred from practising as a lawyer. After being ostracised by the Baader-Meinhof gang, he, along with Dieter Kunzelmann, who was finally released from prison in 1975, had gravitated towards the Maoist KPD.

It was during his time in prison that Mahler rejected the armed struggle. In an interview with *Stern* magazine published to coincide with the tenth anniversary of the killing of Benno Ohnesorg, Mahler called the armed struggle "madness"—the first time a leading figure in the RAF had publicly dissociated himself from the group and its ideology. In an essay published in *Kursbuch* published shortly afterwards, he reflected on how he had ended up making such a tragic mistake. It had all begun, he said, with the Nazi past and the shadow that it had cast over his generation. His motivation for joining the student movement, he realised in retrospect, had been simple. "I wanted to be one of the 'other Germans'".[45] He had found refuge in Marx and Lenin—whose analysis of capitalism, he said, "freed me of all collective guilt" for Nazism—the same point made later by Norbert Elias about the unique attraction of Marxism for the post-war generation in Germany.[46]

Mahler said that he had gradually become disillusioned with the armed struggle, which had been doomed to failure from the start because of a "misunderstanding" of the nature of revolutionary change in a society like West Germany. But as well as the armed struggle, he also rejected the version of Marxism-Leninism on which he said not just the Baader-Meinhof group but also the student movement had been based. In particular he now regarded the Marxist-Leninist theory of revolution, which he said the student movement had subscribed to, as "putschist wishful thinking".[47] It was in essence the same point Jürgen Habermas had made long before the formation of terrorist groups in West Germany when he criticised the student movement's "voluntarist ideology" at the congress in Hanover of June 1967.

Mahler's change of heart must have seemed, at the time, somewhat similar to Fischer's. Like Fischer, his break with the movement seemed to have been prompted by shock at where the increasing radicalisation of the APO since the late sixties had led. Unlike Mahler, of course, Fischer had never been a terrorist. But the two men's essays in 1977—Fischer's in *Autonomie*, Mahler's in *Kursbuch*—represented simultaneous, parallel rejections of the double helix of violence that had emerged out of the West German student movement. If anything, Mahler's change of heart seemed even more thoroughgoing than Fischer's. Neither had yet rejected the continuity thesis that linked the post-war West German democracy to Nazism or accepted the legitimacy of the Federal Republic. But while Fischer had simply questioned the tactical logic of the New Left's confrontation with the West German state, Mahler had rejected its basis in political theory.

But despite the apparent similarities between the two men's thinking, beneath the surface they were being driven by very different impulses. It was not yet clear where Mahler's rejection of the armed struggle left his politics, but there was one clue. If Fischer's Damascus was the Entebbe hijacking, Mahler's was his discovery of Hegel—or so he would later claim.[48] While Mahler was in prison, Otto Schily had given him Hegel's collected works. It was, he said, the turning point in his rejection of the armed struggle. As he delved deeper and deeper into Hegel's metaphysics, he realised that Marx and then Lenin had crucially misunderstood Hegel's logic.[49] Historical contradictions could not simply be resolved by the actions of a revolutionary vanguard—that was what Mahler called "abstract negation".[50] Rather, they would be resolved by history in more complex and cunning ways. From then on, Hegel, not Marx, would be the foundation of Mahler's political thinking. It was the beginning of an ideological transformation that would ultimately take Mahler in a very different, and in a sense opposite, direction to Fischer.

Meanwhile in Stammheim, the high command of the Baader-Meinhof group had no intention of giving up on the armed struggle. They had now been joined on the seventh floor of the prison by Brigitte Mohnhaupt, another member of the group who had until then been held elsewhere but had asked to transfer to Stammheim. Since Mohnhaupt had been convicted of lesser offences and was likely to be released sooner than Baader, Ensslin, and Raspe, she was now given the task of taking over as the leader of the "second generation" of the RAF. Meanwhile, Baader and Ensslin had also assigned Siegfried Haag, Holger Meins' former lawyer, to re-structure the RAF on the outside and to get international support for the armed struggle in West Germany. Together with several other members of the "second generation" of the RAF, Haag travelled to South Yemen, where they made contact with the PFLP.

After the death of Meinhof, the trial of Baader, Ensslin and Raspe had continued in the courtroom in Stammheim. On behalf of the three defendants, Otto Schily attempted to make the case that the actions of the RAF were based on a legal "right to resistance". He called as a witness a former American intelligence agent who he said would show that the IG Farben building in Frankfurt—bombed by the RAF in 1972—had been "a major centre for US activities in the Indo-Chinese war."[51] (IG Farben, coincidentally, was the chemicals corporation that had manufactured the Zyklon B gas that was used in Nazi death camps.)

Responding to the prosecution's application to rule out the testimony as irrelevant, Schily compared the American military to the *Reichssicherheitshauptamt*, or Reich Security Department, the SS agency that was instrumental in organising the Final Solution. He asked the court to

imagine there had been a bomb attack on an institution like the Reich Security Department in the Third Reich. Imagine there was a trial against a defendant who was accused of carrying out the attack. Would you refuse such a defendant the chance to provide proof that the Reich Security Department had co-ordinated and implemented a policy of extermination of Jewish citizens?[52]

Schily went on in similarly emotive style:

Perhaps it is necessary, in order to bring to life why we are here, to remind ourselves of the pictures that we have seen on the television of children who have been burned by napalm. They are the same pictures: the Jewish child in the ghetto with its hands up, walking towards SS men, and Vietnamese children, screaming and burned with napalm from carpet bombing, running towards a photographer. And the evidence for the court to hear centres on this question: should we have tolerated and kept silent about such murder, or was it justified to take action against the mechanisms and the apparatus that carried out such murder? That is the question.[53]

The court declined to hear the testimony. "The Vietnam war is not the subject of this trial," Judge Prinzing said.[54] After the defence's attempt to mount a "political defence" failed, the prosecution made its criminal case against the defendants. It was based largely on testimony by Gerhard Müller, a former member of the Socialist Patients Collective who had joined the RAF, shot a police officer dead in 1971, and then turned against the group while in prison. Müller provided detailed, damning evidence about the RAF's structure and methods, including the planned "executions" of "deserters" like Peter Homann.

While the RAF continued to represent themselves as victims of Nazism in an imaginary gas chamber and to portray their struggle as "resistance", they had themselves also—like the Revolutionary Cells with their "selection" of Jews—assumed some of the features of Nazism. With the RAF's exaltation of "struggle" and death, its division of the world into friends and enemies, the *Führer*-cult around Andreas Baader, the "executions" and the hand-written signs placed around the necks of kidnapped victims paraded before cameras, it seemed almost to mimic the Nazis, intentionally or not. Its end would also contain distant echoes of the downfall of the Third Reich. Just as the Nazis continued to cling to their belief in an imminent final victory even as the "Thousand Year Reich" was collapsing around them, so the "hard core" of the RAF fanatically continued their "struggle" to the bitter end even after they were surrounded by overwhelming evidence that it was doomed to failure. Increasingly cut off from the outside world, Baader continued to give orders that others on the outside continued to follow. In fact, Gerd Koenen suggests, the situation on the seventh floor of Stammheim had, by 1977, come to resemble nothing so much as Hitler's bunker in the last days of World War II.[55]

A couple of weeks before Baader, Ensslin and Raspe were finally convicted of murder and sentenced to life in prison, a group led by

Brigitte Mohnhaupt, who had been released from prison two months earlier, shot dead the West German chief federal prosecutor, 57 year-old Siegfried Buback, as he was driven to work one morning in April 1977. They issued a statement in which they declared that Buback had been "directly responsible" for the "murders" of Holger Meins and Ulrike Meinhof. "For puppets of the system like Buback," the statement said, "history always finds a way."[56] At the end of July they struck again, shooting dead Jürgen Ponto, the chief executive of Dresdner Bank, at his home near Frankfurt. Among the killers was Susanne Albrecht, the daughter of a Hamburg lawyer, whose sister was Ponto's goddaughter. The group had used Albrecht's connections with the Ponto family to gain access to his house.

The finale came that autumn. On 5 September 1977, a group led by Peter-Jürgen Boock, another leading member of the "second generation" of the RAF, kidnapped Hanns Martin Schleyer, the president of the West German Employers' Federation and a member of the board of Daimler-Benz, in Cologne. Armed with HK-43 assault rifles, they killed Schleyer's bodyguard and the three police officers accompanying him. The 62 year-old Schleyer was the perfect embodiment of the student movement's continuity thesis. The highest representative of West German capitalism, whom *Stern* magazine had dubbed "the boss of bosses", he had been a Nazi student leader, joined the SS in 1933 and had worked as an official in Prague during the Nazi occupation.[57] The following day, his kidnappers released a photo of him—the first of many over the next forty or so days—holding a sign with the words "Prisoner of the RAF". They demanded that all of their comrades be freed, given DM 100,000 each and allowed to leave West Germany for a country of their choice.

For the next six weeks, West Germany was gripped by the crisis, the most dramatic in the Federal Republic's short history. Chancellor Schmidt created a so-called "crisis staff"—a kind of war cabinet that included representatives of all the political parties in the *Bundestag* and that in effect ran the country for the duration of the crisis. Among its members was Franz Josef Strauss, the Bavarian Christian Democrat leader who had sued Ulrike Meinhof in 1961. During one session of the cabinet, Strauss, who was apparently drunk, proposed executing one member of the RAF for every hostage they killed.[58] Although Schmidt rejected this suggestion, he took steps that had no basis in West German law—such as completely suspending contact among the

RAF prisoners and between them and their lawyers. The German authorities also considered bugging the cells in Stammheim, though the extent to which this actually happened remains unclear.[59] The·RAF had finally created the state of emergency whose spectre the student movement had raised a decade earlier.

On 13 October, as negotiations continued between the West German authorities and Schleyer's abductors, a Lufthansa Boeing 737 flying from Majorca to Frankfurt with 86 passengers, mainly German holidaymakers returning home, was hijacked and flown east. The hijacking was carried out on behalf of the RAF by four Arab terrorists, two men and two women, affiliated with the PFLP. They called themselves "Martyr Halimeh Commando"—a reference to the Arab codename for Brigitte Kuhlmann in the Entebbe hijacking. After making several stops, including one in Aden, where the pilot, Jürgen Schumann, was shot dead, the aircraft eventually landed in Mogadishu, Somalia. (While the aircraft was on the tarmac at Mogadishu airport, one of the hijackers discovered a Mont Blanc pen belonging to one of the passengers, and, mistaking its logo for a Star of David, threatened to execute her.)

Finally on 17 October Schmidt took action. The West German GSG 9, the police anti-terror unit that had been formed after the 1972 Olympics, stormed the aircraft, killing three of the terrorists, seriously wounding the fourth and successfully freeing the hostages. That night, after hearing the news on the radio, Baader, Ensslin and Raspe killed themselves in their cells on the seventh floor of Stammheim. Baader shot himself with a pistol that had been smuggled into his cell and hidden in a record player. He also fired into the wall and his mattress to give the impression there had been a struggle. Raspe also shot himself with a smuggled 9mm pistol. Ensslin made a noose out of a piece of electric cable and hanged herself from her cell window. Her lawyer, Otto Schily, was among those to be shown the cells with the bodies still lying on the floor.

The following day, Hanns Martin Schleyer's kidnappers took him in the trunk of an Audi 100 to a pine forest near the French border, made him kneel down, and shot him three times in the back of the head—a textbook execution. One of the members of the group that had kidnapped Schleyer later said that to release him would have been "an admission of defeat".[60] Schleyer's body was then put back in the trunk of the car for the police to find. In a communiqué sent to the French newspaper *Libération*, the RAF declared:

We have, after 43 days, ended Hanns Martin Schleyer's miserable and corrupt existence. [...] His death is nothing to us compared to our pain and our rage at the massacres of Mogadishu and Stammheim.[61]

The communiqué added that "the struggle has only just begun."[62]

Baader, Ensslin and Raspe were buried a week later in Stuttgart. Many residents objected to the idea of three terrorists being buried within the city limits. It was the Christian Democrat mayor of Stuttgart, Manfred Rommel—the son of Hitler's favourite general, Field Marshall Erwin Rommel—who insisted they be given permission to be buried in Stuttgart. Demonstrators, many in masks, also attended the funeral, some carrying banners declaring that "the struggle continues"—echoing Rudi Dutschke's words at the funeral of Holger Meins. The RAF continued to operate for another two decades, carrying out increasingly senseless attacks on American soldiers and military bases, representatives of West German business and the West German state.[63] But after 1977, it was never the same again. The "German Autumn", as it came to be known, marked the end of the West German New Left's fascination with terrorism.

By then, even some members of the RAF had come to see the parallels between themselves and the Nazis. Peter-Jürgen Boock, who was finally arrested four years later, said the meeting at which the kidnapping of Hanns-Martin Schleyer had been planned was "our Wannsee conference," referring to the 1942 conference at which the Nazis' "final solution" of the "Jewish question" was organised.[64] The parallels were also clear to Joschka Fischer, who later said that the RAF's statement after the murder of Schleyer, with its "cold, technocratic, lethal language", was reminiscent of the Nazis.[65] With the "German Autumn", Fischer's break with the terrorism of the 1970s, which had begun with the death of Ulrike Meinhof, was complete. But, once again, his change of heart was not instantaneous. In fact, writing in 1978 about the killings of Ponto, Buback and Schleyer, he used some fairly cold language himself: "I do not feel any great sense of grief for those three distinguished gentlemen," he wrote.[66] It seems that, as with the Entebbe hijacking, it would take some time before the full horror of the "German Autumn" hit Fischer.

Even then, as some would later admit, the West German New Left's rejection of terrorism took place largely in silence. In 1985, the writer Peter Schneider, a key figure in the student movement who, in an influential speech at the Free University in May 1967, had urged the students to be more radical in their methods, began corresponding with Peter-Jürgen Boock, who was by then in prison for his part in the kidnapping and murder of Hanns-Martin Schleyer. Schneider wrote to Boock that his generation had repressed its past just as their parents' generation had repressed theirs. Even after the West German New Left ended its "theoretical flirtation with the armed struggle" after 1977, he said, it did so suddenly and without explanation. The post-war generation acted, in fact, as if the entire dark decade that began with Dutschke and Krahl's formulation of the concept of the "urban guerrilla" in 1967 and ended with the "German Autumn" in 1977 had never taken place—just as the "Auschwitz generation" had acted as if the Nazi era had never happened. "As far as dealing with our own past is concerned," he wrote, "the sons barely did better than their fathers."[67]

A decade after the post-war generation had begun its "resistance" against the "Auschwitz generation," West Germany was a very different place. At least partly as a result of the New Left, the stiff conformism of the Adenauer era had given way to a more tolerant society. Schools and universities had become somewhat less hierarchical and disciplinarian. Attitudes towards sex had loosened and alternative lifestyles were flourishing. With the thaw in the Cold War and, in particular, Brandt's *Ostpolitik*, there had also been a lessening of the almost hysterical anti-communism that had defined the Adenauer era, especially in West Berlin. West Germany was, in a word, less "authoritarian" than it had been in 1967.

At the same time, however, the "armed struggle" that had grown out of the student movement had strengthened the repressive tendencies of the Federal Republic. At the time of the "Battle of Tegeler Weg" in the autumn of 1968—the beginning of the 1968 generation's experiment with "counter violence"—the West Berlin police did not even have riot gear. By the time of the "German Autumn" in 1977, the West German police had become centralised and militarised and a vast system of state surveillance had been set up. When Horst Herold retired as president of the BKA in 1981, it had more than double the number of agents than when he took over in 1971 and a budget that was five times as large as it was then.[68] The database of criminal suspects he had developed contained nearly five million names and the fingerprints of over two million people.[69] In retrospect, the West German state

DEATH TRIP

probably over-reacted. It was, nevertheless, a reaction to a real threat.

Perhaps even more corrosive of democracy than the specific measures the Federal Republic had taken to deal with the terrorist threat was the climate of fear that the terrorism of the 1970s had created in West Germany. This played directly into the hands of the political right. By the late 1970s the paranoia about communism that had existed in West Germany in the 1960s had been replaced, to some extent, by paranoia about terrorism. Many liberal politicians became so fearful about being branded as terrorist "sympathisers" that they hesitated to speak out against the expansion of state power.[70] In this sense, the post-war generation had, in fact, helped to make the Federal Republic more like the kind of "authoritarian" state they had always claimed it to be.

A LIFELINE

The first half of the 1970s had been a difficult time for Rudi Dutschke, who was by now in his mid-thirties and slowly recovering from the assassination attempt in 1968. Although his physical condition had stabilised and his epileptic seizures had become less frequent and less severe, he continued to be traumatised by the assassination attempt and would live in fear of a repeat of it for the rest of his life. He had received a generous grant from a West German foundation, which meant he and his family did not have to worry about making a living. But, sequestered in a farmhouse in a remote part of Denmark, he was isolated from the political struggle that, until the assassination attempt, had been his life. Gradually he felt himself drawn back to his homeland.

West Germany had changed dramatically since the spring of 1968 when he had left the country. Dutschke had watched with a sense of frustration and helplessness as the student movement had fragmented and finally dissolved itself. In particular, he was dismayed at the sectarianism of the "K-Groups", which he thought had "no revolutionary future".[1] He remained an optimist, however, and hoped he might be able to help the West German left re-unite and form a new political organisation that could play something like the role the SDS once had. To the surprise of many on the left, the living symbol of the APO had also become open to the idea of a new left-wing party that might stand for election. "Anyone who has a clue about politics talks not just about extra-parliamentary opposition but also about the reality of the parliamentary situation," he said in 1975. "For us, that doesn't mean that the question of organisation and the question of parties is not up for discussion. It is up for discussion."[2] However, Dutschke was no longer the leader of a movement as he had been in 1968. Although he remained an iconic figure on the West German left, his influence over his comrades had waned since he had left the country.

Apart from his openness towards parliamentary democracy, Dutschke's politics had also changed in other ways since the assassination attempt. Away from home, he had become increasingly focused on the "national question"—in other words the division of Germany—which he had discussed only with a handful of friends in the 1960s. He had begun to develop further the ideas that had begun with his pseudonymous article in 1967 proposing a "free city" of Berlin as a "strategic transmission belt for a future reunification of Germany". In 1973, to mark the twentieth anniversary of the uprising of 17 June 1953, he had written his first major article since the assassination attempt, this time under another pseudonym, "R. Bald".[3] It was an attack on Willy Brandt's *Ostpolitik*.

During the era of Adenauer, the West German student movement had criticised the pervasive atmosphere of hysterical anti-communism, which they saw as a symptom of the continuities between the Federal Republic and the Nazi era. With the Brandt government's *Ostpolitik*, there had been a significant reduction in the tension between East and West Germany, which had, amongst other things, allowed exiles like Dutschke to return to the GDR to visit their families. But in common with many other former members of the West German student movement, Dutschke was now as critical of the improvement in the relationship between the two German states as he had been of the earlier standoff. To him, the *rapprochement* between the Federal Republic and the GDR was an indictment of both. Just as he believed democracy in West Germany was a facade, so the Cold War was also a sham masking a deal that had been struck between the United States and the Soviet Union.

To Dutschke, the Social Democrats had yet again betrayed the proletariat. By making an accommodation with the East German state, Brandt had sacrificed the East German proletariat for the sake of a spurious peace in central Europe. The GDR had also sold out, giving up on the possibility of what he called a "socialist reunification" of Germany.[4] The solution, Dutschke thought, was a movement that could unite the working class in East and West Germany. At the same time, he dismissed any idea of a Europe-wide socialist movement as an "abstraction" that did not take account of national identity. Where once Dutschke had regarded the oppressed of the Third World as the true revolutionary subject, it now seemed to have been replaced in his thinking by an "imagined community" of the German nation on both sides of the Elbe river.[5]

Over the next few years, while the West German New Left was increasingly preoccupied with terrorism and the "question of violence", Dutschke began to argue more and more openly for a socialist reunification of Germany.[6] In a series of articles for various left-wing journals, he returned again and again to the connection between the national struggle and the class struggle. He accused the groups that had emerged from the student movement of being "left-wing conservatives" who were blind to the "national question". The most urgent task for the left in the two German "fragment states" was now to co-operate to form an "oppositional network" that could create a national consciousness and ultimately overthrow both regimes and reunify Germany.[7]

Anticipating criticisms from the left, Dutschke referred to Marx's own discussion of the dialectic between nationalism and internationalism. "Though not in substance, yet in form, the struggle of the proletariat with the bourgeoisie is at first a national one," Marx and Engels had written in *The Communist Manifesto*.[8] In other words, although fundamentally internationalist in outlook, the proletariat in each country first had to confront its own bourgeoisie, which represented national interests, and therefore needed to be organised along national lines itself. Yet Dutschke went beyond Marx's dialectic, which implied that a national consciousness was a temporary, tactical feature of the international proletariat's struggle for socialism. Dutschke seemed to see the nation as something essential and substantial, and German reunification as a goal in itself.[9] He began one article in 1977 by complaining about a "comrade" from Hamburg, another member of the post-war generation, who had said in a discussion with him that Portugal was of more relevance for West Germany than East Germany was. Dutschke lamented the fact that he and others on the West German left were not able "to grasp and to feel" that the GDR was "the other part of a country divided into two states."[10]

Throughout, Dutschke remained conspicuously silent about the Nazi past and its connection with the post-war division of Germany. The United States and the Soviet Union appear in his writing merely as "occupying powers" that had colonised and divided Germany in much the same way as they had Vietnam rather than as countries that had also liberated Germany from Nazism. Not only did this have the effect of creating an equivalence between the United States and the Soviet Union, it also, even more importantly, divorced the post-war division of Germany from its wartime aggression. Germany became a victim of its fate in the twentieth century, not an active participant in it. In particular, the Holocaust did not feature at all in Dutschke's version of German history. While mythologising the German working class, Dutschke absolved it of any responsibility for Auschwitz.

These arguments brought Dutschke dangerously close to some on the far right. Henning Eichberg, one of the leading ideologues of the New Right, welcomed Dutschke as a "national revolutionary". By identifying with national liberation movements in the Third World, Eichberg said, the student movement had sought an *Ersatznationalismus*, a "substitute nationalism". In other words, instead of dealing with the difficult question of German national identity after Nazism, the student movement had simply borrowed national identities from the Vietnamese, the Palestinians and other Third World countries—an argument which, given Dutschke's own silence about the Nazi past, carried some weight. With his writings in the 1970s, Eichberg suggested, Dutschke had made explicit what was implicit in the West German student movement all along—that Germany, like its colonised counterparts in the Third World, also required a national liberation movement against foreign occupation.[11]

Years later, the claim that Rudi Dutschke was a German nationalist would outrage many former members of the West German student movement. To them, the student movement was quite the opposite: an "internationalist" movement. In fact, it had always been both. There were some within the student movement who focused above all on the continuities between the Nazi era and the Federal Republic. But others, particularly exiles from the GDR like Dutschke, had little interest in looking back to the Nazi era and tended to be more concerned with the division of Germany. Most of Dutschke's comrades were unaware of the extent of his concern with the "national question" because in the 1960s he had written about it using pseudonyms. Besides, the student movement's much-vaunted "internationalism" was itself deeply ambiguous. In practice, it consisted largely of supporting liberation movements in Third World countries that were themselves nationalist. In other words, nationalism and internationalism were by no means mutually exclusive concepts.

German nationalism had originally emerged at the beginning of the nineteenth century at a time when many of the hundred or so German states had fallen under Napoleonic domination and were engaged in what later became known as the "war of liberation".[12] It included, broadly speaking, two currents, which diverged essentially in their relationship to the Enlightenment and the French Revolution. One was a liberal nationalist current, which aimed to apply the principles of the French revolution to Germany and to unify the patchwork of German states into a democratic, representative nation-state somewhat analogous to the French republic. The other was a romantic nationalist current, which sought to create a sense of German identity defined against the principles of the French revolution and more broadly against the Enlightenment. Both currents, however, contained a strong element of utopianism and a tendency towards what has been called the "haloisation of the nation".[13]

The rise of liberal nationalism in Germany culminated in the unsuccessful revolution of 1848 and after that was increasingly eclipsed by romantic nationalism. Since there was during this period no unified German nation-state around which a civic nationalism along French lines could cohere, German nationalism tended to attribute greater significance to culture in defining the nation than other European nationalisms. Under the influence of Herder and Fichte, it tended to centre on a romantic concept of the German nation based on a distinctively German *Volksgeist* or national spirit, rooted in particular in the German language. In the second half of the nineteenth century and the early twentieth century, German nationalists increasingly defined German *Kultur* against French, or sometimes Western, *Zivilisation*. It was out of this romantic nationalism that the explicitly ethnically-based, rather than culturally-based, *völkisch* nationalism of the Nazis developed, closely linked to ideas of blood.

From its earliest origins until the Nazi era, a key element in the development of German nationalism was thus its tendency to define itself against the West. There was, as Michael Hughes has put it, an "intellectual rejection by some German nationalists of western ideas and models and the search for a specifically 'German Way' in ideas, politics and social organisation."[14] In particular, this included a rejection of political liberalism as it had developed in western nation states such as

Britain, France and the United States. It had also often included a rejection of capitalism, which was also associated with the West, in particular Britain and the United States. In the most extreme version of this idea popularised during World War I, British *Händler*, or traders, were contrasted with German *Helden*, or heroes.[15] Since anti-capitalists on both the right and the left, including Marx himself, also often identified capitalism with the Jews, it was by no means a coincidence that anti-Semitism was often also a by-product of German nationalism.[16]

Rudi Dutschke's socialist version of German nationalism was in many ways alien to this tradition of romantic nationalism, which since the mid-nineteenth century had been mainly associated with the political right and also with militarism. Dutschke's nationalism was certainly and obviously very different from the *völkisch* nationalism of the Nazis. However, like the early German nationalists, Dutschke had developed his ideas at a time when Germany was divided and dominated by foreign powers—in this case, the United States and the Soviet Union—and was defined in opposition to an Other. Dutschke's nationalism was strikingly like romantic nationalism in at least this one sense, that it developed in opposition to foreign rule—hence his tendency to see Germany as a victim.

Dutschke's nationalism also shared several of the other key elements of romantic versions of German nationalism. He was anti-capitalist and in many ways anti-liberal. Although he was not anti-western per se, he, like most in the student movement, was vehemently opposed to the *Westbindung* and to NATO. Despite having an American wife, he was also prone to expressions of anti-American sentiment, for example his references to "Dreckamis". As a corollary to this, he also sympathised with Central and South American victims of American imperialism and tended to see Germany as a colony of the United States—a key feature of German anti-Americanism since the twenties. Finally, Dutschke's thinking—and, to some extent, that of the West German New Left in general—at times seemed to have inherited from romantic nationalism a sense that in finding its own true identity, Germany would not just liberate itself but also redeem the whole world. This sense of a historic German mission had been most memorably expressed in the 1861 poem by Emanuel Geibel, "Deutschlands Beruf" ("Germany's mission"):

> Und es mag am deutschen Wesen
> Einmal noch die Welt genesen.

A LIFELINE

(The essence of the German nation
Will one day be the world's salvation.)[17]

In the second half of the seventies, while the revolutionary left retreated after the spectacular failure of the armed struggle, the mass extra-parliamentary opposition movement it had always hoped for suddenly and unexpectedly became a reality. Against the background of rising oil prices, nuclear power had come to seem more and more attractive to mainstream politicians across the West, who began to plan a new generation of nuclear power stations. But in West Germany even more than elsewhere, politicians were surprised by the breadth and depth of popular opposition to nuclear power. From 1975 onwards, people across West Germany took to the streets in numbers far larger than the student movement had ever been able to mobilise in protest against the expansion of nuclear power.[18]

The movement had begun when the town of Wyhl in a picturesque part of Baden-Württemberg was selected as the site for a new nuclear power station in 1973. When construction began two years later, thousands of protesters occupied the site and eventually an administrative court ordered a halt to construction. In 1976, similar clashes over plans to build new nuclear power plants took place at Brokdorf on the Lower Elbe in Schleswig-Holstein and the following year at two other sites, Grohnde and Gorleben in Lower Saxony. Out of these protests against nuclear power stations, "citizens' initiatives"—local, single-issue campaign groups—began to form. In 1975 two mainstream political figures wrote books on the "ecological crisis": the Social Democrat Erhard Eppler, the environment minister in the Brandt government who had quit shortly after Schmidt took over, and the Christian Democrat Herbert Gruhl. By 1977, opposition to nuclear power had expanded into a radical green critique of capitalism influenced by the ideas of the German Catholic writer Carl Amery and the East German dissident Rudolf Bahro, and the citizens' initiatives around West Germany started to coalesce into a national green movement.

In many ways, this new protest movement had nothing to do with 1968. In fact, parts of it drew heavily on a right-wing, anti-modernist tradition in German politics that went all the way back to the German Romantics.[19] Indeed, some of the key figures in the new movement had backgrounds in the far right, such as August Haußleiter, who as an

18 year-old had taken part in Hitler's failed 1923 *putsch* and in 1950 had formed a "nationalist-neutralist" group called the *Deutsche Gemeinschaft*, or German Community.[20] Unlike the student movement, which had consisted almost exclusively of young people born around the time of the war, the green movement was more diverse and included both older and younger people than the generation of 1968. Moreover, unlike the student movement, which had been based on Marxism and placed the proletariat at the centre of its politics, the green movement was unashamedly middle-class. In fact, the green movement had emerged outside the SPD precisely because the working-class left, particularly the trade unions, had been so uninterested in environmental issues.

In some ways, in fact, the ideas of the green movement were almost the opposite of those of the student movement. Unlike the student movement, which had mythologised *Kampf*, or "struggle", the green movement's rhetoric centred on the concept of "peace". Above all this expressed a rejection of German militarism and technocratic capitalism. But it was also, in some ways, a backlash against the West German student movement that had culminated in the ultra-violence of the "German Autumn" of 1977. The environmentalists replaced the student movement's humanist Utopia with a new naturalist Utopia. The green movement was also even more anti-American than the APO had been. While the APO had had an ambivalent attitude to the United States, which it saw as both liberator and oppressor, the green movement tended to see West Germany simply as an exploited colony of the United States. While the *Achtundsechziger* had seen a deep complicity between West Germany and the United States, the green movement tended to see West Germany simply as a victim of American imperialism.[21] In that sense, the green movement was closer to Rudi Dutschke's view of Germany than that of the student movement as a whole.

Unlike most in the student movement, but like Dutschke, many of the theorists and activists within the green movement also tended to downplay the Nazi past and the Holocaust. They did not see Auschwitz as a crucially significant metaphysical break as, for example, Adorno had; in fact, they saw subsequent developments, in particular the development of nuclear power and weapons, as either an extension of the same phenomenon that created Auschwitz or as qualitatively worse. What fascism was to many of the post-war generation, the bomb was to the greens. The philosopher Günther Anders, a major influence on the West German green movement, wrote that Auschwitz represented an age where "all human beings can be killed", whereas the bomb represented an age where "humanity as a whole can be killed."[22] Some had already noticed this tendency to subsume Auschwitz as a specific historical event within the threat of an even greater evil in the anti-nuclear movement of the fifties and early sixties. In an essay published in 1964, Hans Magnus Enzensberger had written that the bomb was "the present and future version of Auschwitz".[23] Hannah Arendt said that for a German to write this represented a "very cultivated form of escapism."[24]

Given the similarities with his own thinking, it was perhaps not surprising that it was Rudi Dutschke who, of all the *Achtundsechziger*, was the first to commit to the green movement. Dutschke participated in many of the big demonstrations against nuclear power stations, for example in Brokdorf, which he said immediately reminded him of the demonstration following the Vietnam Congress in West Berlin in 1968.[25] "It was the biggest, most impressive and most disciplined demonstration I have ever seen."[26] He had long discussions with green activists, who, he said, had changed his view of the reality of the political situation in West Germany. He sensed an "anti-capitalist feeling" and a "sense of the necessity of resistance" among the anti-nuclear protesters but felt they were not sufficiently socialist.[27] Despite these differences he was enthused by the new movement. He said it was a "second APO".[28]

However, many of the other revolutionary left-wing groups that had grown out of the student movement had mixed feelings about the new extra-parliamentary opposition. They were all fascinated by the political potential of the protest movement against nuclear power plants, but they had little in common with the protesters themselves. To many on the West German New Left, the anti-nuclear activists had an insufficiently theoretical understanding of capitalism. "We thought they were conservatives who were scared of progress," says Hubert Kleinert, at the time a member of a "Sponti" group in Marburg.[29] It was a matter of style as well as ideology: to the battle-hardened Frankfurt "Spontis", the anti-nuclear protesters were, as one member of Revolutionary Struggle put it, "softies".[30] The "Spontis" were happy to participate in demonstrations and battles against the police in places like Brokdorf and Grohnde but at the same time were hesitant about fully committing to the green movement. Their elastic ideology and willingness to undertake experiments as part of a "political learning process" made it easier for them to embrace environmental issues than it was, for example, for the more dogmatic "K-Groups". And yet, the truth was that, deep down, none of the "Spontis" really cared about the environment, least of all Joschka Fischer.[31]

Beyond their indifference about the environment, the emergence of the green movement also presented a deeper problem for many among the 1968 generation which was related to their view of the West German state. By 1978, the citizens' initiatives and other local anti-nuclear organisations had shifted their focus from organising protest to achieving political power. They had begun to get together to form loosely organised "alternative lists" of candidates to stand at local and state elections around West Germany. Many of the revolutionary left-wing groups, including some of the "K-Groups" such as the Maoist KPD in West Berlin, had even begun to join the alternative lists. While some of them had come to terms with parliamentary democracy, others merely made a tactical decision to participate in parliamentary democracy. But what ultimately made it so difficult for many on the West German New Left, such as the "Spontis", to join them was their equation of the Federal Republic with a fascist state—in other words the continuity thesis that went right back to the beginning of the student movement.

For Joschka Fischer, the Entebbe hijacking in 1976 had begun a long, painful process of questioning that thesis. Until then, much of the West German New Left had thought in black and white terms. The Federal Republic was a fascist state. They, in turn, were the "resistance" against the "Auschwitz generation" or perhaps even the "new Jews". The shock of Entebbe had begun to undermine that black-and-white view of their struggle. In particular it had shattered the idea that the war against the Federal Republic that had grown out of the West German student movement qualified as "resistance". That, in turn, raised the possibility that, despite all the apparent structural similarities between the Nazi state and the Federal Republic and despite all the former Nazis like Globke and Schleyer whose biographies seemed to confirm the continuity thesis, the Federal Republic was maybe not a fascist state after all.

Since the "Whitsun congress" of May 1976 when they first began to publicly voice their doubts about the direction the West German New Left had taken, the "Spontis" had gone their separate ways. Daniel

A LIFELINE

Cohn-Bendit had started *Pflasterstrand*, a magazine that functioned as a kind of listings guide to the Frankfurt alternative scene. Thomas Schmid, the group's theoretician, had been the editor of the student magazine *diskus* and then started the radical journal *Autonomie*, in which Fischer published his 1977 essay criticising the armed struggle. But Fischer had taken the failure of the "Sponti" movement harder than all of them and sank into a deep depression from which it would take him years to recover.[32] In the meantime, he sold second-hand books in the basement of a left-wing bookshop near Frankfurt University during the day and worked as a taxi driver at night.

It was Cohn-Bendit who jumped first, setting a pattern that was repeated several times over the next two decades. For Cohn-Bendit, the "child of freedom" who had grown up not in West Germany but in France, 1945 had always represented a greater break with the Nazi past than it had for his German comrades. Perhaps as a result of this, he had never been as passionately committed as them to the idea that the Federal Republic was a fascist state. That, in turn, meant he never had as much of a problem with the idea of participating in the parliamentary system as they did. Cohn-Bendit engaged with the green activists early on and decided to put himself forward as a candidate for the "Green List" in the 1978 Hesse state elections. His candidacy proved so controversial, however—he proposed, among other things, legalising marijuana, which horrified conservative environmentalists—that he withdrew a few weeks later.

Fischer was also tempted by the nascent green movement, not because he cared about the environment, but because he saw in it the possibility of once again being a political activist. In an essay in *Pflasterstrand* in 1978 entitled "Why not?" he complained that

the lack of prospects, the hanging around, the not knowing what to do is getting more and more unbearable. The air in the ghetto is suffocating, and our withdrawal into ourselves has not changed reality either. No wonder then that, to some of us, the possibility of finally doing something *realpolitisch* again, of getting together with other people outside the ghetto, seems like a lifeline.[33]

However, Fischer still could not bring himself to accept parliamentary democracy and with it everything the "Spontis" had once opposed. In the same essay he agonised over the existential question of whether he should now vote:

Are we anarchists, Spontis and objectors supposed to suddenly forget everything and vote or even get ourselves elected? In that case, why didn't we vote for Brandt in 1969? Why not in 1972? Why have we never voted (at least not as a movement, even if some individuals have) and why should we now?[34]

But even as he asked the question, Fischer's radical opposition to the system was softening. In the same essay, he expressed a growing doubt that would eventually lead him to re-define what form his generation's "resistance" should now take:

Perhaps our rejection of parliament is wrong; perhaps it is our left-wing radicalism that is wrong. [...] In short, maybe the path of reform is the only path left open to us because everything else is over? Reformists in reality and radical dreamers? If that's how it is, we should at least say it openly.[35]

This choice between what he would later call "fundamental opposition" to the "system" and *Realpolitik* would come to define both Fischer's internal struggle and then later the struggle between him and many other members of the Green party that eventually emerged out of the environmental movement.

Since the start of Willy Brandt's "social-liberal" coalition in 1969, the SPD had blossomed. By 1976, it had over a million members—the highest number ever.[36] Beneath the surface, however, conflicts had broken out, in particular between the party leadership and the *Jusos*, the youth organisation created after the expulsion of the SDS from the SPD, which included all SPD members under the age of 35. The conflict between the post-war generation and the "Auschwitz generation" that had taken place on the streets in the sixties would now continue within the SPD.[37]

After the Bad Godesberg conference in 1959, the SPD had transformed itself into one of the most pragmatic centre-left parties in Western Europe. Under Brandt, it had moved to the right of many other socialist parties in Western Europe such as the British Labour party and the *Jusos* became simply a "loyal source of logistical support and future leadership for the mother party."[38] However, between 1969 and 1974, with the influx of young people politicised in the sixties, a new left wing formed within it, particularly in the university towns, that considered itself part of the same "movement" as the APO and drew many of its ideas from it. Many of them, in fact, remained members of other revolutionary left-wing groups and saw themselves as infiltrating the SPD and transforming it from within in the spirit of Dutschke's "long march through the institutions". They followed a "double strat-egy" of mobilising people at the grass roots level—much as many of the revolutionary post-1968 groups did—and simultaneously internally reforming the party, which in practice meant moving it to the left, in particular on foreign policy. Their aim was to take over the SPD by the 1980s.[39] Peter Corterier, a moderate who had been ousted as *Juso* chairman in 1969, said the youth organisation had become "the APO's bridgehead inside the SPD."[40]

Within the *Jusos* was a range of factions that paralleled the various radical left-wing groupings outside the SPD. All of them believed, in slightly different ways based on their different ideological positions, that they could use the SPD to radically change the West German political and economic system. The most radical was the "Stamokap" faction, a kind of "K-Group" within the SPD, which believed in the same theory of "state monopoly capitalism" as the DKP and often worked closely with it, forming joint committees on issues such as the *Berufsverbot*.[41] It regarded even the Brandt government as the "agent of monopoly capitalism."[42] Then there were the "anti-revisionists", based in particular in Lower Saxony—the "Spontis" of the SPD. Influ-enced more than any of the other factions by the ideas of the student movement, they believed in building a radical grass roots movement from the bottom up, to which they believed the party should defer. Although there were significant ideological differences between them, the "Stamokap" faction and the "anti-revisionists" often worked together against the more moderate "reform socialists".

Torn between revolutionary fantasies and Brandt's promises of reform, the *Jusos* spent most of the early seventies arguing among themselves about the exact relationship of the party to the proletari-at.[43] With the end of Brandt's reforming government, however, the SPD's new left wing became more openly hostile to the party leader-ship and in particular to Schmidt, beginning a second period of ideo-logical struggle between the wartime generation and the post-war generation—only this time within the SPD. In July 1977, the "Stamo-kap" faction and the "anti-revisionists" joined forces and succeeded in getting a leading member of the "Stamokap" faction, Klaus-Uwe Ben-neter, elected as the leader of *Jusos*—the first time a representative of either of the two more radical factions had done so. The SPD leader-ship was outraged and ejected Benneter and around 150 or so other members of the "Stamokap" faction from the SPD. The following Feb-ruary, with the support of what remained of the "Stamokap" faction,

Benneter was succeeded as leader of the *Jusos* by a 33 year-old "anti-revisionist" lawyer from Lower Saxony named Gerhard Schröder.

Schröder, born in 1944, was of the same age as many in the student movement, but had followed a somewhat different trajectory to most of them. Schröder's father Fritz, a lance corporal in the *Wehrmacht*, had been killed in action in Romania in 1944 when he was six months old. He, his three sisters and a stepbrother were raised by his mother, who made a living as a cleaner. He left school when he was 16 and started an apprenticeship but also took evening classes to complete his education. He finally passed his *Abitur* when he was 22 and began studying law at Göttingen University, where he joined the Social Democrats and became a *Juso* activist. But although Schröder was in Göttingen in 1968, he did not have much time for student politics, which, he would later say, seemed childish and insufficiently practical.[44] As a member of the SPD, he was also a member of the *Sozialistischer Hochschulbund* (SHB), the Social Democrat student organisation, which had joined the SDS in protests against the Vietnam war but had never been as radically opposed to the Federal Republic as the SDS. Schröder had never read Adorno or Marcuse, and the left-wing theories that many students buried themselves in simply did not interest him.

Also, unlike many of his generation but like Rudi Dutschke, Schröder was not troubled by the Nazi past. Even though his father had been a soldier on the Eastern Front—where the *Wehrmacht*, alongside the SS, was routinely involved in atrocities—Schröder did not dwell on what he might have done during the war. "At home the Nazi era was not an issue," he would later write."[45] It was only when he went to university that he began to engage with the Nazi past for the first time. Even then, he never came to see the Federal Republic primarily as a continuation of Nazism, as many among his generation had.[46] Nevertheless, Schröder leant to the left. Growing up with a strong sense of working class identity fuelled both his own ambition and a passionate belief in the importance of social mobility in West Germany.[47] Above all he was driven by what friends of his saw as a deep-seated "instinct for power."[48]

Although he called himself a Marxist, Schröder had little time for the arcane theoretical debates among the various factions within the *Jusos*. "For months, even years, these clashes paralysed the *Jusos'* political work," he would later write.[49] Schröder's strength was not theory but organisation. Although he was known within the *Jusos* as a left-winger, he was in fact a pragmatist who was not attached to any particular theoretical position and could win support from both the dogmatic left—who considered him their best option after Benneter's ejection—and from moderates. Like Fischer within the student movement, Schröder had also emerged within the *Jusos* at a crucial turning point. By the late 1970s, the *Jusos* had ceased to be a significant oppositional force, but their ideas were about to move into the mainstream of the party.

At the same time as he became *Juso* chairman in 1978, Schröder also started his own law practice in Hanover and began to make a name for himself in a series of high-profile political cases. He fought, mostly unsuccessfully, on behalf of left-wing activists who had been prevented from working in the civil service because of the *Radikalenerlaß*. In the summer of 1978—with West German society still reeling from the violent events of the previous autumn—he agreed to represent Horst Mahler, who, having now apparently rejected his terrorist past, had applied for parole. Despite pressure from the party leadership to give up his controversial client, Schröder and Mahler became friends. "If Mahler loses, there will be a political prisoner in Germany," Schröder declared publicly.[50] At the end of 1979, Mahler appeared on the front cover of *Spiegel* after taking part in a discussion with the Free Democrat interior minister Gerhart Baum, in which Mahler once again criticised his former comrades but also called for the state to exercise more leniency towards "ex-terrorists" such as him. "We all have to come out of our trenches," he said.[51] The following year, Schröder secured Mahler's release from prison after completing ten years of a fourteen-year sentence.

By 1979, the green movement was coalescing into a political party. The "5 per cent rule"—the requirement that political parties obtain at least 5 per cent of the vote in elections to gain representation in local or state parliaments or the *Bundestag*—put pressure on local green groups to unite. Lists of green and alternative candidates had been steadily gaining more votes in local and state elections around West Germany, particularly in the regions where nuclear power stations were planned. Although there still remained within the green movement deep resistance to the idea of forming a fully-fledged political party, each electoral success further increased the momentum towards formalisation of the informal lists.

While the Social Democrats were being riven by conflicts between the centre-left and the far left, the nascent green movement was even more heterogeneous. It included, alongside writers like Heinrich Böll, right-wing environmentalists, disillusioned Social Democrats and members of the citizens' initiatives, as well as members of the "K-Groups", especially the Communist League, which had been increasingly successful in infiltrating the rapidly growing green movement as part of a strategy of "entrism".[52] At one extreme were authoritarian environmentalists like Herbert Gruhl, who argued for a kind of eco-dictatorship, and at the other extreme were members of the Communist League like Jürgen Reents, who seemed to see the environmental crisis merely as a catalyst for revolution and the green movement as a vehicle for it.[53] In 1978, Gruhl left the Christian Democrats and formed his own party, Green Action Future (*Grüne Aktion Zukunft*—GAZ)). A battle between the right and left for control of the movement ensued, centred on the question of whether to allow members of the "K-Groups" to join the lists.

In the spring of 1979, a diverse group of green activists, including Gruhl, the artist Joseph Beuys and a disillusioned Social Democrat named Petra Kelly, formed a loose coalition of candidates to stand at the first ever elections for the European Parliament, which were due to take place the following summer. The alliance, whose three spokespersons included Gruhl and the nationalist August Haußleiter, gained 3.2 per cent of the vote—enough to win financial support from the West German state. Galvanised by this success, the momentum to form a fully-fledged party—which would be necessary if they were to stand in a general election in West Germany—became unstoppable.

Rudi Dutschke, who had long campaigned unsuccessfully for the formation of a new left-wing party that could participate in elections and gain political power in West Germany, was also ready to commit to the green movement. He still disagreed with many of the environmentalists about key issues, in particular the relationship between ecology and economics, and believed nuclear power in West Germany could only be stopped by a full-blooded socialist movement. But as the green movement began to transform itself into a fully-fledged political party, Dutschke came to see it as the last best hope for unifying the radical left in West Germany. He began campaigning for the Bremen Green List, which had been formed by a group of 22 former Social Democrats, in the run-up to state elections in October 1979. They gained 5.1 per cent of the vote in the election. It was the first time that a green list had reached the minimum of 5 per cent of the vote needed to gain seats in a state parliament. "We all agree about the most important question," he said in an interview after the election. "We all know that the survival of the human race is at stake."[54]

Fresh from this triumph, a conference was planned for January 1980, at which a national Green party would be formed. It would for the first time put up candidates in the general election scheduled for later that year. Eleven years after the assassination attempt, Dutschke, who had been spending more and more time in West Germany, finally decided to move back permanently with his family and in the middle of December the Bremen Green List elected him as one of their delegates to the conference. Ten days later, however, on Christmas Eve, Dutschke suffered an epileptic seizure while taking a bath and drowned. He was 39 years-old—the same age as his political hero Che Guevara had been when he was killed in Bolivia in 1967.

By the end of the decade, nearly all the leading figures of the student movement were gone. Dutschke, Hans-Jürgen Krahl and Ulrike Meinhof—probably the movement's three leading ideologues—were dead. Others, like Horst Mahler, were in prison. Many others, including Dieter Kunzelmann, had withdrawn from West German politics or even left the country. It would now be people like Joschka Fischer and Gerhard Schröder—peripheral figures in 1968 who were influenced not so much by the events that had led to the rebellion itself but by its failure—who would pick up what was left of the ideas of the student movement and apply them to a world that had already changed and would in the next 20 years change even more dramatically.

One by one, the student movement's inspirations around the world had also collapsed. Whatever illusions some of its members may still have had about the Soviet Union had already been shattered when the Red Army crushed the Prague Spring in 1968. In the 1970s, the New Left's role models in the Third World also turned out to be less emancipatory than they had originally thought. The Cultural Revolution in China, once a model for the student movement, turned out to be a disaster with a cost in human lives that dwarfed even the Holocaust.[55] Illusions had also been shattered about other national liberation movements that the students had once seen as the vanguard of a global socialist revolution such as the NLF in Vietnam. The Shah of Iran—whose visit to West Berlin had led to the death of Benno Ohnesorg and triggered the rebellion in the summer of 1967—had finally been overthrown in 1979. But in his place came not a democracy but a theocracy that would turn out to be as repressive, if not more so, than its predecessor. Joschka Fischer summed up the mood in another essay for *Pflasterstrand* in 1979. "Our revolution simply didn't exist—neither here nor in Vietnam nor in Iran nor in China," he said. "It existed only in us."[56]

With the collapse of the far-flung inspirations of the *Achtundsechziger*, their dream of a socialist Utopia also evaporated. But although most of them had lost their faith in socialism, some of the *Achtundsechziger* took with them on their political journey several other less obvious elements of the thinking of the student movement. In particular, two currents would emerge from the disappointments of the 1970s. Those among the post-war generation who had thought of their struggle as "resistance" against the "Auschwitz generation" and had been horrified by where the West German New Left had ended up, would over the next decade re-define what "resistance" meant. Their fears about Nazism had, in a sense, been radicalised. In 1967, many of them had thought fascism was in the "system". Now, after their experiences of the decade since then that culminated in the "German Autumn", they were haunted by the idea that perhaps it was also in them as Germans. In the sixties, they had felt that they faced an all-or-nothing choice between Utopia and Auschwitz. Instead of a socialist Utopia, they would now pursue a more modest aim: to prevent a recurrence of Auschwitz. This aspiration would come to be epitomised above all by Joschka Fischer.

But there was also a second, less immediately obvious current that emerged from the thinking of the student movement. As well as those who had been obsessed by Auschwitz, there had been some, like Rudi Dutschke, who had had little interest in the Nazi past. They had seen Germany not as a society of perpetrators but as a nation of victims. They had been revolutionary optimists who had focused on the idea of creating a revolution in both West Germany and East Germany, with the eventual aim of re-uniting the two. Over the years, they too would give up on the idea of a socialist Utopia. What remained for them was a kind of left-wing nationalism that they had inherited from Rudi Dutschke. This tendency would come to be epitomised above all by Gerhard Schröder, who, like Dutschke, had little time for dwelling on Germany's Nazi past.

In the 1980s, these two currents of thinking of the student movement would move from the margins to the centre of West German society. Until then, the ideas of the *Achtundsechziger* had remained restricted to intellectual West Germany. They had swirled around the communes of West Berlin and Frankfurt and the university towns of West Germany where the "K-Groups" and other revolutionary groups were based. They had been debated in journals like *Kursbuch*, *neue kritik* and *Autonomie* and finally in the *tageszeitung* (or *taz* for short), the co-operative-owned daily newspaper set up opposite the Springer building in West Berlin in 1978, which was in a sense the fulfilment of the student movement's dream of creating a *Gegenöffentlichkeit*, or "counter public sphere".[57] In the 1980s, however, the ideas of the student movement would be refracted through the SPD and the Greens and begin to penetrate the mainstream of West German society. In particular, the debates of the 1960s and 1970s would be transposed onto West German foreign policy. Out of the post-war generation's ambivalent attitude to the Nazi past would emerge two very different visions of Germany's role in the world.

8

PEACE

At the end of seventies, just as the Green party was about to come into existence, the Cold War heated up. In 1977, the Soviet Union had begun to replace its medium-range nuclear weapons with new SS-20 missiles that directly threatened western Europe and in particular West Germany. Over the next two years, Chancellor Schmidt helped bring about a shift in NATO strategy towards the Soviet Union to meet the new threat and convinced the Americans to station new medium-range missiles of its own in western Europe. In December 1979 NATO agreed to install Cruise and Pershing II missiles in various countries in Europe, including West Germany, if the Soviet SS-20s were not withdrawn by 1983. This so-called *Doppelbeschluß*, or "twin-track decision", eventually tore apart the West German left and ultimately led to the fall of the Schmidt government.

The 1970s had been a decade of *détente* between NATO and the Eastern Bloc. The United States and the Soviet Union had signed the SALT treaties, which limited the numbers of long-range nuclear weapons, and held negotiations about reducing conventional forces stationed in Europe. They had also negotiated other agreements on security, economic co-operation and humanitarian issues, culminating in the Helsinki final agreement of 1975. From an American point of view, the SALT agreements were a great success that had helped to reduce the danger of an all-out nuclear war between the two superpowers. But from West Germany's perspective, things looked a little different. SALT had not included medium-range missiles or other so-called "theatre weapons" that threatened Western Europe, while the Soviet Union continued to have overwhelming superiority in terms of conventional forces. To some West Germans like Schmidt, it seemed increasingly difficult to believe that the United States would use nuclear weapons as a response to a conventional Soviet attack on the Federal Republic. In other words, in West Germany's case, the nuclear deterrent seemed less and less credible, leaving it more vulnerable than ever before in the Cold War. At a speech in London in October 1977, Helmut Schmidt argued that NATO needed to re-arm in Western Europe if the Warsaw Pact countries refused to disarm.

Although West Germany was directly in the firing line—the first battlefield of World War III, as it were—the shifts that took place during the seventies had highlighted how little influence it had over its own security. As West Germany's relative economic power increased in the seventies—Schmidt's success in stabilising the economy after the oil shock had made it something of a model for other western countries—the Federal Republic had also begun to play a greater role in international affairs. It had, for example, signed a series of bilateral agreements with the GDR—which had become increasingly financially dependent on West Germany—that increased trade and eased travel between the two countries. But by the end of the 1970s, and especially following the Soviet invasion of Afghanistan in December 1979, relations between East and West had hardened. With the election of Ronald Reagan as US president in the autumn of 1980, the relationship between the United States and the Soviet Union became even more confrontational. As it did so, West Germany's room for manoeuvre decreased.

The "twin-track decision" would create what two political scientists called the "largest, most heterogeneous mass movement in the history of the Federal Republic", overshadowing not just the student movement but also the anti-nuclear movement of the late 1970s out of which the Green party had emerged.[1] It picked up from where the anti-nuclear movement of the 1950s, in which older members of the student movement such as Horst Mahler and Ulrike Meinhof had been involved, had left off. It was a complex phenomenon: as well as being an expression of moral outrage, it was also a protest against German powerlessness. With it emerged a new German pacifism that was both a direct backlash against German militarism and an expression of German nationalism. In particular, the peace campaigners tended to see Germany as a victim of American imperialism—even though the missile deployment had been largely a response to Schmidt's concerns about West Germany's security. The Green activist Petra Kelly, for example, saw West Germany as a "forward-based colony" which would become a "nuclear launch pad" in the event of a war.[2]

Internal opposition to the missile deployment within the SPD was led by Erhard Eppler, the party's environmental campaigner, but also launched the careers of a new generation of young Social Democrat officials and members of the *Bundestag*, such as Oskar Lafontaine, the former mayor of Saarbrücken. In June 1981, a group of SPD members including Eppler and Lafontaine issued a statement on security policy that was at complete odds with Schmidt's views. It rejected the concept of deterrence through strategic parity and alluded to Germany's special historical and constitutional obligation to peace.[3] Gerhard Schröder, who had been elected as leader of the *Jusos* for a second year in April 1979, also became a vocal critic of US foreign policy and in turn of Schmidt. His arguments centred above all on West German sovereignty and suggested in particular that the stationing of Cruise and Pershing II missiles in West Germany was not in its national interest. In February 1980, he wrote that "the highest principle has to be that the West German government cannot become the United States' deputy sheriff in other regions of the world."[4] Otherwise, he said, West Germany would become the western equivalent of a Soviet satellite state.

Schröder was elected as a member of the *Bundestag* in the general election of 1980 that also confirmed Schmidt as chancellor, and immediately caused a stir by giving his first speech in parliament wearing a sweater instead of a jacket and tie, strengthening the impression that he represented the rebellious generation of 1968. From the beginning, it was on foreign policy, and in particular on American foreign policy, that he was most vocal. As the arms race accelerated under President Reagan, Schröder became increasingly critical of the United States, which, along with many on the West German left, he saw as the major obstacle to *détente*. Although the peace campaigners claimed they were equally opposed to both American and Soviet armament policy—what was called "equidistance"—in practice they were much more critical of the United States.[5] In February 1981 Schröder wrote in *konkret* that the United States was attempting to tie West Germany into a "policy of confrontation" with the Soviet Union that would have "devastating foreign and domestic policy consequences."[6] In August 1981 Schröder, along with Gert Bastian, a former *Bundeswehr* general who had joined the the peace movement, published a pamphlet called *Against NATO's Armament Decision* that controversially accused the Schmidt government of disseminating "misinformation" about nuclear weapons.[7]

These arguments found increasing resonance among the West German population. In October 1981 300,000 people attended a demonstration against the missile deployment in Bonn—the largest ever demonstration in the history of the Federal Republic.[8] That year, nearly half of the West German population expressed a positive attitude towards the peace movement. The following Easter, 500,000 took part in a march against the missile deployment. The campaign culminated in a demonstration in Bonn on the day President Reagan, who had come to symbolise everything wrong with the United States, gave a speech to the *Bundestag* during a NATO summit.

While Schmidt came under attack from the left over the missile deployment, he was also coming under pressure from both left and right over his economic policy. The left of the SPD demanded increased spending, whereas the Free Democrats, the SPD's coalition partner, wanted more cuts. In September 1982 the Free Democrats, led by foreign minister Hans-Dietrich Genscher, resigned from the cabinet. The following month, after a vote of no-confidence in the *Bundestag*, Schmidt was deposed as chancellor and replaced by Helmut Kohl at the head of a new coalition of Christian Democrats and Free Democrats. A general election held the following spring confirmed the new coalition in power. While the Christian Democrats increased their share of the vote to 48.8 per cent, the SPD dropped nearly five points to 38.2 per cent, its worst result in 20 years. With the defection of the Free Democrats to the Christian Democrats, West German politics returned to the configuration that had existed before the grand coalition, in which the centre-right had a virtual monopoly on power in the Federal Republic.

While the "twin-track decision" plunged the SPD into crisis and ultimately ended the Schmidt government, it provided a major boost to the new Green party, which had rapidly become a major force in West German politics. Although it was not the first Green party in the world or even in Europe—the British Ecology Party, for example, had existed since 1973—it soon emerged as the most powerful. As opposition to the missile deployment grew, disillusioned Social Democrats turned to the Greens, who virtually became the parliamentary arm of the peace movement. They in turn used the issue of the missile deployment—and fear about a nuclear war in which Germany would be annihilated—to mobilise voters. In their first general election in 1980, the Greens won only 1.5 per cent of the vote (partly because many disillusioned Social Democrats voted for Helmut Schmidt to stop the right-wing Christian Democrat candidate, Franz Josef Strauss, becoming chancellor) but they subsequently scored a series of successes in state elections that suggested the party would soon be able to reach 5 per cent and therefore enter the *Bundestag*.

The Green party had begun as a heterogeneous movement united only by opposition to nuclear power, but, after its founding conference in Karlsruhe in January 1980, it quickly cohered into a radical left-wing party based on four principles: ecology, social justice, grass roots democracy and non-violence. By that time, most of the "K-Groups" had dissolved themselves, but many of their members had joined the Greens and brought with them their ideas, particularly on foreign policy.[9] Meanwhile the key right-wing figures in the party were marginalised. Herbert Gruhl, the former Christian Democrat, left in 1981 to form a rival right-wing green party, the *Ökologische Demokratrische Partei* (ÖDP). August Haußleiter, the German nationalist, was also forced to step down as party spokesman after more details about his far-right past emerged, though he remained a member of the party until his death in 1989.

The new figurehead of the party was Petra Kelly, who a few years earlier had been almost completely unknown in West Germany. Kelly, born in 1947 in Günzburg, the same Bavarian town as the notorious Auschwitz doctor Josef Mengele, was around the same age as the *Achtundsechziger* but had spent most of her youth in the United States, where she had gone to high school and university. She opposed the Vietnam war and, inspired by Martin Luther King, volunteered for Robert Kennedy's presidential campaign. She moved back to West Germany in 1970, joined the Social Democrats and worked for them in Brussels but quit the party in 1979 in protest at Schmidt's support for the missile deployment. Through the peace movement, Kelly met the former *Bundeswehr* general Gert Bastian, who remained her partner for the rest of her life.

Kelly was a radical eco-feminist who envisioned the Greens as an "anti-party".[10] It would put up candidates for election, but would not have the hierarchical structures of other parties, and, so the theory went, would therefore avoid having professional politicians interested only in power. Instead, the party would remain the parliamentary wing of a political movement, to which it would remain subservient. From the beginning the Greens considered themselves different and morally superior to other political parties in West Germany. They saw themselves as West Germany's conscience.

The programme the party had adopted at a conference in Saarbrücken ahead of the 1980 general election had focused overwhelmingly on the issue of nuclear power and this reflected the party's roots in the citizens' movements against nuclear power stations. The influence of the ideas of the student movement and the radical left-wing groups that had emerged out of it was primarily in foreign policy, which took up only four out of forty-six pages of the programme.[11] The Greens called for an "active peace policy" that rejected the threat or use of violence between states and also called for a "partnership with the peoples of the Third World".[12] At the heart of the Greens' vision for West German foreign policy was the idea of a non-aligned Federal Republic that was could escape the "bloc logic" of the Cold War and the influence of the United States and the Soviet Union. In practical terms, the policy of non-alignment meant a unilateral West German withdrawal from NATO, because, as Petra Kelly put it, "the alliance brings us more harm than good."[13]

The demand for a withdrawal from NATO, which would become the Greens' central foreign policy position for the next decade, was in essence a rejection of the *Westbindung* that went back to Adenauer. Otto Schily, who had also joined the Greens, said Adenauer's policy of integrating the Federal Republic into the West had obstructed the creation of "a different kind of Germany based on an anti-fascist sense of identity".[14] The idea of a non-aligned Germany was familiar in the New Left, much of which had rejected what it saw as both American and Soviet imperialism. In particular, it owed much to Rudi Dutschke. Significantly, however, it was an idea that was also shared by elements on the right that had thrown in their lot with the Greens, such as Haußleiter's "nationalist-neutralist" German Movement. It also appealed to the environmentalists and peace campaigners within the Greens, who regarded NATO as the driving force in the nuclear arms race. Indeed, it was precisely because these ideas were common ground shared by the various factions within the Greens that the party was able to adopt them as part of its platform.

The idea of a peaceful, neutral Federal Republic also allowed the Greens to sidestep the issue of the Nazi past, on which the various factions within the party differed. While Nazism was a kind of negative reference point for the Greens as it had been for the student movement, they tended to draw different lessons from it. The environmentalists and anti-nuclear campaigners who had joined the Greens focused not on the Holocaust but rather on the broader tradition of German militarism, which they thought had continued in a different form in post-war capitalist society.[15] When they talked about the Holocaust, they tended to include it in a list of other twentieth century horrors such as the bombing of German and Japanese cities during World War II. In fact, to activists like Petra Kelly Hiroshima seemed even more important than Auschwitz.[16]

An illustration of this attitude was the "Nuremberg tribunal" on nuclear weapons held by the Greens in the run-up to the 1983 general election, at which Kelly described Auschwitz and Hiroshima as essentially comparable crimes against humanity.[17] Even the choice of Nuremberg as the venue evoked images not just of the trial of Nazi war criminals in 1945 but also of the wartime bombing of the city.[18] In their election manifesto that year, the Greens called for unilateral nuclear disarmament "in memory of the horrors of World War II", horrors which they said would be exceeded in the event of a nuclear confrontation between the two superpowers.[19] At the same time they, like the student movement before them, thought of themselves as being part of a "resistance" movement. "We will never again be able to say 'We didn't know anything,'" Petra Kelly said in a call to organise "non-violent resistance" against nuclear weapons in 1983.[20]

The Greens' tendency to subsume Auschwitz within a list of other real and potential catastrophes and, like the student movement before them, to see their own movement as "resistance", reflected their belief in a fundamental continuity between Nazism and post-war industrial society. It was, in effect, the environmental and peace movement's own version of the student movement's continuity thesis, borrowing this time from E.P. Thompson's theory of the "exterminist" logic of advanced capitalism as well as from Adorno and Horkheimer.[21] The radical pacifists among the Greens saw themselves as belonging to a tradition of anti-fascism, while the student movement, which had itself turned violent, was a product of the same tradition as the Nazis themselves. The Greens' lesson from the Nazi past was encapsulated in the slogan that would become their mantra: "Never again war".

Given the pacifism of the Greens, and their tendency to downplay Auschwitz, it was, in a sense, surprising that former members of the

APO such as Otto Schily, Gudrun Ensslin's former lawyer, would find a home there, because the one thing they had never been was pacifists. But the Green party was essentially nothing more than a vehicle for their political ambitions. With a decade of practice in political in-fighting behind them, the *Achtundsechziger*, led by Joschka Fischer, hijacked the Green party in what one opponent, Jutta Ditfurth, would later call a "hostile takeover."[22] Their goal, above all, was power, in the form of a "red-green" coalition.

At the time of the formation of the Green party in 1980, Joschka Fischer was still in a state of depression. While eking out a living work-ing in his second-hand bookstore in Frankfurt during the day and as a taxi driver at night, he continued to agonize about whether it was pos-sible to achieve political change within the system he had struggled against ever since his politicisation in the late sixties. Later that year, however, he finally made his peace with parliamentary democracy. In an essay published in November 1980 under the title "The Taming of the Shrew", he turned away from what he now called the militant left's "radical ethos of refusal." It was no longer a question of simply destroy-ing the system, as he and the "Spontis" had aimed to do, but of chang-ing it from within. The parliamentary system would, he said, prove to be "stronger than any grass roots democratic or actionist illusions."[23]

Almost as soon as he reconciled himself to the idea of democratic politics, Fischer suggested that he might make a good democratic poli-tician himself. "If you have to have representatives, it's better that someone who is having a hard time with the idea of it becomes a rep-resentative than someone who has never done anything else," he said.[24] It was a kind of justification, in advance, of the political career that was about to begin. A year later, in the summer of 1981, Fischer joined the Greens. For a year or so, however, he remained an observer rather than an active participant. The real beginning of his career in the Greens came a few days before the collapse of the Schmidt government in September 1982. While in Bonn the Christian Democrats were about to take power, the left seemed to be gaining in strength in Hesse. The Greens had just won 8 per cent of the vote in state elections, taking over from the Free Democrats as the third largest party in the state parliament.

The Hesse election opened up an exciting new possibility for the West German left. For almost the entire life of the Federal Republic until then, West German politics had followed the same simple electoral logic. The Christian Democrats had consistently been the biggest party in West Germany. The only way the Social Democrats had been able to form a government was with the support of the third party, the Free Democrats, who held the balance of power. The emergence of the Greens, however, changed everything. On the night of the Hesse election, Willy Brandt, who regarded the Greens as "the lost children of the SPD," spoke of "a new majority to the left of the Christian Democrats."[25] It was above all this prospect of power that enticed Fischer, who now became an aggressive and outspoken advocate for an alliance with the Social Democrats.

There was not yet any talk of forming a "red-green" coalition, but even the idea of co-operation with the Social Democrats was anathema to most of the Greens. At the time, the left-wing but technocratic SPD government in Hesse was planning to build a new runway at Frankfurt airport—against which a major campaign had been organised—and to expand an atomic power station at Biblis, 40 miles south of Frankfurt. To most of the leading Frankfurt Greens such as Jutta Ditfurth, a radical eco-socialist who would become Fischer's arch enemy, propping up an SPD government was unthinkable. To Fischer, however, it was necessary if the Greens were ever to achieve anything.

The month after the election Fischer, Daniel Cohn-Bendit and several of their friends published a manifesto in the name of a "*Realpolitik* working group" in which they laid out a new strategy for the party. They suggested that the Greens should put a series of demands to the Social Democrats—including a one-year moratorium on building the new runway at Frankfurt airport and a halt to the expansion of the Biblis nuclear plant—in return for tolerating the administration. The alternative, which they called "fundamental opposition", would mean "wasting an historic opportunity and giving the SPD the space that the protest movements had actually given to the Greens."[26]

The manifesto was the beginning of what would become a decade-long battle between Green "fundamentalists" and "realists". With it, a tiny minority that had only just joined the Greens succeeded in re-shaping the terms in which the party would see itself, portraying themselves as hard-headed realists and labelling their opponents as quasi-religious "fundamentalists".[27] To the "realists", "fundamentalists" like Jutta Ditfurth were interested only in political posturing rather than concrete change—demonstrating in parliament, as it were.

The "fundamentalists", meanwhile, thought Fischer should just join the SPD. To them, he was simply an opportunist, a man without principles who was prepared to do anything to achieve power—precisely the kind of person whose emergence the Greens' loose structures had been designed to prevent but had instead facilitated.

The rise of the Greens culminated in a triumph at the general election of March 1983. Held precisely at the moment when feelings were running highest about the missile deployment, there was a groundswell of support for the Greens. While the SPD's share of the vote dropped nearly 5 per cent, the Greens ended up receiving 5.6 per cent and thus entered the *Bundestag* for the first time. The morning after, when the electoral mathematics had been done, it turned out that Fischer, who had been in third place in a list of candidates from Hesse to be elected by proportional representation, would also be going to Bonn. Fifteen years after 1968, less than two years after joining the Green party and barely six months after becoming active within it, Fischer was to become one of its first representatives in the *Bundestag*.

Even as he became an elected representative, however, Fischer's radical past caught up with him. In May 1981, the Hesse economics minister Heinz-Herbert Karry had been shot dead in bed at his home in Frankfurt. It was the first time in German post-war history that a government minister had been assassinated. Karry, a Free Democrat who was half-Jewish and had been a slave labourer during the war, had been in favour of expanding the Biblis nuclear plant and of building the new runway at Frankfurt airport. Several weeks later, in a communiqué published in Daniel Cohn-Bendit's magazine *Pflasterstrand*, the Revolutionary Cells claimed responsibility for the killing. The case was never solved. However, it transpired that the 0.22–caliber pistol used to kill Karry, which had been stolen from an American army base in 1970, had been hidden in Joschka Fischer's car three years later. Fischer said that Hans-Joachim Klein, a mechanic, had been repairing the car for him at the time. There was no evidence that Fischer was involved in the murder. But the connection between him and the killing of Karry would hang over his political career for years to come.

The Kohl government did not usher in a period of radical change as under Ronald Reagan in the United States or Margaret Thatcher in Britain. Helmut Kohl himself was hardly a free-marketeer in the mould of Reagan or Thatcher, nor did the consensus-based West German polit-ical system lend itself to the kind of sweeping changes possible in the United States and Britain. The Christian Democrats' coalition partner, the Free Democrats, did support greater economic liberalisation and nominated as economics minister Count Otto Lambsdorff, an aristo-cratic free marketeer whom Genscher predicted would be "the Ludwig Erhard of the 1980s."[28] However, within 18 months of taking office he was forced to resign after it emerged that he, along with leading Chris-tian Democrats, had accepted undisclosed (and therefore, under Ger-man law, illegal) donations from the industrialist Friedrich Karl Flick.

Meanwhile, with Kohl now in the Chancellery instead of Schmidt, the massive campaign against the deployment of Cruise and Pershing II missiles reached its climax. In October 1983, as the decision by the *Bundestag* about the missile deployment approached, 400,000 protest-ers, including Willy Brandt, Heinrich Böll and Günter Grass, took part in the largest ever demonstration in the history of the Federal Repub-lic. Shortly afterwards, the opponents of the missile deployment won the battle within the SPD. At a party conference in Cologne in Novem-ber 1983, the Social Democrats voted by 583 votes to 14 against the missile deployment. The vote not only symbolised the new ascendancy of the post-war generation within the party but also represented a par-tial reversal of the Bad Godesberg conference of 1959, at which the SPD had accepted re-armament and the *Westbindung*. But with the change of government, it no longer made any difference. The same month, the *Bundestag* approved the deployment (Schmidt abstained), which began shortly afterwards. The Greens unsuccessfully challenged the deployment in the Constitutional Court and peace campaigners continued to protest for years at Mutlangen, the US air base near Stutt-gart where Pershing II missiles were stationed.

The 28 Green parliamentarians elected in 1983 were an eclectic bunch to say the least. Other than Fischer there were former members of the APO such as Otto Schily, who became the Greens' parliamen-tary leader; Jürgen Reents, the former editor of the Communist League's newspaper, *Workers' Struggle*; Hubert Kleinert, the "Sponti" from Marburg who, like Fischer, had initially been suspicious of the anti-nuclear protest movement; and Dirk Schneider, the former owner of *Agit 883*, who, it later transpired, had been a Stasi agent. But the Green contingent also included other very different figures, such as Christa Reetz, a pensioner from Wyhl who had been a leading figure in the movement against nuclear power stations, and Antje Vollmer, a left-wing pastor. It had also originally included a 75 year-old environmental activist from the Rhineland named Werner Vogel, who would have been the oldest member of the Bundestag and therefore entitled to give the first speech in the new parliament. However, shortly before the first session of parliament, it emerged that Vogel, who had joined the Greens through Herbert Gruhl's right-wing Green Action Future, was also a former SS officer who had attended the Wannsee conference in 1942, and he was forced to resign.

To the Bonn establishment, the arrival in spring 1983 of the Greens, the first new political party to enter the Bundestag since the 1950s, initially seemed like "an alien invasion."[29] On the first day of the new parliament, the Greens marched through Bonn on their way to the Bundestag carrying banners and beating drums. Petra Kelly, the pale, passionate figure who was the party's unofficial leader, carried with her a small shrub taken from the site of the planned new runway at Frankfurt airport and declared: "We will never betray the movement."[30] Apart from her, it was Fischer, the party whip, who made the biggest impact in what the Greens called "Spaceship Bonn". A month after taking up his seat, he declared in an interview with *Pflasterstrand* that the Bundestag "was an assembly of alcoholics."[31] Fischer said Bonn was stuck in the era of Adenauer and suggested that he would bring the spirit of the student movement to Bonn fifteen years after it had swept through the universities of West Germany. Usually unshaven and wearing a flea-market-bought jacket on top of a t-shirt, he quickly made a name for himself heckling Helmut Kohl and giving sarcastic speeches of his own. On one occasion he was ejected for calling the speaker of the Bundestag an "asshole", albeit "with respect". He rapidly turned into a political celebrity, which created suspicion in the Green party just as Dutschke's celebrity had created suspicion in the SDS.

In fact, the internal conflicts within the Greens, which had begun before they entered the Bundestag and had initially been welcomed as part of a *Streitkultur* (culture of debate) that differentiated them from other parties, got worse in Bonn and threatened to tear the party apart. While their influence on government policy was tiny, they argued among themselves as much as with the government, in particular about the "coalition question". The party was divided three ways between those around Fischer who wanted the Greens to be open to a "red-green" coalition, those around the eco-socialist Rainer Trampert who

ruled out a coalition but were prepared to "tolerate" a Social Democrat government, and those around Rudolf Bahro who ruled out both
possibilities on principle. To Fischer, the "fundamentalists" seemed to
care more about their own identity than achieving change. They, on
the other hand, regarded Fischer and his clique of realists—who they
called the "Fischer gang"—as arrogant opportunists. After two years
in Bonn, Fischer was forced to leave the *Bundestag* as part of the
Greens' policy of rotating office holders—a means of preventing their
elected representatives turning into professional politicians (the rota-
tion principle would later be abandoned after it turned out to be not
just impractical but also unconstitutional).

Although he was forced out of Bonn, Fischer finally won the argument over whether to co-operate with the Social Democrats in Hesse.
In 1985, after two years of tolerating the Social Democrat government
(during which the Greens' share of the vote had dropped from 8 per
cent to 5.6 per cent), the Greens secured the SPD's agreement to build
no new nuclear power stations and in December 1985 formally joined
them in the first ever "red-green" coalition. The Greens were given the
environment ministry and on 12 December, 1985, Fischer, who admitted having little knowledge of environmental issues, became environment minister. To some who had participated in the student movement,
the appointment seemed of monumental symbolic importance. "In
1968 we started out on a long march through the institutions," said
Bernd Messinger, the Green vice-president of the Hesse parliament,
referring to Dutschke's speech at the Vietnam Congress. "The first one
has arrived."[32] (Fischer also brought with him Tom Koenigs, his old
friend from Revolutionary Struggle, who became his chief of staff.)
Fischer was sworn in wearing a pair of brand new white Nike Air
Force Ones that he bought especially for the occasion and from then
on would be dubbed the *Turnschuhminister*, or "sneaker minister". It
was the last time he would wear sneakers on such an occasion—not so
much a act of rebellion as a farewell to rebellion.[33]

As "the first Green minister on the planet", as he put it, Fischer was
even more in the spotlight than he had been as a member of the *Bundestag* in Bonn. The pressure on him increased five months into the
job, when the Chernobyl nuclear disaster took place in April 1986.
With mainstream West Germany suddenly in a panic about the dangers of nuclear power—*Bild* warned that radiation from Chernobyl
might spread to West Germany—the resurgent "fundamentalist" wing

demanded an immediate withdrawal from nuclear power in West Germany. Behind the scenes, Fischer unsuccessfully attempted to coax the Social Democrats to make a concession to the Greens. In public, meanwhile, he remained loyal, keeping silent while the Social Democrat prime minister, Holger Börner, declared there was no reason for Hesse to change its nuclear policy. "Green minister Fischer surrenders to the SPD," headlined the *taz*.[34] Anti-nuclear demonstrators even occupied the environment ministry in Wiesbaden and shouted down Fischer, who had to be rescued by Daniel Cohn-Bendit. Finally, at a party conference in May 1985, Fischer publicly demanded that the Social Democrats take steps to begin phasing out nuclear power by the end of the year. The Social Democrats held firm and even agreed to extend a licence to an existing nuclear power station. The "red-green" coalition finally collapsed in February 1987 after just 14 months. Many thought it would be the last of its kind.

After the bloodbath of the "German Autumn", the New Left had finally ended its war with the West German state. But it was never entirely clear whether the erstwhile revolutionaries who had gone into politics, above all those in the Green party, had done so based on principle or simply tactics—for example as part of the "long march through the institutions" that Rudi Dutschke had called for. Peter Schneider, who had been a leading figure in the West Berlin SDS, wrote that many revolutionaries had undergone a sudden and somewhat disingenuous metamorphosis. "After the defeat we were in a mad rush to be democratic and non-violent and began to read the constitution," he wrote. "From then on we no longer called ourselves Marxist, we were left-wing. We were no longer revolutionary, we were radical. And in this process of re-naming things, we didn't really want to know what we were jettisoning—and what deserved to be jettisoned."[35]

The big debate on the New Left in the late seventies had revolved around the "question of violence" rather than the ideology that had motivated that violence. In particular, few of the former members of the student movement who had thrown themselves into democratic politics had explained how their view of Nazism, and the alleged continuities between Nazism and the Federal Republic, had evolved. Until then, while some among the post-war generation had been almost obsessed with the idea of "resistance" against the "Auschwitz generation", their engagement with the Nazi past had been characterised by a tendency towards "exonerating projection". At the same time, others among the post-war generation, like Rudi Dutschke, had seen the Nazi past as a distraction from the revolution and wanted, essentially, to forget about it. The *Achtundsechziger* liked to think they had forced Germany to face up to its recent history. In reality, their own engagement with the Nazi past had been at best incomplete and at worst flawed.

Gradually, however, some like Joschka Fischer began to think again. The process had begun after Entebbe, when they had begun to face the possibility that fascist and even anti-Semitic tendencies were not restricted to the "Auschwitz generation" but also existed within the thinking of the post-war generation itself. That had shattered the 1968 generation's belief that its struggle was "resistance". They now deepened their engagement with the Nazi past. While in the 1960s and 1970s the post-war generation had reduced Nazism to "fascism", in effect side-lining the specific aspects of German National Socialism and in particular the Holocaust, now they began to put the Holocaust at the centre of their idea of Nazism. In particular, they rediscovered Adorno's exhortation "to arrange one's thoughts and actions so that it will not be repeated, so that nothing similar [to Auschwitz] will happen". Preventing a recurrence of Auschwitz became the essence of the new version of the anti-Nazi campaign, or "resistance", they had always strived for.

What this meant in practice was demonstrated in a furious debate about the lessons for foreign policy from Germany's Nazi past that took place against the backdrop of the deployment of Cruise and Pershing II missiles in the summer of 1983. The debate began after Joschka Fischer and Otto Schily gave an interview to the *Spiegel* in which they defended the Greens' use of their constitutional "right to resistance" in protesting against the missile deployment. In doing so, Schily directly compared the threat of a nuclear war with the Holocaust, saying that a nuclear war would be an "atomic Auschwitz" which could in the worst-case scenario be many times worse than Auschwitz itself.[36] Quoting Adorno and Horkheimer's analysis of fascism, Fischer said that it was "morally terrifying" that it was not a taboo to plan further mass destruction, this time on east-west lines instead of according to the Nazis' racial ideology. "I am not making an analogy with Auschwitz but I am saying that Auschwitz sends us a reminder to denounce this logic wherever it emerges and to fight it politically," he said.[37]

The Christian Democrat cabinet minister Heiner Geißler, like Helmut Kohl a member of the *Flakhelfergeneration* and a vocal critic of "sympathisers" with terrorism in the seventies, took up the debate in the *Bundestag* a few weeks later. He criticised Fischer and Schily for their use of the phrase "atomic Auschwitz" and for inappropriately bringing the Holocaust into a debate about defence policy. He went on to say that the Holocaust would not have happened if the western democracies in the thirties had been tougher. "It was the pacifism of the thirties that made Auschwitz possible," he said.[38] The Greens, along with some Social Democrats and Free Democrats, were outraged at the remarks, particularly about the apparent reduction of non-violent "resistance" by anti-nuclear activists to appeasement. Fischer responded to Geißler in his maiden speech in the *Bundestag*. He said it was not pacifists but the German right that was responsible for Nazism and reminded Geißler of the former Nazis like Globke and Kiesinger who had once been in his own party. "That legacy from another era, which your party always deliberately overlooks, has preserved itself in post-war West Germany," he said.[39] It was a classic statement of the student movement's continuity thesis.

The invocation of Auschwitz in the debate about nuclear weapons represented a subtle shift in the relationship of *Achtundsechziger* like Fischer and Schily to the Nazi past. Where in the sixties, the student movement had tended to marginalise the Holocaust by talking primarily about "fascism", Fischer and Schily now put it at the centre of their thinking about Nazism. But at a deeper level, the concept of an "atomic Auschwitz" was a continuation of the earlier attempts to engage politically with Auschwitz that went back to Martin Walser's 1965 essay in *Kursbuch*. In applying the theory of the "exterminist" logic of modernity, Fischer and Schily were still using the Holocaust to make the case for political change in the present in the same way as the student movement had been when it described the American war in Vietnam as genocide—an approach that would later be criticised as the "instrumentalisation" of Auschwitz. By referring to the Holocaust to alert West Germany and the world to potential future catastrophes such as a nuclear war, they were still, in a sense, relativising Auschwitz.

The New Left's renewed focus on the Holocaust was in fact part of a wider transformation in Germany's attitude to the Nazi past that had been taking place since the 1970s. This transformation paralleled the emergence of the Holocaust as a concept in the West in general. In the United States, for example, the Holocaust had become an increasingly important collective memory since the Six-Day War in 1967 and in particular since the Yom Kippur War in 1973.[40] A central factor that contributed to this change, in West Germany as in the US, was the television series *Holocaust*, which 20 million West Germans watched when it was broadcast in January 1979. The airing of the series became, as Peter Novick puts it, "the turning point in Germany's long-delayed confrontation with the Holocaust".[41] One journalist wrote in the *Spiegel* that "*Holocaust* has shaken up post-Hitler Germany in a way that German intellectuals have been unable to."[42] The following year, the *Bundestag* abolished the statute of limitations on Nazi war crimes, nearly twenty years after the SDS campaign to extend it in the early 1960s.

By the 1980s, a tentative new sense of German identity had emerged that was based not on silence about the past as in the Adenauer era but on an acceptance of responsibility for Nazism and in particular for the Holocaust. How mainstream this "Holocaust identity" had become by the 1980s was illustrated by the way that expressions of atonement for the genocide by West German heads of government and heads of state on behalf of the nation had become more frequent. In November 1977—a month after the end of the "German Autumn"—Helmut Schmidt became the first West German chancellor to deliver a speech at Auschwitz. "We Germans of today are not guilty as individual persons, but we must bear the political legacy of those who were guilty," he said. "That is our responsibility."[43]

Nor was it just the left that had begun to speak openly about Auschwitz and the lessons to be learned from it. Helmut Kohl appeared at times to relativise Nazi war crimes, for example in 1985 when he invited President Reagan to a memorial service at Bitburg cemetery, at which members of the Waffen-SS were buried alongside *Wehrmacht* soldiers. But since the debate about the missile deployment in West Germany in 1983, the right had also begun to actively use Auschwitz to justify its own political positions.[44] The Christian Democrat Wolfgang Schäuble went so far as to claim that his party had been "conceived in the concentration camps".[45] If the left and in particular the Greens tended to reduce Nazism to German militarism, the right in the eighties tended to reduce it to totalitarianism and thus to imply a

183

moral equivalency between Nazi Germany and the Soviet Union. For example the Christian Democrats often used Nazism as a pretext to draw a parallel between appeasement in the thirties and appeasement of the Soviet Union in the eighties, as Heiner Geißler had done during the missile debate.[46]

Perhaps the most eloquent figure on the right on the subject of the Nazi past was Richard von Weizsäcker, the Christian Democrat who had become West German president in 1984. Born in 1920, Weizsäcker served as a soldier on the Eastern Front and was later defence counsel for his father, Ernst von Weizsäcker, a senior diplomat under the Nazis, at the Nuremberg war crimes tribunal.[47] In May 1985, on the fortieth anniversary of the German surrender in World War II, he gave a speech that was to become even more definitive as a statement of contrition about the Nazi past by a German statesman than Schmidt's in 1977. Weizsäcker said that the German surrender in 1945 should be seen not as a defeat but as liberation. He said that the Nazi past could never be "mastered", as the German term *Vergangenheitsbewältigung* implied, but only honestly "accepted". He said the Germans continued to have a national responsibility to remember the Nazi past and the Holocaust in particular, which, he said, was "unprecedented in history".[48] Speeches such as Weizsäcker's helped, as Jeffrey Herf puts it, to entrench the Holocaust in the "national memory of the German political establishment."[49]

But almost as soon as atonement for the Holocaust seemed to have moved to the centre of West Germany's national identity, there was a backlash against it. The summer after Weizsäcker's speech, Ernst Nolte, a right-wing West Berlin historian, argued in an essay published in the *Frankfurter Allgemeine Zeitung* that Nazi atrocities, and in particular the Holocaust, could only be understood in the context of other crimes in the twentieth century, in particular Stalinist terror. Nolte had previously written a book, *Fascism in its Epoch*, which argued that fascism was a European rather than specifically German phenomenon—paralleling, in other words, the student movement's understanding of fascism. He now argued that the Final Solution was in fact a defensive response to the Soviet Union's "class murder" which was its "logical and factual precursor".[50] In other words, the Holocaust was not uniquely evil. Directly contradicting Weizsäcker, who had called for an ongoing process of remembering, Nolte said the Nazi past, like any other, should be allowed to "pass away".

The essay triggered a furious row that subsequently became known as the *Historikerstreit* (Historians' Debate) and was played out in the *feuilletons* of West Germany's leading newspapers for months. Although essentially a historiographical debate that centred on the gruesome details of Nazi and Stalinist terror, it went to the heart of how present-day Germany should confront its dark past. Ultimately, it was a debate about German national identity and what it meant to be German after Auschwitz. The *Historikerstreit* centred on the somewhat technical question of the "uniqueness" of the Holocaust. But the question underlying it was whether it could be correct to draw a *Schlußstrich* (final line) under Germany's Nazi past.

Among Nolte's critics during the *Historikerstreit* was Jürgen Habermas, the Frankfurt University philosophy professor who, like his mentor Theodor Adorno, was on the constant lookout for signs of a re-emergence of irrational German intellectual traditions. In 1967, Habermas had been among the first to see the danger of "left-wing fascism" emerging from the radicalism of the student movement. Now, however, Habermas saw a danger from the right. In a series of articles published in *Die Zeit* in response to Nolte's essay, Habermas accused Nolte and other "neo-conservative" historians (including one, Michael Stürmer, who had also written speeches for Helmut Kohl) of trying to "relativise" the Final Solution as part of a new revisionist nationalist agenda based on a "normalised" German history.[51]

At a first glance, the *Historikerstreit* was a straightforward argument between left and right. It appeared that the right wanted to "relativise"—or, to use their own term, "historicise"—the Nazi past and "normalise" German national identity. The left, on the other hand, insisted on the uniqueness of the Holocaust and the necessity of remembering the Nazi past as a central chapter of German national history. However, the polarised terms of the *Historikerstreit*, the way each side caricatured each other's arguments, and above all the fact that it was almost exclusively a debate among members of the "sceptical generation" and the *Flakhelfergeneration*, obscured the fact that attitudes to the Nazi past did not divide as neatly between left and right as it appeared. For example, it was by no means obvious where the 1968 generation—which was conspicuously silent during the *Historikerstreit*—stood.

- - - - - - - - - - -

Jürgen Habermas saw the attempt by right-wing historians such as Nolte to relativise the Holocaust as part of a broader conservative turn in West Germany that aimed to promote a return to traditional German nationalism.[52] As an alternative to this, Habermas proposed the idea of "constitutional patriotism".[53] The term had been coined by the political scientist Dolf Sternberger, a student of Karl Jaspers, in an essay published to coincide with the thirtieth anniversary of the founding of the Federal Republic in 1979.[54] From the beginning it was a concept that was both descriptive and prescriptive. It theorised the tentative sense of pride in the successful establishment of democracy in post-war West Germany while also attempting to formulate an idealised relationship between a state and its citizens that could be applied in other countries as well as Germany.

In the first place, constitutional patriotism had been a response to the division of Germany and in particular to the problem of how to invest the West German state with legitimacy and to engender loyalty towards a state that represented only half of the German nation. Given the fragmented nature of Germany, Sternberger was attempting, essentially, to show how citizens of West Germany could create a sense of belonging based on republican values and a sense of pride in its democratic institutions rather than classical German nationalism based on a concept of the *Volk* or ethnic community. However, the concept was also implicitly an attempt to articulate a form of patriotism appropriate for Germany after Auschwitz. For Habermas, who would develop and popularise the concept of constitutional patriotism, even Germans born long after the end of the war continued to have a responsibility for remembering the Holocaust because they had grown up in a "context of life" (*Lebensform*) that had created it.[55] "None of us can escape that milieu," he wrote, "because our identity as individuals and as Germans is indissolubly woven into it."[56] Through the concept of constitutional patriotism, Habermas hoped to create a modest sense of pride in having overcome, or at least faced, the past. An ever-present awareness of Germany's terrible history would, so the argument went, guarantee that a republican identity would never become a chauvinistic one.

To Habermas, the real achievement of the Bonn Republic was the way it had westernised Germany. By that he meant not just the strategic *Westbindung* that Adenauer had advocated for reasons of security, but also its belated embrace of the Enlightenment and with it the creation of a liberal democratic culture or public sphere. But he worried that West Germany's citizens had accepted the Federal Republic and its democratic institutions only because of the prosperity it had created. Although the evidence suggested that, by the 1980s, West Germans' sense of pride in their state was based more on its democratic institutions than its economic success, Habermas continued to worry that it remained fragile. To him, the concept of constitutional patriotism was a way of anchoring and deepening the progress that he felt had been made in the Bonn Republic.

But although it had emerged from the specific and particularly disastrous German experience with the nation state, constitutional patriotism was also potentially a universal concept. Germans had committed the worst crimes of the twentieth century. Yet, through the "moral shock" resulting from the way it had belatedly come to terms with the immensity of these crimes, Germany had moved further beyond nationalism than almost any country, to what Habermas called "post-traditional identities". In other words, so the theory went, through learning from its terrible history, Germany had become an exemplary post-national nation—a beacon to other, less enlightened countries with less disastrous national stories. Ironically, though it had developed as a response to German immorality in the past, the concept of constitutional patriotism contained within it a sense of German moral superiority.

There was also another paradox inherent in the concept of constitutional patriotism. Although West Germans had apparently come furthest in developing a "post-national" identity based on republican values instead of ethnicity, they had done so in a country that still had citizenship laws that dated back to 1913 and were based on *ius sanguinis*, or citizenship by blood. As a result, millions of second and third generation immigrants whose parents and grandparents had come to West Germany as *Gastarbeiter* (guest workers) remained foreigners in the country in which they were born. That anomaly was, in turn, partly a function of the division of Germany: it was necessary to define citizenship in terms of blood in order to give an automatic right of return to Germans living in the GDR. In other words, while intellectuals like Habermas could imagine a new "post-national" identity, that did not change the reality that Germans on both sides of the Elbe felt they belonged to the same nation. It was therefore with some justification that critics called constitutional patriotism a "patriotism for professors."[57]

– – – – – – – – – – – –

The concept of constitutional patriotism was also, however, a response to radical left-wing opposition and in particular the "armed struggle" of the 1970s. Sternberger, born in 1907, had been deeply influenced by the experience of the Weimar Republic, Germany's first democracy, which had failed partly because the left had failed to accept it.[58] In order to sensure that the Bonn Republic would not suffer the same fate, he called upon "friends of the constitution"—as opposed to *Verfassungsfeinde* (enemies of the constitution), a term that had been introduced as part of the Decree on Radicals in the 1970s—to support West Germany's democratic institutions and above all the Basic Law.[59] There was therefore in the concept of constitutional patriotism an echo of Habermas's accusation of the student movement's "left-wing fascism" and an implicit critique of the 1968 generation's radical opposition to the West German state.

Although the concept of constitutional patriotism had limited wider resonance in West Germany, it would prove to be a remarkably successful vehicle through which many in the 1968 generation were able to make their peace with the Federal Republic. Those who had once regarded the Federal Republic as a pre-fascist state with a widening democratic deficit now came to identify with it—as many among the "sceptical generation" and *Flakhelfergeneration* who had experienced the end of the war had always done—as a post-fascist state with a narrowing democratic deficit.[60] In doing so, they quietly dropped the continuity thesis and recognised the Federal Republic as a legitimate state. In other words, the key to their change of heart about the Federal Republic was a changed interpretation of its relationship with Nazism. Where they had once seen the Federal Republic as a continuation of Nazism, it was now seen not just as compatible with anti-Nazism but as itself anti-Nazi.

Among the *Achtundsechziger*, no-one would embody this belated embrace of the Federal Republic more than Joschka Fischer, who had attended Habermas's seminars at Frankfurt University in 1968 but, like most in the student movement, had been "outraged" at Habermas's critique of the student movement's "left-wing fascism" in 1967.[61] In the 1970s, Fischer had been more opposed than any of the "Spontis" to the idea of participating in the democratic process. But in the eighties, having rejected the revolutionary socialism of his youth, he now almost imperceptibly became the most thoroughgoing constitutional patriot of all of his former comrades. While he was a Green minister in Hesse in the mid-eighties, Fischer took part in a discussion group led by Habermas in Frankfurt, through which Fischer reconciled himself to the former critic of the student movement—what he would later describe as the beginning of the "part two" of his engagement with Habermas.[62] The concept of constitutional patriotism, which he came to understand largely through Habermas's contributions to the *Historikerstreit*, gave him the "theoretical framework" through which he could articulate his acceptance of the Federal Republic.[63]

By the second half of the eighties, some on the West German New Left had also begun to take a more positive view of the *Westbindung*, as a corollary of their belated acceptance of the Federal Republic. The West German New Left, particularly those who joined the Greens, had always been viscerally opposed to the integration of West Germany into the western alliance that had begun with Adenauer. Since the deployment of Cruise and Pershing II missiles in 1983, the Greens had also broadened their critique of NATO and by the mid-eighties were explicitly calling for a unilateral West German withdrawal from the alliance.[64] "With NATO, there can be no peace," declared the party's election manifesto in 1987.[65] But now some "realists" within the Green party like Joschka Fischer and Otto Schily began to accept the argument—which until then had been made only by the right—that the *Westbindung* was an antidote to the *Sonderweg* (special path), the aberrant trajectory of German history that had diverged from the normative development of western European states, rejected the Enlightenment and culminated in Nazism. The *Westbindung* became for them, as Andrea Humphreys puts it, "a guarantee that the Federal Republic had broken with the aggressive traditions of the German past."[66] Conversely, they believed that calling for a neutral West Germany outside NATO—as some on both the right and left did—was a nationalist demand that would represent an "acceptance of the rebirth of a dangerous German *Sonderweg*."[67]

In the first half of the eighties, as he struggled against the "fundamentalists" in the Green party, Fischer had had little to say about foreign policy. Nor had he been involved in the peace movement and years later would claim he had never supported it.[68] But towards the end of the decade, he and other "realists" such as Hubert Kleinert began, tentatively at first, to make the case for a kind of Green equivalent of the Bad Godesberg conference in 1959 at which the SPD had formally accepted the *Westbindung*.[69] They drew on the arguments of

Jürgen Schnappertz, a pro-American Green foreign policy expert who was the first in the party to begin arguing for an acceptance of the *Westbindung* in a series of essays in 1986 and 1987. Schnappertz argued that the Greens should openly acknowledge that Adenauer's foreign policy had been right—anathema to many on the left. Schnappertz remembers Fischer's reaction after he heard him make the case for the first time. "He said, 'I like that stuff about the *Westbindung*, but you should leave out the stuff about Adenauer.'"[70] Not only did the "realists" now began to campaign for an acceptance of NATO, they also linked it to the "coalition question" by arguing that the Greens would never be accepted as a potential coalition partner until they fully accepted German membership of NATO. In other words, "realists" had to support the *Westbindung*.

The acceptance by some of the Green "realists" of the Federal Republic and the *Westbindung* also went hand in hand with a deepening of their engagement with Auschwitz. In the 1983 debate over the missile deployment, Joschka Fischer and Otto Schily had appeared to relativise the Holocaust by speaking of the threat of an "atomic Auschwitz". But in the second half of the eighties, largely through the effect of the *Historikerstreit* and in particular the argument made by Habermas and others that the Holocaust was "unique", they began to subtly change their position. In 1988, the Green "realists" published a manifesto that carefully expressed their opposition to the relativisation by some Greens of the Holocaust. They said their "historical consciousness" was defined by three historical events—Auschwitz, Hiroshima and Chernobyl—but emphasised, crucially, that Auschwitz should be considered the most important of the three. In foreign policy terms, that meant West Germany had a special responsibility towards countries in which victims of Nazism lived, in particular Israel, Poland and the Soviet Union.[71]

By the end of the eighties, in other words, the Green "realists", led by *Achtundsechziger* like Fischer, had developed a new politics based on three key elements: a reconciliation with the Federal Republic based on the concept of "constitutional patriotism", an acceptance of the *Westbindung* and a belief in the centrality of Auschwitz for West German foreign policy. Fischer expressed this new credo, which would form the basis of his politics for the next twenty years, in an article in *Die Zeit* written to coincide with the fortieth anniversary of the end of the war in Europe in May 1985. In it, Fischer described the long struggle of his generation to identify with the Federal Republic. He echoed Weizsäcker's description of 1945 as "liberation"—an implicit rejection of the continuity thesis—and urged West Germans to develop a "democratic identity" by "consciously remembering" the Nazi past. "Only German responsibility for Auschwitz can be the essence of West German *raison d'état*," he said in conclusion. "Everything else comes afterwards."[72]

As he rose through West German politics over the next decade, Fischer would play a key role in persuading other members of his generation to accept the Federal Republic, and with it the *Westbindung* and the centrality of Auschwitz to post-war German identity. Ironically, however, just as the *Achtundsechziger* had finally reconciled themselves to it, the Bonn Republic was about to come to an end.

NEW REPUBLIC

In the autumn of 1989, almost no-one was seriously expecting German reunification, least of all the West German left. The "national question", which had bubbled under the surface of West German politics in the 1950s and 1960s, had gradually ceased to be a major subject of discussion, especially since Willy Brandt's *Ostpolitik*, which, while relaxing tension between the two German states, had also strengthened the status quo. By the 1980s, even the most fanatical West German anti-communists had given up on the idea of reunification. For example, in August 1989, Axel Springer's newspapers had stopped referring to the GDR in quotation marks, in effect recognizing the East German state just over a year before it ceased to exist.[1]

The rapid emergence of the possibility of reunification in the weeks following the fall of the Berlin Wall in November 1989 was driven initially by nationalist sentiment among the East German population. Within weeks, in fact, what had begun as a movement for free elections and the right to travel had metamorphosed into a movement for German unity. By the end of the month, the protesters who gathered in Leipzig on Monday evenings—the demonstrations that began the movement that had led to the fall of the Wall—were not just chanting "Wir sind das Volk" ("We are the people") but also "Wir sind ein Volk" ("We are one people"). It was a clear demonstration of an aspiration for national unity.[2] Chancellor Kohl, who was as surprised as anyone by the fall of the Wall, quickly seized the initiative. At the end of November, by which time thousands were leaving East Germany, he presented his Ten-Point Plan, which outlined a framework for a transition towards a reunified Germany. In December, he was greeted as a saviour by thousands of East Germans in Dresden.

The West German left, meanwhile, was completely wrong-footed by the events on the other side of the Wall. Since Brandt's *Ostpolitik*, the SPD had developed a working relationship with the *Sozialistische Einheitspartei Deutschlands* (SED), the East German Communist party, and had in turn distanced itself from East German opposition groups.[3] By 1989 it had become almost completely cut off from the East German dissidents. The Greens had maintained contacts with opposition groups in eastern Europe, including Charter '77 in Czechoslovakia and Solidarity in Poland, but had even less interest in the "national question" than the Social Democrats. Many on the left considered the aspiration to German reunification included in the pre-amble to the Basic Law "not as a serious political project but as an antiquated element of tradition", as Ludger Volmer puts it.[4] In other words, East Germany was for them just another eastern European country. Many, in fact, felt they had more in common with the left in Italy or France than with the opposition movements in "the other German state".

This meant that when the Wall fell, much of the West German left looked on, as one East German writer put it, "with open mouths, empty hands and empty brains."[5] The 75 year-old Willy Brandt lent his support to reunification the day after the Wall fell, declaring that "what belongs together will grow together."[6] But the younger leaders of the SPD—often referred to as "Brandt's grandchildren"—simply did not know how they should respond to what Gerhard Schröder later described as an "unexpected earthquake."[7] To many on the left, the sudden nationalist sentiment in the East was simply embarrassing. A consensus on the West German left regarded reunification as a "dream of old men," as the Green politician Antje Vollmer put it.[8] Many on the West German left hoped the "citizens' movements" that had emerged in East Germany would develop a new form of socialism that some East German intellectuals referred to as a "third way" between capitalism and communism. It very quickly became clear, however, that after two dictatorships, the majority of East Germans were more interested in the Deutschmark and western consumer goods than a new socialist experiment.

Moreover, for many on the West German left, as also for some abroad, the prospect of reunification awakened ghosts from the German past. In particular, it re-opened the "German question", which had been closed, or rather submerged within the wider context of the Cold War, since the end of World War II. Since Adenauer, the Federal

Republic had been part of the western alliance and by the 1980s it was also firmly integrated into the European Economic Community (EEC), the forerunner of the European Union (EU). A broad historiographical consensus had developed—now shared by many of the *Achtundsechziger* like Joschka Fischer—that the *Westbindung* meant that the Federal Republic had left behind Germany's disastrous *Sonderweg*. Dark fears loomed, both inside and outside the country that a reunified Germany would embark on a new German *Sonderweg*.

To Jürgen Habermas, the momentum towards reunification represented a threat—perhaps the greatest threat yet—to West Germany's post-national republican consciousness. To Habermas, 1989 was merely a "catching up revolution" for the eastern half of Germany that, as he put it, "shed no new light on the old issues facing the Federal Republic."[9] He believed that there was, however, a danger that the integration of 17 million East Germans, whom he regarded, in terms of their political consciousness, as stuck in the stage of development that West Germans had been in during the Adenauer era, could have a corrosive effect on the Federal Republic's political culture.[10] He hoped that the East Germans could evolve into good constitutional patriots, but worried that instead they might drag the Federal Republic back in a historic regression to the 1950s, or worse. Habermas worried that much of the West German right had accepted the *Westbindung* only for strategic reasons that had disappeared with the collapse of communism. Therefore, if Germany reunified in the wrong way, there was a danger of a return to an older, more traditional German nationalism based on "pre-political" values such as the idea of the German *Volk* as a "community of fate."

Chancellor Kohl's strategy—which turned out to be brilliantly successful—was to press ahead with German reunification as rapidly as possible while reassuring West Germany's neighbours and allies that reunification would not mean a fundamental change in Germany's geopolitical identity.[11] "We have learned from the history of this century," he insisted. "Reunification and integration with the West, German policy and European policy, are like two sides of the same coin."[12] But Habermas argued that the Kohl government was forcing the pace of reunification from the top down by deliberately destabilising the GDR. The East Germans, meanwhile, seemed to him to simply crave West Germany's currency rather than its democratic institutions. To Habermas, reunification seemed to be being driven above all by the Deutschmark—what he called "DM nationalism".[13] Instead of pressing ahead with reunification as a *fait accompli*, Habermas pleaded for a patient, genuinely democratic decision-making process in both halves of Germany that would deepen the Federal Republic's republican consciousness rather than undermine it.

In practical terms, Habermas argued that reunification should take place through a referendum based on Article 146 of the Basic Law—in effect the adoption of a new constitution—rather than through an "annexation" (Habermas used the term *Anschluß*) based on Article 23, which allowed for the accession of "other parts of Germany". The irony, however, was such a referendum would call into question the "constitution" on which constitutional patriotism was based. In fact, that was precisely what the Basic Law required: it was not a constitution at all but a provisional document which was supposed to be replaced by a new, permanent constitution if and when reunification took place. Habermas said this situation made it even more essential for Germany to renew its commitment to constitutional patriotism, which, because of the Holocaust, was "the only possible form of patriotism" for West Germans:

For us in the Federal Republic constitutional patriotism means among other things pride that we have succeeded in permanently overcoming fascism, establishing the rule of law and anchoring it in a somewhat liberal political culture. But our patriotism cannot hide the fact that it was only after Auschwitz—and in a certain sense only through the shock of this moral catastrophe—that democracy took root in the motives and the hearts of our citizens, or at least of the younger generation.[14]

The Berlin Wall fell almost exactly ten years after the death of Rudi Dutschke, who had always dreamed of German reunification. However, although he would no doubt have welcomed the fall of the Wall, it is unlikely that he would have found much to be joyful about in what followed. He had wanted a reunification from below, in which the proletariat on both sides of the Berlin Wall would overthrow their respective governments and create a new socialist Germany. Instead, it appeared that capitalism was about to extend its reach eastwards and that the Federal Republic was about to simply swallow up the GDR— the last thing, presumably, that Dutschke would have wanted.

In the decade since his death, Dutschke had become an iconic figure for much of the West German left and especially for the Green party, which he had helped to create in the late seventies. The Greens had canonised Dutschke as a kind of patron saint whose vision corresponded to their own four founding principles, which of course included non-violence, while ignoring other less convenient aspects of his political thinking. Aspects of Dutschke's nationalism, such as his tendency to see Germany as the victim of American imperialism, which were also shared by figures on the right such as August Haußleiter, had subtly influenced the party, particularly through the peace movement in the early eighties. But the less palatable aspects of Dutschke's nationalism, in particular his preoccupation with reunification, had been quietly forgotten.

There had been others on the New Left who had attempted to discuss the "national question" in the decade since Dutschke's death. The West Berlin Alternative List, the West Berlin branch of the Greens, had maintained a "nationalist-neutralist" foreign policy that was very much in line with Dutschke's thinking on the "German question". The group, co-founded by the former RAF lawyer Hans-Christian Ströbele, was dominated by former members of the Maoist KPD, which in turn had been set up by the former SDS activists Jürgen Horlemann and Christian Semler. In the seventies, influenced in particular by Mao's "three worlds theory", Semler had argued for an "independent, united and socialist Germany".[15] Within the Green party in the eighties, the West Berlin Alternative List had continued to argue for German reunification as a necessary precursor to liberation from domination by the United States and the Soviet Union.[16] The group also included Willy Brandt's son Peter, who, together with Herbert Ammon, had edited an influential book urging the left "not to leave the 'German question' out of the discussion about the future of Europe".[17] However, such left-wing nationalists had been a minority, even within the Greens.

Meanwhile, the other main current within the 1968 generation's thinking—the idea of "resistance" against Nazism—had, through politicians like Joschka Fischer, come to dominate the West German New Left. Like many others on the left, Fischer feared a resurgence of German nationalism, which he had come to regard as the "number one main enemy" for the Federal Republic.[18] For him and others like him among the *Achtundsechziger*, German nationalism, together with its apparently inevitable corollary, militarism, had replaced capitalism as the root cause of Nazism. As a result, "Never again Germany" had become for them almost as central and reflexive an axiom as "Never again war." The Greens, for example, were opposed to the call for reunification in the pre-amble to the Basic Law and boycotted commemorations of the 17 June 1953 uprising in East Germany, which until reunification had been the German "national" day. In effect, they had replaced their earlier anti-fascism with anti-nationalism. This meant that, by the time the Berlin Wall fell, many *Achtundsechziger* like Fischer, "lacked a conceptual framework to deal with the phenomenon of the nation-state", as Jan-Werner Müller puts it.[19]

Like Jürgen Habermas, many among the 1968 generation also saw in the possibility of German reunification a danger that the progress that had been made in developing democratic values and in particular in "working through the past" in the Federal Republic would be undermined. This fear was typified by Joschka Fischer, who, perhaps more than any of the *Achtundsechziger* since Ulrike Meinhof, had come to embody the idea of *ex post facto* resistance against Nazism. Under the influence of Habermas, Fischer had almost imperceptibly shifted from believing that the Federal Republic was a fascist state to believing that it was, in fact, an anti-Nazi state. To put it another way, what he understood by "resistance" had changed: it had once meant overthrowing the West German state; now it meant defending it. A week after the Berlin Wall fell, he wrote an article for the *taz* in which he described the division of Germany as the logical consequence of Nazism. He reminded the German left that:

We are living and making politics as left-wingers in a country that built the gas chambers and crematoria of Auschwitz-Birkenau and that loyally followed its *Führer* Adolf Hitler to self-destruction.[20]

Fischer also saw the division of Germany as a corollary of the *Westbindung*. During the debate within the Green party on West German membership of NATO in the late eighties, he had rejected the idea of leaving the alliance and the possibility of reunification as revisionist.[21] Both the *Westbindung* and the division of Germany were, in his view, the consequence of World War II and were therefore irreversible. He said the "German question" was now closed, leaving only a "new German question": "How do we get out of this aggressive military confrontation between two military blocks on our common border that threatens our existence? What can we contribute to it? And, in doing so, can we positively influence others?"[22] This view of the division of Germany echoed that of Günter Grass, one of the most outspoken opponents of reunification, who believed that it would create "a colossus loaded with complexes" in the centre of Europe.[23] To Grass, the division of Germany was both a way of protecting Germany from itself and an eternal punishment for Auschwitz, which, in a kind of negative German essentialism, he seemed to see as an almost inevitable result of the existence of the German nation-state. To challenge the division of Germany, he seemed to suggest, automatically entailed forgetting German history and in particular the Holocaust.

As a result of their anti-nationalism, the 1968 generation stood on the sidelines of the tumultuous events that followed the fall of the Berlin Wall. Elsewhere in eastern Europe and in particular in Czechoslovakia, the revolutions of 1989 could be understood, as Timothy Garton Ash has suggested, as a kind of completion of the failed revolutions of 1968 and in particular of the Prague Spring.[24] In Germany, however, the influence of 1968 on 1989 was less significant. The leaders of the citizens' movements in East Germany were not veterans of the protest movement of 1968 as they were in Czechoslovakia. In West Germany, meanwhile, where the collapse of communism had automatically raised the question not just of political reform but also of German national identity, the veterans of the student movement played almost no part in the historic events that followed the fall of the Wall.

In some ways, the left, and in particular the Social Democrats, ought to have been ideally placed to benefit from reunification. Industrial eastern Germany, and in particular Saxony, had once been the heartland of German social democracy. Like the other West German political parties, the SPD quickly founded an East German sister party in preparation for the elections for the *Volkskammer*, the East German parliament, in the spring of 1990. But unlike in the West, where the trade unions were able to mobilise voters on its behalf, the SPD failed to win the support of the working class, which gravitated instead towards the Alliance for Germany, a pro-reunification electoral alliance that included the Christian Democrats. In the election held in March 1990, the Christian Democrats won 48 per cent of the vote, including around half of the working class vote.[25] The East German citizens' movements, which had joined together to form a grouping called *Bündnis '90* (Alliance '90), won just 2.9 per cent of the vote. This result effectively ended the dream of a "third way" between capitalism and socialism and made reunification inevitable.[26]

Following the March election, a coalition government led by the Christian Democrats under Lothar de Maizière was formed and negotiations on reunification between the two German states and the four Allied powers—the so-called "two plus four"—began. On 1 July, an economic and monetary union came into effect, creating a single economic area with the Deutschmark as its currency. In September, both German parliaments accepted a unification treaty under which the German Democratic Republic would cease to exist and its five states would become part of the Federal Republic under Article 23 of the Basic Law. On 3 October, 1990—eleven months after the fall of the Wall—Germany was reunified.

Two months later, the first all-German general election took place. The Social Democrats' candidate for chancellor was Oskar Lafontaine, the prime minister of Saarland, who had authored the party's new programme in 1989. Lafontaine, who shared the fears of many on the left about reunification, had opposed economic and monetary union and even suggested restricting the free movement of East Germans to the West. "They are pulling walls down and you are trying to put them up again," the party chairman, Hans-Jochen Vogel, told him. The Greens were even more dismissive of the prevailing mood. Their election slogan—a somewhat flat parody of the famous SDS poster of the sixties—was: "Everyone is talking about Germany. We are talking about the weather." They co-operated with Alliance '90, but because of their reservations about the perceived western takeover of the east, stopped short of merging with them as other parties had done—a decision that would prove to be disastrous.

The left was routed in the election of December 1990. The electorate of the newly reunified Germany rejected the SPD and the Greens even more comprehensively than the East German electorate had done in March. The Christian Democrats won nearly 44 per cent of the vote, while the SPD sunk to 33 per cent—its lowest share of the vote since 1957. In the east, it won just 24 per cent of the vote. The Greens did even worse: they failed to receive the minimum 5 per cent of the vote in the west and therefore dropped out of the *Bundestag*. In the east, Alliance '90 received 6 per cent, which meant that, if it had merged with the Greens, the Greens would have also have remained in parliament. It was the biggest setback for the party since its formation in 1980.

After reunification Germany did not immediately become more outwardly aggressive as some on the left such as Günter Grass had feared.

After a long and heated debate the following summer, the *Bundestag* voted to re-locate from Bonn to Berlin, the new capital.[27] But the decision to return to Berlin was not the catalyst for the beginning of a new German *Sonderweg*. In fact, under Chancellor Kohl, the Federal Republic's foreign policy continued much as before. Germany signed a treaty with Poland which recognised the Oder-Neiße line as the border between the two countries and amended Article 23 of the Basic Law, which had in effect left open the question of Germany's frontiers. Together with the French president François Mitterrand, Kohl also continued to press ahead with European integration. The Maastricht Treaty of 1992 completed the creation of a single European market and laid the foundation for European Monetary Union and with it the ultimate replacement of the Deutschmark by the Euro, which would become a reality in 1999.

In fact, far from a resurgence of bellicosity, there seemed to be an increase in pacifism in Germany after reunification, especially on the left. During the Gulf war in 1991, what the political scientists Andrei S. Markovits and Philip S. Gorski called a "wave of apocalyptic fear" swept through Germany and in particular the German left.[28] Another foreign observer described a "barely contained hysteria in the air."[29] To many on the German left, particularly among the Greens, the images of burning oil in the Arabian desert represented not just a political mistake but also an ecological catastrophe. Protest against the war in Germany was, according to Markovits and Gorski, "quantitatively and qualitatively more pronounced than in any other country in the advanced industrial world."[30]

But, although generally pacifist in tone, this protest against the war in the newly reunified Germany was also tinged with nationalism and anti-Americanism. To most on the left, it was clear that the political and ecological catastrophe in the Gulf was caused not by Iraq but by the United States. While criticism of the United States during the peace movement in the eighties had been balanced to some extent by criticism of the Soviet Union within the context of the Cold War, it now became even more explicit and aggressive.[31] Criticism of US policy also often evoked images of German victimhood during World War II. For example, the coalition assembled by the US was often referred to as the "Allierten", or the Allies, especially when referring to bombing raids—a term which conjured up images of the British and American wartime bombing of German cities.[32] Conversely, many on the left seemed to regard "peace" as a specifically German virtue. The feminist writer Alice Schwarzer, for example, said she was proud to be German because of Germany's post-war pacifism.[33] This kind of rhetoric hinted at the development of the kind of German nationalism that had already manifested itself during the peace movement in the eighties. It was based on the idea that Germany had learned the lessons of its terrible history in the twentieth-century and was therefore now morally superior to other countries—and above all the United States.

The Gulf War also brought to the surface a conflict over Israel that had been developing on the left and in particular within the Green party in the 1980s.[34] By the end of the 1980s, most leading Greens had accepted Israel's right to existence as a Jewish state but nevertheless remained fiercely critical of Israeli policy and in particular tended to dismiss the threat to Israel's security from terrorism and from its Arab neighbours. At the same time, as part of their pacifist foreign policy, the Greens had also campaigned against arms exports by German companies to Israel.[35] However, there was also a minority within the Green party, particularly among the "realists", that was more sympathetic to Israel. The conflict between the two groups had already flared up in 1982 following of Israel's invasion of Lebanon, when Joschka Fischer wrote an article for *Pflasterstrand* defending Israel against the German left's attacks—the first statement of his new post-Entebbe view of the Middle East.[36]

At the end of January 1991, against the background of an agreement by the German government to provide a package of aid to Israel that included an offer to supply it with anti-aircraft missiles, a Green delegation that included Hans-Christian Ströbele visited Israel. Ströbele, the former RAF lawyer and co-founder of the West Berlin Alternative List, had been a Green member of parliament in the eighties and was elected as one of the Greens' three party spokesmen in 1990. During the trip, Ströbele told a journalist, Henryk M. Broder, that Iraqi missile attacks on Israel were "the logical, almost compelling consequence of Israeli policies."[37] Ströbele was forced to resign. Joschka Fischer, who had also opposed the war but was in favour of supplying arms to Israel, called him "Saddam Hussein's lackey."[38]

Meanwhile, as the initial euphoria of reunification passed, economic problems began to emerge that would dominate German politics for the next decade. Wages in the east had been quickly brought up to western levels, creating an initial boom for the West German economy as it suddenly found a new market of 17 million people with Deutschmarks in their pockets. In the first year after reunification the West Germany economy grew by 4.5 per cent as it responded to the new demand. The construction industry in particular boomed as the German government invested massively in infrastructure in the so-called "new states". But as the initial surge in consumer demand in the east passed and uncompetitive factories previously owned by the East German state were forced to shut down, Germany plunged into recession. The economy grew by only 1.1 per cent in 1992 and shrank by 1.1 per cent in 1993. During the election campaign in 1990, Kohl had promised "blooming landscapes" in the former GDR. But by the spring of 1993, 15.5 per cent of the workforce in the east was unemployed. Prospects, especially for young people, seemed to be diminishing. The East Germans who had voted overwhelmingly for Kohl in 1990 became increasingly disillusioned and began to look elsewhere. Many turned to the far left—in the form of the former East German communist party that had reinvented itself as the Democratic Socialist Party (*Partei des Demokratischen Sozialismus* (PDS))—and to the far right.

Like other western European countries, West Germany had recruited workers from abroad in the 1960s to fill shortages in its labour market. But while the United Kingdom, France and Holland had been able to meet their needs for labour largely from their former colonies, West Germany turned initially to southern and south-eastern Europe and, from 1960 onwards, to Turkey. Partly because of this difference, the Federal Republic lagged behind its European neighbours in integrating these immigrants, whom it continued to regard as "guest workers" long after it had become clear they were in Germany to stay. In particular, the German citizenship law, which dated back to 1913 and was based on the principle of *ius sanguinis*, or citizenship by blood, meant that second and third generation immigrants remained foreigners and therefore, amongst other things, that they could not vote.

West Germany had stopped recruiting foreign labour in 1973, although family members of immigrants who had arrived before then were allowed to join them. But since it was so difficult for the children and grandchildren of immigrants who had arrived in the 1960s and 1970s to acquire West German citizenship, the "foreign" population continued to increase even without further immigration. In addition,

Article 16 of the Basic Law guaranteed a right of asylum for those flee-ing political persecution—a response to Germany's Nazi past—as a result of which increasing numbers of refugees had been arriving in Ger-many. By 1989, there were nearly five million foreign citizens living in the Federal Republic.[39]

Immigration had already become a political issue even before reuni-fication. In the 1980s, the West German right had begun to campaign on the issue. The CSU, the Bavarian Christian Democrats, were par-ticularly vociferous in campaigning against further immigration and for a tightening of the asylum law. In the late 1980s, the *Republikaner*, a new far-right party led by former Waffen-SS officer Franz Schönhuber, emerged as a political force in Bavaria. Campaigning in particular against the asylum law, it began to win increasing support, culminating in the 1989 European elections, where it won 7 per cent of the vote (and 14 per cent in Bavaria). It was the first major success by a far-right party in the Federal Republic since the NPD in 1968.[40]

After reunification, racial violence increased dramatically, beginning in the former GDR. In 1991, neo-Nazis set fire to a hostel in which asylum seekers were housed in Hoyerswerda in Saxony. When a simi-lar attack took place in Rostock the following year, bystanders applauded. But although the problem had initially been confined to the East, it was soon followed by even more gruesome attacks in the West directed not just against asylum seekers but also foreigners who had lived in Germany for decades. In November 1992, a Turkish woman and two children were killed when their house in Mölln in Schleswig-Holstein was set on fire. In November 1993, a similar attack took place in Solingen in the Rhineland, killing five Turkish women and children. Habermas's fears about the corrosive effect that the East Ger-mans might have on West German democracy had apparently become a reality.

Although the attacks were directed not just against asylum seekers but against minorities in general, Germany's political establishment reached a consensus that it was necessary to reduce the number of asylum seekers, which had risen from 120,000 in 1989 to 440,000 three years later. The Christian Democrats and the Social Democrats agreed to reform Germany's asylum law and in particular to abolish the guarantee of asylum for victims of political persecution under Arti-cle 16 of the Basic Law, which required a two-thirds majority in both houses of parliament. In the summer of 1992, the two parties reached a compromise whereby refugees who had arrived in Germany via a safe "third country"—which the vast majority of asylum seekers in Germany had—could no longer apply for asylum in Germany. Günter Grass, who had campaigned for Willy Brandt in the 1960s, left the SPD in disgust. Meanwhile, nothing was done to reform the antiquated German citizenship law, which meant second and third generation immigrants remained "foreigners" in Germany.

Among those who spoke out most eloquently against the abolition of the right to asylum and for the need for reform of German immigration law were the *Achtundsechziger* and in particular the former members of the Frankfurt "Spontis", who had been interested in the issue of immigration since their time working at Opel in the seventies. Daniel Cohn-Bendit had since become the City of Frankfurt's Director of Multicultural Affairs. Cohn-Bendit and Thomas Schmid, his former comrade from Revolutionary Struggle and now an "eco-libertarian" member of the Greens, wrote a book in which they pleaded for Germany to finally accept that it was an "immigration country", and, among other things, proposed introducing dual citizenship to ease the integration of Turkish immigrants.[41] To them, the wave of racial attacks and the abolition of the right to asylum was a betrayal of Germany's history. Article 16, they said, was a "small compensatory answer to the guilt" of Germany for the huge wave of refugees it had created during World War II.[42] The Greens would take on Cohn-Bendit and Schmid's proposals and turn them into a key part of their domestic policy agenda. This attempt to liberalise Germany's citizenship law—justified by reference to the Nazi past—would be one of the party's few domestic policy demands that had anything to do with 1968.

As the reality of German reunification kicked in and the Kohl government struggled to deal with the new problems it had created and the old problems it had exacerbated, the left began to recover from the disaster of 1990. Following the election debacle, Joschka Fischer's "realists" took control of the Green party. Joining forces with Antje Vollmer, a centrist who had previously been a critic of his, Fischer began to "professionalise" the Greens and make them "capable of governing"—in other words to turn them into a "normal" party instead of the "anti-party" Petra Kelly had wanted to create. At a party conference in Neumünster in 1991, the Greens agreed to centralise decision-making and abolish the principle of rotating office holders. The party remained committed to the four principles on which it had been founded and in particular remained opposed to nuclear power and committed to abolishing NATO but, in a crucial shift, began to see those principles not as absolutes but as aspirations. The Greens would continue to define themselves in opposition to the SPD, but they were now prepared to compromise on their principles in order to achieve change. It was a clear sign that the Greens were now preparing themselves for a "red-green" coalition.

An exodus of "fundamentalists", who insisted that the Greens should offer a radical alternative to capitalism, followed. A month after the Neumünster conference, the radical ecologist Jutta Ditfurth, Fischer's arch enemy and an opponent of arms exports to Israel, left the party in disgust at what she saw as its move to the right. Jürgen Reents, the former member of the Communist League who had become one of the leading figures in the Greens' eco-socialist wing, also quit and joined the PDS. The following year, Petra Kelly, who had been gradually marginalised within the party since the defeat of the campaign against the missile deployment in 1983, was shot dead at their house on the outskirts of Bonn by her partner, the former *Bundeswehr* general Gert Bastian, who then killed himself. It was several weeks before their bodies were found. Meanwhile several leading "realists" such as Otto Schily and the former SDS chairman Udo Knapp also left the Greens and joined the SPD. With many of big names from the first crop of members of parliament now gone and with his supporters now in key positions in the party, Fischer emerged as the Greens' unofficial leader.

While the Greens were becoming more "realist", the Social Democrats were becoming more open to the idea of co-operating with them. Under Oskar Lafontaine and Rudolf Scharping, who became party leader in 1993, SPD policy had moved to the left and was increasingly converging with that of the Greens. Lafontaine was among those who favoured phasing out nuclear power—the Greens' key demand—and also supported them on large areas of social policy. In fact, the Social Democrats' shift to the left and in particular its increasingly green environmental policy probably helped put the Greens out of the Bundestag in the 1990 election. It also meant, however, that as it moved to the left and the Free Democrats lined up behind the Christian Democrats, the SPD's only hope of regaining power was through a "red-green" coalition.

"Red-green" coalitions were, in fact, now springing up in various states across Germany. The Social Democrats had already formed a short-lived coalition with Hans-Christian Ströbele's West Berlin Alternative List in 1989. In the spring of 1990, after four years as opposition leader in the state parliament, Gerhard Schröder ended fourteen years of Christian Democrat-led government in Lower Saxony and took over as prime minister at the head of another "red-green" coalition. This time both coalition partners were led by members of the post-war generation—Schröder for the Social Democrats and Jürgen Trittin, who had been a student activist and a leading member of the Communist League in Göttingen, for the Greens—and the coalition agreement centred on phasing out nuclear power.[43] It was also particularly significant because it gave the SPD a majority in the *Bundesrat*, the upper house of the German parliament, which represents Germany's state governments. The Social Democrats therefore had an effective veto on government policy.

The following year, Joschka Fischer once again became environment minister in another "red-green" coalition in the state of Hesse, this time headed by Hans Eichel, who had already led a "red-green" coalition as mayor of the city of Kassel and was more sympathetic to the Greens than Holger Börner had been. Fischer was also better prepared than he had been in 1985 and made sure the coalition partners agreed their policy on nuclear power beforehand. When an incident took place at the Hanau plutonium processing plant, Fischer succeeded where he had failed in his first stint as environment minister and closed the plant—a demonstrable success that strengthened the position of the "realists" within the party. In 1995, after the Social Democrats lost their absolute majority in North Rhine Westphalia, one of Germany's largest states, Johannes Rau also formed a "red-green" coalition, albeit reluctantly.

While Lafontaine and Scharping remained the two most powerful figures within the party, Gerhard Schröder was becoming the most popular Social Democrat politician in Germany. Since leaving Bonn and returning to Lower Saxony in the mid-eighties, Schröder had transformed himself from far-left radical to centre-left pragmatist. He now wore Italian suits instead of the frayed sweaters he had in the early 1980s, and smoked Cohiba cigars. His policy positions had also changed. As the prime minister of Lower Saxony, he had become a member of the board of Volkswagen, and as the party's spokesman on economic policy, he was increasingly pro-business. Whereas in 1990 he had wanted to phase out nuclear power, he now advocated compromise with the nuclear industry. He insisted that he remained in favour of "intervention on behalf of minorities and for the weak in society."[44] But he now styled himself as a man of the centre who was not left-wing or right-wing but simply "modern". It was an image that seemed to appeal to German voters. In the spring of 1994 Schröder went one better than in 1990, winning an absolute majority in Lower Saxony—a personal triumph that confirmed him as a vote-winner who had the potential to defeat Kohl.

But although Schröder was increasingly popular among the electorate, Scharping continued to control the SPD and was nominated as the party's candidate for the election due to take place in the autumn of 1994. With unemployment now at 3.8 million, the opinion polls indicated that the SPD stood a good chance of defeating Kohl. But although Schröder and Lafontaine presented a united front, campaigning alongside Scharping in a so-called "troika", tensions remained beneath the surface. Over the summer the signs seemed to indicate the post-reunification recession was coming to an end and Kohl began to recover in the opinion polls. In the end Kohl narrowly won the election, with the Christian Democrats slipping two points to 40 per cent and the SPD at 36 per cent—a three-point increase on the disastrous 1990 election but not enough to bring the Kohl era to an end. The big winners were the Greens, who bounced back spectacularly from the debacle of 1990. Having now merged with Alliance '90, the Greens won 7.2 per cent of the vote—apparently at the cost of the SPD—making them the third-biggest party in the *Bundestag* for the first time.

Despite losing the election, Scharping continued to hold on to power within the party and made no secret of his ambitions to stand again in 1998. But the tensions that had been simmering before the election campaign—Schröder believed he could have won the election had he been the candidate, and said so publicly—now came out into the open.[45] Schröder became ever more open in advocating a pro-business economic policy that diverged from the official party line. After a newspaper interview in which he said that "the question is no longer whether to follow a social democratic or a conservative economic policy but whether to follow a modern or an unmodern economic policy"—an implicit criticism of Scharping—he was forced to resign as the party's economic spokesman.[46] The power struggle culminated in a party conference in Mannheim in 1995, at which Oskar Lafontaine, with Schröder's support, suddenly and spectacularly deposed Scharping as party leader. From then on Schröder and Lafontaine controlled the SPD between them. In fact, the political differences between them were even greater than those between Schröder and Scharping, but for the next three years they would function remarkably well as a team. While Schröder was the public face of the Social Democrats, Lafontaine, the SPD's leader in the *Bundesrat*, blocked the Kohl government's attempts to introduce economic reforms.

Things were also looking up for the Greens. With their success in the 1994 election, Fischer returned to Bonn, this time as the party's undisputed, albeit unofficial, leader. He was now a heavyweight, both politically and physically.[47] He had begun to eat and drink excessively and put on weight, finally reaching nearly 240 pounds. He also became the *de facto* leader of the opposition in the *Bundestag*, overshadowing even Lafontaine, and his duels with Helmut Kohl became known as "the battle of the bellies".[48] In the summer of 1996, his third wife Claudia, whom he had married in 1987, left him. It prompted him— after a period of depression—to radically change his life. He stopped drinking, began to eat more healthily and started jogging along the Rhine, first secretly and then accompanied by journalists and photographers. By the spring of the following year he had lost over 60 pounds and returned to what he called his "fighting weight" of 165 pounds. A year after that, he ran the Hamburg marathon in under four hours.

By that time, Fischer had his sights set firmly on the job of foreign minister in a future "red-green" government. The Greens had moved away from the "fundamental opposition" that had animated them in the early eighties—a betrayal, some thought, of the idealism that had grown out of the protests against nuclear power in the seventies. Fischer, however, had never shared the environmentalist vision of many of the Greens. Rather, he and his friends had used the Green party to advance their own very different agenda that had grown out of the failure of the student movement and its aftershocks. He insisted that his "realist" strategy was at attempt to implement the utopian hopes not of the environmental movement but of the student movement. "We are fighting to govern this country so we can change it," he said in 1994. "It's the old dream of 1968. Back then we dreamed it in a revolutionary way and now we dream it in a reformist way."[49]

- - - - - - - - - - - -

Over the next three years, Gerhard Schröder did everything he could to present himself as the future of Germany. He hoped to be able to emulate the success of Bill Clinton, who won a second term in office in the 1996 presidential election, and Tony Blair's New Labour, which won a landslide election in the United Kingdom in May 1997. The key figure in his plan to reinvent the SPD was Bodo Hombach, a former business executive and economics minister in the state of North Rhine Westphalia, who was to become Schröder's closest adviser, election strategist and spin doctor. Borrowing heavily from the campaigning methods that worked so successfully for New Labour in 1997, Hombach attempted to make Schröder, and the Social Democrats, electable.

Hombach distilled his vision for the SPD into what he called the "Neue Mitte" (New Centre), an idea that was part political philosophy and part electoral strategy. It was born out of the need to regain the support of key sections of the electorate, in particular middle-class swing voters in the West and East Germans who had voted for Kohl in 1990 but had become disillusioned when the "blooming landscapes" he had promised had failed to materialise. Despite the failures of the Kohl government, many voters still distrusted the SPD, partly because of the way they had come to be dominated by the generation of 1968. In addition, there remained scepticism from business. For Hombach, the key was therefore a more business-friendly economic policy—what he called a "supply-side economics of the left"—that would help to stimulate Germany's sluggish economy and in particular reduce unemployment.[50]

Although Schröder seemed at a first glance similar to Clinton in the United States or Blair in the United Kingdom, he was in fact a very different figure who was responding to a specifically German situation. Kohl had been no Reagan or Thatcher—partly at least because of Lafontaine's success in blocking his attempts at reform—and the German economy was still heavily regulated. Although Schröder knew he would need to undertake long overdue reforms of Germany's rigid labour market, overstretched pensions system and arcane tax system—it was often said that there was a "reform logjam"—he had no intention of deregulating the German economy along Anglo-Saxon lines. The challenge, as Hombach put it, was "to pursue a third way between a superficial laissez-faire liberalism and the old ideals of the Federal Republic as it developed after the Second World War".[51]

It was significant that Hombach's inspiration was not a Social Democrat at all but Ludwig Erhard, the former Christian Democrat chancellor and father of Germany's post-war Social Market Economy. Hombach argued that the Christian Democrats of the Kohl era had abandoned Erhard's pragmatic approach and that the most urgent priority for Germany was the recovery of the consensus that lay at the heart of the Social Market Economy. In that sense, Hombach's proposals for economic reform remained firmly within a German corporatist tradition. He stressed the need to retain social cohesion, drawing on the Netherlands as an example as much as the United States. "Erhard's skill lay precisely in striking a balance between economic and welfare policies," he later wrote.[52]

With this move to the centre, Schröder cut whatever ties still existed between himself and the socialist ideals of the APO. In domestic terms, his politics no longer had anything to do with the impulses of 1968. For the moment, however, his centrism was still balanced by Lafontaine's more left-leaning economic and social policy. In fact, between 1995 and 1998, there had effectively been two parallel versions of the SPD developing alongside each other. But the two men reached an agreement that if Schröder won a further term as prime minister of Lower Saxony in the election in March 1998, he would become the SPD's candidate in the general election—making the state election a kind of primary. Schröder won 48 per cent—nearly 4 per cent more than four years earlier and the SPD's best ever result in the state. Schröder's nomination as the candidate for chancellor completed the shift of the SPD from the far left to the centre.

Schröder's opponent in the 1998 election was Helmut Kohl, who declared on his sixty-seventh birthday in 1997 that he would once again stand. Although his stature and power within the party were such that there was nothing anyone could do to stop it, many of the younger Christian Democrats considered it a huge error. Although respected for his achievements, in particular German reunification, he was considered a man of the past—"300 pounds of history made flesh," as Fischer had put it in the *Bundestag* in 1995.[53] With unemployment increasing since 1996, Kohl was fighting a losing battle. This time there was no economic recovery as there had been in 1994. The SPD also kept their nerve. They ran a professional election campaign of a kind that had not been seen in Germany before, even giving voters a "pledge card" with their key manifesto promises—an electoral gimmick borrowed from New Labour's successful 1997 campaign. They ran two parallel campaigns, with Schröder attempting to convince the centre ground and swing voters while Lafontaine secured the SPD's left wing. Schröder later described their strategy as "Oskar for the soul and Schröder for the head."[54]

Fischer, meanwhile, was simply attempting to prevent the Greens—a party that he thought had a "relationship with reality that was still in need of improvement"—from "committing suicide."[55] Although he was the Greens' unofficial lead candidate, Fischer did not hold an official party position. This meant that he was not involved in drafting the electoral programme, which the Greens' leadership, dominated once again by the party's left wing, put together. At a party conference in Magdeburg in March 1998—at which the Greens came under more scrutiny than ever before—it agreed a programme that included a demand for the price of petrol to be increased to DM5 per litre, which unsurprisingly horrified many Germans. Fischer, who was hoping to become foreign minister and had managed to get the party to agree to soften its anti-NATO rhetoric, was forced to accept the policy. In the summer, another leading Green, Jürgen Trittin, compared the *Bundeswehr* with the *Wehrmacht*—another blunder, particularly with Fischer apparently set to become foreign minister.[56]

But the election, which took place on 27 September, turned out to be a landslide. The Social Democrats won 41 per cent of the vote—making it the largest party in terms of the popular vote for the first time since 1972. The Greens won nearly 7 per cent—less than in 1994 but enough to remain the third-biggest party in the *Bundestag*. Together the Social Democrats and the Greens had a comfortable overall majority for the first time. For the Christian Democrats, who won 35 per cent of the vote, it was their worst election result since 1953 and the first time a German chancellor had been voted out of office by the electorate. The 16–year Kohl era was over and the "new majority to the left of the Christian Democrats" that Willy Brandt had spoken of in 1982 had finally become a reality—the first time Germany would be run by two parties of the left. In fact, with eleven out of sixteen state governments also led by the Social Democrats, it seemed as if the left—led by members of the 1968 generation—was on the verge of a new hegemony in Germany.

10

POWER

The election of Gerhard Schröder as German chancellor in the autumn of 1998 seemed to represent a momentous generational and cultural shift in German society. Exactly thirty years after they had marched in the streets, the *Achtundsechziger* had come to power. In one sense, the 1968 generation seemed to have completed the "long march through the institutions" that Rudi Dutschke had called for at the Vietnam Congress in West Berlin in February 1968. But what Dutschke would have made of it was something not even the *Achtundsechziger* themselves could agree on. The Maoist long march Dutschke had in mind was part of a global guerrilla strategy that would subvert and transform the institutions themselves.[1] Whether that had happened was highly debatable. Little, for example, remained of Dutschke's, or the student movement's, commitment to revolutionary socialism. In more complex ways that would only become fully apparent over the next seven years, however, the "red-green" government, and in particular its foreign policy, would bear the imprint of 1968.

Only two members of Schröder's cabinet had been directly involved in the events of 1968: Otto Schily, Gudrun Ensslin's former lawyer, who became interior minister, and Joschka Fischer, who became foreign minister. Several other members of the cabinet had been involved in the radical left-wing groups that had grown out of the student movement in the seventies, such as Jürgen Trittin, the former member of the Communist League, who became environment minister. In addition, other former members of the student movement and its offshoots would be appointed as behind-the-scenes advisers. But the real influence of 1968 on the "red-green" coalition was both broader and more subtle. Aspects of the student movement's thinking had filtered through

213

the *Jusos* into the SPD and via the "Spontis" and the "K-Groups" into the Green party. Even the idea of a "red-green" government was itself a project of the *Achtundsechziger* that had been driven in particular by "realists" within the Green party, like Joschka Fischer, who had turned it from an "anti-party" into a potential coalition partner for Social Democrats.

While many on the left believed that Fischer and Schröder had moved so far away from the ideals of the student movement that they no longer had anything to do with 1968, to some on the right, they remained dangerous radicals who had infiltrated the Federal Republic's highest institutions. Over the summer of 1998, as it had become increasingly likely that there would be a "red-green" government, conservative newspapers like the *Frankfurter Allgemeine Zeitung* and *Die Welt*, Axel Springer's flagship broadsheet, revived the issue of the still unresolved murder of Heinz-Herbert Karry. "How did the murder pistol end up in Joschka Fischer's car?" asked *Die Welt*.[2] Christian Democrat politicians also demanded that Fischer respond to the charge that he encouraged others to use Molotov cocktails at the demonstration after Ulrike Meinhof's death in 1976 at which Sergeant Jürgen Weber had been critically injured.[3]

Nor was it just in politics that, by 1998, what had once been the counter-culture had become the establishment. According to the *Spiegel*, former radicals, now entering their fifties, were in positions of power "everywhere—in politics, in the media, in the arts and culture, even in business."[4] There was perhaps no better example of this than Thomas Schmid, Fischer's former comrade in Revolutionary Struggle. When the Frankfurt "Spontis" had gone their separate ways, Schmid had worked for Klaus Wagenbach's publishing house and then for the *taz* and various other newspapers. In the eighties he joined the Greens and worked in Frankfurt with Daniel Cohn-Bendit, who, meanwhile, had returned to France and been elected as a Green member of the European parliament. Now, Schmid, who like Fischer had accepted the *Westbindung*, had become one of the few genuine libertarian conservatives in Germany and an advocate of a "black-green" coalition of Christian Democrats and Greens. He said he no longer thought of himself as left-wing or right-wing but simply "liberal".[5] In 1998, Schmid, who had demonstrated against the Springer corporation over the Easter weekend in 1968, went to work for the Springer broadsheet *Die Welt*. He later became its editor.

While many former members of the APO had risen to positions of power, others were living in obscurity. Dieter Kunzelmann had completed his five-year prison sentence for the bombing campaign of the late 1960s and 1970s and was released in 1975. For two years in the early eighties, he had been a member of Berlin's Senate. In the nineties he worked as archivist in Hans-Christian Ströbele's law firm in West Berlin. In 1997, he was sentenced to just under a year in prison for throwing an egg at Eberhard Diepgen, the mayor of Berlin. Just as he was about to begin his prison sentence, however, he disappeared. There were rumours that he had committed suicide, but no-one really knew for sure. Meanwhile his former comrades from Kommune 1, Rainer Langhans and Fritz Teufel, had withdrawn from politics altogether. Langhans had rejected politics for spiritualism and lived in an all-white one-room apartment in Munich. After spending five years in prison for his involvement in the kidnapping of Peter Lorenz, Teufel had become a bicycle courier in Berlin.

Finally, a few months before Schröder became chancellor came news that even what remained of the RAF had given up on its "struggle". In May 1998, an eight-page declaration was sent to Reuters in Cologne in which the RAF apparently declared its own dissolution. The declaration, which the German authorities believed to be genuine, began:

Nearly 28 years ago, on 14 May, 1970, the RAF was created in an action to free Andreas Baader. Today we are ending this project. The urban guerrilla in the form of the RAF is history.[6]

The declaration went on to say that although the armed struggle had not been successful, it had been "fundamentally right to counter the continuities of German history with resistance".[7] It listed the 28 members of the RAF, the 2 June Movement and the Revolutionary Cells—the three main terrorist groups that had grown out of the student movement—who had been killed during the course of the armed struggle. No mention was made of their victims. The declaration ended, paraphrasing Rosa Luxemburg, with the words:

The revolution says:
I was
I am
I will be.[8]

— — — — — — — — — — —

The handover of power in 1998 seemed so significant not just because several members of the Schröder government had backgrounds in radical left-wing politics but also because it represented a shift from the generation that had experienced World War II to the post-war generation. Schröder's predecessor Helmut Kohl was born in 1930 and thus belonged to the *Flakhelfergeneration*. Although members of this generation bore no responsibility for the Nazi era—on a visit to Israel in 1984 Kohl had referred to his generation as having "the blessing of a late birth"—they had nevertheless experienced first hand the disaster of 1945 as young men and women. On the other hand, Schröder, who was born in 1944, and the rest of his generation had no memories at all of Germany's "hour zero." It was this generational difference, as much as the idea that former revolutionaries were about to take over, that created an expectation in 1998 that a new era was beginning, above all in German foreign policy.

For Kohl's generation, 1945 was the key caesura in German twentieth-century history. For many of them, Germany's role in the world was defined essentially by its responsibility for World War II—that, for example, was the basis of their belief in European integration. Joschka Fischer also seemed to share this preoccupation with the Nazi past and the lessons to be learnt from it. But Schröder could not have been more different. German history did not seem to loom as large for him as it did for Fischer, nor had he gone through the successive crises of conscience that Fischer had. In particular, Schröder seemed to have a casual, almost careless attitude to the Nazi past and showed little interest in the Holocaust. In this respect, in fact, if he resembled anyone at all from the student movement, it was Dutschke himself, who considered the Nazi past a distraction from the revolution.

Thus even before his election as chancellor, Schröder came to be associated with the idea of a new "uninhibited" nation less encumbered by historical guilt. Where, for example, Kohl had talked about European integration as a matter of war and peace and the Euro as a necessary condition of German reunification, the more pragmatic Schröder called for a European policy "without visions." With major reforms of the EU budget looming, Schröder complained about Germany's disproportionate payments to the EU and said Germany should adopt the Euro "not in order to overcome our past but as an option for our future."[9] In doing so, Schröder, as Daniel Cohn-Bendit and others pointed out, seemed to be jettisoning Kohl's principle that European integration was a trade-off for German reunification.[10] Schröder thus came to embody the idea of German "normalisation" and with it a new, more assertive German foreign policy that would pursue Germany's national interests—though what exactly these were had yet to be defined.

During the election, Schröder, whose campaign centred on the idea of change, found it politically useful to associate himself and the "red-green" coalition with the sense of a new era in German politics. After his election he also made much of the fact that it had been the first time in the history of the Federal Republic that a change of government had been brought about by an election, as opposed to a back-room deal between coalition partners—and explicitly connected it to the "normalisation" of Germany. "The change [of government] is an expression of democratic normality and of growing democratic self-confidence," he declared in his first speech as chancellor.[11] In an appearance on a television talk show shortly afterwards, he said that under his leadership Germany would be more "uninhibited" and "in a good sense maybe even more German."[12] Above all, the difference between Kohl and Schröder seemed to be illustrated by the debate about the planned Holocaust memorial in Berlin, which had become almost a litmus test of attitudes to the Nazi past. In contrast to Kohl, who supported the plans to build a vast memorial in the former no-man's land in the new centre of the re-unified city, Schröder had been critical of the project. His designated culture minister, Michael Naumann, went so far as to compare the design by the American Peter Eisenman to Albert Speer's monumental architecture.

In October 1998, against the background of the ongoing discussion about the Holocaust memorial, the writer Martin Walser gave a controversial speech that further intensified the already heated debate about German "normalisation". Walser's speech sharpened the argument, which he had first made 33 years earlier in his 1965 essay in the first issue of *Kursbuch*, that conscience was essentially private. He criticised what he regarded as the empty rituals of contrition about the Nazi past—"the continual presentation of our shame", as he put it.[13] Walser, who had also been one of the few West German intellectuals of his generation who had consistently argued for German reunification, criticised figures like Günter Grass who used the Holocaust as a "moral cudgel" to justify particular political positions—what he called the "instrumentalisation of Auschwitz".[14] He also singled out for criticism the planned Holocaust memorial in Berlin—the ultimate public expression of contrition for the Nazi past—which he described as a "football field-sized nightmare" that "monumentalised shame."[15] The memorial represented what he called the "banality of good"—a reference to the concept of the "banality of evil" that Hannah Arendt had developed in her account of the Eichmann trial, *Eichmann in Jerusalem.*[16]

The debate resulting from Walser's speech, which ran for several months on the pages of the *feuilletons* of German newspapers, was in essence a continuation of the *Historikerstreit* a decade earlier. To many people, Walser seemed to be suggesting it was time to draw a so-called *Schlußstrich* (final line) under the Nazi past. Although Walser's argument was directed against the ritualisation of memory rather than memory itself, he was widely criticised for appearing to suggest that it was time to stop remembering Auschwitz. The chairman of the Central Council of German Jews, Ignatz Bubis, who as a real estate developer in the seventies had been caught up in the Frankfurt *Häuserkampf*, described Walser's speech as "intellectual arson."[17] Schröder himself became embroiled in the controversy when he was asked about Walser's speech and said flatly that "a writer must be allowed to say things like that, but the chancellor can't."[18] The remark, which seemed to suggest he sympathised with Walser, led some commentators to think that it might be the generation of 1968 that would draw the *Schlußstrich.*[19]

The sense that a new era in German history was beginning was further heightened by the fact that in 1999, nine years after reunification, the German parliament moved from Bonn to Berlin, where it sat in the Reichstag building built at the end of nineteenth century and newly renovated by Sir Norman Foster, the British architect. Even before it had begun, it had already been dubbed the "Berlin Republic", though it was unclear what, if anything, the phrase meant.[20] In theory, nothing would change except the physical location of parliament—a fact often emphasised by those opposed to the use of the term. Nevertheless, the contrast between the old and new capitals could not have been greater: Bonn, the leafy Rhineland university town in the far western corner of West Germany, and Berlin, the chaotic metropolis in the far east of the re-unified Germany.

The geopolitical idea implicit in the concept of the "Berlin Republic", in so far as there was one, was that, with the re-location of the capital from Bonn to Berlin, Germany's centre of gravity would move to the east. Some feared that this might weaken the *Westbindung* and in particular undermine the two fundamental principles that had formed the basis of the Federal Republic's foreign policy consensus stretching back from Adenauer through to Kohl: the Atlantic alliance and European integration. Ultimately, it might mean a return to Germany's *Mittellage*, its position as a central European power in conflict with its neighbours in both the East and the West. Behind these dark fears about the move to Berlin were the memories of the city as the capital of the *Kaiserreich* and then, after the brief interlude of the Weimar Republic, the Third Reich.[21] But although Berlin seemed to embody the idea of a bigger, more confident Germany, and had been the Nazi capital, Hitler himself had always disliked the city. And whatever Berlin's past, some also said that its vibrant, multicultural present, in particular its large Turkish population, would have a liberalising effect on German politics.

The Reichstag building itself was an even more ambivalent symbol. Built after German unification in 1871 with a portico inscribed with the words "Dem deutschen Volke" (To the German People), it represented both German nationalism and parliamentary democracy. Norman Foster's renovation of the building skillfully negotiated this tension. The glass dome, which had been destroyed in the fire of 1933 that the Nazis had used as a pretext to begin dismantling democracy in Germany, was reconstructed in such a way that it looked almost like a foreign body sitting on top of the building. Foster also built into the cupola a spiral staircase, so that the public could walk up it, the *Bundestag* chamber beneath them, and literally look down on democracy in action, thus turning it into a symbol of transparency. Cyrillic graffiti written by Soviet soldiers was even left on the walls as a reminder of World War II.

Meanwhile, across from the Reichstag, a massive, new Federal Chancellery was also built. A 1,000–foot long, 120 foot-high stone and glass box, it was described by one foreign observer as "an exuberant expression to German power."[22] Unlike the Reichstag, which carefully juxtaposed Germany's dark past and democratic present—so-called "critical engagement" with history—the bland new Chancellery, which was later nicknamed the "washing machine", seemed to erase all trace of history beneath it. Although it had actually been commissioned by Helmut Kohl, it seemed strangely appropriate that Schröder, who more than anyone seemed to embody the idea of the forward-looking "Berlin Republic," would be the first chancellor to use it.

Like the Chancellery, the German foreign office was also due to move into a controversial new home in Berlin in 1999. The monolithic, curved Reichsbank building had been built by the Nazis in the 1930s and used during World War II to store gold taken from the Jews of Europe, including gold melted down from the teeth of concentration camp inmates.[23] After the war, the building was used by the SED, the East German Communist party. In fact, Fischer moved into the office once occupied by Erich Honecker, the former general secretary of the party's central committee. Like Schröder, Fischer had not chosen the location of his new office. But it was nevertheless a building that was, like the new Chancellery, strangely appropriate for its first occupant. For whereas Schröder was apparently oblivious to German history, Joschka Fischer was haunted by it.

Although it was in foreign policy that the new era of "normality" that Schröder seemed to represent was expected to manifest itself, the new foreign minister stood for the opposite of "normality." After all, one of the most outspoken critics of the idea of the "normality" of the Berlin Republic was Jürgen Habermas, who had been a major influence on Fischer since the *Historikerstreit* in the mid-eighties.[24] On the other hand, of all the new appointments in the "red-green" government, none seemed to promise a greater culture clash than that between the straight-talking former taxi driver without an *Abitur* and a department filled with refined aristocratic diplomats. According to some of his old Frankfurt friends, Fischer had talked about becoming foreign minister way back in the late seventies. Fischer himself claimed he had started preparing for the job in 1992, when he moved from his position in the Hesse state government in Wiesbaden back to the *Bundestag* in Bonn.[25] And although his views had changed dramatically since then, many still expected a radical new direction in foreign policy. Fischer was, after all, a Green.

Until Fischer's appointment, the foreign office had been held by the liberal Free Democrats continuously for nearly thirty years—in other words, almost since 1968 itself. In particular, it had been dominated by the figure of Hans-Dietrich Genscher, who had been foreign minister from 1974 to 1992, when he was succeeded by his party colleague Klaus Kinkel. Genscher, who, like Helmut Schmidt, had been a soldier in the *Wehrmacht* in World War II, had also been interior minister when the Baader-Meinhof group had begun its bombing campaign in the early seventies. However, to the surprise of many people, Fischer kept most of the senior staff, including the head of the political department, Wolfgang Ischinger, who was unexpectedly appointed as Fischer's state secretary. "I thought of myself as a symbol of continuity," Ischinger says.[26] Fischer brought only three of his own people with him—two advisers, Achim Schmillen and Georg Dick, and Sylvia Tybussek, his longtime secretary. (He would later also bring in Joscha Schmierer, the former Heidelberg SDS leader.) The career diplomats in the foreign office were impressed.

In fact, as soon as he took office Fischer began to look and sound very much like a traditional German foreign minister, much to the relief of some and the disappointment of others. Instead of his usual suit and t-shirt combination, he took to wearing ministerial three-piece suits. And while Schröder created an expectation of change, Fischer did all he could to stress the continuities of German foreign policy. "The most important change is that nothing will change in the fundamentals of German foreign policy," he told *Die Zeit* in November 1998, a few days into the job. His task, he said, was to "complete what others have begun" in European policy.[27] As to those who expected a radical environmental turn in German foreign policy, Fischer was emphatic: "There is no such thing as a green foreign policy, only a German foreign policy."[28]

In November 1998, while Schröder was getting his feet under the desk at the Chancellery, his old friend and client Horst Mahler sat down in his study in his villa in Kleinmachnow, an affluent suburb southwest of Berlin, to write a pamphlet that would announce another new turn in his political journey. The "Pamphlet to the Germans Who Want to Stay German, on the State of their Nation" was a bitter polemic against mass immigration to Germany, which, he said, had already turned neighbourhoods such as Kreuzberg and Wedding in Berlin—where Mahler himself had lived after coming out of prison—into foreign settlements and was now threatening the future of the German *Volk* itself. He was particularly vexed by the "red-green" government's plans to introduce legislation to give second and third generation immigrants, including Germany's Turkish population of more than two million, an automatic right to citizenship. "The planned new citizenship law could permanently bury the chance of a relatively humane and peaceful solution to this problem," he wrote apocalyptically.[29]

The fact that Germany was allowing itself to be swamped by immigrants, Mahler said, was a sign of a deeper identity crisis. The "re-education" of Germany undertaken by the Allies after the end of World War II had aimed to "destroy Germany's spiritual foundation—its religion, its sense of history, its traditions and its philosophy—in order to rob it of its identity."[30] What he called an "intellectual Morgenthau Plan", referring to the short-lived Allied proposal to de-industrialise Germany after the end of the war, had transformed the Germans into "a people without God, but also without hope and mercy and forgiveness, without the will to be a nation, forever cowed and conscious of our guilt, in penitential robes, submitting to every possible unreasonable demand, ready even to give up our homeland."[31]

Mahler said this intellectual and spiritual humiliation of Germany had been masterminded by the Allies and implemented by none other than Adorno and Horkheimer—the intellectual fathers of the student movement. He said the Frankfurt School's theory of the "authoritarian character" had been imposed on the Germans so successfully that by the nineties the German character was regarded as the primary cause of Nazism. Echoing the comments of Martin Walser a month earlier—but also those of Ernst Nolte, the right-wing historian whose intervention had triggered the *Historikerstreit*—Mahler said the Holocaust was being used to permanently humiliate Germany. He said German pride had been eroded through a "cult of Holocaust remembrance" that had been imposed on Germany.[32] Behind it, Mahler said, was a conspiracy by American capitalism, which had turned Germany into "a laboratory for an experiment in how a great nation can be 'peacefully' ruined."[33]

But the tide was turning, Mahler said. More and more Germans were beginning to sense the threat from immigration and creating a new kind of cultural revolution in which Germans would recover their identity. Mahler now called upon Germans to rise up and organise a "national resistance" against the foreign takeover of their homeland:

One cannot expect us Germans to be driven from our homes without resistance. No one will be able to persuade me to change my mind about this. And no one will be able to persuade me that I am a "bad person" for saying it. The right to a homeland is a human right. It is justified for anyone—even Germans—to defend this right.[34]

For a former leader of the West German student movement that had begun as "resistance" against the "Auschwitz generation", these were astonishing claims made in extravagant language. The tone of Mahler's arguments echoed that of Franz Schönhuber, the former Waffen-SS officer and leader of the far-right *Republikaner*—with whom Mahler subsequently published a book on Germany's "national masochism."[35] Despite Mahler's past history of political extremism, former friends were shocked and baffled. "I never predicted he would make an about-turn like this," said Ulrich K. Preuss, another left-wing lawyer who had worked with Mahler in the 1960s and subsequently become a professor at the Free University in Berlin.[36]

Mahler, now 62 years-old, had once been, along with Ulrike Meinhof, the most respectable figure in the West German student movement. Like Meinhof, he had rejected his bourgeois life and joined the armed struggle. Eight years after he was released from prison in 1980, Gerhard Schröder had helped him win the right to practice law again. Since then he had revived his commercial law practice in Berlin and seemed to have put his terrorist past behind him. In an interview with *Die Zeit* in May 1997, he looked back on his time in the RAF as a period of madness and said he and his generation had been "poisoned" by its view of the Federal Republic as a fascist state.[37] Few readers probably noticed that although he had apparently reconciled himself to the Federal Republic, he also gave a vague prediction of a future revolt against it.[38] A year before Schröder was elected as chancellor, he and Mahler had met with a right-wing Stuttgart philosophy professor named Günter Rohrmoser, who had visited Mahler while he was in prison and whom Mahler now considered as his intellectual mentor.[39] In fact, it was in a speech at a celebration for Rohrmoser's 70th birthday in December 1997 that Mahler first began to tentatively air his new right-wing views.[40]

Initially, Mahler had had high hopes for the "red-green" government. Schröder's comments about an uninhibited Germany unencumbered by guilt led him to believe Schröder's government would begin the national revival he wanted. Just days after the election, Mahler wrote a newspaper article in which he described Schröder as the saviour of the German nation. While his predecessor Kohl had wanted to "dissolve Germany as a nation within a united Europe", Schröder would challenge the world financial system and re-assert German national identity.[41] But a few weeks later, Mahler's hopes were dashed.

Amid growing controversy about the article, Schröder distanced himself from Mahler's views, finally ending the friendship between the two men. It was then that Mahler's rhetoric sharpened.

Mahler's new worldview was a strange mixture of New Left and New Right rhetoric. He claimed his politics had not fundamentally changed since 1968 and pointed out that the targets of his wrath—the Federal Republic, American and Israeli imperialism and the Springer press—remained the same.[42] In fact, like many veterans of 1968 who had remained on the far left, he regarded his former comrades who had made their peace with the Federal Republic and were now in power—like Fischer and above all his old friend and lawyer Otto Schily—as "traitors" who had betrayed the ideals of the student movement.[43] He had not made his peace with the West German state after all. Unlike Fischer and Schily, he still believed in the revolution.

But there was one big difference: the revolution Mahler now advocated was an explicitly nationalist one. As a Marxist, he had always seen the "people"—the *Volk*—as the victims of capitalism, but he now apparently defined the "people" not in class terms but in cultural and ethnic terms. He also now agreed with the idea, originally propounded in the 1960s by right-wing thinkers like Caspar von Schrenck-Notzing, that the Americans, with the assistance of the Frankfurt School, had, through "re-education", undermined German national identity as a means of subjugating Germany—what in typically provocative language he called "the final solution of the German question".[44] Germany, he seemed to suggest, was the victim of a bizarre alliance of American capitalism—controlled, in his mind, by the Jews—and the Frankfurt School.

However, although Mahler's ideas seemed to be unmistakeably right-wing, they also had antecedents on the left and specifically in the student movement. Mahler inevitably claimed that his anti-Semitism was derived from Marx himself and in particular the essay "On the Jewish Question", in which Marx had identified the Jews with capitalism itself.[45] His arguments about Germany's "cult of Holocaust remembrance" also clearly echoed his old friend Dieter Kunzelmann's justification of the bombing of the Jewish Community Centre in 1969. In fact, Mahler picked up exactly where Kunzelmann had left off with his "Letter from Amman" in 1969. He continued to see it as essential to provoke, as Kunzelmann had always done, in order to "break through the spiral of silence."[46] Anti-Semitism was of course the biggest provocation of all in post-war Germany.

The worldview Mahler had developed was almost diametrically opposed to that of Joschka Fischer. Fischer had also been accused of moving to the right, but in a very different way to Mahler. As the left-wing terrorism of the 1970s reached its climax, both had gone through an intellectual crisis and had rejected the armed struggle. But their journeys had taken them in quite different directions. While Fischer had become a liberal, Mahler had gone directly from extreme left to extreme right. Through Jürgen Habermas's concept of constitutional patriotism, Fischer had come to accept the Federal Republic. Mahler, on the other hand, saw it as a "vassal state" of the "occupying powers", above all the United States. Although he had rejected terrorism as a means of overthrowing the Federal Republic, he still wanted to overthrow it. Whereas Fischer had rejected the student movement's continuity thesis, Mahler had as turned it on its head. In the sixties the student movement had regarded the Federal Republic as illegitimate because it believed it was a continuation of Nazism; Mahler still regarded it as illegitimate, but because it represented too much of a break with Germany's pre-1945 traditions.

More than anyone, though, Mahler's ideas were directed against Jürgen Habermas, who had influenced Fischer so much since the eighties. Mahler had first argued with Habermas at the congress in Hanover after the death of Benno Ohnesorg back in June 1967. Mahler now saw Habermas—whom he called the "spiritual leader of the Frankfurt School"—as the key architect of Germany's ongoing identity crisis.[47] For Habermas, the Federal Republic's westernisation was one of its most important achievements. Mahler, on the other hand, saw it as a sign of how far Germany had been brainwashed and lost its soul. For Habermas, "constitutional patriotism" was, because of the Nazi past, the only appropriate form of patriotism for Germany. For Mahler it was simply another tool to erode Germany's real national pride.

Mahler's view of the events of 1989 was also a kind of mirror image of Habermas's. Whereas Habermas worried about the effect that the authoritarian East Germans would have on West German political culture, to Mahler they were the Federal Republic's last hope. They had escaped the influence of the Frankfurt School and had not undergone the same "re-education" as the citizens of the Federal Republic had and therefore remained more German. While Habermas thought the East Germans needed to "catch up" with the West Germans, Mahler thought it was the West Germans who needed to learn from the East Germans. The East Germans had overthrown their "occupying power", the Soviet Union, in 1989. The West Germans, on the other hand, had yet to overthrow their own occupying power, the United States, and were in fact barely even aware of their own colonisation.

Both Fischer and Mahler had spent much of their adult lives fixated on the question of the meaning of Auschwitz for their identity as Germans but had ultimately found very different answers. After the shock of Entebbe, Fischer had gradually made his peace with the Federal Republic and come to see atonement for the Holocaust as central to German identity after Auschwitz. After his decade in prison, Mahler felt he had solved what he called the "riddle" of German identity after Auschwitz in a different way. "We have to straighten out our relationship with our parents," he wrote in his book with Franz Schönhuber. Instead of demonising the people who "gave us life", he said it was time to recognise the idea of a "perpetrator generation" for what it was—"a crime against our humanity."[48] Buried deep in Mahler's bitter rhetoric, there was, in other words, a desire for reconciliation with his parents—the "Auschwitz generation."

Both Fischer and Mahler would be accused of betraying the ideas of the student movement, albeit in very different ways. Fischer had rejected the revolutionary impulse of 1968 but attempted to fulfil the student movement's exhortation to fight a permanent anti-Nazi campaign. Mahler, on the other hand, had retained the student movement's revolutionary impulse but—in what was surely the most bizarre journey of any member of the 1968 generation—become a neo-Nazi. Fischer and Mahler represented opposite extremes of the spectrum of political positions taken by the *Achtundsechziger*. Where they had ultimately diverged was in their view of post-war West German liberal democracy, which in turn centred on their view of the Nazi past and the lessons to be learned from it.

What made Mahler so disturbing to many on the left was not just his turn to the far right, but his claim that his views were the logical conclusion of the student movement's thinking. Several other former members of the student movement shared this view. One was Reinhold Oberlercher, a former member of the SDS whom the *Spiegel* had described in 1967 as "Hamburg's Dutschke".[49] Another was Günter

Maschke, a former member of Subversive Action who had married Gudrun Ensslin's sister Johanna and, after spending two years in Cuba, had also moved to the far right and become a student and close friend of Carl Schmitt, the former "crown jurist of the Third Reich". In the spring of 1999, Mahler, Oberlercher and Maschke published a manifesto on 1968 which declared that the APO represented "the second German uprising against an occupying power"—the western counterpart of the 1953 uprising against the Soviet occupation of East Germany. The Red Army Faction, which they now described as the "Waffen-SDS", had made "tactical" mistakes but had attacked "legitimate targets" such as American military bases and German "collaborators" in its struggle for German national liberation.[50]

Mahler and Oberlercher subsequently formed the *Deutsches Kolleg*, a kind of think tank that they hoped would lay the theoretical groundwork for Germany's national rebirth and eventually replace the Federal Republic with a Fourth Reich. The "national question", they said, now took a different form than at the time of the student movement. Reunification meant that the division of Germany that had so pre-occupied Dutschke was no longer the main issue (though there remained the outstanding issue of lost former German territories in central and eastern Europe). On the other hand, in the sixties, they had not realised that millions of "guest workers" would remain in West Germany. To Mahler and his colleagues, the attacks on asylum-seekers in Hoyerswerda and Rostock in 1991 and 1992 were "uprisings" and young East German neo-Nazis who had been imprisoned for racial attacks were "political prisoners". In fact, they said, these youths were the spiritual heirs of the *Achtundsechziger*, continuing the same struggle for German national liberation begun by the students Mahler had represented as a lawyer in 1968 and demonised by the media in the same way as they had been. As one of the *Deutsches Kolleg*'s pamphlets put it, "Dutschkism lives on in these youths."[51]

Mahler's ideas seemed so outrageous that it would have been easy to disregard them, except for the fact that he was not the only former member of the student movement who was re-interpreting 1968 as a nationalist uprising. At the beginning of December 1998—the month after Mahler wrote his pamphlet excoriating the "red-green" government for its plans to reform Germany's citizenship laws—Bernd Rabehl gave a speech to a right-wing student fraternity in Munich called "Danubia". In it, Rabehl echoed Mahler's warnings about the dissolution of German national identity through immigration, but also, looking back at the 1960s, claimed that he and Dutschke had in fact been "national revolutionaries."[52] The speech was later reprinted, albeit without Rabehl's permission, in the right-wing newspaper *Junge Freiheit*.

Rabehl, now a 60 year-old professor at the Free University in Berlin, where he had studied in the 1960s and where the West German student movement had begun, did not go as far Mahler in his political views and in particular did not share his anti-Semitism or defend neo-Nazis. But Rabehl's claims about the nationalist nature of the student movement were in some ways even more unsettling than Mahler's because he had been closer than Mahler—as close to anyone, in fact—to the icon of the West German student movement, Rudi Dutschke. His claims about the real nature of "Dutschkism" could not be dismissed quite as easily as those of Mahler.

Dutschke and Rabehl had been best friends since they met in West Berlin in the mid-1960s. Like Dutschke, Rabehl had grown up in Brandenburg and had come to West Berlin to study. Together they had joined Subversive Action and then formed the "anti-authoritarian" faction within the West Berlin SDS. But by the time of the assassination attempt on Dutschke in April 1968, they had become estranged. Rabehl had never got along with Dutschke's American wife Gretchen, who he regarded as a "hippy chick" who was distracting Dutschke from the revolution.[53] Rabehl was furious about Dutschke's plans to move to the United States with her—he was one of the few to know about them—and never visited him in hospital after the assassination attempt. In fact, he did not see him again until two years later in London.[54]

Rabehl now claimed that the student movement had always been a nationalist movement. Whether or not the other members of the SDS knew it, he said, what motivated him and Dutschke was a visceral desire to rid Germany of "foreign rule". "Germany was occupied by two foreign powers—by the Soviet Union, which exercised power over the GDR, but also occupied by the United States, which exercised power over West Germany," he claimed. "The struggle in Germany was a part of the anti-colonial struggle."[55] In other words, Rabehl claimed, it was not just that he and Dutschke had supported national liberation movements in the Third World. They also regarded the West

German student movement as a national liberation movement. He and Dutschke saw the Germans, despite their relative prosperity in comparison to the colonies of Asia, Africa and Latin America, as a colonised people too. In fact, Germany was most similar to Vietnam, which was also divided in two by the Cold War. They saw the government of the Federal Republic as a corrupt puppet government—"something like the Thieu regime in South Vietnam."[56] He and Dutschke hoped for an uprising against the United States that would be a kind of western equivalent to the 17 June 1953 uprising in East Berlin.

Unlike Mahler, Rabehl did not see the Jews as being at the heart of a plot against Germany. However, he did share with Mahler a nationalist concept of Germany as a "community of fate". He also, like Mahler, had a sense of Germany as a victim of history that depended on an almost wilful rejection of the significance of the Holocaust. Like Mahler, Rabehl would take this sense of German victimhood to extraordinary extremes and in particular implicitly compare the Germans to the Jews. The Allies, he suggested, divided Germany out of revenge. "They wanted to say, 'There is a chosen people in a negative sense and that people is the German people,'" he would later say.[57]

Other former members of the student movement were horrified about the way Mahler, Rabehl and others had attempted to claim the legacy of Rudi Dutschke.[58] Numerous former members of the SDS, among them Dutschke's widow Gretchen, Klaus Meschkat and Hans-Christian Ströbele, who had again been elected as a Green member of the *Bundestag* in the 1998 election, signed a petition declaring that "We were never nationalists!" They said Mahler and Rabehl were distorting the aims of the student movement, which had been above all an anti-nationalist movement motivated by opposition to the war in Vietnam. "The 68er movement was not a specifically German matter but a worldwide youth revolt which was committed to a collective struggle against global exploitation, oppression and racism," their petition stated.[59] They insisted the student movement could not have been a nationalist movement, as Rabehl claimed, because it was an internationalist movement. "Solidarity with the underdeveloped countries of the Third World formed an essential part of our political identity," the petition stated.[60] Rudi Dutschke, they went on, "was a determined internationalist who fought with us for social liberation in all countries."[61]

However, the student movement's much-vaunted internationalism had consisted largely of supporting nationalist movements in other parts of the world. In other words, nationalism and internationalism were not mutually exclusive. In fact, to Rabehl, the student movement's internationalism was also evidence of its nationalism. He argued that the student movement's identification with nationalist movements in other parts of the world was a kind of "substitute nationalism", as the New Right ideologue Henning Eichberg had argued in the 1970s. The reality was that the student movement had been both nationalist and internationalist and that the relationship between nationalism and internationalism was simply never thought through in 1968. Even other former members of the student movement who did not share Rabehl's views, let alone Mahler's, admitted that the "national question" may have played a "subliminal" role in the SDS, especially in West Berlin.[62] "It was always an aspect of the student movement, but not yet a conscious aspect," says Tilman Fichter. "We simply didn't theoretically develop the question, partly because we didn't have a majority. We didn't want to tear the SDS apart."[63]

The Holocaust had played an equally complex role in the student movement. Some, like Ströbele, claimed that forcing West Germany to face the Nazi past and in particular the Holocaust was "one of the essential motivating forces" of the student movement.[64] There was never any doubt that for many of the post-war generation in West Germany, the student movement was a revolt against the "Auschwitz generation" that would force Germany to engage with the Holocaust in a way it had not done until then. But there were also others—Dutschke among them—who simply regarded the Holocaust as a distraction and wanted to draw a line under it, to use the term that defined the debate in the 1990s.

By the time Gerhard Schröder came to power, it had become clear—even if it hadn't been thirty years earlier—that the student movement had been a complex phenomenon that had contained within it deeply contradictory impulses. It was at once both internationalist and nationalist. It saw Germany both as a perpetrator and as a victim. It was an attempt to engage with Germany's Nazi past and the Holocaust in particular, and at the same time an attempt to draw a line under it. At the end of 1998, it was not yet clear which of these contradictory elements of the student movement's thinking would most influence the Schröder government. In fact, the "red-green" coalition would be influenced by both, in particular in its foreign policy. In the end, it would turn out to be as contradictory as 1968 itself.

One of Gerhard Schröder's first initiatives as chancellor was to set up a fund to pay compensation to former slave labourers who had been forced to work in German industry during World War II. The decision followed a series of class action lawsuits in the United States against leading German companies such as Deutsche Bank, which had helped to finance the construction of Auschwitz. In February 1999, following months of negotiations between the German government, companies including Daimler-Benz and Volkswagen, the US State Department and Jewish organisations, Schröder announced the creation of a foundation to adjudicate claims. He said it showed that Germany was dealing responsibly with the Nazi past. However, the agreement, which was intended to guarantee an end to legal claims against German companies for their activities during the Third Reich, could also be seen as an attempt to draw a line under the Nazi past. In fact, Schröder said that until a way could be found to prevent further lawsuits, the fund would not start operating.[65]

Meanwhile, the "red-green" government's plans to reform Germany's citizenship laws quickly ran into trouble. The reform of the citzenship law had been one of the Greens' pet projects since the early nineties when Daniel Cohn-Bendit had been Frankfurt's Director of Multicultural Affairs. However, because many Turkish-Germans did not want to give up their Turkish citizenship, it was not enough to simply make naturalisation easier. The Greens' proposals focused on the concept of dual citizenship, to which many Germans objected because it seemed to imply immigrants were not fully committed to Germany. In Hesse, a traditionally left-wing state with a "red-green" government where an election was about to take place in February 1999, the opposition Christian Democrats started a petition against the proposal, with enormous success.[66] On the back of the campaign against the new citizenship law they defeated the Social Democrats in the election and the Christian Democrat Roland Koch took over as the new prime minister of the state where the "red-green" experiment had begun.[67]

With this disastrous election defeat, the "red-green" coalition also lost its majority in the *Bundesrat* almost as soon it had come to power. It created an exact reversal of the situation that the Christian Democrats under Kohl had been forced to live with since the Social Democrats took control of the *Bundesrat* in 1990. It meant that in order to pass legislation—including the new citizenship law itself—the "red-green" government would from now on need the agreement of the Christian Democrats. In the end, a compromise was reached on the citizenship law whereby children of non-Germans born in Germany could get dual citizenship up to the age of 23, at which point they would have to choose between German citizenship and the citizenship of their parents' country of origin. Despite the compromise, it was one of the "red-green" government's main domestic policy successes. But from then on—just a few months into the administration—the "red-green" government faced an uphill struggle to make the radical reforms it had promised during the election campaign.

A power struggle was also taking place within the SPD itself as Gerhard Schröder and Oskar Lafontaine battled for control of the new government. The two men had always differed, particularly over economic policy: while Schröder was a centrist who believed in Bodo Hombach's idea of a "supply-side economics of the left", Lafontaine was an old-fashioned Keynesian who believed in stimulating demand to reduce unemployment. In opposition and during the election campaign in 1998, they had worked together remarkably well despite their political differences. But as soon as they were in power, they faced hard choices, particularly about how to reduce unemployment, which by the end of 1998 had risen to nearly 11 per cent. Appointed by Schröder as finance minister as well as party leader, Lafontaine immediately put together a tax reform bill that lowered tax rates for people on low incomes and closed lucrative tax loopholes for large companies. Lafontaine also called for taxes to be harmonised across the European Union, which led the British newspaper *The Sun* to begin a campaign against him, calling him "the most dangerous man in Europe". Schröder feared Lafontaine's proposed measures would lose him the trust of business and voters.

With Schröder and Lafontaine feuding with each other behind the scenes, the first three months of the "red-green" government were chaos. As well as the lack of clarity over economic policy, the government had to backtrack on a series of poorly planned policy initiatives, for example over plans to phase out nuclear energy, which Schröder publicly blamed on the Green environment minister Jürgen Trittin. Stuck in an almost permanent state of crisis, Schröder was widely criticised in the media for a lack of leadership. At the end of the government's first 100 days in power, the *Spiegel*'s cover story asked simply, "Where's Schröder?" Schröder's subsequent attempts to take control, often by secretly briefing journalists against Lafontaine, created even more friction.

On 10 March, a rumour circulated that Schröder had threatened to resign during a cabinet meeting that morning. Then, the following day, Lafontaine suddenly and dramatically resigned, not just as finance minister but also as party leader. He was quickly replaced as finance minister by Hans Eichel, the recently deposed Social Democrat prime minister of Hesse. Schröder himself took over as party leader. A week after Lafontaine's sudden departure, Bodo Hombach, who Schröder had appointed as his Chancellery minister and was blamed by many in the party for the internal struggle, also resigned. For the moment, it secured the survival of the "red-green" coalition. But it now also faced a major foreign policy crisis and it would be a long time before Schröder was able to get his economic policy plans back on track.

11

A WAR AGAINST THE PAST

The fundamentals of German foreign policy, which Fischer had insisted would not change under a "red-green" government, were, in fact, already in flux even before he became foreign minister. Since reunification, Germany had remained within its multilateralist framework, centred on the two fundamental principles of Atlanticism and European integration that went back to Adenauer. But because of its size and position, it had almost inevitably re-emerged as Europe's de facto "central power".[1] As ethnic and regional conflicts flared up, particularly in the Balkans, the question of what Germany's political and in particular military role in the post-Cold War world should be had become an increasingly pressing one.

Multilateralism, which had been an existential necessity in the earliest days of the Federal Republic and later during the Cold War, had over the years become a cross-party foreign policy consensus. Within that basic multilateral framework, what Germany was expected and not expected to do was defined by parameters that had also been accepted by Germany and by its international allies for decades. The Federal Republic was a *Zivilmacht*—a "civilian power" (as opposed to a *Großmacht*—a great power) that used multilateral institutions and economic co-operation rather than military power to achieve its foreign policy goals.[2] Its role as "an economic giant and a political dwarf", as it was often described abroad, was formalised in the Federal Republic's Basic Law: Article 26 prohibited the Federal Republic from fighting wars of aggression; Article 87a, added after West Germany joined NATO in 1955, restricted Germany's armed forces to a defensive role. It meant Germany could use its military only if it or another NATO country was directly attacked.

For most of the Cold War, West Germany had been relatively happy with this role, and so had its allies. In fact, the only time there had been a major rift between West Germany and its partners was during the Vietnam war. In 1965, as the war escalated, President Johnson had demanded that Germany send a battalion of soldiers and 200 medical orderlies to southeast Asia. The then chancellor Ludwig Erhard refused—though his stand against Washington meant little to the students who were soon marching in the streets of West Berlin and Frankfurt. With the end of the Cold War, however, the expectations of Germany's allies began to change. After reunification, Germany had not just become a larger country but had also re-gained full sovereignty and in that sense, at least, become a "normal" country. While some in Europe worried about the power of the new, re-unified Germany, others, particularly in the United States, actually wanted it to play a more active role in resolving conflicts around the world, to become, as President Bush put it, a "partner in leadership". There therefore emerged an increasing tension between Germany's reluctance to use military force, and its commitment to multilateralism and in particular the Atlantic alliance.

This tension, which would define the foreign policy debates of the nineties in Germany, first came to the surface during the Gulf War in 1991, which the German public overwhelmingly opposed. By referring to Article 87a—which specified that Germany could not participate in "out of area" operations—Helmut Kohl was able to hold off American pressure for German military involvement. So, for the moment, Germany reverted to its Cold War role: it would foot the bill—in this case DM 16 billion—while other countries did the fighting. However, the Cold War compromise was no longer sustainable. Washington made it clear that next time, a cheque would not be enough.

During the string of post-Cold-War conflicts that flared up over the next decade, Germany would take a series of baby steps towards a more interventionist foreign policy. The first were in Cambodia in 1992 and Somalia in 1993, where Germany sent troops as part of unarmed UN humanitarian operations. It was above all in the Balkans, however, that the shift from a strictly civilian foreign policy to a more interventionist approach played out. As Yugoslavia had begun to disintegrate from 1991 onwards—helped along, some argue, by Germany's unilateral recognition of an independent Croatia in 1991—ethnic conflicts between the Serbs, Croats and Muslims, particularly in Bosnia, had re-emerged. In 1992, as President Slobodan Milosevic began to try to create a geographically contiguous and ethnically pure Greater Serbia, the United Nations dispatched a peacekeeping force to the region.

Helmut Kohl's approach was, essentially, to push Germany to take greater responsibility on the global stage but to try to remain within the traditional post-war German foreign policy "culture of restraint." That meant, firstly, that any military deployment should be within a multilateralist framework and in particular be subject to the approval of the United Nations. Secondly, Germany should deploy its military with extreme caution and in particular take into account sensitivities about German history. This approach coalesced into the so-called "Kohl doctrine", according to which German troops could serve "out of area", but not in any territory occupied by the *Wehrmacht* in World War II. The former Yugoslavia was, of course, precisely such a territory.

As the situation in the Balkans worsened and Germany came under increasing pressure to play its part in peacekeeping operations, the Kohl government was itself forced to go beyond the "Kohl doctrine", beginning in mid-1992 with the enforcement of UN sanctions against Yugoslavia. Initially, German crews were used to man AWACS reconnaissance aircraft monitoring and later to enforce the "no-fly" zone in Bosnia. In 1994, NATO asked Germany to use its Tornado jets in support of its operations and for German assistance in a non-combat role for the event of an evacuation of UNPROFOR, the United Nations' peacekeeping force in Bosnia. The same year, the Constitutional Court clarified the constitutional position, ruling that Germany's armed forces could participate in any "out of area" operations sanctioned by the UN, subject to specific *Bundestag* approval.

This incremental shift in German foreign policy—sometimes described as "modified continuity"—was driven largely by events and pressure from Germany's allies.[3] German politicians generally followed events rather than shaped them, often equivocating and passing the buck to the judiciary where possible. For example, Klaus Kinkel, Fischer's predecessor as foreign minister, simultaneously pushed for the use of AWACS aircraft to support the "no-fly" zone in Bosnia and challenged the constitutional legality of the decision—in effect taking himself to court. However, in so far as German politicians influenced events at all, it was the right that drove the change. More than anyone, it was the Christian Democrat defence minister Volker Rühe who made the case for the use of the German military to resolve international conflicts and for the transformation of the *Bundeswehr* for that role. He even referred to the Holocaust and in doing so echoed Heiner Geißler's use of Auschwitz to justify the missile deployment in West Germany in 1983. Just as the victims of Nazi concentration camps had been liberated only by the Allies, Rühe said, so foreign intervention was required to liberate the victims of concentration camps in Bosnia.

Meanwhile, the left opposed change every step of the way, raising the spectre of a "militarisation" of German foreign policy. Although most of the leading figures in the Social Democrats had reconciled themselves to German membership of NATO by the mid-nineties, they still resisted the idea of "out of area" operations or of the *Bundeswehr* becoming an "army of intervention." They were suspicious of the idea of German "normalisation," which at that time was still very much associated with the right. And their sensitivities about German history were even greater than the right's. In the debate in the *Bundestag* on the use of Tornados in June 1995, passed by 386 votes to 258, Rudolf Scharping, then the Social Democrat leader and subsequently defence minister in the "red-green" government, argued that sending Tornados to the Balkans would be inappropriate because of German history.

Among the Greens, opposition was even more fundamental than among the Social Democrats. The proliferation of regional conflicts in the early 1990s presented a particularly difficult issue for the Greens because it in effect forced them to choose between two of their most fundamental Cold War-era principles—pacifism on one hand and a commitment to human rights on the other.[4] While the Greens were in no doubt that Milosevic was primarily to blame for the deteriorating situation in the former Yugoslavia, they rejected military intervention in the region, in particular by NATO. In fact, the party was also still in favour of dissolving the alliance, as well as abolishing the *Bundeswehr*, as part of its "consistently pacifist" approach to foreign policy.[5] Instead, they hoped regional conflicts could be resolved by other multilateral organisations such as the United Nations and the Conference on Security and Co-operation in Europe (CSCE), later to become the Organisation for Security and Co-operation in Europe (OSCE)—a hope that was to become increasingly unrealistic during the course of the decade.

Joschka Fischer had himself been one of the harshest critics of the Kohl government's foreign policy. Although he and the other "realists" had by the late eighties come to accept the *Westbindung* along with the Federal Republic, they had done so when NATO was still a purely defensive Cold War alliance, not a "community of shared values" whose troops, including those from Germany, might be deployed in post-Cold War conflicts around the globe.[6] Like Rühe, Fischer used arguments from German history and specifically the Holocaust. He believed German responsibility for Auschwitz should be the basis of the Federal Republic's foreign policy. But, like most on the left at the time, he still assumed that meant above all preventing a re-militarisation of German foreign policy and a gradual transformation of Germany back into a *Großmacht*. In his 1994 book on foreign policy, *Risiko Deutschland (The German Risk)*, which warned of the dangers created by a re-unified Germany in the centre of Europe, he depicted the Kohl government's tentative steps in the direction of a more activist foreign policy as a slippery slope that would end in a militaristic Germany armed with nuclear weapons:

It starts with calls for "more responsibility". Then combat troops will be deployed for the first time. Then there will be the first deaths and the first patriotic rituals will follow. Then the generals will want more freedom of action. The war heroes will be celebrated. [...] Simultaneously, Germany will get a permanent seat on the United Nations Security Council, in which at the moment only nuclear powers sit. A debate will begin in Germany about "complete" sovereignty, which in today's world means nuclear sovereignty.[7]

There were, however, some on the German left who saw things differently. One was Fischer's old friend Daniel Cohn-Bendit, who, as the child of German Jews who had fled from Nazism, had good reason to believe that military intervention was sometimes necessary, especially in the face of genocide. Together with Marieluise Beck, a founding member of the Greens who had worked with refugees from the Balkans, her partner Ralf Fücks, and Gerd Poppe, a former East German dissident who had become a leading figure in Alliance '90, Cohn-Bendit began trying to persuade the Greens to re-think their attitude to military intervention. In a panel discussion in Frankfurt in 1993 organised to coincide with the twenty-fifth anniversary of 1968, Cohn-Bendit attacked those on the left, including Fischer, who talked about human rights but opposed military intervention in Bosnia, describing himself as a "child of D-Day" who would not have existed without the Allied invasion of occupied France—an anti-fascist military intervention.[8] Fischer was shocked by Cohn-Bendit's views and responded by challenging Cohn-Bendit to send his own son to fight in Bosnia.[9]

The Greens' "pacifism debate" continued for much of that year. In an article for the *taz*, Cohn-Bendit said he was "ashamed" at the way his generation, which had condemned its parents for their political failure, was now "helplessly, powerlessly and sanctimoniously watching" the persecution of the Bosnian Muslims just as the world had stood by as the Jews were exterminated under Nazism.[10] At an extraordinary Green party conference in Bonn later that year, he compared Bosnia to the Warsaw ghetto and warned the Greens about putting themselves in the tradition of the appeasement that "led to the destruction of the Jews".[11] Fischer, however, could still not understand it. To him, Cohn-Bendit's views just seemed "out of date".[12]

Joschka Fischer's conversion to the idea of German involvement in "out of area" military interventions came two years later and three years before he became foreign minister. The event that prompted his dramatic change of heart was the massacre by the Serbs of 7,000 Bosnian Muslims at Srebrenica in 1995, the worst atrocity in Europe since World War II. Srebrenica, a former mining town in eastern Bosnia just 10 miles from the Serbian border, had been designated a "safe area" by the UN along with five other Bosnian towns in April 1993. Throughout the early 1990s, Bosnian Serb soldiers and paramilitaries had "ethnically cleansed" the surrounding areas, driving as many as 200,000 Muslims from their homes, many of whom had sought refuge in Srebrenica. By the summer of 1995, the enclave was overcrowded with thousands of refugees, was short of food and medical supplies and was being subjected to artillery bombardment by the Serbs.

By designating it a "safe area", the UN had committed itself to protecting it, but, fearful of its troops being drawn in on one side of the conflict or the other, it was in no position to keep its promise. The peacekeeping force on the ground consisted of a battalion of 429 Dutch United Nations troops, many of whom were medical and support personnel and who were only lightly armed. They also lacked a clear mandate and were unsure if they were able to defend the Bosnian Muslims or even themselves. The UN's real power lay in the threat of NATO air strikes, but European politicians had been reluctant to authorise them while their troops remained on the ground, vulnerable to being taken hostage by the Serbs. The compromise was "pin-prick" bombing, which had proved ineffective in curbing Serb incursions.

In July 1995, the Serbs attacked. They took 30 of the Dutch troops in Srebrenica hostage, putting their commander, Colonel Ton Karremans, in an impossible situation. Unable to get either clear orders or effective air support, he was forced to surrender and watch as the Serbs marched into the town. General Ratko Mladic's paramilitaries separated the women and children, who were taken away on buses. Over five days, Mladic's troops systematically executed the remaining men—all 7,000 of them—with Kalashnikovs and buried them in mass graves.

In London, Paris and in particular in Washington, the fall of Srebrenica prompted a change of strategy that led directly to NATO's more aggressive response to the situation in Kosovo four years later. The UN embargo had lost all credibility along with the idea of providing humanitarian aid to the victims of a civil war without taking sides. From now on, humanitarian intervention would mean enforcement—in other words providing more robust military force against the Serbs, with the aim of reaching a decisive victory. Only then could aid be effectively provided to the victims on the ground. In practice, this meant massive, sustained air strikes against Serb military targets.

In Germany, however, Srebrenica raised not just strategic but also deeper, existential questions, particularly for the generation of 1968. Unlike many of his Green colleagues, Fischer had never been a pacifist, but he had adopted their mantra of "never again war." He especially opposed the idea of a German military presence in a place where, as he put it, "Hitler's soldiery had rampaged."[13] But the echo of Auschwitz in the Srebrenica massacre was unavoidable. Here, for the first time since 1945, genocide was taking place in Europe. Fischer would later say that, for a few days after news emerged of what had happened in Srebrenica, he had difficulties looking at himself in the mirror.[14] "I would look at myself in the mirror in the morning while I was shaving and ask myself, 'How could it happen? What have you done?'" he remembers. "I was asking myself the same question that I had once asked my parents."[15]

After thinking about it for several days, Fischer decided that he and his peace-obsessed colleagues in the Green party had drawn entirely the wrong lesson from Germany's history. If responsibility for Auschwitz really was Germany's *raison d'état* as he had claimed, it was not good enough to simply avoid war at all costs. Other "safe areas" like

Sarajevo, Gorazde and Bihac remained. If the struggle of the post-war generation over the past thirty years meant anything, how could they stand by and allow them to also be overrun by the Serbs? "I decided I had to do something," he remembers. "I told myself, 'You can no longer look away, there can be no more compromises, otherwise you too will be guilty.'"[16] Fischer's Green colleague Hubert Kleinert, who along with Daniel Cohn-Bendit, had unsuccessfully attempted to persuade Fischer to re-think his position on the use of the *Bundeswehr* in "out of area" operations, remembers Fischer calling him a few days after news emerged about the massacre in Srebrenica and asking him what he thought. "I think we are a bunch of cowards," Kleinert said. Fischer replied that he too thought it was now time to for the Greens to re-think their position.[17]

In July 1995, after further discussion with Kleinert and others, Fischer wrote a 6,000–word open letter to his party colleagues and, more broadly, his generation. In it he made the case for humanitarian intervention, echoing the arguments that Cohn-Bendit had used against him two years earlier. After Srebrenica, he said, the West was faced with a simple choice: "retreat or resistance".

Europe is now faced by the same question it faced sixty years ago: where does appeasement of a policy of violence end? Some in Germany believe that Bosnia is our generation's Spain, that in the Bosnian war a new and at the same time familiar Balkan fascism is bloodily rampaging, which, for political as well as moral reasons, we cannot afford not to stop. If we do not draw a line of "here and no further" in Sarajevo, Gorazde and Bihac, we will have to draw one in the not too distant future after there have been countless further victims, because this kind of fascism with its politics of force will not stop by itself. Does the German left not run a massive risk of losing its moral soul if it cowers before this new fascism and its politics of force, regardless of the rhetorical excuses we make? [...] If we do not stand up to this terror with all the means at our disposal and do not do everything humanly possible to prevent further victims, will our generation not have morally and politically failed, just as our parents' and grandparents' generation in the thirties did?[18]

The "Bosnia letter" represented a new Damacus for Fischer. He had joined the student movement in 1968 as a form of rebellion against the West German state. But as the state responded with a mixture of repression and recuperation, he, along with many others among the post-war generation, had found himself drawn into a spiral of violence, until finally it seemed that they themselves had become a grim parody of the Nazis. Then, after a period of retreat in the late seventies, he had gone to the other extreme, joining the Greens, who rejected the violence of the student movement's offshoots. But, with real political power now beckoning, their fundamental opposition to violence had taken them to another dead end where they found themselves justifying inaction as a new genocide took place in Europe. For Fischer, it was time to re-define his anti-Nazism once again. Military intervention to prevent genocide was now "resistance." Strikingly, the arguments Fischer used, particularly in reference to the thirties, echoed those that the Christian Democrat Heiner Geißler had used against him in the debate over the missile deployment in 1983.

Fischer's "Bosnia letter" sparked an intense debate in the Green party that would last for the next six months.[19] Beneath the surface of the question of military intervention was the equally explosive issue of the *Westbindung*. NATO remained problematic for many Greens not just because it was a military alliance that was in their view inimical to peace but also because of the closeness to the United States that membership of it implied. Some on the moderate left of the Greens had softened their earlier opposition to NATO. Although it had not changed in the way they had wanted, they no longer regarded the alliance as they did during the Cold War. "We could live with it," says Ludger Volmer, the party leader in the early nineties who described himself as a "political pacifist" and subsequently became a junior minister under Fischer in the "red-green" government.[20] But even Greens such as Volmer who had reconciled themselves to NATO in principle could not yet jettison their pacifist convictions and bring themselves to to support military intervention in the Balkans.[21]

Meanwhile, after Srebrenica, the tide turned in Bosnia. US bombing of Serb military targets, together with a joint Croat/Bosnian offensive, forced the Serbs to the negotiating table. The Dayton peace accords of November 1995 partitioned Bosnia-Herzogovina, creating a Bosnian-Croat Federation and, surrounding it, a Bosnian Serb Republic. Meanwhile, in Germany, mainstream opinion also shifted. German Tornados took part in Operation Deliberate Force against the Bosnian Serbs in August and September 1995, again in a supporting role. With the backing of the Constitutional Court, the Kohl government also committed Germany to sending troops to Bosnia as part of IFOR, the NATO-led peacekeeping force that was given the task of enforcing the Dayton agreement. This time, there was overwhelming support in the *Bundestag*, with 543 members voting in favour and only 107 against.

After the shock of Srebrenica, the majority of the parliamentary SPD, led by Rudolf Scharping, backed the decision. Only the Greens remained adamantly opposed.

A few days before the *Bundestag* debate, the Greens had met at a party conference in Bremen—the culmination of the long debate that had been sparked by Fischer's "Bosnia letter". With the issue of *Bundeswehr* participation in IFOR, the Greens were forced to face the question of German involvement in military intervention—a question Fischer had, for tactical reasons, left out of the "Bosnia letter". The motion in favour of *Bundeswehr* participation proposed by the "realist" Hubert Kleinert was rejected by the party in favour of an alternative motion that called for "sustainable alternatives to military conflict resolution" and a "demilitarisation of international politics"—a major defeat for the "realists" around Fischer.[22] Even as late as the spring of 1998—by which time a "red-green" government seemed imminent—the Greens were still agonising over whether German troops should be part of SFOR, the successor to IFOR.

For the moment, Fischer had failed to persuade his party, or for that matter his generation, about the correct lessons to draw from German history. Still haunted by the spectre of the *Wehrmacht*'s crimes in Yugoslavia in World War II, as Fischer had been until Srebrenica, they could not bring themselves to contemplate the idea of sending German troops there even as peacekeepers, let alone to fight. Fischer believed he was remaining true to Adorno's categorical imperative to do everything possible to prevent another Auschwitz. But to many in the Greens, Fischer and his "realist" supporters, whom they now dubbed "Olive Greens", were simply opportunists who had abandoned their principles for power.

Although the use of greater force against Milosevic had stopped the war in Bosnia, many of the key questions in the Balkans had not been answered. Milosevic was still in power and indicted war criminals like Ratko Mladic and Radovan Karazdic remained at large. The assistant US secretary of state Richard Holbrooke, the American negotiator at Dayton, later said that the agreement had not created peace in the Balkans but merely "the absence of war."[23] It would return just as the Social Democrats and Greens came to power.

By the autumn of 1998, Kosovo, which had not even been formally discussed at Dayton, let alone dealt with, had emerged as the new flashpoint in the Balkans. 90 per cent of the province's population consisted of ethnic Albanians, but, as the site of the epic battle of Kosovo in 1389 against the Turks, it was the crucible of Serb nationalism and considered sacred land by the Serbs. In 1989, on the 600th anniversary of the battle, Milosevic had begun his campaign for a Greater Serbia there and had withdrawn the province's autonomous status. By the late 1990s, the non-violent movement for Kosovar autonomy led by Ibrahim Rugovar had given way to the more aggressive tactics of the UCK (KLA—Kosovo Liberation Army), a guerrilla group that had emerged after the end of the war in Bosnia. In January 1998 the situation escalated with a pattern of KLA attacks followed by massive Serbian reprisals. Another humanitarian disaster loomed as Kosovar Albanians fled their towns and villages to escape the Serb soldiers and paramilitaries. Some in the Clinton administration, in particular the new Secretary of State, Madeleine Albright, whose own family had been killed in the Holocaust, were in favour of a renewed military intervention against the Serbs.

By the time Helmut Kohl was voted out of office on 27 September, 300,000 Kosovar Albanians had been driven from their homes and preparations were being made for a NATO attack on Yugoslavia.[24] On 9 October, Schröder and Fischer, who were still negotiating the coalition agreement and had not yet been sworn in, visited Washington. They hoped to keep German troops out of any military operation in Kosovo, at least until the new *Bundestag* was constituted.[25] Initially, President Clinton agreed. But a few days later, after they had returned to Bonn, the American position changed: it was now believed that German participation was essential in order to demonstrate to Milosevic that NATO was united.[26] They reluctantly agreed. After the war, Schröder said that Germany had freely decided to participate in the military intervention, whereas Fischer said that, as a junior coalition partner, he had no choice but to accede to the American demand. "It was a question of whether, simply because of the international situation, the red-green experiment would fail before it had even started," he wrote. Of all the times to be in government, he asked himself, why did it have to be now?[27]

On 12 October, the North Atlantic Council agreed to give a go-ahead for possible military action against Yugoslavia—a so-called "activation order", or ActOrd. Four days later, the decision—and with it the question of German involvement in military action—was put to a vote in the *Bundestag*. 500 members voted to support military action, with 62 against and 18 abstentions—while the vast majority of Social Democrats supported the motion, the Greens were still split. The vote removed the last barrier to German participation in NATO air strikes. Meanwhile, efforts continued to find a diplomatic solution. In mid-January 1999, the Serb police killed 40 Kosovar Albanian men in the village of Racak, a massacre that also convinced many in the United States and in Europe that what had happened in Bosnia would be repeated in Kosovo unless they took decisive action now. Fischer would later say that Racak was also the turning point for him. Before this, he had still believed that a peaceful solution to the Kosovo crisis might be possible; after, he believed only military intervention would stop Milosevic.[28]

Even after Racak, however, Fischer continued to work energetically to find a peaceful way out. In fact, partly because of the political pressure on the coalition, Germany probably did more than any other member of the Contact group of countries (the United States, Russia, Britain, France, Germany and Italy) to find a diplomatic solution to the crisis in the first three months of 1999. It was largely as a result of Fischer's efforts that another attempt was made to negotiate an agreement with the Serbs and Kosovo Albanians. However, at the subsequent conference held in February at Rambouillet, just outside Paris, the Germans soon found themselves marginalised.[29] In any case, the conference was doomed to failure because of the Serbs' refusal to accept a NATO presence in Kosovo. "The parties," as two historians later put it, "were on a collision course for war."[30] Fischer himself went to see Milosevic on 8 March. He seemed to Fischer to be a man who was "prepared to walk over corpses".[31]

In one sense, the groundwork for German participation in the Kosovo war had been laid by the incremental shift towards interventionism that had taken place during the Kohl administration. That it represented merely the final step in a direction already taken by the right was illustrated by the fact that in October 1998 the Kohl government had already agreed in principle to the American request for German participation in military intervention. It is almost certain, therefore, that a "black-yellow" government of Christian Democrats and Free Democrats would have pursued the same policy as a "red-green" one. Nevertheless, German involvement in NATO air strikes on Serbia still represented a major break with the past. Firstly, although Germany had gradually reconciled itself to the idea of using its military abroad, it had until then only been used for peacekeeping purposes. This, however, was explicitly a combat operation, which was a very different proposition. Secondly, the 1994 Supreme Court decision had cleared the German military to participate in "out of area" operations, but only with UN approval. However, because of Russian opposition, there was not yet a Security Council resolution authorising military action, nor did there seem any prospect of securing one.

To many people, both on the left and the right, this set a dangerous precedent. Indeed, Fischer himself had always seen a UN mandate as a minimum requirement for German participation in military intervention, even after Srebrenica. Some argued that the lack of a Security Council resolution made it, in legal terms, a war of aggression. However, from a broader perspective, a refusal to participate in military action would also have violated one of the most fundamental principles of German post-war foreign policy by causing a major rift within NATO. Indeed, *Bündnistreue*, or loyalty to the Atlantic alliance, was, in some ways, an even more important aspect of Germany's post-war multilateral framework than its commitment to the UN—albeit one to which many of the 1968 generation had only recently converted. It was, in effect, a double bind.

Commentators frequently pointed to the irony of a "red-green" government being the first to take Germany to war since 1945. It was particularly ironic that it should be a foreign minister from the Green party, the party that had grown out of the peace movement, who would send the *Bundeswehr* into combat for the first time. On the other hand, given the political journey of the 1968 generation, it was strangely appropriate that the "red-green" government should find itself in power during the Kosovo war. For thirty years the *Achtundsechziger* had been haunted by Auschwitz. Now that they were finally in power, it had come back to haunt them again.

The Kosovo war split the left almost everywhere around the world. Some accepted the argument that it was legitimate to undertake a military intervention, unilaterally if necessary, where crimes were being committed that, as Michael Walzer put it, "shock the moral conscience of mankind".[32] A significant number of those on the left around Europe who most eloquently and loudly made this case for humanitarian intervention were veterans of the student movements of 1968 like

Bernard Kouchner, the founder of *Médecins sans frontières* and a friend of Daniel Cohn-Bendit, who would become the first permanent UN administrator in Kosovo after the war was over and later the French foreign minister. Beginning in the early nineties, Kouchner had been one of the first to propound the idea of humanitarian intervention, or *ingérence*. This would lead some observers like Paul Berman to describe Kosovo as "the 68ers' war".[33]

However, the *soixante-huitards* were by no means unanimously in favour of the military intervention in Kosovo. Tariq Ali, once the leader of the British anti-Vietnam war movement, thought that NATO's real, "sordid" aim in 1999 was to extend American hegemony by establishing "a bridgehead against Russia".[34] He called those on the left who supported the war "Tomahawk liberals".[35] Writing in a special issue of the *New Left Review* on "the imperialism of human rights," he dismissed the parallels that some in Britain were also drawing between Milosevic and Hitler. "The only function of the Hitler analogy is to obfuscate political discourse and to incite a stampede to reckless military action," he wrote.[36]

In Germany, it was Joschka Fischer who, more than any other member of the "red-green" government, made the case for the NATO military intervention and for German participation in it. Given his stand on Srebrenica—indeed given his entire biography—it was hardly surprising that he chose to support German involvement in the military intervention as passionately and vocally as he did, nor that he did so above all by referring to the parallels between Kosovo and Auschwitz. For Fischer, it was not only a just war; it was "resistance." The arguments for intervention seemed so powerful to him that they even overcame the need for a UN mandate. Fischer would certainly have preferred the backing of the UN, but if Germany had to intervene without UN approval in order to prevent genocide—the central theme of his thinking since Srebrenica—it would. "If people are being massacred," he bluntly told the *New York Times* in January 1999, "you cannot mutter about having no mandate."[37] Fischer would later make this reasoning more explicit than ever before when, during the war, he declared, "I didn't just learn 'never again war.' I also learned, 'never again Auschwitz.'"[38]

Some on the left in Germany, including Jürgen Habermas, agreed with Fischer, while others, especially foreign policy realists like the former chancellor Helmut Schmidt, opposed the war. The war also split the 1968 generation down the middle. Some veterans of the West German student movement like Klaus Meschkat, one of the "traditionalists" in the SDS, saw it not as a new kind of humanitarian intervention at all but rather as an old-fashioned imperialist war and criticised it in terms that paralleled the student movement's critique of the Vietnam war in the sixties. Just as they had thought that in 1968 fascism had hidden behind a democratic mask in West Germany, so now they thought that imperialism hid behind a mask of humanitarian intervention. Meschkat agreed with Tariq Ali that the comparisons of Kosovo to Auschwitz were simply a pretext for the real goal, which was an expansion of American power.[39]

In Germany, those comparisons were even more central to the debate about the war than elsewhere. Frank Schirrmacher, the editor of the *feuilleton* of the *Frankfurter Allgemeine Zeitung* would later write that "in Germany, unlike in other countries, people justify this war almost exclusively on the basis of Auschwitz."[40] The invocation by Fischer and others of Auschwitz turned the public argument about the war into a hyper-moral one that crystallised essentially around Germany's own past, and turned a debate about a crisis in a foreign country into a somewhat narcissistic debate about German identity. The Kosovo war could be seen as yet another act of the 1968 generation's *ex post facto* resistance against Nazism. Unlike the debate about the missile deployment in 1983, in which Fischer and Schily had spoken of an "atomic Auschwitz", Fischer did not this time directly compare Kosovo and Auschwitz. Nevertheless, the mere invocation of it could also be seen as yet another example of the 1968 generation's tendency towards "exonerating projection".

Many in the Greens were outraged at Fischer's invocation of Auschwitz in what they believed should have been a more sober debate about war and peace. Angelika Beer, the party's defence spokesperson, had been a member of the Communist League in Hamburg in the seventies and had campaigned for Germany to quit NATO in the eighties. But after a series of trips to the Balkans in the nineties, she changed her mind and was prepared to consider German involvement in military intervention. To her, the resort to the Holocaust to justify the military intervention in Kosovo showed "the political helplessness of the coalition".[41] Even some of the senior diplomats in the German foreign ministry were uneasy about the comparison of Milosevic's policy of ethnic cleansing with the Holocaust, while recognising that it was a "killer argument" that might be necessary to win support, particularly on the German left, for involvement in NATO military action. "They overplayed the argument in order to win domestic support," says Wolfgang Ischinger, then the state secretary in the foreign office.[42]

Whether or not Fischer had relativised Auschwitz (a claim which he denied) the implication of his logic was that Germany's history, and in particular the unique significance of the Holocaust, gave it, for some unspecified period and perhaps forever, a special responsibility to intervene to prevent genocide. It was, in effect, a kind of German exceptionalism, though an unusual one—a sort of inverted German *Sonderweg*, which argued that Germany now had to live up to higher ideals than other "normal" countries precisely because, in the past, it had sunk to greater depths. And yet, at the same time, the aspiration to prevent a repetition of Auschwitz by any means was one that Germany had to pursue within a multilateral framework—if not through the UN, then at least through NATO.

Schröder's reasons for supporting the war, on the other hand, were more opaque. During the debate about the Kosovo war, he too had used arguments about the need to intervene militarily to protect human rights, but he did not mention Auschwitz as Fischer had done. Although he did not feel able to publicly contradict Fischer at the time, Schröder did not share Fischer's reasons for the supporting the military intervention and specifically German participation in it. He would later say that he too thought Fischer went too far in bringing up Auschwitz to justify the military intervention. "I thought it was wrong," he says. "Despite the brutality of the Milosevic regime, I thought there was a difference between what happened in Serbia and the Holocaust. Auschwitz is something very unique and to make a comparison is to question the uniqueness of Auschwitz."[43]

In fact, although he too supported German participation in military intervention, Schröder's thinking was almost diametrically opposed, in terms of its implications for German history, to Fischer's. For Schröder, there was no categorical imperative for Germany to intervene to prevent genocide. It was now once again a "normal" country and with that came the responsibilities of a "normal" country—no more, no less. Thus, like other middle-sized developed European countries, it should be willing, and able, to back its foreign policy with armed force. Both Fischer and Schröder frequently used the word "responsibility". But while for Fischer it meant primarily responsibility for Auschwitz, for Schröder it generally meant responsibility as a "normal" country.

Within the ruling coalition there were thus two very different, in fact contradictory, versions of German identity that reflected the two different attitudes among the 1968 generation in Germany to the Nazi past: on the one hand Fischer's Holocaust identity and on the other Schröder's normal identity. The difference between them revolved around the significance of the Holocaust in determining Germany's present and future role in the world. Schröder, who just a few months earlier had appeared to tacitly approve of Martin Walser's criticism of the "instrumentalisation of Auschwitz", now stood alongside a foreign minister who appeared to be doing exactly that. Fischer would later, in fact, be widely criticised for "instrumentalising Auschwitz."[44] Years later, Fischer would continue to dismiss this criticism, pointing out that many on the left who later criticised him for bringing up Auschwitz in the context of the Kosovo war had themselves brought up Auschwitz in debates about the wave of racist attacks in Germany in the early nineties.[45]

The two diametrically opposed views of Fischer and Schröder happened to coincide on the question of German involvement in the intervention in Kosovo for two reasons. Firstly, it was an intervention that was supported, indeed led, by the United States and the European powers. Participating in it did not, therefore, put Germany at odds with any of its key partners or undermine either the Atlantic alliance or European integration. On the contrary, a German refusal to participate would have created a rift between Germany and its key allies. That meant that, for the moment, multilateralism in fact implied a more assertive, interventionist foreign policy. Secondly, it could be justified, both legally and morally, as a humanitarian intervention. In other words, in this case, preventing genocide went hand in hand with an expansion of Germany's military role.

Conversely, there were also two diametrically opposed arguments for rejecting German involvement in the intervention in Kosovo, and, more broadly, an interventionist German foreign policy. Particularly among the Greens, there were those such as Hans-Christian Ströbele who still believed that precisely because of its history, Germany could still not be trusted to play the same role in international affairs as other "normal" countries. On the other hand were those who implied that, precisely because Germany was a "normal" country, it had no special obligation to undertake a humanitarian intervention.

There would later be much discussion in Germany about whether Schröder and Fischer had been too quick to accede to American demands in October 1998 for German agreement to participate in the war. Some wondered whether, in agreeing to German participation in the NATO operation just as they were in the process of forming the first ever "red-green" government, their political principles had proved less important than their desire for power. But the reality was that, for both of them, agreeing to German involvement in the military intervention in Kosovo did not fundamentally conflict with their basic political convictions.

At around 6.45 pm on 24 March, 1999—the first night of Operation Allied Force—four German Tornados armed with HARM anti-radar missiles flew from San Damiano airbase near Piacenza, Italy, to attack Serbian anti-aircraft defences. For the first time since 1945, Germany was at war. In the following weeks, the four Tornados flew almost daily missions; all the aircraft and crews returned home safely. It was, all in all, a tiny contribution to the NATO operation. German crews would fly 436 out of a total of 37,565 sorties during the war and launch one-thousandth of the total missiles used during the conflict.[46] German crews were also, for historical reasons, excused from bombing runs on Belgrade. Nevertheless, it was, for Germany, a huge step. "The German government did not take the decision lightly," Schröder said as he announced the commencement of the bombing campaign.[47]

The Clinton administration had expected it to be a brief campaign. What no one really knew, however, was what would happen if the air strikes did not work. There was what Fischer later called a "strategic-political vacuum" at the heart of the NATO strategy.[48] In the United States there were also major reservations about the war, though not so much on moral, legal or historical grounds as in Germany but rather because of fears about American casualties. As a result, the Clinton administration had "tiptoed" into the war, indicating publicly that it had no intention of putting American troops on the ground.[49] Nevertheless, as the bombing continued, the prospect of some kind of invasion became ever more likely. To what extent Schröder and Fischer had agreed in principle to sending German ground troops to Kosovo, if it came to that, is still unclear.

Meanwhile, the humanitarian crisis in Kosovo worsened as the Serbs stepped up their attacks on the Albanians, for which some now blamed NATO. As pressure for a unilateral ceasefire increased from the left of the SPD and the Greens, the Schröder government continued to emphasise the genocidal character of the enemy to justify the intervention. On 8 April, defence minister Rudolf Scharping informed reporters of details he had received of the "Horseshoe Plan," an alleged Serbian plan to ethnically cleanse Kosovo in a semi-circular sweep. With its echoes of the Nazi plans agreed at the Wannsee conference to clear Europe of Jews, Scharping said it offered "proof that as early as December 1998 systematic ethnic cleansing and the expulsion of Kosovo Albanians had been planned."[50] Scharping also spoke of "serious indications of the existence of concentration camps" in Kosovo.[51] The "Horseshoe Plan" made the comparison with the Holocaust even more explicit than it had been until then. When he looked at what was happening in Kosovo, Scharping said he saw "the grimace of our own history."[52]

With the pressure for the deployment of ground troops increasing, and with it anxiety in Germany, the historian Daniel Goldhagen intervened in the debate about the war and made the parallels between Milosevic's Serbia and Hitler's Germany yet more explicit. Goldhagen's book *Hitler's Willing Executioners* about the role of "ordinary Germans" in the Holocaust had caused a major controversy three years earlier, with many German historians accusing him of resurrecting the thesis of "collective guilt" and even of an "anti-German quasi-racism".[53] In an article written originally for the *Guardian* at the end of April and reproduced a few days later in the *Süddeutsche Zeitung*, Goldhagen argued that Milosevic was not Hitler but was a "genocidal killer" who was pursuing an "eliminationist" project"—the same language he had used about the Holocaust. He said that a "large majority" of the Serbian population supported "an ideology which called for the conquest of *Lebensraum* and the vanquishing of the putative enemies". Therefore, he went on, NATO should not simply continue bombing until Milosevic surrendered but should "defeat, occupy and reshape" Serbia as the Allies had Germany. "If people accept that it was both morally correct and wise to occupy and transform Germany and Japan in 1945," he wrote, "then it follows that they must endorse, in principle, the desirability of pursuing a similar course in the Serbia of 1999."[54]

Many in Fischer's own party, however, were still not convinced—despite months of wooing by senior Greens such as the joint parliamentary leader Rezzo Schlauch, who went from one local party meeting to another to keep the Greens' grass roots informed of developments and to attempt to persuade them to support the party leadership.[55] But by the time of the Greens' extraordinary party conference in Bielefeld on 13 May, they no longer had any influence over the war. By that time, what the Greens decided would certainly not affect NATO, which had no intention of stopping the bombing campaign and thus taking the pressure off Milosevic. Nor, as the junior coalition partner, could the Greens end Germany's participation in the war. Their decision would not even affect the role of Fischer, who made it clear that he would resign from the party rather than quit as foreign minister. It was simply a vote about the fate of the Green party and, perhaps, the extent to which the generation of 1968 had accepted Fischer's conception of German identity after Auschwitz.

In truth, there was also never much doubt that, just six months into the "red-green" coalition that most of them had worked for years to bring into existence, enough of the Greens would support the party leadership to remain in power. Most senior figures in the party knew they would win by at least a small majority.[56] In the end, nearly every senior Green voted in favour of the leadership's motion to continue the bombing, including Ludger Volmer, Fischer's old adversary, and Angelika Beer, the party's defence spokesperson, who had abstained in the vote in the *Bundestag* in October 1998. Typically, Daniel Cohn-Bendit went a step further than even Fischer, calling for the deployment of ground troops in Kosovo if necessary. In reality, however, the conference was a piece of political theatre, albeit a spectacular one.[57]

Four weeks later, the war was over—in no small measure through Fischer's own efforts. A week before the Bielefeld conference, Fischer had put a six-point peace proposal to the foreign ministers of the G8 group of countries. According to what would become known as the "Fischer Plan," all Serb troops and paramilitaries would withdraw from Kosovo and a NATO peacekeeping force would guarantee security and the return of ethnic Albanian refugees—"Serbs out, NATO in, refugees back", as Madeleine Albright would later summarise it.[58] Fischer had also done much to secure Russian co-operation, thus removing Milosevic's last source of support. The weekend after the Bielefeld conference, the so-called "troika" of the EU, the United States and Russia met for the first time. The Finnish president Martti Ahtisaari subsequently took the proposal to Milosevic along with the Russian envoy Viktor Chernomyrdin. This kind of proactive diplomacy was a new departure for Germany and, according to German officials, would not have happened without Fischer. "We would not have had the confidence," Wolfgang Ischinger says.[59] It was therefore somewhat annoying for Fischer that, at the press conference at a European summit in Cologne at the beginning of June where the success of the proposal he had worked so hard on was announced, Ahtisaari suggested it be called the "Schröder plan."

For Fischer, Kosovo had been a war not just against the Serbs but also, in a sense, against Germany's past. Kosovo, he had said during the war, was "the first war in which a united Europe stood opposed to the nationalist Europe of the past."[60] A failure to stand up to Milosevic would not just have caused a humanitarian catastrophe on the ground but would also have had disastrous implications for the future of Europe itself. "If we accept this kind of politics, we will not recognise Europe," he said. "It won't be the Europe that we struggled for". Consciously echoing Woodrow Wilson after World War I, Fischer said he hoped it would be "the last war in Europe".[61] However, the reality was that Europe would not have been able to take military action at all without the United States. Thus, although Fischer had successfully held the coalition together as Germany went to war for the first time since 1945, it was hardly a triumph for him. In fact, the war had been a humbling experience, exposing a major transatlantic gap in military power. "Europe saw in the Kosovo war that it was not in a position to solve its own problems," Fischer said shortly after the end of the bombing campaign.[62]

The lack of German influence not only over military decisions but also over the international diplomacy before and during the war—itself a consequence of the military gap—had come as a shock to many in Germany, including Fischer himself.[63] German diplomats had also been taken aback. "It was a major wake-up call for us," says Wolfgang Ischinger.[64] The Americans, meanwhile, felt that the political and legal concerns of European NATO members had constrained their ability to conduct the war effectively. In a meeting of NATO defence ministers a few months after the war, one minister remarked that the biggest lesson of Kosovo was that "we never want to do this again."[65] Some in Europe now saw an opportunity to create a more coherent European foreign policy that could act as a counterweight to American power.[66]

Following Kosovo, discussions about the development of a European Security and Defence Policy (ESDP) intensified, leading to the creation of a rapid reaction force of 60,000 men at the Nice summit in December 2000. But for Fischer, the problem went deeper. Although Europe had been relatively united in the war itself, major divisions remained within the EU. In fact, in March 1999, just as the war was beginning, European leaders were squabbling about EU budget reform at a summit in Berlin.

Fischer's response was the bold speech on the "completion" of European integration that he delivered at the Humboldt University in Berlin in May 2000, almost a year to the day after the Bielefeld conference on the Kosovo war, which sparked the debate leading to the abortive European constitution. He had already, in January 1999, given a speech at the European Parliament in Strasbourg, in which he called for more democracy and transparency in the EU, in particular by strengthening the role of the European Parliament in decision-making. He now went further, calling for a complete overhaul of the EU institutions and the creation of a directly elected president.

It was, in many ways, a speech that Helmut Kohl himself might also have delivered. "European integration was the response to centuries of a precarious balance of power on this continent which again and again resulted in terrible hegemonic wars culminating in the two World Wars between 1914 and 1945," he began.[67] With enlargement about to expand the EU to a union of up to 30 member states, a reversal or stagnation of European integration "would demand a fatal price of all EU member states and of all those who want to become members." For Fischer, the only option was therefore to move forward to a federal Europe, if necessary through the motor of a "core Europe", in other words a vanguard of member states fully committed to further integration. The speech represented a renewed attempt to deepen European integration in the tradition of German foreign policy that went from Adenauer to Kohl. Fischer's proposals were aimed at making Europe more democratic but also more *handlungsfähig*, in other words able to act, and in particular able to deal with foreign policy crises in the future.

Fischer's vision of a federal Europe, like his justification for the war itself, was rooted in the European, and in particular the German, experience in the dark twentieth century. Enlargement and further deepening of integration, he said, would solve the historic problem of the

Mittellage: "It will be possible to lastingly overcome the risks and temptations objectively inherent in Germany's dimensions and central situation." Thus, for Fischer, the "completion" of European integration would, in a sense, represent the end of German history. "To me, 'normality' doesn't mean drawing a *Schlußstrich* under our past," he said in a debate shortly after the Humboldt speech. "But European normality means to have arrived at our destination within firm borders."[68] For Fischer, it also represented the culmination of the struggle of the *Achtundsechziger*. "To complete European integration is the task of our generation," he said.[69]

The speech also once again illustrated the difference between Fischer and Schröder. Although their views had coincided on the Kosovo war, the differences between their views of Germany's role in the world that had already emerged in the first few months of the "red-green" government were still there, particularly as Schröder began to play a greater role in foreign policy. There was a stark contrast between, on one hand, Fischer's grand vision of an integrated Europe that would be able to intervene on its own against nationalism and genocide, and, on the other, Schröder's pragmatic European policy "without visions". A month after Fischer's Humboldt speech, Schröder, who had been informed about it only at the last minute, dismissed Fischer's vision of a federal Europe as a "total illusion."[70]

By the middle of the "red-green" government's first term, German foreign policy looked very different than before Schröder and Fischer had taken office. With the Kosovo war, one leading journalist wrote, Germany had become, in terms of foreign policy, "a different republic."[71] German foreign policy remained rooted in a multilateral framework. But the gradual shift from a non-military foreign policy to a more activist one that had begun during the Kohl government had apparently been completed, although, crucially, Fischer insisted that the lack of a UN mandate in Kosovo must remain an exception.[72] Germany was also no longer shy about playing an active role in international diplomacy. Its previous diplomatic initiatives, such as those undertaken by Helmut Schmidt during the 1970s, had focused on Germany's own security. During the Kosovo conflict, Germany had for the first time acted as an *Ordnungsmacht*, a power that intervened to maintain the global order.[73] In short, the "culture of restraint" was dead. The *Econ-*

omist said that Germany had "come out of its post-war shell" and was "at last starting to punch at its full political weight in the world."[74] However, although it had gone further than ever before in the use of military force, it had done so in concert with NATO and could therefore still claim to be a "civilian power".[75]

Fischer himself had become one of the leading evangelists for humanitarian intervention. Germany went on to play a key role in KFOR, the NATO-led UN peacekeeping force in Kosovo, with a contingent of 8,500 troops—the largest ever deployment in a peacekeeping operation by the Federal Republic. Meanwhile, Tom Koenigs, Fischer's old friend from Revolutionary Struggle in Frankfurt became the first head of the UN civilian administration in Kosovo under Bernard Kouchner. Some, like Paul Berman, saw this as a quintessential New Left project. Others, including many commentators in Germany, thought the Kosovo war represented the end of the dreams of the generation of 1968, which had exchanged its principles for power. "Like many of his generation, Fischer had wanted to change the institutions," wrote three *Spiegel* reporters of the decision to go to war. "But in the end the institutions changed the one-time street fighter almost beyond recognition."[76] Some former members of the student movement agreed. Klaus Meschkat said the war had unmasked Fischer and Schröder as the "*Realpolitiker* of the generation of 1968" whose loyalties lay with the US government rather than the anti-war movement.[77]

If 1968 was primarily about opposition to American power, supporting a US-led war did represent an obvious about-turn. In fact, however, whether or not one agreed with the war, the "red-green" government's attitude to it reflected two key, albeit contradictory strands of the political thinking of 1968. In Fischer's rhetoric about the need to intervene to prevent genocide, using force if necessary, one could hear clear echoes of the students' slogans about "resistance" against the "Auschwitz generation" in 1968. Conversely, in the tendency towards a "normalisation" of German foreign policy, most clearly represented by Schröder's attempt to move on from the Nazi past, one could see the amnesia of the post-war generation that went all the way back to Dutschke. These two very different visions—Fischer's attempt to base German foreign policy on responsibility for Auschwitz, and Schröder's quest for "normalisation" that drew a line under the Nazi past—came together on the use of the German military in Kosovo and created an historic shift in German foreign policy.

Then came September 11.

THE RETURN OF HISTORY

At 2.45 pm on Tuesday, 11 September, 2001, Joschka Fischer was on his way back to the foreign ministry after a lunch meeting with the Yemeni foreign minister at the Hotel Adlon beside the Brandenburg Gate in Berlin. When he arrived back at his office on the fourth floor of the former Reichsbank building a few hundred yards away shortly before 3 pm, he found his colleagues glued to the television. The screens showed black smoke pluming from the World Trade Centre in New York.[1] A plane had crashed into the north tower.

"Was it an accident?" Fischer immediately asked.[2] No one knew. A few minutes later, just after 3 pm, when a second aeroplane crashed into the south tower, the question was answered. At that moment, Fischer immediately sensed the scale of what was happening. "We were facing a new kind of terrorism," he later remembered.[3] He called Gerhard Schröder, who had been working in his office on his budget speech that was due to be delivered the next day when he had heard the news, and went immediately to the Chancellery.[4] By the time Fischer got there, the twin towers had collapsed.[5]

If, with the return of genocide to Europe in the form of "ethnic cleansing" in the former Yugoslavia, the ghosts of the Nazi past had come back to haunt the 1968 generation, then with the terrorist attack on America, the ghosts of the 1968 generation's own past had come back to haunt it. The threat represented by Islamist terrorism was in many ways an entirely new one, as Fischer said. But at the same time, al-Qaeda was a movement that, despite its Islamist ideology, was remarkably similar in its methodological thinking to left-wing terrorist groups such as those that had proliferated in West Germany in the 1970s. It too saw itself as a revolutionary vanguard.[6] It too attributed the lack of support for its radical views to the masses' "false consciousness".[7] And it too believed in the use of spectacular, theatrical violence to rouse the masses from their false consciousness—in other words, Bakunian "propaganda by deed".[8]

Nor was it just that large parts of the West German New Left had, like al-Qaeda, for a long time believed in the use of violence to achieve political ends. The similarities went deeper. Islamism was an ideology that shared two key enemies with the West German far left in the 1970s: the United States and Israel. In fact, in the seventies, West German and Palestinian terrorists had had an almost symbiotic relationship with each other that culminated in the Entebbe hijacking in 1976. And, in case anyone was not yet aware of the 1968 generation's problematic past or had forgotten about it by 2001, it had returned and intruded into the present just a few months before September 11. In January 2001, Fischer's time as a street fighter in Frankfurt in the seventies, which by then had come to seem like ancient history, had suddenly become news again and nearly forced his resignation.

In January 2001, Hans-Joachim Klein, Joschka Fischer's old friend from Revolutionary Struggle, was due to go on trial for murder. Ever since the attack on the OPEC oil ministers meeting in Vienna in 1975, "Klein-Klein" had been in hiding. Seriously wounded in the shootout with the Austrian police, he had soon afterwards become disillusioned with his boss Carlos and quit the group. In 1979 he had written a memoir entitled *Return to Humanity* in which he distanced himself from terrorism—he had even sent his pistol to the *Spiegel*.[9] However, he was still wanted for his part in the terrorist attack that had caused the deaths of three people. He was finally arrested in 1998 in France at the age of 53. His trial was due to begin in mid-January 2001, and, sensationally, Fischer had been called to testify.

On 3 January, to coincide with the trial, the news magazine *Stern* published a set of five photographs that showed Fischer beating up the police officer Rainer Marx at a demonstration in Frankfurt in April 1973. The first picture in the sequence showed the 25–year-old Fischer, wearing a black motorcycle helmet and leather jacket, crouching as he approached Marx, who was also wearing a helmet and was armed with a nightstick and riot shield. The subsequent images showed several of Fischer's comrades joining him and attacking the policeman. By the last of the five images, the officer was on the ground being punched and kicked by several people. The photos had been taken by a photographer named Lutz Kleinhans, who at the time was working for the *Frankfurter Allgemeine Zeitung*, but they had been long forgotten. They were rediscovered 28 years later and provided to *Stern* by Bettina Röhl, one of Ulrike Meinhof's two daughters, whom Meinhof had planned to send to a Palestinian refugee camp in 1970.

Until the publication of the photos in *Stern* in January 2001, Fischer's radical past had ceased to be politically significant in Germany. After the initial flurry of analyses of the 1968 generation's political journey after the "red-green" government came to power in 1998, the radical pasts of politicians like Fischer had receded into the background. 1968, it seemed, was just another chapter in into the history of the Federal Republic. As for Fischer, although he had rejected violence and made his peace with the Federal Republic, he had never apologised for his actions in the 1970s or given any reason to think he was ashamed of anything he had done. On the contrary, Fischer seemed to be proud of his radical past, which had, in fact, become part of his unique appeal and distinguished him from less colourful colleagues in German politics. And yet, with the publication of the photos in *Stern*—which were reproduced around the world, causing Fischer's past to be dissected not just in Germany but also abroad—that past was suddenly called into question again. The images did not reveal anything substantial about Fischer's biography that was not already known. But they brought it to life. The contrast between the foreign minister in the three-piece suit and the street fighter in the motorcycle helmet and leather jacket could not have been greater.

In the interview with Fischer that accompanied the photos in *Stern*, Fischer was once again unapologetic about his radical past. Asked whether he didn't feel it was unpleasant for the German foreign minister to have to testify at the trial of a terrorist, he replied:

No. I don't see it as unpleasant. This is my biography. This is who I am, Joschka Fischer. Without my biography I would be a different person today than I am, and I don't think that would be a good thing.[10]

Fischer insisted that although he had been a "militant" in the 1970s, he had always opposed the "armed struggle".[11] He admitted there had been among the *Achtundsechziger* a "fascination with revolutionary violence". But he said that he, like most in the scene, had stopped before what he called the "abyss".[12] He had fought with the Frankfurt police but only in self-defence. He argued that what the "Spontis" had practised was "counter-violence"—a response to the state's violence that could only be understood in the context of his generation's suspicion of continuities between Nazi Germany and the Federal Republic. The left's militancy had developed as a response to the violence of the state and the "hate" the students experienced when they had demonstrated non-violently.[13] "German democracy showed a face that made it appear as if it was a continuation of National Socialism," Fischer said.[14]

Over the next month, Fischer came under increasing pressure as his controversial past was put under the spotlight as never before. Day by day, new allegations emerged. Five days after the publication of the photographs of Fischer in *Stern*, the *Spiegel* published details of Fischer's participation in the Fatah congress in Algiers in 1969. Another former member of Revolutionary Struggle, Elisabeth Heidenreich, said Fischer had been in favour of using Molotov cocktails in defending occupied houses, which he denied. Soon there were calls for Fischer's resignation as the Christian Democrats and the Springer newspapers picked up the campaign against Fischer they had begun in the summer of 1998. Others also called for his resignation. If Fischer were to remain in office, the historian Michael Wolffsohn argued, it would set a dangerous precedent that would mean former neo-Nazis might also become ministers in future. The Green environment minister Jürgen Trittin was also dragged into the affair after it emerged that, as a student at Göttingen University in 1977, he had defended the publication of a notorious "obituary" written by an anonymous "Mescalero" that expressed "secret joy" at the murder by the RAF of the federal prosecutor Siegfried Buback. What became known as the "Fischer affair" quickly put, "the whole 1968 generation under the spotlight", as Daniel Cohn-Bendit put it.[15]

Some—in particular former members of the student movement—saw in the "Fischer affair" an attempt to discredit the New Left as a whole. They argued that Adenauer's West Germany was a deeply authoritarian society and that the student movement had helped to deepen democracy in West Germany and even "re-founded" the Federal Republic. The former West Berlin SDS member Christian Semler, now a commentator at the *taz* who had criticised Fischer's foreign policy, defended him from what he called "68er bashing."[16] The APO, Semler said, was radically democratic. The problem was not that it was totalitarian, as some on the right now alleged, but that it was too utopian.[17] But other former left-activists admitted that the student movement—and certainly its offshoots in the 1970s—had had anti-liberal, anti-democratic and anti-western tendencies.[18] One of the sharpest critics of Fischer, in fact, was his old friend and comrade from Revolutionary Struggle, Thomas Schmid, now at the *Frankfurter Allgemeine Zeitung*, a bastion of German conservatism. Schmid said the movement to which he had once belonged was totalitarian and wanted to destroy democracy through the use of violence.[19] Ralf Dahrendorf, who had been a prominent critic of Dutschke in 1968, distinguished between the student movement itself, which he said was democratic, and the successor groups of the 1970s, including Fischer's "Spontis", which he said were simply violent for violence's sake.[20] Dahrendorf pointed out that the photos of Fischer beating up a policeman were taken not during the era of Adenauer but that of Willy Brandt—whose portrait now hung in Fischer's office in the foreign ministry.

By the time Fischer finally testified on 16 January, however, his poll ratings had dropped only slightly despite the media furore. It seemed that Germany had reconciled itself to the 1968 generation's past. In court, he evaded most of the questions put to him, saying he did not remember what happened 25 years earlier. He denied—but was later forced to admit—that the RAF terrorist Margrit Schiller had visited the "Spontis" at their commune in Frankfurt in 1973. The following day, Fischer was questioned in the *Bundestag* and was asked whether he had met Carlos. He denied once again that he had ever thrown Molotov cocktails and defended the student movement and its offshoots. "1968 and what followed led to more freedom, not less freedom, in this country," he said.[21] Backed up by Schröder, Fischer rode out the storm. Klein, meanwhile, was sentenced to nine years in prison.

Ultimately, the reason so many members of the post-war generation had gone to such extremes—from beating up policemen to kidnapping business leaders—was that, going back to the beginning of the student movement, they had seen the Federal Republic as a fascist state. This—the continuity thesis—was the 1968 generation's real mistake. One of the few former members of the student movement to admit this during the "Fischer affair" was Daniel Cohn-Bendit, who had also known Hans-Joachim Klein and testified in his trial. Fischer did not say that the continuity thesis was wrong, but rather that the Federal Republic had changed since the sixties, not least because of the student movement's own actions. Like Fischer, Cohn-Bendit saw the militancy of the revolutionary left as a response to what they perceived as the developing fascism of the Federal Republic. But unlike Fischer he said that that had been a mistake:

For us Auschwitz was a kind of madness that tormented our thoughts. The militant, militaristic manner of the police provoked false associations. And that made any kind of resistance legitimate.[22]

Cohn-Bendit said Jürgen Habermas had been right about the "left-wing fascism" of the student movement. It had from the beginning been anti-authoritarian and libertarian but also authoritarian and totalitarian. His generation therefore bore a "moral responsibility" for the left-wing terrorism of the 1970s.[23] At the same time, Cohn-Bendit said, the 1968 generation had also helped to "civilise an authoritarian society."[24] He said the fact that Fischer had become foreign minister—and remained in office—was a symbol of reconciliation between the generations in Germany and "a blessing for this country". At some point, he said, the past should be allowed to pass away, even in Germany.

This, of course, was exactly what Ernst Nolte had argued in relation to the Nazi past during the *Historikerstreit*.[25] In fact, the debate about the place of 1968 in German history directly paralleled earlier debates about the place of the Third Reich in it. The post-war generation, some commentators pointed out, was now using the same kinds of arguments to explain their involvement in the student movement as its parents' generation had used to evade their responsibility for Nazism.[26] The *Achtundsechziger*, in other words, now found themselves playing the same role that the "perpetrator generation" had once played. Again and again they had pointed out the continituies between Nazism and the Federal Republic. Now others were pointing out the continuities between Nazism and the *Achtundsechziger* themselves.

Not least because of the biographies of its leading figures like Joschka Fischer, the "red-green" government had to be seen to unambiguously support the American government in its response to the terrorist attacks on the United States. By the time of September 11, Germany also no longer had the option of taking a back seat as it had done earlier in the post-Cold War era. Since the Kosovo war, which was not only the first time it had sent troops into combat since World War II but also the first time in the post-war era that it had acted as an *Ordnungsmacht*, Germany had begun to play a greater role in resolving conflicts around the world. Although this process had begun during the presidency of Bill Clinton, it had continued apace after the election as president in 2000 of George W. Bush, whose administration appeared to be sceptical of the kind of humanitarian intervention to which the Clinton administration had been committed, which it regarded as "nation-building". "I don't like genocide and I don't like ethnic cleansing," Bush had said in a television interview in January 2000. "But the president must set clear parameters as to where troops ought to be used and where they ought not to be used."[27]

Perhaps the most remarkable of all the places in the world where Germany had by the time of September 11 begun to play a more active role was the Middle East. Germany had provided financial support to Israel since the Adenauer era but had also, through the European Union, become a major provider of aid to the Palestinian Authority, which had been created in 1994 as part of the Oslo Agreement between Israel and the PLO. By 2000, the peace process that President Clinton had brokered in the 1990s had stalled. That autumn, after Ariel Sharon made a controversial visit to the Temple Mount in Jerusalem, violence escalated. The formerly anti-Zionist Joschka Fischer might have seemed like an unlikely figure to win the trust of the Israelis, but his unique political journey, and in particular the engagement with the Nazi past that formed such a key part of his political persona, enabled him to do things in the Middle East that no previous German foreign minister had done.

Fischer's own views on the Middle East had come almost full circle since he had attended the Fatah conference in Algiers in 1969. He would later say that after the Six-Day War in 1967 he had struggled to reconcile his consciousness of German responsibility for the Shoah with an anti-Zionist position.[28] Influenced by Daniel Cohn-Bendit, he had adopted the position of the Israeli anti-capitalist group Matzpen.[29] Although he denied that he had ever questioned Israel's right to existence, the shock of Entebbe made him uncomfortable even with what he would later call a "post-Zionist" position and brought him to the conclusion that "there can be no ambiguity" about Israel.[30] "It was clear to me after that that anti-Zionism was ultimately the same thing as anti-Semitism," he would later write.[31] He had publicly defended Israel at the time of its invasion of Lebanon in 1982 and by the time he became foreign minister in 1998 he had reconciled himself to Adenauer's pro-Israeli position as well as to Adenauer's commitment to the *Westbindung*. In practical terms, this meant a strong commitment to Israel's security as well as an acceptance of the Palestinians' right to self-determination.

Largely through Fischer's personal intervention, Germany took a more active role in the Middle East conflict under the "red-green" government than it ever had before. Germany, which by the nineties had become Israel's second largest trading partner after the United States, continued to define its Middle East policy within the framework of the European Union as it had done under the Kohl government. But, as violence in the Middle East escalated from the autumn of 2000 onwards, Fischer also began to act as an ad hoc mediator between Israel and the Palestinians, a role that was unprecedented for a German foreign minister. In June 2001, Fischer travelled to Israel to meet with both the Israeli prime minister Ariel Sharon and the Palestinian Authority president Yasser Arafat, who Fischer had first seen in person at the Fatah conference in Algiers in 1969. On the day he arrived, a suicide bomb attack at the Dolphinarium disco in Tel Aviv killed 21 people, mostly teenagers. After shuttling between Arafat and Sharon in the days following the attack, Fischer helped to negotiate a temporary cease-fire between the Israelis and Palestinians.[32]

During the following weeks and months, Fischer travelled back to the Middle East and continued to mediate between Arafat and Sharon, leading eventually to the resumption of direct talks between the two sides.[33] The following April, Fischer presented a seven-point "idea paper" for a new European peace plan for the Middle East, an attempt to revitalise the Middle East peace process that led eventually to the three-phase "Road Map" agreed by Israel and the Palestinians in 2003.[34] Gerhard Schröder, who was less interested in the Middle East, responded to the Fischer paper, which included a "security component," by suggesting he would be prepared to send German troops to the region as part of multi-national peacekeeping force.

Germany also continued to play an active role in the Balkans. Although Kosovo had been stabilised, the ethnic conflicts in the region had by 2001 spread to neighbouring Macedonia, where fighting had broken out between ethnic Albanian paramilitaries and the government. Fischer was initially worried that he would face another big battle within his party to commit German troops to a NATO operation in Macedonia, which was first suggested by the British foreign secretary Robin Cook in 2000.[35] But after a visit to Macedonia in the spring of 2001, Fischer decided that the participation of the *Bundeswehr* was essential in order to maintain Germany's credibility.[36] In July 2001, after a ceasefire was agreed in Macedonia, NATO sent troops to the country to collect weapons from the Albanian rebels in a mission codenamed Operation Essential Harvest. The following month, Germany agreed—after another heated *Bundestag* debate—to contribute 500 soldiers as part of the 4,500–strong British-led mission. At the end of the 30–day operation, it was Fischer, once again the advocate for humanitarian intervention, who urged the United States and Europe to create a new NATO-led force with a United Nations mandate to keep Macedonia from descending further into civil war.[37]

Perhaps as a consequence of the more active role in international affairs that it had begun to play under the "red-green" government and in particular since the Kosovo war, Germany now also began to call more loudly than previously for a permanent seat on the United Nations Security Council—what one foreign policy analyst would later describe as the "modern day version of a 'place in the sun,'" a reference to Bismarck's demand for a German empire in Africa at the end of the nineteenth century.[38] Ironically, Fischer had himself explicitly warned against a German demand for a Security Council seat in the early nineties before Srebrenica changed his mind on military intervention. In his 1994 book *The German Risk*, he had said that a demand for a permanent seat on the Security Council would inevitably follow a "re-militarisation" of German foreign policy.

By the autumn of 2001, Germany had developed a new, more activist foreign policy that had carefully straddled continuity and change, *Bündnistreue* and greater "responsibility". But once again, just as Fischer appeared to have completed one part of his political journey, yet another dramatic change took place that would force him to think again. The terrorist attacks of September 11 would present a radically different challenge from the problems in the Balkans in the nineties. Until then, Fischer's thinking, from Entebbe to Srebrenica, had been guided largely by the lessons of the Nazi past. But in the radically different world that would emerge out of the terrorist attacks on the United States, German history provided fewer obvious answers.

Gerhard Schröder said later that he knew instantly, as he watched the World Trade Centre collapse on television, that "nothing would be the same as it was before."[39] Schröder, whose wife Doris had lived in New York for two years, said he was deeply moved and cried as he watched television that afternoon.[40] Quickly, however, his thoughts shifted to the political implications of the attacks. Schröder wrote later that he felt the attack on America was a "declaration of war against the whole civilised world" and decided immediately that "Germany needed to act as decisively as possible and fulfil its responsibility to NATO just as decisively."[41] The following day, Schröder told the *Bundestag* that he had spoken to President Bush and promised him "our unlimited—and I emphasise unlimited—solidarity".[42] At the same time, he confided in a colleague that he was worried that Bush was about to "start something that will get us all in a mess."[43]

Joschka Fischer shared Schröder's fears. According to Ludger Volmer, Fischer declared at a meeting in the evening of September 11 that "this is the first Huntington war", a reference to the American political scientist Samuel P. Huntington, who in an influential book published five years earlier had predicted a "clash of civilisations" between the West and Islam.[44] A week after September 11, Fischer travelled to Washington, where he met with President Bush, Secretary of State Colin Powell and Deputy Secretary of Defence Paul Wolfowitz. He was alarmed by the new mood in the United States, where the Bush administration and in particular "neo-conservatives" like Wolfowitz seemed not just to be planning an attack on Afghanistan, where al-Qaeda was based, but also seemed to have further targets in mind, in particular Iraq.

Fischer says the neo-conservatives in Washington immediately reminded him of the left-wing ideologues he had known in West Germany back in the seventies. "Because of my own radical past I could smell it immediately," he says. "It all seemed very familiar to me."[45] Fischer was torn. On the one hand, he felt passionately that Germany should be aligned with United States and wanted to avoid a transatlantic estrangement. But at the same time, he was convinced that a war with Iraq, even with United Nations Security Council approval, would be a disaster. "As a member of the Vietnam generation, I knew America could make great mistakes with fatal consequences," he says. "And from the beginning I knew this was one of those mistakes."[46]

Fischer and Schröder hoped that the United States would choose to respond to the terrorist attacks with non-military means. But despite their reservations, both of them appear to have decided immediately that if the United States did decide to invade Afghanistan they would support it—and German participation in it. At the end of September, Germany agreed to take over the leadership of a new NATO force in Macedonia—a move that some observers interpreted as an attempt to avoid involvement in military operations in response to the September 11 attacks.[47] But both Fischer and Schröder would later say that they had by then already decided to support German involvement in such operations. It was, as Schröder put it, "not a question of whether Germany would take part in military action but exclusively a question of how."[48] However, as in the case of Kosovo and Macedonia, deploying German troops to Afghanistan once again required the approval of the *Bundestag*.

In some ways, it was easier than in the autumn of 1998 when the "red-green" government had come to power. The war in Kosovo had established a de facto precedent for German participation in "out of area" operations—although Fischer had insisted at the time that it did not. Moreover, the humanitarian work the *Bundeswehr* had done in Kosovo and Macedonia had helped to soften the left's innate suspicion of the military. "The ice had been broken," says Rezzo Schlauch, the Greens' joint parliamentary leader.[49] In addition, even most Greens recognised that the United States had a right to self-defence. On 12 September, the UN Security Council had passed resolution 1368 which authorised the United States to take military action against states such as Afghanistan that had supported the terrorists who had carried out the September 11 attacks—a mandate in international law that the Kosovo war never had. On the other hand, this was not a primarily humanitarian intervention to prevent genocide but a shooting war to remove a tyrannical regime—a problem above all for the Greens. According to Ludger Volmer, the discussion this time was not so much about whether the war was legal and legitimate as it had been over Kosovo but about whether it was smart and effective.[50]

For the next two months, the Greens agonized over Afghanistan as they had done over Kosovo. After returning from his visit to Washington a week after September 11, Fischer attempted to woo the Greens' grass roots. This time, there was no genocide to which Fischer could point. But as well as invoking the principle of *Bündnistreue*, he once again also made the case for German involvement in military action in moral terms. In an interview with the *taz*—the Greens' favourite daily newspaper—he said he wanted to face the "totalitarian challenge" presented by al-Qaeda together with the Greens and said the debate within the party was "important for the whole country."[51] But, he went on, "this kind of terrorism, which consciously mass murders civilians, has to be fought politically and economically but also militarily." To refuse to assist the United States in military action would be a "historic mistake" that would "break a 50–year long line of integration with the West that stretches from Adenauer through Brandt to Schröder."[52]

At the beginning of October, following the invocation of Article 5 of the North Atlantic Treaty, which in effect defined the attack on America as an attack on all NATO states, Operation Enduring Freedom began with the American and British bombing of targets in Afghanistan. Air attacks continued for the next month as the Northern Alliance, together with US Special Forces, began operations on the ground. At the beginning of November, as the ground forces prepared to move towards Kabul, Schröder called for Germany to provide military support in the war on terror. Unlike Fischer, he framed the question not in moral terms but in terms of *Realpolitik*. The language, in fact, was very similar to the language he had used during the Kosovo war. "By making this contribution, the unified and sovereign Germany will be meeting its growing responsibilities," he told the *Bundestag*.[53]

With the Christian Democrats in favour of supporting the war, Schröder did not technically need the support of the Greens. He hinted that if he did not have a "red-green" majority—and it would take only a handful of Social Democrat and Green members of parliament opposing him—he would dissolve the coalition and either form a grand coalition with the Christian Democrats or hold a new election. But with a "red-green" majority looking in doubt, he decided to take a radical step and call a motion of confidence in conjunction with the vote on the Afghanistan deployment, thereby calling the rebels' bluff and forcing them to make a simple choice: support him on Afghanistan or end the "red-green" experiment after just two years in power. Helmut Schmidt had successfully used the same strategy in 1982 to bring his own party in line, although it had only won him an extra seven months in power.

The gamble worked. On 13 November—the day the Northern Alliance entered Kabul—the *Bundestag* voted. With anti-war campaigners demonstrating outside the Reichstag, just enough Social Democrats and Greens voted for Schröder to give him a majority without the opposition. It cleared the way for a limited number of German troops to be used as part of Operation Enduring Freedom, including, as well as medical and support personnel, 100 members of the *Kommando Spezialkräfte* (KSK), a German special forces unit that had been created in 1996. It was the largest combat operation in the history of the Federal Republic and the first time that troops had been sent into combat outside Europe, although with the war now all but over, they would function largely in a defensive and protective role. Nevertheless, Schröder said it represented the beginning of a new era in which Germany would play a full military role in guaranteeing international security instead of providing exclusively financial support.[54]

Finally, a week later, the Greens met in Rostock for a party conference—a reprise of the fraught conference on Kosovo in Bielefeld in April 1999. Fischer was once again prepared to resign if defeated. Opponents once again accused him and his "Olive Greens" of being "warmongers". "Do you want total war?" shouted one delegate from the floor—an implicit reference to the famous speech made by Joseph Goebbels in 1943.[55] But in the end, after a ten-hour debate, the party once again endorsed Fischer and military action—this time by a two-thirds majority. It passed a convoluted resolution that "accepted" that Greens in the *Bundestag* had backed German participation in Operating Enduring Freedom without, however, endorsing their decision. It emphasized that although only four of its representatives had voted against Schröder in the *Bundestag*, another four were opposed to the Afghanistan mission but had voted for it to keep the coalition going. The Greens further insisted that despite their acquiescence, they remained bound by their "pacifist tradition"—a paragraph inserted at the insistence of Hans-Christian Ströbele, who led the internal opposition to Fischer and the "red-green" government. And in a subtle but significant difference to the language Schröder had used immediately after September 11, they said their attitude to the United States was one of "critical"—as opposed to "unlimited"—solidarity.[56] It was, as two German commentators put it, "dissent without consequences."[57]

The key concept according to which German participation in the Operation Enduring Freedom was justified by both Fischer and Schröder was the principle of *Bündnistreue*, or loyalty to the Atlantic alliance. For both Fischer and Schröder, the decisive factor which made

German participation in the operation inexorable was the invocation of Article 4 of the Atlantic Treaty—the basis of the *Westbindung*. Although Operation Enduring Freedom remained an American-led rather than a NATO operation, Article 4 made German participation in the war in Afghanistan even more essential than it had been in the intervention in Kosovo. Once again, there were the subtle differences between the way that Fischer and Schröder made the case for German participation in the American-led invasion of Afghanistan. Fischer tended to point to the dangers of a new kind of totalitarianism, whereas Schröder once again emphasised German "normality". But where Milosevic's policy of "ethnic cleansing" had provided an additional moral case for intervention in Kosovo, no such argument about preventing genocide in Afghanistan could be made. Therefore, in Afghanistan, the principle of "never alone" was the key determinant of German policy.[58]

Although Fischer and Schröder had, on the basis of this appeal to *Bündnistreue*, forced their parties into line, they remained under pressure, in particular to bring the conflict in Afghanistan onto a more multilateral footing. This pressure actually increased once the Americans had reached their initial aim of removing the Taliban regime in Kabul at the end of November. The month after the *Bundestag* approved the deployment of German troops to Afghanistan, Afghan leaders met at the Petersberg hotel on the Rhine near Bonn to plan the reconstruction of their country. They signed the so-called Bonn Agreement, which set up the Afghan Interim Authority (AIA) to manage the transition to post-Taliban democracy and a commission to create a new constitution and a supreme court. The Petersberg conference also created ISAF, the multi-national stabilisation force designed to support the provisional government in creating security in Kabul and its surroundings, which was approved by the UN Security Council at the end of December. With the UN mandate, the American-led operation in Afghanistan was put on a multilateral basis, which made it easier for Germany to participate as it had agreed to the previous month. It was a skilful piece of German diplomacy that reconciled *Bündnistreue* with Germany's traditional commitment to the United Nations, and Germany's international obligations with the needs of domestic public opinion. NATO subsequently also took over leadership of ISAF, further embedding the operation into Germany's multilateral framework.

With its participation in the American-led operation in Afghanistan, Germany had taken another dramatic step away from its non-military post-war tradition, albeit one that was once again forced by objective developments. This time Germany had not only sent troops into combat outside Europe for the first time, it had also taken part, not in a humanitarian intervention, but a full-scale war to remove a hostile regime. Crucially, however, Germany had once again acted in concert with its allies and in particular NATO—perhaps the most important aspect of the Federal Republic's multilateral tradition. In addition, the operation was in two senses more legitimate than Operation Allied Force. Firstly, it had a mandate from the United Nations. Secondly, it was a response to an attack on a member of NATO. In fact, because of the invocation of Article 4 of the Atlantic Treaty, a German refusal to participate in the operation would have represented a dramatic, almost unthinkable, break with NATO—especially after Germany had participated in the intervention in Kosovo. In that sense, although Germany appeared at the end of 2001 to have gone further than ever in the use of military force, it could still claim to be a "civilian power".

But although Fischer and Schröder had for now managed to maintain the balancing act between international obligations and domestic pressure, that balancing act would become increasingly difficult during the "second phase" of the Bush administration's "war on terror". With the removal of the Taliban regime, the United States had achieved its initial objective. The United States and Germany differed over what to do next. The Germans wanted to shift the focus onto reconstruction in Afghanistan and also onto resolving other conflicts, such as that between the Israelis and the Palestinians. The Bush administration, however, clearly had other plans.

In the weeks after September 11, as the "red-green" government faced its second major foreign policy crisis, it also became clear that the attack on the World Trade Centre had, in fact, been planned in Germany—adding to the multiple ironies of a government with a history linked to the left-wing terrorism of the seventies facing a terrorist threat of its own. Mohammed Atta, the Egyptian-born ringleader of the 9/11 plot, had arrived in Hamburg as a graduate student in 1992 and had assembled around him a group of disaffected young men from the Middle East that would form the core of the group of nineteen that carried out the hijackings on September 11. The Hamburg cell took advantage not only of Germany's generous asylum policy but also of its lax anti-terror laws, which allowed terrorists to plan operations outside Germany with impunity. These laws had been conceived as a reaction against excessive police powers under Nazism, but had also survived the left-wing terrorism of the 1970s. "In recoiling from its own extremist past," the American journalist Lawrence Wright would later observe, "Germany inadvertently became the host of a new totalitarian movement."[59]

The job of tightening Germany's anti-terror laws after September 11 would fall to, of all people, Otto Schily, the interior minister who had made his name defending terrorists like Gudrun Ensslin in the 1970s. Schily had always had a more distanced relationship with his terrorist clients than some of his colleagues—he had never, for example, been convicted of smuggling notes out of Stammheim like Hans-Christian Ströbele. Nevertheless, he had, like the other members of the legal team, mounted a "political defence" of the RAF and become an outspoken critic of the surveillance state. In particular, he had repeatedly drawn parallels between the Federal Republic and the Nazi state and argued that through their actions the RAF were exercising a "right to resistance" in West Germany.

A somewhat aloof, irascible figure who, like Horst Mahler, was already in his thirties and working as a lawyer by the time the student movement got going, Schily had never quite fitted the culture of the *Achtundsechziger*. He had been the only member of the Greens to wear a tie in the *Bundestag* and, if anything, been even more of a "realist" than Joschka Fischer. After leaving the Greens in 1989, he had moved to the right wing of the Social Democrats and seemed a natural choice as interior minister in 1998. After months of negotiations, he had finally reached a compromise with the opposition on the new citizenship law—one of the "red-green" government's few successful, albeit watered down, reforms. He had also proposed a new, more open immigration law that would encourage skilled workers to come to Germany.[60]

After September 11, Schily responded to the terrorist threat with a series of tough new security measures that shocked many on the left. By the end of 2001 he had introduced two packages of anti-terror measures that made changes to over 100 laws.[61] They gave the foreign and domestic intelligence services sweeping new powers to intercept phone conversations, obtain information from internet service providers and to obtain details from banks about financial transactions involving possible terror suspects. Where, just a few months earlier, Schily had proposed liberalising immigration law, he now proposed tightening it, extending data collection on foreign citizens in Germany and making deportations easier. He also proposed introducing biometric passports and finally changed the criminal law to close the loophole that allowed terrorists to plan operations that would take place outside Germany.

Most of the new powers were ones that law enforcement agencies in many other western countries took for granted. However, in Germany, where the spectre of the SS state, and the Stasi state, loomed, they alarmed many people. Many argued that Schily's anti-terror measures were creating another intrusive "big brother" state—echoing the arguments that Schily had himself made in the 1970s. Among those making such arguments now was Hans-Christian Ströbele, who had represented Andreas Baader while Schily represented Ensslin. For Ströbele, Schily's transformation into the embodiment of law and order was incomprehensible. "I ask myself, why, why, why?" he said.[62] Even Gerhart Baum, the former Free Democrat interior minister, said Schily's anti-terror laws were the "most serious attack on civil liberties that I have ever seen."[63] Schily dismissed such criticisms, arguing that freedom was meaningless without security and that the state had a responsibility under the Basic Law to protect people from crime.[64] Schily said his critics' fears about the anti-terror laws were misplaced. "The strange misconception that the dangers we face come from the state, from the police and from the law and not from those who were responsible for September 11 and other crimes—that is what I find scary."[65]

Whether or not Schily was right about the correct response to the threat posed by Islamist terrorism in the twenty-first century, it was an extraordinary turnaround for a man who had once himself defended terrorists. There was, in Schily's transformation from opponent of state power to the embodiment of law and order, something almost eerie. He would later, after further terrorist attacks in Europe, also strengthen the BKA, whose expansion in the seventies he had vehemently opposed. What was extraordinary was not just how much his views had changed but the fact that he spoke as if he had never held different views in the first place. Unlike Joschka Fischer, who had a tendency to mythologise every step in his own political metamorphosis, the much more private Schily simply refused to discuss his previous life. It was reminiscent of the description by Alexander and Margarete Mitscherlich of the attitude of Germans in the immediate post-war period. Like them, Schily seemed to act as if the past had simply never happened.

Horst Mahler, meanwhile, had a somewhat different take on September 11. The following day, he wrote another polemic—entitled "Independence Day Live"—in which he celebrated the spectacular attack on the United States. For Mahler, it was not terrorism at all but an act of self-defence by an oppressed people that would bring about "the end of the American century and the end of global capitalism." The "air attack", as he called it, had "struck the heart of this beast and paralysed it for a day. The symbolic power of this military operation shattered the complacency of western civilisation which is based on hypocrisy."[66]

It was not yet clear who had carried out the attack on the United States. But whoever it was, to Mahler it was part of the same war between Anglo-American capitalism and the oppressed peoples of the world that he himself was engaged in. According to Mahler's version of history, this war—of which Germany was a prime, but not the only target—had been running since 1914. The representatives of American capital, led by the Jews and assisted by collaborators around the world, including Germany's own "vassal regime", aimed to

secure the hegemony of the USA as a guarantor of predatory free trade by destroying the German *Reich* for eternity and decimating the great and powerful German *Volk* in the centre of Europe, and, subsequently, by repopulating it, wiping it out as a cultural nation and a world historical power factor.[67]

Now, for the first time in this long war, the "globalists" had suffered a defeat on their own—American—soil.

The Cold War, Mahler wrote in another essay written the following month calling for a "global Vietnam", had allowed the United States to disguise its plan for world domination as a struggle against communism. But with the end of the Cold War and 9/11, its real aims had been exposed:

The flag of smoke rising from the towers of the World Trade Centre could be seen around the world. It inscribed in the sky the question, "What is the reason the peoples of the world are attacking globalism on American soil?" This question is now being answered with unrelenting rigour. The answer will reduce to ruins the walls that have been built around our thinking. It is the end of the USA as a global power, whose rule depends not on an arsenal of material weapons but on a state of consciousness.[68]

For Mahler, who had also opposed the Kosovo war, World War III had begun in earnest with the US air strikes on Afghanistan. What he called the "Judeo-American Imperium" was intent on a "global genocide" against all peoples of the world.[69] He called for the Germans and all the other oppressed peoples of the world to resist. "Any attack anywhere on earth or even in space directed against American installations, functionaries or collaborators," he wrote, were "acts of revenge permitted by the laws of war."[70] Mahler was subsequently prosecuted under German hate-crime laws for his remarks about 9/11. His anti-American rhetoric, which sharpened after September 11, expressed an extreme version of Rudi Dutschke's view of the Germans as victims of American imperialism.

In the summer of 2000, Mahler had opened up another front in his war against his former comrades from the student movement by joining the far-right NPD. After its electoral successes in the late 1960s, culminating in Baden-Württemberg in 1968, the NPD had disappeared into obscurity for two decades and then began to re-emerge after German reunification, particularly in eastern Germany. It now had around 6,500 members and was being closely watched by the *Bundesverfassungsschutz*, Germany's domestic intelligence agency.[71] Though the NPD remained electorally insignificant in comparison to other far-right parties like the *Deutsche Volksunion* (DVU), it had close links to neo-Nazis, whom it could mobilise for demonstrations and rallies, and was believed by some to be responsible for racial attacks.[72]

Although Mahler had much in common with the NPD—it also campaigned against American imperialism, globalisation and immigration—he did not believe in political parties. Now, as in 1968, Mahler believed in overthrowing the entire political system, not attempting to work within it. Instead of standing for elections, he hoped to build a movement—a "national extra-parliamentary opposition" (*Nationale Ausserparlamentarische Opposition*), or "NAPO". Actually, as he himself admitted, Mahler had joined the NPD for one reason alone, which was that Otto Schily wanted to ban it as unconstitutional.[73] Mahler saw in the impending proceedings before Germany's highest court a chance for even greater publicity for his ideas, and, perhaps even more importantly, a chance for a head-to-head battle with Schily, whom he once called his friend and now called "scum".[74]

The calls for a ban of the NPD had begun after a series of racist and anti-Semitic attacks in Germany in 2000.[75] Although the NPD was not implicated in any of the attacks, it had been increasingly visible, demonstrating in Berlin and even, in a provocative evocation of the Nazis' torchlit parades, marching through the Brandenburg Gate. Schily was initially sceptical about a ban.[76] But after an arson attack on a synagogue in Düsseldorf in October 2000 (which was initially assumed to have been the work of the far right but later turned out to have been carried out by two Arab youths), he changed his mind. In January 2001, supported by conservatives like Günter Beckstein, the hardline Bavarian interior minister, he officially applied to the Constitutional Court, arguing that the NPD was anti-democratic and therefore unconstitutional under Article 21 of the Basic Law.[77] The NPD appointed Mahler, who, in any case, regarded the Basic Law as a "temporary document for the transition period until the ability of the German *Reich* to function is restored," as its lawyer.

If the application was successful, it would be the first time a political party had been outlawed in the Federal Republic since the KPD in 1956. The debate about banning the NPD was reminiscent not only of the debate about banning the KPD but also the debate in the 1970s about banning left-wing radicals from the civil service.[78] At that time, the 1968 generation was on the receiving end of such bans. This time, with Schily driving the ban and Mahler fighting it, it was on both sides. Inevitably, the spectre of Nazism also hung over the debate. Proponents of the ban argued that the NPD resembled the Nazi party and threatened democracy in Germany—the "Weimar argument". Opponents of the ban in turn argued that the real lesson of Nazism was the need to protect freedom of speech and that the place to defeat the NPD was not in court but at the ballot box.

At the beginning of 2002, shortly before the court was about to begin hearing the case, it emerged that several witnesses who were due to testify against the NPD were in fact intelligence agents who had infiltrated the party. One of them was Wolfgang Frenz, a senior party official, whose anti-Semitic remarks the government had pointed to as evidence of the NPD's unconstitutionality. Schily came under pressure to resign, not least of all from Hans-Christian Ströbele, who had also assisted Schily in defending Mahler in the 1970s and who insisted that, of the three of them, he was the only one who had remained true to his principles.[79] The Constitutional Court postponed the case, which seemed likely to collapse, until after the general election due to take place in September 2002. It was a triumph for Mahler and for the NPD. "You cannot ban Germany" would become its election slogan.

Joschka Fischer would also come to see 9/11 as the beginning of a new era, albeit a very different one from the one about which Mahler fantasised. Fischer entitled his book about the challenges of the post-9/11 world *The Return of History*—a reference to Francis Fukuyama's theory that history had ended with the triumph of capitalism over communism in 1989. The terrorist attacks, Fischer said, made it clear that the West now faced a threat from a new kind of totalitarianism in the form of Islamic terrorism, which made every conflict around the world, however remote, a strategic one. With the threat of terrorism, the West was in danger of being plunged into what he called a "permanent state of emergency"—an echo of the "undeclared state of emergency" that the student movement, haunted by the spectre of Nazism, had feared in 1968.[80]

September 11 also changed his views about Europe. In his Humboldt speech in 2000, he had described European integration as a response to the continent's own troubled history. He argued that, with the creation of the European Union, the continent had quietly but decisively rejected the system of balance-of-power politics that had emerged after the Peace of Westphalia in 1648 and culminated in the disaster of World War II. In its place, Europe had created a new system of co-operation and shared sovereignty—and in the process solved the "German question" once and for all. He almost seemed to believe that with what he called the "completion" of the process of European integration, Europe would reach its own version of Francis Fukuyama's "end of history".

The shock of September 11 changed that. Fischer remained an evangelist for European integration and in particular for the draft constitution that had emerged out of the debate he had stimulated with his Humboldt speech in the summer of 2000. But instead of focusing primarily on Europe's internal development, he now focused on its "strategic dimension"—its security and its relationship with its neighbours. He argued that terrorism was, in fact, an even more urgent issue for Europe than it was for the United States because of the greater proximity of the Middle East to Europe. "The decisive question for the security of Europe in the 21st century is whether the Mediterranean will be a sea of co-operation or a sea of confrontation," he wrote.[81] As a result, Fischer now rejected the idea of a "core Europe" that he had endorsed at the time of the Humboldt speech and argued for the accession of Turkey to the EU for strategic reasons. "After September 11 and in view of the strategic danger that emanates from the Middle East region that neighbours Europe, the integration and modernisation of Turkey is even more important for Europe's security interests than Turkey's military power was for the security of Western Europe during the Cold War."[82]

As Fischer began to view Europe in increasingly strategic terms, he apparently also retrospectively revised his thinking about the justification for the military intervention in Kosovo. At the time of the war, Fischer had argued that Germany's history gave it a special responsibility to intervene to prevent genocide taking place in Europe and was criticised in Germany for "instrumentalising" Auschwitz. Several years on, Fischer argued in strategic as well as moral or humanitarian terms, in particular pointing out the dangers for the stability of the region and the possibility of a war involving the entire Balkans.[83] In other words, Europe and especially Germany had not just had a moral responsibility to act in Kosovo, but also needed to do so for reasons of *Realpolitik*.

But although he was apparently thinking in increasingly strategic terms, Fischer's view of international affairs remained an idealist one based on the lessons of German history, as it had been since he entered parliament. In fact, whereas earlier he had tried to teach those lessons to Germans and Europeans, he now seemed to want to teach them to the entire world and in particular the United States, where neo-conservatives seemed to be increasingly dominating foreign policy. Fischer said that neo-conservatism—by which he really meant a unilateral pursuit of American national interest—was in fact alien to the American foreign policy tradition, which was rooted in a rejection of European balance-of-power politics. After the shock of 9/11, he said, "the intellectual margins became the mainstream" in America.[84] Ironically, in other words, the United States had adopted the Westphalian system just as Europe, which had created it, had rejected it. Fischer urged the United States to now follow Europe's lead in rejecting balance-of-power politics. "The choice is whether to go back to the Westphalian system or move forward to a global system of co-operation," he said.[85]

The implication was that the rest of the world needed to catch up with Europe and in particular with Germany, which, because of its history, had advanced further than any other country in rejecting hegemonic ambitions. In particular, Fischer said the European Union should be seen as "a model for the other regions of the world in the twenty-first century."[86] Just as the concept of "constitutional patriotism" was a model for other nation states, so European integration, whose justification was for Fischer itself derived from the Holocaust, was now also a model for the rest of the world. In a way somewhat reminiscent of Emanuel Geibel's poem "Germany's Mission", Fischer seemed to want everyone to learn from German's tragic history just as his own generation—the children of the "perpetrator generation"—had done. For Fischer, in other words, Auschwitz was no longer just Germany's *raison d'état*: it was the whole world's.

13

A GERMAN WAY

In the summer of 2002, things were not looking good for the "red-green" government. With a general election due to take place in September, Gerhard Schröder's chances of being re-elected for what he liked to call a "second half" looked slim. An apparently Europe-wide rightward shift in public opinion had already swept out the centre-left governments in France, Italy and the Netherlands that at the beginning of Gerhard Schröder's chancellorship had seemed to signal a new progressive hegemony across the continent. The economic outlook in Germany was worsening and unemployment—which Schröder had himself made the acid test of his government—had hit four million at the beginning of the year.

After the end of the war in Kosovo, Schröder had attempted a fresh start in economic policy, this time taking the government in a more centrist direction. The new finance minister, Hans Eichel, began a series of cost-cutting measures and reforms of Germany's tax system and welfare state that he hoped would stimulate the economy. At the end of 1999, the government had been given some breathing space when the Christian Democrats were engulfed by a party financing scandal that forced Wolfgang Schäuble, Helmut Kohl's successor as party leader, to step down and sent them tumbling in the opinion polls. But by the beginning of 2002, with a new leader, Angela Merkel, who had grown up in the GDR, the Christian Democrats had recovered and had once again overtaken the Social Democrats in the opinion polls. That summer, the defence minister, Rudolf Scharping, a key figure in Schröder's "war cabinet" in 1999, was forced to resign after he was pictured in a women's magazine on vacation in Majorca with his new girlfriend just as the *Bundeswehr* was about to begin its mission in

Macedonia. He was replaced by Peter Struck, until then the Social Democrats' parliamentary leader.

The main cause of the loss of popular support for Schröder, however, was his government's failure to create jobs. Schröder had come to power promising economic renewal after the stagnation of the Kohl era. On taking office, he had gone so far as to say he did not deserve to be re-elected if he had not significantly reduced unemployment, which then stood at 3.9 million, or 10.2 per cent. Hans Eichel's tax reforms had initially seemed promising. But as the dot-com bubble burst and Germany's economy took a turn for the worse, unemployment had continued to climb. As Schröder's government's first term came to an end, he asked his friend Peter Hartz, the personnel director of Volkswagen, to chair a commission to look into ways to reform the labour market and report back in mid-August—just five weeks before the election.

As the election approached, it looked as if the "red-green" coalition was about to come to an end after just one term in office. The SPD was consistently trailing the Christian Democrats in the opinion polls, which reported that the SPD had lost support particularly among its traditional working-class voters and in eastern Germany. Although Schröder's personal popularity ratings remained high, the Christian Democrats' candidate, the Bavarian Edmund Stoiber, was rapidly catching up. Stoiber's reputation was built on Bavaria's mix of economic dynamism and social conservatism—the so-called "laptops and lederhosen" model. At a meeting in May, one senior Social Democrat wondered whether they could pull a rabbit out of a hat to save the "red-green" coalition. Another senior Social Democrat replied that they needed not one but three rabbits. The following day, Franz Münterfering, the SPD general-secretary and Schröder's campaign manager, told journalists off-the-record, "There is no rabbit."[1]

By the beginning of August 2002, however, it had also become clear that, as Fischer and Schröder had feared since shortly after September 11, the United States was planning to invade Iraq. In his State of the Union address at the end of January 2002, President Bush had said that Iraq, together with Iran and North Korea, formed an "axis of evil". The day after the speech, Schröder and Fischer, who happened to be on a visit to Washington at the time, met with Bush in the White House. During the meeting, Iraq did not come up. At a dinner that evening, however, Schröder attempted to explain to Bush in diplomatic language that Europeans, because of their history, had a "special relationship to war" and also said he believed that the West should not divert resources from the ongoing "war on terror".[2] At the end of the discussion, Schröder believed Bush had assured him he would consult the Europeans before he took any action against Iraq.[3] Bush, meanwhile, believed Schröder had told him he "understood" the United States might have to go to war.[4]

In subsequent meetings during 2002, Schröder and Fischer attempted to impress upon their American counterparts their reservations about an attack on Iraq, which opinion polls showed a vast majority of Germans opposed.[5] At a meeting in Washington in April, Fischer explained to Colin Powell that an attack on Iraq would endanger the Social Democrats' and Greens' chances in the upcoming elections. In May, when President Bush visited Berlin, 100,000 people protested against him—a reflection of the animosity towards him in Germany less than a year after September 11. At a press conference after speaking at the *Bundestag*, Bush declared that he had no plans to invade Iraq. But Schröder was not so sure. The following month, Bush outlined a new doctrine of military pre-emption in a speech at West Point, which seemed to make military action both more likely and imminent.[6] Schröder and his advisers began to discuss how he might move from his promise of "unconditional solidarity" with the United States in September 2001 to opposition to military action in Iraq.[7]

At some point during 2002, though it is not clear exactly when, Schröder appears to have decided to oppose an invasion of Iraq, regardless of the circumstances under which such an invasion might take place. He later said that the decisive factor in his decision was the way that the arguments used by the Bush administration to justify the invasion appeared to shift during the course of 2002. Initially, it had claimed a link existed between Iraq and al-Qaeda. Schröder says that, if the United States had been able to prove such a connection, he would have argued for German participation in military action, though whether he would have been able to persuade his party or the country is another question.[8] However, that claim was subsequently dropped and the focus shifted to Saddam Hussein's alleged possession of weapons of mass destruction, which, however, could not yet be proven.[9] That, for Schröder, left only the argument that Saddam Hussein's regime was an evil one which the West should remove on principle.

"It was clear to me that that wasn't enough to justify an invervention," he says.[10]

Whenever the decision was taken, by the beginning of August, Schröder's mind was made up. On 5 August, he formally launched his election campaign—three weeks earlier than originally planned—with a rally on the Opernplatz in Hanover. There, in front of 5,000 supporters, he declared that:

The era in which we look to America and others as a model for our economy is over. The way things are in the United States, with bankruptcies and the exploitation of little people who now have to worry about who will take care of them when they are old—I say to you, that is not the German Way that we want for our people.[11]

He further elaborated on the concept of the "German Way"—the "Deutscher Weg"—and finally came to the subject of Iraq:

We want to show solidarity. [...] But I will not lead this country into adventures. [...] And in regard to the discussion about a military intervention in Iraq, I say this: I warn you not to speculate about war and military action and I say to those who have plans in this situation: anyone who wants to do this needs not just to know how they are going to get in, but needs a political conception for what happens next. Therefore I say: pressure on Saddam Hussein, yes, but playing around with war and military intervention... I can only warn against it. We won't be part of it.[12]

The audience at the Opernplatz cheered. "Thank God," said Uwe-Karsten Heye, Schröder's spokesperson.[13]

The speech in Hanover was unprecedented in the context of post-war German foreign policy. Never before in the history of the Federal Republic had a chancellor so publicly distanced himself from the United States. It was also the first time a post-war German chancellor had used such openly nationalist rhetoric. For half a century, the Federal Republic had sought to submerge its national interest within the broader interests of Europe or the West. Hans-Dietrich Genscher, for example, had famously said that Germany had no national interests apart from European interests. Schröder, on the other hand, was now asserting not only that there was such a thing as a German national interest but that it was at odds with that of the United States. What made Schröder's speech even more extraordinary was the break it represented with the foreign policy of the "red-green" government up to that point, which had been distinguished by an emphasis on the importance of multilateralism and in particular the Atlantic alliance. Schröder had insisted on the principle of *Bündnistreue*, even where that meant taking unprecedented steps such as sending German troops into combat and where it created political problems within Schröder and Fischer's own parties, for example during the wars in Kosovo and in Afghanistan. Schröder could not have made it plainer that the period of "unconditional solidarity" with the United States after 9/11 was now over.

The concept of the "German Way" had been originally been thought up by Kajo Wasserhövel, a spin doctor who worked for Franz Müntefering, the general-secretary of the SPD and Schröder's election campaign manager.[14] With the SPD behind in the polls, Schröder's campaign team wanted to develop an election strategy that would crystallise the differences between themselves and the Christian Democrats. In particular, they wanted a slogan that would express Schröder's opposition to American plans to invade Iraq.[15] At a brainstorming session of campaign strategists and pollsters at the SPD campaign headquarters in Berlin a few days before the speech in Hanover, Wasserhövel had suggested the phrase, which Müntefering and others at the meeting liked.[16] Müntefering presented the concept to Schröder later that evening at a meeting of senior Social Democrats that also included cabinet ministers and several state prime ministers. They, in particular Schröder, liked it too.[17]

In using the concept of the "German Way" with its deliberate contrast with the "American Way", Schröder was striking an unmistakably nationalist tone, although he would later deny this was his intention. Looking back after he left office, he claimed that he had intended firstly, to contrast the German "social market economy" with the Anglo-Saxon free market economic model, and, secondly, to refer to "Willy Brandt's peace policy".[18] He said that, in foreign policy terms, he was attempting to draw a contrast not so much with the United States as with the opposition Christian Democrats, who had been less openly critical of American foreign policy.[19] Nevertheless, the search for a "German way", distinct in particular from western ideas and models, had been a key motif of German nationalism going back to the nineteenth century. It defined Germany in opposition to a Western Other and seemed to both be motivated by, and play upon, anti-western *ressentiment*. Specifically, by associating Germany with peace, and therefore by implication the United States with war, the concept of the "Deutscher Weg" represented a continuation of the nationalism of the peace movement of the eighties.

The *Deutscher Weg* inevitably also recalled the idea of a German *Sonderweg* or "special path," the aberrant historical trajectory which, according to some historians, had diverged from the normative development of western European states, had rejected the Enlightenment, and which had culminated in Nazism. According to Germany's mainstream foreign policy consensus, by embedding itself firmly within a multilateralist framework, above all NATO and the European Union, the Federal Republic had put this path behind it. But with his reference to a *Deutscher Weg*, Schröder seemed to suggest that it was time for Germany to once again follow its own, unique path. Unlike previous incarnations of the *Sonderweg*, this, however, was to be a peaceful path. Indeed, this deliberately ironic contrast with the classical German *Sonderweg* was part of the thinking behind the concept.[20]

If the *Deutscher Weg* did represent a new German *Sonderweg*, it was also one that rested precisely on the idea of German "normalisation"—a concept that was closely associated with Schröder and often thought of as the opposite of the *Sonderweg*. After sixty years of contrition for Nazism, Schröder seemed to imply, Germany had now put the past behind it. It should therefore now be free to act in its national interest in precisely the same way as any other nation unencumbered by historical guilt, although what that national interest might be was less clear. In that sense, the speech took Schröder back to the rhetoric of the 1998 election campaign and the first 100 days of the "red-green" government, when he had seemed to represent a new, self-confident Germany unencumbered by the Nazi past.

With the Kosovo war, the idea of a new, uninhibited German foreign policy had seemed to recede as Schröder, along with Fischer and Scharping, insisted on the need for *Bündnistreue*. Although by sending German troops into combat the "red-green" government had broken new ground, at a deeper level, its participation in the NATO intervention represented a continuation of the multilateral and in particular Atlanticist tradition of German foreign policy. The adherence to *Bündnistreue* as the highest principle of German foreign policy continued with Germany's participation in the "war on terror", which Schröder had put his own job on the line to secure. But with the decision to publicly oppose the United States over Iraq that had now all changed. Nor did Schröder's stance even represent a return to Germany's role before the "red-green" government, when it did not participate in "out of area" interventions but supported them financially and logistically. Schröder made it clear that he was not just refusing to send troops to Iraq but also to provide other support.

Schröder insisted that the United States was acting unilaterally in its threat to invade Iraq. It was certainly true that the Bush administration had increasingly given the impression that it was prepared to take military action with a "coalition of the willing" or, if necessary, alone—not least because of the frustrating experience of the NATO intervention in Kosovo.[21] But in August 2002, the situation in relation to Iraq was still both uncertain and fluid. At that point, it was not clear whether Iraq did, in fact, have weapons of mass destruction, as the United States claimed. Weapons inspectors, led by the head of the United Nations Monitoring Verfication and Inspection Commission (UNMOVIC), Hans Blix, had not even yet begun, let alone completed, the renewed search for weapons of mass destruction in Iraq that subsequently took place.

Furthermore, neither the United States on the one hand, nor France and Russia on the other, had committed themselves one way or the other on the question of military action. By publicly declaring his opposition to military action, Schröder alone seemed to have pre-empted the decision of the UN Security Council. As two American critics later put it, he thereby "wrote himself out of the diplomacy over Iraq."[22] In effect, Schröder was acting as unilaterally as Bush, who by the beginning of September had in fact been persuaded by Tony Blair and Colin Powell to take his case to the United Nations.[23] Schröder not only risked isolating Germany but also went against the consistent multilateralism of the "red-green" government up to that point.[24] Schröder, the *Washington Post* editorialised in September, "appears prepared to trample some of the most important principles of his government in order to pander to Germany's leftist voters."[25]

As Iraq displaced the economy as the number one theme of the election campaign, Schröder became even more unequivocal in his stance, saying flatly that "under my leadership Germany will not be part of any military action against Iraq."[26] At the beginning of September, he spelled out exactly what that meant. In an interview with the *New York Times*, he declared that the arguments against a war with Iraq—

the lack of evidence of a threat from Iraq and the danger of creating instability in the Middle East and of dividing the coalition in the "war on terror"—were so compelling that he would oppose it even if the United Nations Security Council approved it. "These arguments make me say 'Hands Off,'" he said.[27] After the war was over, Schröder would claim that the decisive moment for him was a speech given by Vice President Dick Cheney before the Veterans of Foreign Wars in Nashville, Tennessee, on 16 August, which convinced him that the decision to invade Iraq had already been taken.[28] In the speech, Cheney expressed scepticism about continuing to contain Saddam Hussein's regime through weapons inspections and said that "there is no doubt that Saddam Hussein has weapons of mass destruction".[29] However, the speech took place three weeks after Schröder's 5 August election rally in which he had declared that "we will not be part of" an invasion of Iraq.

The Iraq crisis once again illustrated the differences between Schröder and Fischer. Like Schröder, Fischer was also opposed to military intervention in Iraq and had worried that an attack on Iraq was imminent ever since he had met with President Bush and with Deputy Secretary of Defence Paul Wolfowitz in Washington a week after September 11. From the beginning, Fischer felt that Iraq was of marginal importance and that military action would be a diversion from the war on terror. "There was a terrible regime in power in Baghdad, but I was convinced that Iraq should not be at the centre of the answer to this crisis," he said later.[30]

Fischer also had good reason to use Iraq to win votes. After all, his party had, if anything, even greater anti-American tendencies than Schröder's. But unlike Schröder, Fischer did not resort to anti-American rhetoric and in fact repeatedly said how much he liked America and Americans, stressing the role of the United States in liberating Europe in World War II.[31] For Fischer, the transatlantic relationship remained "the central pillar for peace and security in the twenty-first century." He said it would be "unprecedented idiocy to question our relationship with the USA and this transatlantic zone of stability."[32] At election rallies he went out of his way to stress that "anti-Americanism will get us nowhere."[33] As for Schröder's concept of the "German Way", Fischer initially said nothing. A month after the election, however, in an interview with *The Guardian*, he dismissed the concept. "I don't want to comment for the chancellor, but I tell you: Forget it," he said. "There is definitely, in foreign policy, no German way".[34]

Years later, Fischer said that he was amazed at Schröder's use of a term like "German Way". "I thought, 'He's lost it'", he says. "'Are they nuts?'"[35] But just as Schröder did not criticise Fischer for bringing up Auschwitz during the debate about the Kosovo war, Fischer did not criticise Schröder for his use of the concept of the "German Way". Although Fischer disapproved of the nationalist tone of Schröder's rhetoric, his hands were tied, especially because it was the middle of an election campaign. Fischer says that although he did not publicly contradict Schröder, he nevertheless tried to indicate that he did not share his thinking. "You can contradict someone without directly contradicting them," he says. "I couldn't directly contradict him, because it would have become an issue during the election campaign, but I could preach the opposite of the 'German Way', and that's what I did."[36]

Schröder's blunt opposition to the Iraq war seemed to resonate with German voters and things started to look up for the Social Democrats. In mid-August, a sudden, massive flood in eastern Germany allowed the chancellor to appear on television wearing rubber boots and a look of grim determination on his face, demonstrating his crisis management skills. By the end of August, the SPD had caught up in the opinion polls, which reported that Schröder's stance on Iraq had worked particularly well on the left, the far-right and in eastern Germany.[37] The left wing of the SPD itself was also energised and even the *Jusos*, who had been bitter critics of the chancellor ever since the resignation of Oskar Lafontaine, praised him.[38]

The Christian Democrats, meanwhile, were unable to respond to Schröder's late surge. Edmund Stoiber had been reluctant to make Iraq an election issue. He too was opposed to the war, but argued that Germany should be led by the decision of its allies—essentially, the view that the "red-green" coalition had adopted during the Kosovo war. However, this more nuanced position did not go over well in the cut and thrust of an election campaign. During the second of two television debates, Schröder challenged Stoiber to simply "say yes or no" to the question of whether Germany should support an invasion of Iraq.[39] According to an opinion poll carried out after the debate, 50 per cent of viewers found Schröder more convincing, compared to 28 per cent who preferred Stoiber.[40] Speaking in the *Bundestag* ten days before the election, Schröder reiterated that he was opposed to military action regardless of what happened in New York. "Decisions about the existential questions of the German nation will be made in Berlin and nowhere else," he declared.[41] A few days later—and just two days before the election—came perhaps the most extreme attack on Bush of all. At a campaign stop, the justice minister Herta Däubler-Gmelin, whose father had been a Nazi official and after the war had become mayor of Tübingen—another embodiment of the student movement's "continuity thesis"—said that Bush was using Iraq to divert attention away from domestic problems. "It's a popular method," she told a German newspaper reporter. "Hitler did it too."[42] The US national security adviser Condoleezza Rice said German-US relations had been "poisoned" as a result of the remark. "How can you use the name of Hitler and the name of the president of the United States in the same sentence?" she said. "Particularly, how can a German, given the devotion of the US in the liberation of Germany from Hitler?"[43]

The election wound up being the closest in the history of the Federal Republic. When the votes had finally been counted late in the night of 22 September, the Social Democrats and the Christian Democrats were neck-and-neck with 38.5 per cent each. It marked a slight shift from the left to right, but given the apparently hopeless situation for the Social Democrats just a few weeks earlier, it was a triumph for Schröder. The decisive factor, however, was the fact that the Greens—who this time had run a campaign based almost exclusively around the figure of Joschka Fischer, still the most popular politician in Germany—won nearly 9 per cent of the vote, nearly 2 per cent more than in 1998 and their best ever result in a general election. With that, they guaranteed the survival of the "red-green" coalition—albeit with a majority of only five seats.

After the election, Schröder sought to re-build the damaged relationship with the United States as best he could while keeping his word to the German electorate on Iraq. At the beginning of November, after eight weeks of negotiations, the UN Security Council unanimously passed Resolution 1441, which reiterated that Iraq would face "serious consequences" if it did not comply with its disarmament obligations under previous resolutions and sent UN weapons inspectors back to Iraq. At a NATO summit in Prague later that month, Bush and Schröder shook hands for the cameras, but the stalemate over Iraq remained. In January 2003, as the French pressed for a continuation of inspections and the United States and Britain pressed for a further UN resolution sanctioning military action against Iraq, Germany took up a non-veto-bearing seat on the UN Security Council and, the following month, the rotating chairmanship of the Security Council. The last chance of a compromise between the United States and Germany disappeared on 21 January, however, when, at an appearance in the north German town of Goslar in the run-up to another election, this time in the state of Lower Saxony, Schröder stated publicly that Germany would vote against military action in the Security Council.

Fischer disapproved of this. For him, it was a strategic blunder that made Germany a hostage to fortune. "There was a danger that we would ultimately have to face off against all of our western partners," he would later say. "If Russia and France had agreed to the war, we, along with Syria, would have been the only ones [on the Security Council] saying no."[44] Fischer claimed that he told Schröder that if that happened, he would resign.[45] Schröder's own position would also have become extremely difficult and perhaps untenable. Schröder said later that, although he was confident that Presidents Chirac and Putin would eventually back him, he had no guarantees from them.[46] In other words, he was taking a huge risk. Fortunately, from his point of view, the French and the Russians (which, as permanent members, had veto rights) made it clear at the beginning of February that they would also vote against a further Security Council resolution sanctioning military action against Iraq. By doing so, they saved the "red-green" coalition. At the beginning of March, the three countries signed a joint declaration opposing a resolution authorising the use of force in Iraq.

Europe was split. Towards the end of January, in answer to a question from a Dutch journalist at a press conference, US Secretary of Defence Donald Rumsfeld described France and Germany as "old Europe".[47] A week later, eight EU states, including the United Kingdom, Spain and Poland, published a letter in support of the United States in newspapers across Europe. The next month, Fischer publicly took on Rumsfeld at an annual security conference in Munich. With anti-war protesters led by the city's mayor outside and Rumsfeld sitting in the front row of the audience, Fischer once again restated his government's reservations about attacking Iraq and said the United States had failed to convince its allies to support the war. Then, mid-speech, he broke suddenly into heavily-accented English. "You have to make the case in a democracy," he said. "Excuse me, but I'm not convinced."[48] On 20 March, the United States began bombing Bagh-

dad. The day afterwards, Schröder went on German television to publicly reiterate his opposition to the war. "The wrong decision has been
made," he declared. "The logic of war has prevailed over the chance
of peace."[49]

However, despite Schröder's loud opposition to the war since the
previous summer, Germany was in fact already quietly providing the
United States with significant military assistance. Germany allowed the
United States full access to its airspace, agreed to send German AWACS
reconnaissance aircraft to patrol the skies over Turkey and, after initial
opposition, provided missiles for Patriot missile batteries that were
also sent to Turkey in case it was attacked by Iraq. The German navy,
which had been deployed to the Horn of Africa as part of Operation
Enduring Freedom, also helped safeguard waterways for American
ships en route to the Persian Gulf. The Pentagon thus classified Germany as "noncoalition but cooperating."[50] In addition, it would later
emerge that two German intelligence agents had remained in Baghdad
during the war and secretly provided information they gathered—including details of Iraqi military units and weapons located in the
city—to the US military. The information was passed through another
German intelligence officer, who was stationed in the headquarters of
General Tommy Franks, the American commander of the invasion, in
Qatar. The intelligence sharing arrangement was approved by both
Fischer and Frank-Walter Steinmeier, Schröder's chief of staff.[51]

Gerhard Schröder's nationalist rhetoric coincided with yet another re-
assessment of the Nazi past in Germany and with it a shift in the balance of the competing collective memories that defined its post-war
identity. There was during the second half of 2002 and the first half of
2003 what one American reporter called "an outpouring of memory"
that had the effect of "changing the public view of World War II" and
"strengthening the German opposition against a threatened war in
Iraq".[52] This outpouring of memory centred on German suffering during the war, particularly as a result of the Allied bombing of German
cities, and reflected a shift in German identity. "For the first time,
many Germans are openly considering themselves not just as perpetrators of wars, but as victims of war," wrote the American reporter.[53]

The catalyst for this process was the publication in November 2002
of a book called *The Fire* (*Der Brand*), written by an author named

Jörg Friedrich, about the Allied bombing of German cities in World War II.[54] The book, which was serialised in *Bild*, the newspaper with the biggest circulation in Germany, and quickly became a bestseller, described the Allied bombing campaign in a way that was not just vivid and emotive but that also used language normally used for the Holocaust. Friedrich, himself a member of the post-war generation who had been on the far left as a student, wrote of the Allied *Vernichtung*, or annihilation, of German cities. He referred to the Allied bombing crews as *Einsatzgruppen* (the term used for the SS killing squads which operated behind the lines on the Eastern Front, which had already been applied to American GIs in Vietnam), German air-raid shelters as "crematoria" and the death of civilians from carbon monoxide poisoning as "gassing". It thus implicitly equated the suffering caused by Germany and the suffering experienced by Germans during World War II.[55]

As if meeting a pent-up need to engage with German suffering during World War II, a string of television documentaries, covering everything from the Allied bombing of German cities to the fate of German soldiers in Stalingrad, followed the publication of Friedrich's book. Even Günter Grass, who had earlier criticised others for any signs of relativising Germany's wartime crimes, seemed to think it was time to talk about German wartime suffering. Earlier that year, he published a novel, *Crabwalk (Im Krebsgang)* about the Soviet sinking of the Wilhelm Gustloff, a cruise ship that was carrying thousands of German civilians and wounded soldiers from the Eastern Front when it was sunk by a Russian submarine in January 1945, with the loss of more than 9,000 lives, including several thousand children. Named after a Nazi official killed by a Jewish student in 1936, it had been the flagship of the "Strength Through Joy" (*Kraft durch Freude* (KdF)) organisation that provided leisure activities and vacations for German workers.

While it was of course true that Germans suffered greatly during World War II, the equation of the suffering experienced by Germans with the suffering caused by Germany contained a danger of "exonerating projection". Although German suffering had featured rarely in the mainstream, even as the Holocaust had come to assume a central place in German identity, it had long been discussed on both the far right and the far left, in particular among the 1968 generation.[56] In fact, Friedrich's description of the bombing of German cities and its implicit comparison of it with the Holocaust picked up where Ulrike

Meinhof's 1965 column about the bombing of Dresden, in which she had written that "the Anti-Hitler war degenerated into what it was supposed to be fighting against", had left off.[57] It also echoed the rhetoric of the New Right in Germany, for which alleged Allied war crimes had long been a favourite subject.

The sudden interest in German wartime suffering dovetailed with opposition to the Iraq war in the autumn of 2002 and the first half of 2003.[58] During the build-up to the Iraq war, German television frequently showed images of the bombing of German cities during World War II, creating what Andreas Huyssen has called a "false sense of simultaneity" between the two conflicts.[59] The collective memory of the Allied bombings during World War II thus strengthened and intensified German opposition to the expected American war on Iraq.[60] In particular, some Germans suggested that, having learned from their own terrible past, they were now in a better position than others to judge the justness of wars in the present—and especially better than Americans who had carried out air raids but had never suffered the effects of them. "Germans have a deeper knowledge on matters of bombing campaigns," Jörg Friedrich told the *Wall Street Journal*.[61]

The debate on the Iraq war at the end of 2002 and the beginning of 2003 thus became, like the debate on the Kosovo war, a narcissistic one that was as much about German identity as the fate of Iraq. While the debate about the Kosovo war had focused on parallels with the Holocaust and therefore centred on German guilt, the Iraq war evoked collective memories that highlighted German suffering. The debate on Kosovo, and the decision to send German troops into combat as part of Operation Allied Force, could be seen as the culmination of the "Holocaust identity" that had emerged in the eighties and which, perhaps more than anyone else, Joschka Fischer had come to embody. But as the world had changed after September 11 and in particular as an invasion of Iraq became more likely, the narrative of "resistance" against the "Auschwitz generation" had given way to a new identity based on the collective memory of German suffering in World War II. In terms of the two currents of the thinking of the post-war generation that had emerged out of the student movement in the sixties, Germans had come to think of themselves much less as perpetrators and much more as victims.

- - - - - - - - - - -

The "red-green" government's opposition to the war in Iraq created the biggest rift between the United States and Germany since the founding of the Federal Republic in 1949. To many, both inside and outside Germany, it seemed apt for a government that included members of the 1968 generation. Many elements of the crisis did indeed echo the sixties. Then, as now, Germany's baby boomers were in opposition to what seemed to them to be an unjust American war, with Donald Rumsfeld reprising the part of Robert McNamara, the US Secretary of Defence during the Vietnam war. It was therefore perhaps also fitting that the campaign against the war in Germany included, on the eve of the election in 2002, an equation of the United States' foreign policy with Nazism—a real throwback to 1968 itself. To some former members of the student movement like Tilman Fichter, Schröder spoke and acted like a true *Achtundsechziger* during the Iraq crisis—perhaps for the first time ever.[62]

After Fischer's clash with Rumsfeld, which had seemed to encapsulate the stand off between "old Europe" and the United States, Germany's opposition to the Iraq war came to be associated with Fischer as much as Schröder, and Fischer's radical past once again came under scrutiny. Some foreign observers saw the German government's opposition to the war as directly connected to Fischer's background in the West German New Left. In an acidic column in the *Washington Post* in February 2003 entitled "Germany's Mr. Tough Guy", the American journalist Michael Kelly, who was killed less than two months later while covering the war in Iraq, wrote that Fischer "rose in public life as an important figure in the anti-American, anti-liberal, neo-Marxist, revolution-minded German radical left of the generation of 1968," the same left that had "produced and supported the Baader-Meinhof gang."[63]

While it was true that Fischer had been more radical in the sixies and seventies than Schröder ever had, Kelly's accusation of anti-Americanism actually more accurately fitted Schröder than Fischer. It was Schröder's loud opposition to the war in Iraq, and in particular the nationalist tone of his rhetoric in the summer of 2002, that marked the real departure from the previous solidarity of the "red-green" coalition with the United States from the war in Kosovo through to the "war on terror". Schröder repeatedly emphasised during the Iraq crisis that Germany had made a major contribution to the "war on terror", with 8,000 German peacekeepers serving in Afghanistan, Kosovo and Macedonia, and that he had put his own job on the line over German involvement in Operation Enduring Freedom.[64] But the Iraq war illustrated that there were limits to his belief in multilateralism. Apart from the political and electoral calculations that motivated his opposition, he appeared to want to create a specifically German foreign policy distinct from that of the United States.

Fischer, on the other hand, continually stressed the need for multilateralism and above all for a UN mandate for military action. Of course, the Kosovo war, which Fischer had supported, did not have a UN mandate either. But in that case, the parallels between Milosevic's policy of "ethnic cleansing" in the former Yugoslavia and the Holocaust overrode that need for Fischer. Fischer was also able to see parallels between Islamist ideology and Nazi ideology—not least because of their shared anti-Semitism—and therefore supported the invasion of Afghanistan. But the war in Iraq was not a war against Germany's past in the same way. Though Saddam Hussein was a tyrant, Fischer did not regard him as a fascist.[65] Rather than revealing Fischer's anti-Americanism, the Iraq crisis illustrated how much he still viewed international relations though the prism of German history. "The Americans had no Verdun on their continent," he told the *Spiegel* a few days after the war had started. "In the United States there is nothing comparable to Auschwitz or Stalingrad or any of the other terrible symbolic places in our history."[66] Because of his passionate defence of the Kosovo war, he had come to be seen as an evangelist for humanitarian intervention. But unlike some others on the left like Bernard Kouchner who made a case for a humanitarian intervention in Iraq, Fischer was far less willing to send German troops into combat when the parallels with Auschwitz were less compelling.

In a sense, Germany responded to the Iraq crisis in almost the opposite way to the way it had responded to the invasion of Afghanistan. In the case of Afghanistan, Germany had used the principle of *Bündnistreue* to justify taking part in military action. In the case of Iraq it appeared to downgrade the importance of *Bündnistreue*—the principle that had been a key determinant in Kosovo and *the* key determinant in Afghanistan. Although Germany had opposed the Iraq war in the name of its post-war scepticism about the use of military force, it had in doing so departed from Germany's multilateralist tradition and in particular the principle of "never alone" that had guided policy up to that point. That multilateralism was a key aspect of the concept of a "civilian power". In that sense, as Hanns W. Maull has argued, the war in Iraq represented a break with the Federal Republic's foreign policy identity as a "civilian power".[67]

While Fischer tried to repair the rift with the United States, reality quickly caught up with Gerhard Schröder. Within a few months of the 2002 election, Schröder's approval ratings, which had climbed above 50 per cent in the autumn of 2002 against the background of the impending war in Iraq, once again plummeted. In elections in February 2003, the SPD suffered heavy losses in Hesse and in Lower Saxony, Schröder's own backyard, where his successor as prime minister and an up-and-coming star of the SPD, Sigmar Gabriel, was voted out of office. It was the beginning of a series of election defeats for the Social Democrats that put the chancellor under increasing pressure. The economic outlook had also continued to worsen. In particular, despite Hans Eichel's cost-cutting measures, Germany's budget deficit had exceeded the 3 per cent permitted under the European Stability Pact.

In March 2003, Schröder presented Agenda 2010, a package of reforms that represented the biggest reform of the German social security system since the Federal Republic began. Most controversially, the package included cuts in unemployment benefit based on recommendations by Peter Hartz, the personnel director of Volkswagen whom Schröder had appointed as the head of the commission to modernise the labour market in 2002. The reforms also cut state health care benefits, reduced state pension levels and made it easier for companies to fire employees. While some on the right thought the measures did not go far enough in reforming Germany's overstretched welfare state, the left, including many Social Democrats, saw the proposals, which were approved by the *Bundestag* later that year, as neo-liberal. Led by the powerful trade unions, opponents of "Hartz IV", as the cuts to unemployment benefit became known, began protesting. From the summer of 2004, demonstrations took place on Mondays in cities across Germany, just as they had done in East Germany in 1989. Oskar Lafontaine formed a new left-wing party whose support rose as anger about economic reform grew. The party subsequently joined forces with the PDS, the former East German communists, to become the *Linke*, or Left party.

Increasingly unpopular within his own party, Schröder resigned as party chairman, a position he had held since the resignation of Oskar

Lafontaine in the spring of 1999, and was replaced by Franz Müntefering, his campaign manager in the 2002 election. Peter Hartz was subsequently also forced to resign when it emerged that he had been involved in a massive corruption scandal involving paying kickbacks to union bosses and even paying for prostitutes for them. Despite the economic reforms, however, growth remained slow and unemployment—the self-imposed litmus test of Schröder's government—continued to rise. By the end of 2002 it had risen to 4.2 million and by the summer of 2003 to 4.6 million. By the beginning of 2005, unemployment was over five million for the first time in the history of the Federal Republic.

While Germany's economy went from bad to worse, Schröder focused on improving economic ties with China and Russia. Schröder helped to secure Chinese investment in Germany while remaining conspicuously silent about human rights abuses by the Chinese government. He also offered his support for lifting the European Union's embargo on selling arms to China that had been in place since the Tiananmen Square massacre in 1989. At the same time, he developed an increasingly close personal relationship with President Vladimir Putin, who he described as a "flawless democrat" despite his increasingly authoritarian tendencies. When Putin visited Germany in December 2004 and Schröder was asked at a press conference about the war in Chechnya, he responded glibly that it had been over for three years.[68]

While Germany's economic interests seemed to be at the heart of Schröder's foreign policy, he sought a reconciliation with Russia that paralleled its earlier reconciliation with France. While on a visit to Russia in May 2005 to commemorate the sixtieth anniversary of the end of World War II in Europe, Schröder visited a German military cemetery near Moscow. He seemed to think of it as his equivalent of Willy Brandt's genuflection at the Warsaw ghetto uprising memorial in 1970, except of course in this case it was a monument commemorating not the victims of Germans but German victims. Schröder later wrote that he was moved by "how young the soldiers were when they gave their lives for Hitler's criminal regime."[69] His father, of course, had been one of them.

Meanwhile Joschka Fischer's influence on German foreign policy appeared to diminish during the second term of the "red-green" government. He had problems of his own to deal with. In April 2005 he faced a parliamentary hearing on his involvement in the secret relaxation of visa requirements in 1999 that allowed tens of thousands of Ukrainians to enter Germany. In March 2005, Fischer caused another controversy when he ordered the foreign ministry to stop publishing obituaries honouring German diplomats who had been members of the Nazi party in its internal magazine, *InternAA*.[70] Fischer took the decision after a former foreign ministry interpreter informed him that Franz Nüsslein, a former consul in Barcelona who had died in 2003 and received an obituary in the magazine, had been a state prosecutor in Prague during the Nazi occupation and was responsible for the execution of political opponents—something the obituary had omitted. "I was furious," Fischer says.[71] Fischer's personal intervention to stop the magazine publishing obituaries of such men—just the kind of "old Nazis" whose rehabilitation the student movement had once protested against—was perhaps the final, posthumous battle in the post-war generation's struggle against the "Auschwitz generation".

In May 2005, the Social Democrats and Greens were defeated in an election in the state of North Rhine Westphalia, where a "red-green" government had been in power for a decade. Claiming he no longer had a mandate, Schröder decided to call an early general election by proposing a no-confidence motion—a move whose constitutionality was questionable but which was approved by the president, the Christian Democrat Horst Köhler. The Christian Democrats nominated Angela Merkel as their candidate. Born in 1954 and raised in East Germany, she had risen through the Christian Democrats after the fall of the Berlin Wall. She had been a protégée of Helmut Kohl but had also been one of the first to turn against him during the party funding scandal in 1999. She was also the first female candidate for a major party in the history of the Federal Republic.

The election took place on 18 September. The Social Democrats did surprisingly well, winning 34 per cent of the vote but not enough seats in the *Bundestag* to give them a majority with the Greens, who won 8 per cent of the vote. Nor, however, did the Christian Democrats, the biggest party, have enough seats to form a coalition with their preferred partner, the Free Democrats, who, along with the new left-wing party led by Oskar Lafontaine, were the big winners. It appeared to be a stalemate. At the beginning of October, Schröder finally conceded defeat and stepped down. Angela Merkel became chancellor at the head of a grand coalition—the first in the Federal Republic since the

Kiesinger government from 1966 to 1969. The student movement had seen in that grand coalition the beginning of a transition from democracy to fascism. The final irony of the "red-green" government, a project brought into existence by the 1968 generation, was that it, too, ultimately produced a grand coalition.

Two very different visions of Germany's role in the world emerged from the seven years of the "red-green" government, which Fischer described in retrospect as "formative years" for German foreign policy. During those years, German foreign policy had undergone some fundamental changes. Under Schröder and Fischer's leadership, Germany had taken an historic step towards "normalisation", which many thought would not have been possible without their attempts to convince the German left of the humanitarian justification for military intervention. Many foreign observers welcomed this change. According to the director of a leading British centre-left think tank, for example, they "had the courage to argue that Germany should, like other middle-sized developed countries, be willing to reinforce foreign policy with the deployment of armed force."[72] But behind this apparent "normalisation" lay two distinct visions of Germany's future.

Fischer's vision remained one based on the prevention of a recurrence of Auschwitz—Adorno's new categorical imperative applied to German foreign policy. Ever since the 1980s, Fischer had regarded Auschwitz as the basic premise of Germany's national interest. From that followed, in the first instance, a commitment to Atlanticism and European integration. Fischer had reformulated the argument beyond that, particularly in relation to the use of military force, several times during his political career. First he had argued that, because of Auschwitz, Germany should not use its military at all in "out of area" interventions. After Srebrenica, he argued not just that Germany could participate in "out of area" interventions but that its history meant it had a moral obligation to do so. Finally, during the debate over the war in Iraq it began to look as if Fischer only believed in German participation in military intervention when the parallels to Auschwitz were overwhelming. But throughout all these shifts in his thinking, he remained committed to the idea of Germany as a "civilian power." Although he was considered a "realist" within the Greens, in foreign policy terms he remained an idealist whose conception of German foreign policy centred on Germany's responsibility for World War II and in particular for the Holocaust. For him, Auschwitz was, as one critic put it, "the founding myth of a new German sense of mission."[73] Crucially, Fischer remained an Atlanticist. The transatlantic relationship remained for him "the central pillar for peace and security in the twenty-first century."[74] He devoted a long chapter of his book *The Return of History*, published a few months before the "red-green" government came to an end, to the transatlantic relationship, which he thought urgently needed to be renewed after the Iraq crisis. He stressed the common interests of the United States and Europe and likened the disagreement over Iraq to a dispute within a family. An increasing erosion of the relationship, he wrote, "is not in the interests of either North America or Europe and therefore it cannot be allowed to happen."[75] For Fischer it was essential that European integration should be achieved with America, not against it—a crucial difference.[76]

In the first phase of the "red-green" government, Schröder had appeared to share Fischer's Atlanticism. But as the likelihood of an American invasion of Iraq increased in 2002, Schröder seemed to jettison the principle of *Bündnistreue* that had guided German foreign policy in Kosovo and even after September 11 for a realist foreign policy that, in the end, undermined Germany's role as a "civilian power". Perhaps even more striking than Schröder's anti-American rhetoric during 2002 and 2003 was his attitude to the United States after the war was over. Unlike Fischer, Schröder did not seem to regret the estrangement between the United States and Germany that had resulted from the differences of opinion over Iraq. In his memoirs, which were published the year after he left office, Schröder wrote that it would be a mistake for Germany to "give up its newly-won foreign policy freedom and independence" from the United States.[77] To do so, he said, would have "fateful consequences for the interests of Germany in Europe and for the interests of Europe in the world."[78] Far from creating a crisis in transatlantic relations, Schröder seemed to think that the Iraq war had created an historic opportunity for Germany to emancipate itself from the United States. Nor was Schröder's disagreement only with the policies of the Bush administration but rather with the "American Way". It was therefore time to "re-think the transatlantic relationship".[79]

In contrast to Fischer's belief in the importance of the transatlantic West, Schröder believed Germany had what he called a "European mission".[80] During the course of the Iraq crisis, Germany had become closer to both France and Russia—countries Schröder seemed to regard as more appropriate allies for Germany than the United States. Schröder regarded Germany's "special relationship" with Russia, which he had done so much to develop while in office, as being of particular importance. He seemed to think that, together with France and Russia, Germany could create a European foreign policy distinct from, and perhaps opposed to, that of the United States. The joint declaration that the three countries signed in March 2003 was the first attempt to formalise this new alliance and an illustration, Schröder said, that when they acted together they could stand up to the United States.

Schröder always denied that he was calling the *Westbindung* into question. Rather, he says, he was simply declining to affirm something that, unlike Fischer, he took as a given. "No-one asks the British or the French if they are part of the West," he said. "Why do they ask us?"[81] However, the implication of his statements on German foreign policy was that Germany's geopolitical role would no longer be defined by the *Westbindung*, as it had been from Adenauer to Kohl. Looking back on his time in power three years after leaving office, he claimed that under the "red-green" government, the Federal Republic had finally become fully "sovereign". "My government reclaimed independence in decision-making," he says.[82] He seemed to suggest that he had left Germany free for the first time to pursue a truly independent foreign policy.

By de-emphasising the *Westbindung*, Schröder seemed to suggest that Germany should return to its pre-war geopolitical role as a central European rather than a western power. The new role that Schröder envisaged for Germany was, however, very different from the pre-war concept of the *Mittellage*. Instead of facing enemies in both the East and the West, as had been traditional, Schröder's vision for Germany centred on close friendships with both France and Russia (though he seemed less concerned about Germany's relationship with Poland, which inevitably felt threatened by Germany's alliance with Russia). In this sense, it was no new German *Sonderweg* at all. But at the same time, Schröder's vision for Germany did include hints of the anti-western *ressentiment* that had characterised earlier incarnations of German nationalism, directed this time primarily against the United States.

Above all Fischer and Schröder differed in their views of German history and its role in German foreign policy. While Fischer's vision of

German foreign policy focused on the collective memory of Auschwitz, in other words on German guilt, Schröder focused on the history of Europe in the twentieth-century as a whole—"everything that the war and post-war period, the Iron Curtain and the division of Europe have left behind in the collective consciousness of Europe," as he put it.[83] It was a vision, in other words, in which perpetrators and victims were reconciled and Germans were no more guilty than anyone else. Schröder's vision of Germany was as a "normal" country that had "overcome" the Nazi past.[84]

Between them, Fischer and Schröder had begun to define what Germany's post-Cold War national interest might be. Hans-Dietrich Genscher had argued that Germany had no national interests apart from European interests. That era was now over. The question was what Germany's national interest in the twenty-first century was. Fischer suggested that Germany's national interest should be deduced from the basic premise of Auschwitz. Schröder on the other hand seemed to suggest that Germany's national interest lay in a tripartite alliance with Russia and France in opposition to the "American Way." Although these two visions of Germany's national interest were to some extent in conflict during the "red-green" government's seven years in power, they had intersected on the three key foreign policy crises—Kosovo, Afghanistan and Iraq—that it had to face.

What the legacy of the "red-green" government will be for Germany's foreign policy in the twenty-first century remains very much an open question. According to the most sympathetic reading, the "red-green" government led Germany towards a foreign policy in which global leadership and responsibility is balanced with an acute awareness of German history and the lessons drawn from it. According to a somewhat less sympathetic reading, its references to the Holocaust simply eased the transition to a new era in which Germany is once again able to pursue its own national interest like any other country. In the former interpretation of the "red-green" government's foreign policy, Joschka Fischer emerges as an heroic figure who led his own generation and the German left towards an understanding of its responsibility for Auschwitz. In the latter interpretation, his idealist rhetoric about Auschwitz simply made Schröder's realist foreign policy politically viable, both in Germany and abroad. It was, in any case, an ambivalent legacy. Schröder's successor Angela Merkel would pursue a foreign policy that was both less fixated on the Holocaust and also less nationalist.

— — — — — — — — — — —

With the end of the "red-green" government, Germany's 1968 genera-tion exited the stage. In December 2005—just two months after leav-ing office—Gerhard Schröder was appointed as the chairman of the board of Nordstream, the consortium set up to build a controversial Baltic Sea gas pipeline that was majority-owned by the Russian energy company Gazprom. Schröder and President Putin had signed the deal to build the pipeline, which would run from Russia to Germany, by-passing Poland, just two weeks before the election. Schröder later claimed he had initially declined the offer but was subsequently per-suaded by Putin to take the job.[85] In an editorial entitled "Gerhard Schröder's sellout", the *Washington Post* slammed the former chancel-lor, pointing out that while in office he "went out of his way to ignore the gradual suppression of political rights in Russia and to play down the significance of Russia's horrific war in Chechnya" and "thwarted attempts to put unified Western pressure on Russia to change its behaviour."[86]

Joschka Fischer also quit politics. In an interview with the *taz* a few days after the election, he styled his departure as the end of an era. "I was one of the last rock 'n' rollers of German politics," he said.[87] Now a 57–year-old grandfather, he said he was passing the torch to the next generation in the Green party. "Younger people, above all those under 40 years-old will have to write the next chapter," he said, promising that he would not criticise from the balcony like Statler and Waldorf on *The Muppet Show*.[88] A month after the election, he got married for the fifth time, to Minu Barati, the 29 year-old daughter of an Iranian opposition figure. The following summer he moved to the United States as a visiting professor in international relations at the Woodrow Wilson School at Princeton University.

Dieter Kunzelmann, the former patriarch of Kommune 1 who had been presumed dead, turned out be alive after all. In fact, he had faked his suicide in one last prank and gone underground for the second time in his life in 1997. "I apologise to all those who seriously mourned for me," he told *Stern*.[89] He said he had originally planned to "resurrect" himself in time for the 1999 Berlin mayoral election. "I wanted to see what would happen if a corpse would stand against the other corpses," he said.[90] Instead he served his year-long prison sentence and was released in 2000. Since then, he has lived a quiet life in Berlin. Now a grandfather like Joschka Fischer (his daughter Grischa, who had grown up in Kommune 1, had herself had children), he refused to discuss his past and in particular his responsibility for the bomb in the Jewish community centre in November 1969.[91]

Horst Mahler, on the other hand, continued to seek as much publicity as possible. After Otto Schily dropped his attempt to ban the NPD in 2003, Mahler left the party. Over the next few years, he repeatedly made anti-Semitic remarks, incited racial hatred and gave the Hitler salute in public, accumulating a series of criminal cases against him, much as the members of Kommune 1 he had once represented had done in the sixties. In fact, of all the former members of the student movement, Mahler seemed to be the only one who still believed in provocation—albeit for different political purposes than back then. As a result of his criminal convictions, he once again lost the licence to practice law that Gerhard Schröder had helped him win back in the 1990s. In January 2006, the German authorities withdrew his passport to stop him attending a planned conference on the Holocaust in Tehran, to which he, along with other members of European far-right groups, had been invited. In any case, when the conference took place in December 2006, Mahler, now 70 years-old, was back in prison.

What effect this tiny group of Germans born around the end of the war—the so-called 1968 generation—had had on Germany would continue to be debated in all sorts of paradoxical ways over the next few years. In fact, four decades on from 1968, there was little more consensus in Germany about whether the revolution they had created had been a good or bad thing than there had been at the time. On the fortieth anniversary of 1968—which also happened to be the 75th anniversary of the Nazi seizure of power—the *Achtundsechziger* were both blamed for, and given credit for, almost every change, real or perceived, that had taken place in Germany since the sixties.[92] Some said the student movement had made Germany more liberal, even though it had in many ways been anti-liberal. Some of the *Achtundsechziger* insisted they had deepened democracy in Germany, while others insisted they themselves had been essentially anti-democratic. Although the student movement had defined itself as anti-authoritarian, some said it was in fact authoritarian. Although Rudi Dutschke had been a nationalist, some praised the 1968 generation for creating a post-national identity and others criticised it for undermining German national identity. Perhaps the only thing one could say unequivocally about the 1968 generation was that it had, for better or worse, broken taboos.

The reality was that the revolutionary movement the post-war generation had created in the 1960s was a deeply contradictory—and perhaps ultimately incoherent—one that contained within it disparate and opposing impulses. Many among the post-war generation—from Ulrike Meinhof to Joschka Fischer—were driven by the idea of "resistance" against the "Auschwitz generation". But this *ex post facto* resistance against Nazism had been accompanied by an undercurrent of anti-Semitism that started with Dieter Kunzelmann, ran through the left-wing terrorism of the 1970s and found its ultimate, most extreme expression in Horst Mahler's neo-Nazism. In fact, it seems as if the most anti-Semitic of the *Achtundsechziger* were some of those who had been most haunted by the Nazi past. In that sense, anti-Semitism could be seen as the flipside of "resistance": if the idea of "resistance" was an expression of a need by some among the post-war generation to reject their parents, anti-Semitism was an expression of their desire for a final reconciliation with them.

At the same time, there was also among Germany's post-war generation a nationalist current that went back to Rudi Dutschke, who wanted to reunify Germany, and found its way through the peace movement into the politics of Gerhard Schröder, most obviously during the Iraq war. This left-wing nationalism was both different from, and similar to, classical German nationalism. It had rejected the militarism of German nationalism in the nineteenth century and first half of the twentieth century, but shared other less obvious elements of the German nationalism of that period. It was defined above all by a tendency to ignore the Nazi past and see Germany as a victim, particularly of American power. It expressed a desire among some of the post-war generation to see their parents—and by extension Germany—not as perpetrators but as victims of their fate in the twentieth century.

These currents had flowed in and out of each other in complicated ways over the forty years since 1968. In the end, the only way to characterise the 1968 generation and its effect on Germany is to describe its contradictions, above all in relation to the Nazi past. It is only half true to say that it was the 1968 generation that forced Germany to confront its Nazi past. In fact, it had an ambivalent attitude to the Nazi past. While some among the *Achtundsechziger* such as Fischer wanted to put Auschwitz at the centre of German identity indefinitely, others, from Dutschke through to Schröder, wanted to move on from it and perhaps even forget it. The 1968 generation both intensified Germany's engagement with the Nazi past and drew a line under it.

EPILOGUE

A NEW GENERATION

One Saturday in September 2007, the Greens met in Göttingen to discuss war and peace once again. This time the crisis was in the Hindu Kush rather than the Balkans, but the issue was essentially the same as eight years earlier: What role should Germany—and in particular its military—play in the world? The Greens had called yet another extraordinary party conference ahead of a *Bundestag* vote on whether to renew the mandate for the deployment of the *Bundeswehr* in Afghanistan. Inevitably, it was seen as a repeat of the conference in Bielefeld in April 1999 at which the Greens had voted to support NATO's military intervention in Kosovo. This time, however, the Greens were in opposition and had even less influence on events than they did then. This time, there was also no Joschka Fischer. Although he had returned to Germany from the United States where he had been living for a year, he had no intention of attending the conference.

Eight years after Germany had sent its troops into combat in Kosovo, the world was a different place. The "war on terror" had made questions of humanitarian intervention even more complicated than they were before. German troops—around 3,000 in total—were on the ground in Afghanistan as part of the multi-national ISAF stabilisation force that had been there since the beginning of 2002 and was now, partly as a result of German pressure, being led by NATO. While American, British, Canadian and Dutch troops were fighting the Taliban in southern and eastern Afghanistan, the Germans were confined to the country's relatively peaceful north, where they were engaged largely in reconstruction work. Nine German soldiers had been killed in action in Afghanistan since the beginning of the deployment, including three killed by a roadside bomb in August 2007. They were a fraction of the casualties other NATO countries had suffered, let alone the United States, but for Germany, and above all for the Greens, they were shocking losses.

In addition, for the previous six months, German Tornado aircraft had been carrying out reconnaissance operations in the skies over Afghanistan, including over the south of the country where the fighting was heaviest. This in particular had riled the grass roots of the Greens who had called the conference. Most of the party was in favour of the *Bundeswehr* continuing to carry out reconstruction work in the north of Afghanistan. But if the Tornados were deployed in the south, even for reconnaissance purposes, that meant they were no longer involved in a humanitarian operation with a UN mandate but in Operation Enduring Freedom, the American-led war against the Taliban. That, in turn, meant they were complicit in the "collateral damage" caused by air strikes on Afghan villages. And if the 51 Green members of the *Bundestag* voted in favour of continuing the mandate, that meant that they too, and with them the whole party, were responsible for civilian casualties in Afghanistan. Once again Hans-Christian Ströbele was calling for a ceasefire exactly as he had done eight years earlier. "We must end the offensive strategy," he said on television a few days before the conference.

Just as in Bielefeld on Ascension Day in 1999, the conference took place amid massive protests. Oskar Lafontaine, now the joint leader, together with the former East German communist Gregor Gysi, of the new Left party, was speaking at a demonstration in Berlin on the same day, demanding an immediate withdrawal of the *Bundeswehr* from Afghanistan. There were also protesters outside the Lokhalle in Göttingen, the conference venue, carrying placards that said "*Bundeswehr* out of Afghanistan!" Others wore badges with the words "Tornados? No thanks!"—an updated version of the Greens' anti-nuclear power slogan from the eighties.

Inside, the 700 Green delegates—each with an apple placed on the table in front of him—debated for four hours. In Fischer's absence, it was left to the party's joint leaders Claudia Roth and Reinhard Bütikofer to make the case for continuing the deployment. Standing in front of a huge yellow sunflower—the Green party's symbol—they criticised the United States's flawed strategy in Afghanistan, which they said Angela Merkel's government had uncritically backed. They said the *Bundeswehr* was needed in Afghanistan for reconstruction but should not be involved in Operation Enduring Freedom, which was creating a spiral of violence and hate in Afghanistan. "No single German soldier has any place in such a mission," Roth said. Nevertheless, they said, the party should back the continuation of the mandate, including the deployment of the Tornados, which the government had insisted would be separate from Operation Enduring Freedom and would not be used to assist in air strikes in the south. "Giving up on Afghanistan is not an alternative," Bütikofer said.

As usual, Daniel Cohn-Bendit went even further, urging Germany to play a greater role in Afghanistan both by sending more troops to fight the Taliban and by spending more on reconstruction, which he said went hand in hand. "I want—and even dream—that the Greens will be the party that actively makes the case for NATO to do the right thing," he said. He said it was impossible for German troops to reconstruct Afghanistan as part of the ISAF mission without the support of troops in the south and east—and the Tornados. "If you want to protect ISAF, we need the Tornados!" he said. He was booed and heckled. This time, however, there were no paint bombs.

After a four-hour debate, repeatedly interrupted by anti-war protesters, the Greens rejected the party leadership's motion and voted against the deployment of the Tornados by 361 to 264. With that, the party seemed to have made a dramatic about-turn in its foreign policy. A disgusted Daniel Cohn-Bendit called the Greens a "kindergarten".[1] Above all, the vote in Göttingen was a defeat for the absent Joschka Fischer and a rejection of the transformation in the party's foreign policy that he, more than anyone else, had helped to create. Cohn-Bendit said that with the vote, the party had "aborted" the foreign policy of the "red-green" government and "buried" Joschka Fischer.[2] Hans-Christian Ströbele said gleefully that "there is a new generation of Greens that has nothing to do with Joschka Fischer."[3]

For the time being, Fischer himself stayed silent. A month later, however, when the first volume of his memoirs was published, he responded in an interview with the *Spiegel*. "A look at the history of the Greens shows us that the road to oblivion was always paved with illusory or radical decisions," he said. "I think we have a difficult time ahead."[4]

NOTES

PROLOGUE: WAR, AGAIN

1. Joschka Fischer, *Die rot-grüne Jahre. Deutsche Außenpolitik vom Kosovo bis zum 11. September* (Köln, 2007), p. 222.
2. Interview with Rezzo Schlauch.
3. Fischer, *Die rot-grünen Jahre*, p. 185.
4. Ibid., p. 223.
5. Heribert Prantl, *Rot-Grün. Eine erste Bilanz* (Hamburg, 1999), p. 113.

CHAPTER 1: CHILDREN OF MURDERERS

1. Stefan Aust, *Der Baader-Meinhof Komplex* (München, 1998), p. 57.
2. Ibid., p. 58.
3. Ibid., p. 59.
4. Aust, p. 60. This story was originally told in Jillian Becker's book *Hitler's Children. The Story of the Baader-Meinhof terrorist gang* (London, 1977). Some have subsequently questioned whether the blonde woman Fichter remembers was in fact Gudrun Ensslin. See Gerd Koenen, *Das rote Jahrzehnt. Unsere kleine deutsche Kulturrevolution 1967–1977* (Frankfurt am Main, 2002), p. 383. See also Willi Winkler, *Die Geschichte der RAF* (Berlin, 2007), pp. 88–90.
5. Paul Berman, *A Tale of two Utopias. The Political Generation of 1968* (New York, 1997), p. 25.
6. Tariq Ali/Susan Watkins, *1968. Marching in the Streets* (London, 1998), p. 7.
7. Tom Brokaw, *The Greatest Generation* (New York, 1998).
8. Tariq Ali for example says that while he and others on the left used the term "fascist", "this was not intended as a serious accusation". Tariq Ali, *Street Fighting Years. An Autobiography of the Sixties* (London, 2005), p. 28.
9. Interview with Tariq Ali.

10. On the 1968 generation as a "political generation", see Heinz Bude, *Das Altern einer Generation. Die Jahrgänge 1938–1948* (Frankfurt am Main, 1997).
11. Interview with Rainer Langhans.
12. Ibid.
13. Ibid.
14. Ibid.
15. Interview with Karl-Dietrich Wolff.
16. "Vaterlose Gesellen: Alexander Mitscherlich über den Frankfurter SDS-Kongreß und die Studentenrebellion", *Der Spiegel*, 8 April, 1968.
17. Norbert Elias, *Studien über die Deutschen. Machtkämpfe und Habitusentwicklung im 19. und 20. Jahrhundert* (Frankfurt am Main, 1989). Translated as: *The Germans. Power Struggles and the Development of Habitus in Nineteenth and Twentieth Centuries* (Cambridge, 1996).
18. Jan-Werner Müller, *Another Country. German Intellectuals, Unification and National Identity* (New Haven/London, 2000), p. 137.
19. Elias, *The Germans*, p. 230.
20. Elias, *Studien über die Deutschen*, p. 537.
21. See Norbert Frei, *Vergangenheitspolitik* (München, 1997).
22. Jens-Christian Wagner, "Der Fall Lübke," *Die Zeit*, 19 July, 2007.
23. Hannah Arendt, *Eichmann in Jersualem. A Report on the Banality of Evil* (Harmondsworth, 1977), p. 19.
24. Alexander und Margarete Mitscherlich, *Die Unfähigkeit zu trauern. Grundlagen kollektiven Verhaltens* (München, 1980), p. 23.
25. On the exhibition, "Ungesühnte Nazijustiz," see Tilman Fichter/Siegward Lönnendonker, *Kleine Geschichte des SDS. Der Sozialistischer Deutsche Studentenbund von 1946 bis zur Selbstauflösung* (Berlin, 1977), p. 109.
26. Peter Novick, *The Holocaust and Collective Memory* (London, 1999), p. 33.
27. Martin Walser, "Unser Auschwitz", in: *Kursbuch 1* (Berlin, 1965), p. 189.
28. Ibid., p. 195.
29. Interview with Christian Semler.
30. Andrei S. Markovits/Philip S. Gorski, *The German Left. Red, Green and Beyond* (Cambridge, 1993), p. 56.
31. Hans Magnus Enzensberger (hrsg.), *Kursbuch 12. Der Nicht erklärte Notstand. Dokumentation und Analyse eines Berliner Sommers* (Berlin, 1968).
32. Knut Nevermann (hrsg.), *Der 2. Juni 1967. Studenten zwischen Notstand und Demokratie. Dokumente zu den Ereignissen anlässlich des Schah-Besuches* (Köln, 1967), p. 98.
33. Thomas Schmid, "Ein deutsches Wunder," *Frankfurter Allgemeine Zeitung*, 3 February, 2001.
34. For a more detailed discussion of theories of Nazism as fascist or totalitarian, see Ian Kershaw, *The Nazi Dictatorship, Problems and Perspectives of Interpretation* (London, 2000), pp. 20–46.

35. Quoted in Ruth Wittlinger, "Taboo or Tradition? The 'Germans as victims' theme in the Federal Republic until the mid-1990s," in: Bill Niven (ed.) *Germans as victims. Remembering the past in contemporary Germany* (2006), pp. 62–75. Here p. 68.
36. Götz Aly, *Unser Kampf. 1968—ein irritierter Blick zurück* (Frankfurt am Main, 2008), pp. 151 ff.
37. Aly, *Unser Kampf*, p. 149. The sole case which attracted the attention of the student movement was that of Hans-Joachim Rehse, a Nazi judge at the People's Court in Berlin who had signed at least 231 death sentences and was acquitted in December 1968. Aly argues that even the campaign against his release was part of a broader attempt to discredit the entire West German justice system, with which the student movement was by then in conflict.
38. Aust, p. 35.
39. Interview with Stefan Aust.
40. Joachim Fest, *Begegnungen. Über nahe und ferne Freunde* (Reinbek, 2004), p. 250.
41. Willi Winkler, "Tragisch, selbstgerecht, mörderisch," *Süddeutsche Zeitung*, 26 November, 2007.
42. Ibid.
43. Aust, p. 38.
44. Aust, p. 52.
45. Ulrike Meinhof, *Die Würde des Menschen ist antastbar* (Berlin, 1994), p. 62.
46. Ibid., p. 64.
47. Correspondence with Karl-Heinz Metzger, Bezirksarmt Charlottenburg-Wilmersdorf, July 2003.
48. Heinz Höhne, *The Order of the Death's Head. The Story of Hitler's SS*, (Harmondsworth, 2000), pp. 308 ff. See also Hans Buchheim, "Rechtsstellung und Organisation des Reichskomissars für die Festigung deutschen Volkstums," *Gutachten des Instituts für Zeitgeschichte*, Band 1 (München, 1958).
49. On *neue kritik*, see Fichter/Lönnendonker, pp. 72 ff.
50. Ernest R. May, "America's Berlin. Heart of the Cold War," *Foreign Affairs*, July/August 1998, p. 148.
51. David Clay Large, *Berlin* (New York, 2000), p. 455.
52. Interview with Bernd Rabehl.
53. Bernd Rabehl, *Am Ende der Utopie. Die politische Geschichte der Freien Universität Berlin* (Berlin, 1988), pp. 33–44.
54. Jürgen Habermas, *Protestbewegung und Hochschulreform*, (Frankfurt am Main, 1969), p. 155.
55. Uwe Bergmann/Rudi Dutschke/Wolfgang Lefèvre/Bernd Rabehl, *Rebellion der Studenten oder die neue Opposition*, (Reinbek, 1968), p. 20.
56. Bergmann/Dutschke/Lefèvre/Rabehl, p. 21.
57. Martin Jay, *The Dialectical Imagination. A History of the Frankfurt School and the Institute of Social Research, 1923–1950* (London, 1973), p. 156.

58. Jay, *The Dialectical Imagination*, p. 166.
59. Martin Jay, *Adorno* (London, 1984), p. 38.
60. Theodor Adorno, "Was heißt: Aufarbeitung der Vergangenheit?" in: *Eingriffe. Neun kritische Modelle* (Frankfurt am Main, 1963).
61. Jay, *Adorno*, pp. 19ff.
62. Theodor Adorno, *Negative Dialektik*, (Frankfurt am Main, 1975), p. 358. Quoted from: Theodor Adorno, *Negative Dialectics* (London, 1966), p. 365.
63. Interview with Arno Widmann.
64. Detlev Claussen, *Theodor W. Adorno. Ein letztes Genie* (Frankfurt am Main, 2005), p. 395.
65. Interview with Tilman Fichter.
66. Ibid.
67. Interview with Detlev Claussen.
68. Ibid.
69. Wolfgang Kraushaar, "Von der Totalitarismustheorie zur Faschmismustheorie—Zu einem Paradigmenwechsel der bundesdeutschen Studentenbewegung," in: Alfons Söllner/Ralf Walkenhaus/Karin Weiland (hrsg.), *Totalitarismus. Eine Ideengeschichte des 20. Jahrhunderts* (Berlin, 1997), p. 272.

CHAPTER 2: REVOLUTIONARY OPTIMISM

1. Bergmann/Dutschke/Lefèvre/Rabehl, p. 18.
2. Fichter/Lönnendonker, *Kleine Geschichte des SDS*, p. 123.
3. David Clay Large, *Berlin*, p. 441. See also Lawrence Freedman, *Kennedy's Wars. Berlin, Cuba, Laos and Vietnam* (Oxford, 2000).
4. May, "America's Berlin."
5. Interview with Bernd Rabehl.
6. Interview with Hans-Christian Ströbele.
7. Ibid.
8. Interview with Klaus Meschkat.
9. Jürgen Horlemann/Peter Gäng, *Vietnam—Genesis eines Konflikts* (Frankfurt am Main, 1966).
10. The concept of "collective memory" was first used by the French sociologist Maurice Halbwachs in the 1920s. According to Halbwachs, collective memory is essentially a reconstruction of the past in the light of the present. In other words, it is memory that is selective, determined by present concerns rather than simply by the nature of the past itself. See Peter Novick, *The Holocaust and Collective Memory* (London, 1999), pp. 3 ff.
11. Siegward Lönnendonker, "Die Studentenrevolte und die Freie Universität Berlin." *Berliner Zeitung*, 30 January, 2001.
12. Markovits/Gorski, p. 53.
13. Aly, *Unser Kampf*, p. 147.

14. Dan Diner, *Feindbild Amerika. Über die Beständigkeit eines Ressentiments* (München, 2002), p. 138.
15. Bergmann/Dutschke/Lefèvre/Rabehl, p. 19.
16. Meinhof, *Die Würde des Menschen ist antastbar*, p. 110.
17. Interview with Hans-Christian Ströbele.
18. Aust, p. 47.
19. Interview with Tilman Fichter.
20. Michael 'Bommi' Baumann, *Wie alles anfing* (München, 1988), p. 41.
21. Gretchen Dutschke, *Wir hatten ein barbarisches, schönes, Leben. Rudi Dutschke. Eine Biographie* (Köln, 1996), p. 28.
22. Jürgen Miermeister, *Rudi Dutschke* (Reinbek, 1986), pp. 17 ff.
23. Interview with Bernd Rabehl.
24. Frank Böckelmann/Herbert Nagel (hrsg.), *Subversive Aktion. Der der Organisation ist ihr Scheitern* (Frankfurt am Main, 2002), p. 127.
25. Ulrich Enzensberger, *Die Jahre der Kommune 1. Berlin 1967–1969* (Munich, 2006), p. 27.
26. Arno Münster (hrsg.), *Tagträume vom aufrechten Gang. Sechs Interviews mit Ernst Bloch* (Frankfurt am Main, 1978), p. 118. I am grateful to Peter Thompson for this reference. On the influence of Bloch on Dutschke, see Jürgen Miermeister, *Ernst Bloch, Rudi Dutschke* (Hamburg, 1996).
27. Interview with Bahman Nirumand.
28. Rudi Dutschke, *Aufrecht gehen. Eine fragmentarische Autobiographie* (Frankfurt am Main, 1981), p. 29.
29. Interview with Tilman Fichter.
30. Gretchen Dutschke (hrsg.), *Rudi Dutschke. Jeder hat sein Leben ganz zu leben. Die Tagebücher 1963–1979* (Köln, 2003), p. 11.
31. Ibid.
32. Interview with Arno Widmann.
33. Herbert Marcuse, *One-Dimensional Man* (Boston, 1964), Introduction.
34. Marcuse, *One-Dimensional Man*, Ch. 10.
35. Ibid.
36. Herbert Marcuse, "Repressive Toleranz," in Robert Paul Wolff/Barrington Moore/Herbert Marcuse, *Kritik der reinen Toleranz* (Frankfurt am Main, 1966), p. 127. Quoted from: Robert Paul Wolff/Barrington Moore, Jr./ Herbert Marcuse, *A Critique of Pure Tolerance* (Boston, 1965).
37. Bergmann/Dutschke/Lefèvre/Rabehl, p. 73.
38. Bergmann/Dutschke/Lefèvre/Rabehl, p. 88.
39. Wolfgang Kraushaar, "Rudi Dutschke und der bewaffnete Kampf," in: Wolfgang Kraushaar (hrsg.), *Rudi Dutschke, Andreas Baader and die RAF* (Hamburg, 2005), p. 41.
40. Bergmann/Dutschke/Lefèvre/Rabehl, p. 89.
41. Bergmann/Dutschke/Lefèvre/Rabehl, p. 82.
42. Wolfgang Kraushaar, "Denkmodelle der 68er-Bewegung", in: *Aus Politik und Zeitgeschichte*, B22–23/2001, p. 23. The German translation, by Traugott König, was published as Frantz Fanon, *Die Verdammten dieser Erde* (Frankfurt, 1966).

43. Frantz Fanon, *The Wretched of the Earth*, (Harmondsworth, 1967), p. 27.
44. The key figure in the student movement's analysis of the Shah's regime was Bahman Nirumand, an Iranian opposition figure living in West Berlin. Nirumand had returned to Iran in the early sixties after studying in West Germany but was forced to leave again in 1965. In 1967, with the help of Hans Magnus Enzensberger, he had published a book on Iran that became a key text for the student movement. See Bahman Nirumand, *Persien. Modell eines Entwicklungslandes oder die Diktatur der Freien Welt*, (Reinbek, 1967).
45. *Das Ende der Utopie. Herbert Marcuse diskutiert mit Studenten und Professoren West-Berlins an der Freien Universität Berlin über Möglichkeiten einer politischen Opposition in den Metropolen im Zusammenhang mit den Befreiungsbewegungen in den Ländern der dritten Welt* (Berlin, 1967), p. 15.
46. Letter from Rudi Dutschke to Dieter Kunzelmann, 9 January, 1966. Quoted in: Kraushaar (hrsg.), *Rudi Dutschke, Andreas Baader and die RAF*, p. 29.
47. Kraushaar (hrsg.), *Rudi Dutschke, Andreas Baader and die RAF*, p. 33.
48. Wolfgang Kraushaar, *1968 als Mythos, Chiffre und Zäsur* (Hamburg, 2000), p. 121.
49. Gaston Salvatore/Rudi Dutschke, Einleitung zu: Che Guevara, *Schaffen wir zwei, drei, viele Vietnams* (Berlin, 1967).
50. Bergmann/Dutschke/Lefèvre/Rabehl, p. 69.
51. Wolfgang Kraushaar, *1968 als Mythos, Chiffre und Zäsur* (Hamburg, 2000), p. 103.
52. Gretchen Dutschke (hrsg.), *Rudi Dutschke. Jeder hat sein Leben ganz zu leben*, p. 55. On the use of the term *Machtergreifung*, see Norbert Frei, "Machtergreifung. Anmerkungen zu einem historischen Begriff," *Vierteljahrshefte für Zeitgeschichte*, 31/1983, pp. 136–145. Frei shows that although post-war historians' use of the term *Machtergreifung* identified it closely with Hitler's seizure of power, the Nazis themselves generally used the term *Machtübernahme*.
53. Enzensberger, *Die Jahre der Kommune 1*, p. 170.
54. Interview with Arno Widmann.
55. Diner, *Feindbild Amerika*, pp. 71–81.
56. Enzensberger, *Die Jahre der Kommune 1*, p. 156.
57. Ibid., p. 160. See also Wittlinger in Niven (ed.), p. 69.
58. Detlev Claussen, "Der kurze Sommer der Theorie" (unpublished paper provided by author), p. 4.
59. Bernward Vesper (hrsg.), *Bedingungen und Organisation des Widerstandes. Der Kongreß in Hanover* (Frankfurt am Main, 1967), p. 75.
60. Ibid., p. 78.
61. Gretchen Dutschke, *Wir hatten ein barbarisches, schönes, Leben*, p. 188.

62. Vesper (hrsg.), *Bedingungen und Organisation des Widerstandes*, p. 82.
63. Ibid., p. 101.
64. Ibid., p. 104.
65. Ibid.
66. Ibid.
67. Gretchen Dutschke (hrsg.), *Rudi Dutschke. Jeder hat sein Leben ganz zu leben*, p. 45.
68. For a more detailed account of the Six-Day War, see Michael B. Oren, *Six Days of War. June 1967 and the Making of the Modern Middle East* (Harmondsworth, 2003).
69. The Soviet Union had supported Israel since its creation but in 1954 switched its allegiance to the Arab states and in particular Syria. See Oren, p. 8.
70. Enzensberger, *Die Jahre der Kommune 1*, p. 158. See also Oren, p. 24.
71. Martin Kloke, "'Das zionistische Staatsgebilde als Brückenkopf des Imperialismus'. Vor vierzig Jahren wurde die neue deutsche Linke antiisraelisch", *Merkur*, June 2007.
72. On relations between West Germany and Israel, see Michael Wolffsohn, *Ewige Schuld? 40 Jahre deutsch-jüdisch-israelische Beziehungen* (München, 1988).
73. Enzensberger, *Die Jahre der Kommune 1*, p. 158.
74. Michael Jürgs, *Der Fall Springer* (München, 1995), p. 261.
75. Jürgs, p. 268.
76. Ibid., p. 274.
77. Wolffsohn, p. 97.
78. Dietrich Wetzel (hrsg.), *Die Verlängerung von Geschichte. Deutsche, Juden und der Palästinakonflikt* (Frankfurt am Main, 1983), p. 115. I am grateful to Martin Kloke for this reference.
79. Enzensberger, *Die Jahre der Kommune 1*, p. 157.
80. Tilman Fichter, "Der Staat Israel und die neue Linke in Deutschland." In: Karlheinz Schneider/Nikolaus Simon, (hrsg.), *Solidarität und deutsche Geschichte. Die Linke zwischen Antisemitismus und Israelkritik. Dokumentation einer Arbeitstagung in der Evangelischen Akademie Arnoldshain, August 1984* (Berlin, 1987), p. 92.
81. Letter of 8 June, 1967, by Eberhard Sommer. Quoted in Martin Kloke, "Antisemitismus in der deutschen Linke", *Tribüne*, March 2006, p. 124.
82. Kloke, "'Das zionistische Staatsgebilde als Brückenkopf des Imperialismus.'"
83. Meinhof, *Die Würde des Menschen ist antastbar*, p. 101.
84. Kloke, "'Das zionistische Staatsgebilde als Brückenkopf des Imperialismus.'"
85. Ibid.

CHAPTER 3: FROM PROTEST TO RESISTANCE

1. Interview with Bernd Rabehl.
2. Fichter/Lönnendonker, p. 115.
3. Gerd Koenen, *Das rote Jahrzehnt*, p. 18.
4. Baumann, p. 21.
5. Interview with Rainer Langhans.
6. Enzensberger, *Die Jahre der Kommune 1*, p. 70.
7. Ibid., p. 97.
8. Enzensberger, *Die Jahre der Kommune 1*, p. 101.
9. Jörg Lau, *Hans Magnus Enzensberger. Ein öffentliches Leben* (Frankfurt am Main, 2001), p. 245. See also Diner, *Feindbild Amerika*, pp. 141 ff.
10. Ibid.
11. Interview with Rainer Langhans.
12. Ibid.
13. Ibid.
14. Enzensberger, *Die Jahre der Kommune 1*, p. 22.
15. Dieter Kunzelmann, *Leisten Sie keinen Widerstand* (Berlin, 1998), p. 49.
16. Enzensberger, *Die Jahre der Kommune 1*, p. 160.
17. Ibid., p. 123.
18. Meinhof, *Die Würde des Menschen ist antastbar*, p. 93.
19. Ibid., p. 93.
20. Enzensberger, *Die Jahre der Kommune 1*, p. 123.
21. Fichter/ Lönnendonker, p. 105.
22. Enzensberger, *Die Jahre der Kommune 1*, p. 242.
23. Fichter/Lönnendonker, p. 129.
24. Ibid.
25. Aust, p. 49.
26. www.krahl-seiten.de.
27. Interview with Detlev Claussen.
28. Hans-Jürgen Krahl, *Konstitution und Klassenkampf. Zur historischen Dialektik von bürgerlicher Emanzipation und proletarischer Revolution* (Frankfurt am Main, 1971), p. 20.
29. Kraushaar (hrsg.), *Frankfurter Schule und Studentenbewegung*, vol. 1, p. 254.
30. Stefan Müller-Doohm, *Adorno. A Biography* (Cambridge, 2005), p. 452.
31. Ibid., p. 451.
32. Ibid., p. 456.
33. Ibid., p. 454.
34. Krahl, *Konstitution und Klassenkampf*, p. 285.
35. Müller-Doohm, p. 456.
36. Rudi Dutschke/Hans-Jürgen Krahl, "Organisationsreferat," quoted in Miermeister, p. 85.
37. Ibid.
38. Wolfgang Kraushaar, *Die Bombe im jüdischen Gemeindehaus* (Hamburg, 2005), p. 81.

39. Kloke, "'Das zionistische Staatsgebilde als Brückenkopf des Imperialismus.'"
40. Paul Berman, "The Passion of Joschka Fischer," *The New Republic*, 27 August, 2001.
41. It emerged in May 2009 that Kurras had been a Stasi agent from 1955 until 1967. A gun enthusiast, he applied to move from West Germany to East Germany in 1955 when he was already a policeman. The East German authorities asked him instead to remain in West Berlin and spy on his colleagues for the Stasi, which he did under the codename "Otto Bohl" until the shooting of 2 June, 1967. See "Verrat vor dem Schuss," *Der Spiegel*, 25 May, 2009; Stefan Reinicke, "Der Untertan", *die tageszeitung*, 24 May, 2009; Jana Simon, "Ein Verräter, der die Verräter verriet", *Die Zeit*, 28 May, 2009; Götz Aly, "Wir alle haben uns geirrt", *Die Zeit*, 28 May, 2009.
42. Aly, *Unser Kampf*, p. 81.
43. Enzensberger, *Die Jahre der Kommune 1*, p. 248.
44. See for example the banner depicted in Gerd Koenen/ Andres Veiel, *1968. Bildspur eines Jahres* (Köln, 2008), p. 125.
45. Fichter/Lönnendonker, *Kleine Geschichte des SDS*, p. 121.
46. Gretchen Dutschke, *Wir hatten ein barbarisches, schönes, Leben*, p. 195.
47. Interview with Alain Krivine.
48. Interview with Bernd Rabehl.
49. Gretchen Dutschke, *Wir hatten ein barbarisches, schönes, Leben*, p. 489.
50. Ibid., p. 178.
51. Ibid.
52. Ibid., p. 180.
53. Bahman Nirumand, *Mein Leben mit den Deutschen* (Reinbek, 1989), p. 112.
54. Kraushaar, *Andreas Baader, Rudi Dutschke und die RAF*, p. 25.
55. Interview with Bernd Rabehl.
56. Gretchen Dutschke, *Wir hatten ein barbarisches, schönes, Leben*, p. 181.
57. Ali/Watkins, p. 47.
58. Gretchen Dutschke, *Wir hatten ein barbarisches, schönes, Leben*, p. 177.
59. Ali, *Street Fighting Years*, p. 245.
60. Interview with Alain Krivine.
61. Aust, p. 76.
62. Aust, p. 75.
63. Gerd Koenen, *Vesper, Ensslin, Baader. Urszenen des deutschen Terrorismus* (Frankfurt am Main, 2005), pp. 46, 52.
64. See Michael Kapellen, *Doppelt leben. Berward Vesper und Gudrun Ensslin. Die Tübinger Jahre* (Tübingen, 2005).
65. Koenen, *Vesper, Ensslin, Baader*, p. 28. The magazine *Die neue Literatur* was published from 1933 to 1943 and in particular attacked Jewish publishers.
66. Michael Kapellen points out that the anthology also included right-wing authors like Hans Baumann, who had written songs for the Hitler Youth (Kapellen, p. 147).

67. Dorothea Hauser, *Baader und Herold. Beschreibung eines Kampfes* (Berlin, 1997), p. 48.
68. Koenen, *Vesper, Ensslin, Baader*, p. 106.
69. Hauser, *Baader und Herold*, p. 79.
70. Ibid., p. 111.
71. Aust, p. 63.
72. Aust, p. 61.
73. Hauser, *Baader und Herold*, p. 112.
74. Aust, p. 65.
75. Aust, p. 66.
76. Enzensberger, *Die Jahre der Kommune 1*, p. 270.
77. Meinhof, p. 154.
78. Aust, p. 67.
79. Kraushaar, *Andreas Baader, Rudi Dutschke und die RAF*, p. 25.
80. Ali/Watkins, pp. 74ff.
81. Kraushaar, *Die Bombe im jüdischen Gemeindehaus*, p. 239.
82. Ibid.
83. Miermeister, p. 94.
84. Ali/Watkins, p. 79.
85. Fichter/Lönnendonker, p. 127.
86. Baumann, p. 47.
87. Enzensberger, *Die Jahre der Kommune 1*, p. 284.
88. Meinhof, p. 138.
89. Meinhof, p. 140.
90. Ibid.
91. Ibid.

CHAPTER 4: AN ABOMINABLE IRRATIONALISM

1. Miermeister, p. 106.
2. Fichter/Lönnendonker, p. 131.
3. Fichter/Lönnendonker, p. 133.
4. Fichter/Lönnendonker, p. 134.
5. Krahl, *Konstitution und Klassenkampf*, p. 149.
6. Ibid., p. 151.
7. It has frequently been pointed out that it was in Germany, Italy and Japan—in other words the three leading Axis powers of World War II-that the protest movement of the sixties turned particularly violent. See, for example, Dorothea Hauser, "Deutschland, Italien, Japan. Die ehemaligen Achsenmächte und der Terrorismus der 1970er Jahre", in: Wolfgang Kraushaar (hrsg.), *Die RAF und der linke Terrorismus* (Hamburg, 2006).
8. Stefan Reisner (hrsg.), *Briefe an Rudi D.* (Berlin, 1968), p. iv.
9. Reisner (hrsg.), *Briefe an Rudi D.*, p. v.
10. Miermeister, p. 104.

11. Aust, p. 82.
12. Interview with Horst Mahler.
13. Aust, p. 81.
14. Koenen, Vesper, Ensslin, Baader, p. 182.
15. Aust, p. 77.
16. Hauser, *Baader und Herold*, p. 151.
17. Fichter/Lönnendonker, p. 137.
18. Letter from Herbert Marcuse to Theodor Adorno, 5 April, 1969. Quoted in: "Correspondence on the German student movement", *New Left Review*, January/February 1999, p. 125.
19. Herbert Marcuse, *Versuch über die Befreiung* (Frankfurt am Main, 1969), p. 80.
20. Interview with Detlev Claussen.
21. Ibid.
22. Ibid.
23. Müller-Doohm, p. 461.
24. Ibid.
25. Müller-Doohm, p. 464.
26. Müller-Doohm, p. 464.
27. Claussen, *Adorno. Ein letztes Genie*, p. 399.
28. Koenen, p. 201.
29. Letter from Herbert Marcuse to Theodor Adorno, 5 April, 1969. Quoted in: "Correspondence on the German student movement", *New Left Review*, January/February 1999, p. 125.
30. Interview with Detlev Claussen.
31. Müller-Doohm, p. 475.
32. Letter from Theodor Adorno to Herbert Marcuse, 19 June, 1969. Quoted in Müller-Doohm, p. 477.
33. Ibid. Quoted in Müller-Doohm, p. 478.
34. Interview with Joschka Fischer.
35. Dietrich Thränhardt, *Geschichte der Bundesrepublik Deutschland* (Frankfurt am Main, 1996), p. 181.
36. Interview with Jochka Fischer.
37. Ibid.
38. Ibid.
39. Ibid.
40. Ibid. See also Fischer, *Die rot-grünen Jahre*, p. 410.
41. Geis/Ulrich, p. 24.
42. Gretchen Dutschke, *Wir hatten ein barbarisches, schönes, Leben*, p. 159.
43. Matthias Geis/Bernd Ulrich, *Der Unvollendete. Das Leben des Joschka Fischer* (Berlin, 2002), p. 36.
44. Geis/Ulrich, p. 37.
45. Interview with Joschka Fischer.
46. Wolfgang Kraushaar, *Fischer in Frankfurt. Karriere eines Außenseiters* (Hamburg, 2001), p. 80.

NOTES

Die Bombe im jüdischen Gemeindehaus, p. 292.

ation au pouvoir: Entretien de Jean-Paul Sartre avec Daniel dit," *Le Nouvel Observateur*, 20 May, 1968. The interview is :d in full in German in Rudolf Sievers (hrsg.), *1968. Eine* *ädie* (Frankfurt am Main, 2004), pp. 263–271.

49. Alain i .nkielkraut, *The Imaginary Jew* (Lincoln, 1994), p. 17. See also Wittlinger in Niven (ed.), p. 69.

50. Daniel Cohn-Bendit, *Der grosse Basar* (München, 1975), p. 102.

51. Daniel Cohn-Bendit, *Wir haben sie so geliebt, die Revolution* (Frankfurt am Main, 1987), p. 114.

52. Koenen, *Das rote Jahrzehnt*, p. 190.

53. Markovits/Gorski, p. 60.

54. The KPD/AO was established in 1970. The initials AO were subsequently dropped from the party's name and it became the KPD until it was dissolved in 1980. In the remainder of the text I will refer to the group as the Maoist KPD. See Karl Schlögel/Willi Jasper/Bernd Ziesemer, *Partei kaputt. Das Scheitern der KPD und die Krise der Linken* (Berlin, 1981).

55. Koenen, *Das rote Jahrzehnt*, pp. 464 ff.

56. Interview with Helke Sander.

57. Fichter/Lönnendonker, p. 142. For the full text of the speech, see Helke Sander, "Rede des 'Aktionrates zur Befreiung der Frauen' bei der 23. Delegiertenkonferenz des 'Sozialistischen Deutschen Studentenbundes' (SDS) im September 1968," in: Sievers (hrsg.), pp. 372–378.

58. Interview with Helke Sander.

59. Baumann, p. 37.

60. Kraushaar, *Die Bombe im jüdischen Gemeindehaus*, p. 242.

61. Inga Buhmann, *Ich habe mir eine Geschichte geschrieben* (Munich, 1977), p. 289.

62. Baumann, p. 56.

63. Baumann, p. 55.

64. Baumann, p. 59.

65. Baumann, p. 52.

66. Baumann, p. 65.

67. See Kraushaar, *Die Bombe im jüdischen Gemeindehaus*, pp. 86–104.

68. Ibid., p. 121.

69. Ibid., p. 46.

70. Ibid., p. 48.

71. Ibid., p. 68.

72. Ibid.

73. Enzensberger, *Die Jahre der Kommune 1*, p. 343.

74. Baumann, p. 79.

75. Diner, *Feindbild Amerika*, p. 138.

76. The concept of *Schuldabwehrantisemitismus* was introduced in Institut für Sozialfoschung (hrsg.), *Gruppenexperiment. Ein Studienbericht* (Frankfurt am Main, 1955).

77. Koenen, *Das rote Jahrzehnt*, p. 179.
78. Ibid.
79. I would like to thank Udi Greenberg for this formulation.
80. Kraushaar, *Die Bombe im jüdischen Gemeindehaus*, pp. 239–240.
81. Ibid., p. 248.
82. Ibid., p 248.
83. Ibid.
84. Dietrich Thränhardt, *Geschichte der Bundesrepublik Deutschland* (Frankfurt am Main, 1996), p. 198.
85. Fichter/Lönnendonker, p. 140.

CHAPTER 5: THE STRUGGLE CONTINUES

1. Enzensberger, *Die Jahre der Kommune 1*, p. 86.
2. Kraushaar, *Die Bombe im jüdischen Gemeindehaus*, p. 160.
3. Ibid., p. 156.
4. Günter Langer, "Der Berliner 'Blues.' Tupamaros und umherschweifende Haschrebellen zwischen Wahnsinn und Verstand," in: Eckhard Siepmann u.a., *Che Schah Shit. Die sechziger Jahre zwischen Cocktail und Molotov* (West-Berlin, 1988), p. 196.
5. Aly, *Unser Kampf*, p. 166.
6. Siepmann, *Che Schah Shit*, p. 167.
7. Kraushaar, *Die Bombe im jüdischen Gemeindehaus*, p. 122. On the campaign for *Bundeswehr* deserters, see Horst Mahler/Ulrich K. Preuss, *Deserteur Kollektiv. BIG LIFT oder die Freiheit der Deserteure* (Frankfurt, 1969).
8. Kraushaar, *Die Bombe im jüdischen Gemeindehaus*, p. 186.
9. On Kommune 2, see Jan-Carl Raspe (hrsg.) *Kommune 2. Versuch einer Revolutionierung des bürgerlichen Individiuums* (Berlin, 1969).
10. Aust, p. 84.
11. Koenen, *Vesper, Ensslin, Baader*, p. 219.
12. Aust, p. 118.
13. Aust, p. 125.
14. Aust, p. 133.
15. Willi Winkler, "'Der Staat war das Böse.' Ein *Zeit*-Gespräch mit dem Ex-Terroristen Horst Mahler über die APO, den Weg in den Terror und die Versöhnung mit dem Grundgesetz," *Die Zeit*, 2 May, 1997.
16. Aust, p. 129.
17. Aust, p. 141.
18. Interview with Tilman Fichter.
19. Aust, p. 144.
20. Kraushaar, *Fischer in Frankfurt*, p. 80.
21. Cohn-Bendit, *Der grosse Basar*, p. 69.
22. Ibid., p. 97.
23. Ibid., p. 34.

24. Ibid., p. 35.
25. Sibylle Krause-Burger, *Joschka Fischer. Der lange March durch die Illusionen* (Stuttgart, 1997), p. 100.
26. Kraushaar, *Fischer in Frankfurt* (Hamburg, 2001), p. 29.
27. Knapp, the last chairman of the SDS, described the trip many years later. Udo Knapp, "Die Reise nach Algier. Mit Joschka Fischer in Nordafrika: Wie es war, was uns bewegte," *Frankfurter Allgemeine Zeitung*, 15 January, 2001. Like Fischer, Knapp later joined the Greens.
28. Kraushaar, *Fischer in Frankfurt*, p. 212.
29. Interview with Klaus Lange.
30. Michael Schwelien, *Joschka Fischer. Eine Karriere* (Hamburg, 2000), p. 153.
31. See Revolutionärer Kampf, "Betriebsarbeit bei Opel-Rüsselsheim: Abbau gerwerkschaftlichter Herrschaftsinstrumente durch Massenagitation", in *diskus—Frankfurter Studentenzeitung*, December 1971.
32. Interview with Ulrich Enzensberger.
33. Enzensberger, *Die Jahre der Kommune 1*, p. 216.
34. Interview with Ottmar Schreiner.
35. Ibid.
36. Fichter/Lönnendonker, p. 187.
37. Thränhardt, p. 223.
38. Thränhardt, p. 224.
39. Thränhardt, p. 197.
40. Interview with Joschka Fischer.
41. Jeffrey Herf, *Divided Memory. The Nazi Past in the two Germanys* (Cambridge, Massachusetts, 1997), p. 345.
42. Aust, p. 139.
43. Rote Armee Fraktion, "Das Konzept Stadguerrilla."
44. Ibid.
45. Aust, p. 245.
46. Aust, p. 249.
47. Simon Reeve, *One Day in September* (London, 2000), p. 12.
48. Aust, p. 272.
49. Aust, p. 273.
50. Koenen, *Das rote Jahrzehnt*, p. 410.
51. Ibid.
52. Aly, *Unser Kampf*, p. 158.
53. Koenen, *Das rote Jahrzehnt*, p. 372.
54. Aust, p. 204.
55. Karl-Dietrich Wolff (hrsg.), *15 Jahre Almanach aufs Jahr 1968* (Basel/Frankfurt am Main, 1985), p. 18.
56. Koenen, *Das rote Jahrzehnt*, p. 338. See also Martin Klimke, "Black Panther, die RAF und die Rolle der Black Panther-Solidaritätskomitees," in Wolfgang Kraushaar (hrsg.), *Die RAF und der linke Terrorismus* (Hamburg, 2006), pp. 562–582.

57. Interview with Karl-Dietrich Wolff.
58. Koenen, *Das rote Jahrzehnt*, p. 339.
59. Ibid., p. 367.
60. Kraushaar, *Fischer in Frankfurt*, p. 242.
61. "Ein Segen für dieses Land," *Der Spiegel*, 29 January, 2001.
62. Margrit Schiller, *Es war ein harter Kampf um meine Erinnerung. Ein Lebensbericht aus der RAF* (München, 2001), p. 116.
63. Schwelien, p. 38.
64. Koelbl, p. 34.
65. Aust, p. 494.
66. Koenen, *Das rote Jahrzehnt*, p. 362.
67. Koenen, *Vesper, Ensslin, Baader*, p 9.
68. Koenen, *Vesper, Ensslin, Baader*, p. 197.
69. Ibid., pp. 14–15.
70. The unfinished book was published by März, a left-wing publisher, in 1977. The definitive edition is Bernward Vesper, *Die Reise. Romanessay. Ausgabe letzter Hand* (Reinbek, 1983). März was founded in Frankfurt in 1969 by Jörg Schröder, who also sold pornographic books and magazines to subsidise his literary publications. Joschka Fischer occasionally translated English-language pornography into German for Schröder.
71. Kraushaar, *Fischer in Frankfurt*, pp. 38ff.
72. Ibid., p. 43.
73. Interview with Klaus Lange.
74. Ibid.
75. Koenen, *Das rote Jahrzehnt*, p. 346.
76. Kraushaar, *Fischer in Frankfurt*, p. 69. In 1985 Rainer Werner Fassbinder directed a play in Frankfurt, "Der Müll, die Stadt und der Tod" ("Garbage, the City and Death"), which was based on the Frankfurt *Häuserkampf*. Some saw the Jewish property speculator in the play, who is referred to simply as "The Rich Jew", as a thinly veiled portrait of Ignatiz Bubis. Bubis was among protesters who accused Fassbinder of anti-Semitism and walked on to stage on the opening night to prevent the play from being performed. On anti-Semitism in the Frankfurt squatting movement, see Kraushaar, *Fischer in Frankfurt*, pp. 76–79.
77. Kraushaar, *Fischer in Frankfurt*, p. 72.
78. Koenen, p. 406.
79. Aust, p. 270.
80. Aust, p. 292.
81. Aust, p. 293.
82. Aust, p. 302.
83. Aust, p. 302.
84. Aust, p. 305.
85. Aust, p. 306.
86. Aust, p. 311.
87. Gretchen Dutschke, *Rudi Dutschke. Jeder hat sein Leben ganz zu leben*, p. 213.

88. Miermeister, p. 112.
89. Aust, p. 312.

CHAPTER 6: DEATH TRIP

1. Thränhardt, p. 207.
2. Ibid.
3. The concept of the "sceptical generation" originates with the German sociologist Helmut Schelsky and usually refers to those born between 1910 and 1926—in other words, the parents of the "1968 generation". Schelsky argued that their experience of the war made them pragmatic and anti-ideological. Helmut Schelsky, *Die skeptische Generation. Eine Soziologie der deutschen Jugend* (Düsseldorf, 1957).
4. Thränhardt, p. 209.
5. Thränhardt, p. 207.
6. Aust, p. 315.
7. Aust, p. 319.
8. Aust, p. 313.
9. Aust, p. 313.
10. Aust, p. 325.
11. Koenen, *Das rote Jahrzehnt*, p. 407.
12. Hauser, *Baader und Herold*, p. 172.
13. Dorothea Hauser, "Der Kriminalphilosoph," *Die Zeit*, 23 October, 2003.
14. See Hauser, *Baader und Herold*.
15. Koenen, *Das rote Jahrzehnt*, p. 374.
16. Aust, p. 330.
17. Aust, p. 337.
18. Aust, p. 357.
19. Aust, p. 386.
20. Aust, p. 391.
21. Aust, p. 392.
22. Aust, p. 396.
23. Cohn-Bendit, *Wir haben sie so geliebt, die Revolution*, p. 166.
24. Kraushaar, *Fischer in Frankfurt*, pp. 133 ff.
25. Ibid., pp. 136 ff.
26. Koenen, *Das rote Jahrzehnt*, p. 331.
27. Ibid., p. 332.
28. Ibid., p. 333.
29. Joschka Fischer, "Vortoß in 'primitivere' Zeiten—Befreiung und Militanz," in: *Autonomie. Materialien gegen die Fabrikgesellschaft*, Nr. 5, 2/77.
30. Ibid.
31. Koenen, *Das rote Jahrzehnt*, p. 331.
32. Interview with Karl-Dietrich Wolff.

33. Interview with Thomas Schmid.
34. Koenen, *Das rote Jahrzehnt*, p. 412.
35. Interview with Joschka Fischer.
36. Cohn-Bendit, *Der grosse Basar*, pp. 11–17.
37. Fischer, *Die rot-grünen Jahre*, p. 412.
38. Interview with Joschka Fischer.
39. Krause-Burger, p. 110.
40. Ibid.
41. Schwelien, p. 180.
42. Ibid.
43. Interview with Horst Mahler.
44. Kraushaar, *Die Bombe im jüdischen Gemeindehaus*, p. 176.
45. Horst Mahler, "Ausbruch aus einem Mißverständnis," in: *Kursbuch* 48, 1977.
46. Ibid.
47. Horst Mahler, "Appell aus dem Knast," *das da*, November 1977.
48. Horst Mahler/Franz Schönhuber, *Schluss mit deutschem Selbsthass. Plädoyers für ein anderes Deutschland* (Berg am Starnberger See, 2001), p. 38.
49. Interview with Horst Mahler.
50. Mahler/Schönhuber, *Schluss mit deutschem Selbsthass*, p. 38.
51. Aust, p. 399.
52. Aust, p. 400.
53. Aust, p. 401.
54. Ibid.
55. Koenen, *Das rote Jahrzehnt*, p. 390.
56. Aust, p. 454.
57. Lutz Hachmeister, *Schleyer. Eine deutsche Geschichte* (München, 2007), p. 12. It is sometimes claimed that Schleyer worked closely with Reinhard Heydrich, the Protector of Bohemia and Moravia. As Hachmeister shows, this is not quite true. Schleyer was in fact an assistant to Bernhard Adolf, the head of the Industrial Federation of Bohemia and Moravia, which played a key role in the "Aryanisation" of Czech industry and the organisation of slave labour for the German war machine. After three years' internment after the end of the war, Schleyer was classified as a *Mitläufer*, or fellow traveller.
58. Aust, p. 514.
59. "Geheimeoperation im Ländle", *Der Spiegel*, 8 September, 2008. Stefan Aust/Helmar Büchel, "Der letzte Ake der Rebellion," *Der Spiegel*, 10 September, 2007.
60. Koenen, *Das rote Jahrzehnt*, p. 364.
61. Aust, p. 646.
62. Ibid.
63. Aust, p. 647
64. Aust, p. 479.

65. Koelbl, p. 34.
66. Schwelien, p. 180.
67. Peter-Jürgen Boock/Peter Schneider, *Ratte—tot... Ein Briefwechsel* (Darmstadt und Neuwied, 1985), p. 9.
68. Aust, p. 216.
69. Ibid.
70. Thränhardt, p. 234.

CHAPTER 7: A LIFELINE

1. Miermeister, p. 113.
2. Gretchen Dutschke, *Wir hatten ein barbarisches, schönes Leben*, p. 362.
3. Kraushaar, *1968 als Mythos, Chiffre und Zäsur*, p. 108.
4. Ibid.
5. Ibid. On the concept of an "imagined community", see Benedict Anderson, *Imagined Communities. Reflections on the Origin and Spread of Nationalism* (London, 1991).
6. Rudi Dutschke said surprisingly little about the "German Autumn" of 1977. In an article for *Die Zeit* shortly after the kidnapping of Hanns Martin Schleyer in September 1977 he condemned acts of "individual terror", which, he said, "blur terribly the real contradictions and possibilities for political class struggle," and also criticised attempts to blame the New Left for terrorism, which he said "can only be understood as a witch hunt against intellectuals" (Dutschke, *Mein Langer Marsch*, p. 104). But apart from that he remained strikingly silent, even in private. There is for example, only one entry in his diary in September 1977, in which he once again criticises attempts to "make us in the SDS responsible for terrorism", and none at at all in October 1977 (Gretchen Dutschke (hrsg.), *Rudi Dutschke. Jeder hat sein Leben ganz zu leben*, p. 289).
7. Kraushaar, *1968 als Mythos, Chiffre und Zäsur*, p. 115.
8. Karl Marx and Friedrich Engels, *The Communist Manifesto* (Harmondsworth, 1985), p. 92.
9. Wolfgang Kraushaar, "Zur Dimension des Nationalen bei Rudi Dutschke" (unpublished paper).
10. Rudi Dutschke, "Die Deutschen und der Sozialismus", in: *das da*, July 1977.
11. Kraushaar, *1968 als Mythos, Chiffre und Zäsur*, p. 116.
12. On the development of German nationalism, see for example John Breuilly (ed.), *The State of Germany. The national idea in the making, unmaking and remaking of a modern nation-state (London, 1992); Michael Hughes, Nationalism and Society. Germany, 1800–1945* (London, 1988); Hagen Schulze, *The Course of German Nationalism. From Frederick the Great to Bismarck, 1763–1867* (Cambridge, 1991). On nationalism in general see Benedict Anderson, *Imagined Communities. Reflections on the Origin and Spread of Nationalism* (London, 1991), Ernest Gellner, *Nations and*

Nationalism (Oxford, 1983); Anthony Smith, *National Identity* (Harmondsworth, 1991).

13. Hughes, p. 22.
14. Hughes, p. 12.
15. The contrast comes from the 1915 book by the German sociologist Werner Sombart, *Händler und Helden: Patriotische Besinnungen* (München/Leipzig, 1915).
16. On Marx's view of the special role of the Jews in capitalism, see in particular his essay "On the Jewish Question," in Karl Marx, *Early Writings* (Harmondsworth, 1992), pp. 211–241.
17. I would like to thank Karen Leeder for helping me with the translation of these lines.
18. On the emergence of the anti-nuclear movement in the late 1970s, see Markovits, Andrei S./Gorski, Philip S. *The German Left. Red, Green and Beyond* (Cambridge, 1993).
19. On right-wing currents within the environmental movement in Germany, see Jonathan Olsen, *Nature and Nationalism. Right-Wing Ecology and the politics of identity in contemporary Germany* (London, 1999).
20. In 1965 the *Deutsche Gemeinschaft* merged with two other far-right parties, the *Deutsche Freiheitspartei* (DFP) and the *Vereinigung Deutsche Nationalversammlung* (VDNV), to form the *Aktionsgemeinschaft Unabhängiger Deutscher* (UAD). The UAD believed in a neutral, reunified Germany nonaligned to the United States or the Soviet Union and "employed a language shared by the New Left" (Olsen, *Nature and Nationalism*, p. 92). In the 1970s it also began to campaign on environmental issues.
21. Markovits/Gorski, p. 171.
22. Markovits/Gorski, p. 133.
23. Lau, p. 192.
24. Lau, p. 193. On Hannah Arendt's attitude to the West German student movement, see Wolfgang Kraushaar, "Hannah Arendt und die Studentenbewegung. Anmerkungen zum Briefwechsel zwischen Hans-Jürgen Benedict und Hannah Arendt," *Mittelweg 36*, 1/2008.
25. Gretchen Dutschke-Klotz/Helmut Gollwitzer/Jürgen Miermeister, *Rudi Dutschke. Mein langer Marsch. Reden, Schriften und Tagebücher aus zwanzig Jahren* (Reinbek, 1980), p. 196.
26. Ibid.
27. Ibid.
28. Ulrich Chaussy, *Die drei Leben des Rudi Dutschke. Eine Biographie* (Berlin, 1993), p. 326.
29. Interview with Hubert Kleinert.
30. Interview with Klaus Lange.
31. Kraushaar, *Fischer in Frankfurt*, p. 173.
32. Geis/Ulrich, p. 76.
33. Krause-Burger, p. 114.

34. Kraushaar, *Fischer in Frankfurt*, p. 172.
35. Ibid, p. 173.
36. Thränhardt, p. 224.
37. On the continuation of the struggle between the wartime and the post-war generations within the SPD in the 1970s, see Andrei S.Markovits, Andrei S./Philip S. Gorski, *The German Left. Red, Green and Beyond* (Cambridge, 1993).
38. Markovits/Gorski, p. 94.
39. Interview with Klaus-Uwe Benneter.
40. Koenen, *Das rote Jahrzehnt*, p. 203.
41. Interview with Klaus-Uwe Benneter.
42. Markovits/Gorski, p. 97.
43. Koenen, *Das rote Jahrzehnt*, p. 205.
44. Interview with Gerhard Schröder.
45. Gerhard Schröder, *Entscheidungen. Mein Leben in der Politik* (Hamburg, 2006), p. 32.
46. Interview with Gerhard Schröder.
47. Schröder, *Entscheidungen*, p. 28.
48. Interview with Manfred Bissinger.
49. Schröder, *Entscheidungen*, p. 34.
50. Béla Anda/Rolf Kleine, *Gerhard Schröder. Eine Biographie* (München, 2002), p. 36.
51. "Spiegel-Streitgespräch zwischen Bundesinnenminister Gerhart Baum und Ex-Terrorist Horst Mahler über den politischen Untergrund," *Der Spiegel*, 31 December, 1979.
52. Koenen, *Das rote Jahrzehnt*, p. 309.
53. Volmer, p. 52.
54. Dutschke-Klotz/Gollwitzer/ Miermeister, *Rudi Dutschke. Mein langer Marsch*, p. 204.
55. Götz Aly has recently argued that the student movement chose to ignore information about "the murderous side of the Cultural Revolution" that was readily available in West Germany even in the sixties. See Aly, *Unser Kampf*, pp. 104–115.
56. Krause-Burger, p. 117.
57. On the history of the *taz*, see Jörg Magenau, *die taz. Eine Zeitung als Lebensform* (München, 2007).

CHAPTER 8: PEACE

1. Markovits/Gorski, p. 106.
2. Markovits/Gorski, p. 170.
3. Markovits/Gorski, p. 109.
4. Ansgar Graw, *Gerhard Schröder. Der Weg nach oben* (Düsseldorf, 1998), p. 39.

5. This was at least partly because of the influence of the East German state, which had, through the Stasi, extensively infiltrated the peace movement. See Hubertus Knabe, *Die unterwanderte Republik. Stasi im Westen* (Berlin, 1999), pp. 243–255.
6. Graw, p. 49.
7. Graw, p. 50.
8. Markovits/Gorski, p. 110.
9. On the influence of the "K-Groups" on the early foreign policy of the Greens, see Ludger Volmer, *Die Grünen und die Außenpolitik. Ein schwieriges Verhältnis* (Münster, 1998), pp. 51–65.
10. Thränhardt, p. 256.
11. Volmer, p. 66.
12. Volmer, p. 69.
13. Volmer, p. 79.
14. Volmer, p. 226.
15. On the attitude of the Greens towards Nazism and how it related to the debate about the missile deployment in West Germany, see Andrea Humphreys, "'Ein atomares Auschwitz': Die Lehren der Geschichte und der Streit um die Nachrüstung," *Jahrbuch Grünes Gedächtnis 2008* (Berlin, 2007).
16. See Petra Kelly (hrsg.), *Laßt uns die Kraniche suchen. Hiroshima—Analysen, Berichte, Gedanken* (München, 1983).
17. Humphreys, "'Ein atomares Auschwitz': Die Lehren der Geschichte und der Streit um die Nachrüstung,", *Jahrbuch Grünes Gedächtnis 2008* (Berlin, 2007), p. 51. On the "Nuremberg trial," see Die Grünen, *Tribunal gegen Erstschlags-und Massenvernichtungswaffen in Ost und West 18.2.83 Nürnberg Meistersingerhalle* (Bonn, 1983).
18. Nuremberg was chosen for the tribunal in 1945 because it had been the scene of Nazi rallies but also because it was "among the dead cities" of Germany—in other words, those that had been destroyed by wartime bombing. A.C. Grayling, *Among the Dead Cities* (London, 2006), p. 12.
19. Humphreys, "'Ein atomares Auschwitz': Die Lehren der Geschichte und der Streit um die Nachrüstung,", p. 40.
20. Ibid., p. 41.
21. Ibid., p. 40; Volmer, p. 46. On the concept of "exterminism", which was taken up by the East German dissident and environmental activist Rudolf Bahro, see E.P. Thompson, "Notes on exterminism, the last stage of civilization", *New Left Review*, May-June 1980. Thompson's essay was reproduced in an anthology produced by the Green party leadership in 1981. Die Grünen, *Entrüstet Euch. Analysen zur atomaren Bedrohung. Wege zum Frieden* (Bonn, 1981).
22. Jutta Ditfurth, *Das waren die Grünen* (München, 2001).
23. Geis/Ulrich, p. 78.
24. Kraushaar, *Fischer in Frankfurt*, p. 175.
25. Ibid., p. 177.

26. Ibid., p. 178.
27. Until then, the main conflict within the Greens had been between "rationalists" (a group which included eco-socialists and eco-libertarians as well as "realists" like Fischer) on one hand and "spiritualists", "naturalists" and "symbolists" like Petra Kelly on the other. See Volmer, p. 149.
28. Thränhardt, p. 264.
29. Geis/Ulrich, p. 84.
30. Geis/Ulrich, p. 87.
31. Geis/Ulrich, p. 88.
32. Schwelien, p. 227.
33. Joschka Fischer, *Regieren geht über Studieren. Ein politisches Tagebuch* (Frankfurt am Main, 1987), p. 32.
34. Schwelien, p. 223.
35. Boock/Schneider, p. 10.
36. Humphreys, "'Ein atomares Auschwitz': Die Lehren der Geschichte und der Streit um die Nachrüstung," p. 42. The interview with Fischer and Schily was published as "'Wir sind ein schöner Unkrautgarten'. Die grünen Abgeordneten Joschka Fischer und Otto Schily über die Auseinandersetzungen in ihrer Partei," *Der Spiegel*, 13 June, 1983.
37. Humphreys, "'Ein atomares Auschwitz': Die Lehren der Geschichte und der Streit um die Nachrüstung," p. 42.
38. Ibid., p. 43.
39. Ibid., p. 44.
40. Novick, *The Holocaust and Collective Memory*, p. 3.
41. Novick, p. 213.
42. Ibid.
43. Herf, *Divided Memory*, p. 346.
44. For a longer discussion of the use of the Nazi past in *Bundestag* debates, see Helmut Dubiel, *Niemand ist frei von der Geschichte. Die nationalsozialistische Herrschaft in den Debatten des deutschen Bundestages* (München, 1999).
45. Humphreys, "'Ein atomares Auschwitz': Die Lehren der Geschichte und der Streit um die Nachrüstung," p. 46.
46. Ibid., p. 42.
47. Ernst von Weizsäcker was state secretary in the foreign office from 1938 to 1943 and German ambassador to the Vatican from 1943 to 1945. Although he was a member of the Nazi party and held SS rank, he claimed he had in fact supported the resistance against Hitler. He was sentenced to five years' imprisonment as a war criminal in 1949, but was released the next year on an amnesty.
48. Speech to the *Bundestag* on 8 May, 1985.
49. Herf, *Divided Memory*, p. 372.
50. *"Historikerstreit." Die Dokumentation der Kontroverse um die Einzigartigkeit der nationalsozialistischen Judenvernichtung* (München, 1987), p. 45.

51. Charles S. Maier, *The Unmasterable Past. History, Holocaust and German National Identity* (Cambridge, Mass., 1997), p. 2.
52. Maier, *The Unmasterable Past*, p. 47.
53. For an introduction to the concept of constitutional patriotism, see Jan-Werner Müller, *Constitutional Patriotism* (Princeton, 2007).
54. Dolf Sternberger, "Verfassungspatriotismus," *Frankfurter Allgemeine Zeitung*, 23 May, 1979.
55. On Habermas's development of Sternberger's concept of constitutional patriotism, see Müller, *Constitutional Patriotism*, pp. 26 ff.
56. Maier, *The Unmasterable Past*, p. 57.
57. Müller, *Another Country*, p. 109.
58. Müller, *Another Country*, p. 93.
59. Ibid.
60. Müller, *Another Country*, p. 138.
61. Interview with Joschka Fischer.
62. Ibid.
63. Ibid.
64. Volmer, p. 199.
65. Volmer, p. 201.
66. Humphreys, "'Ein atomares Auschwitz': Die Lehren der Geschichte und der Streit um die Nachrüstung," p. 55.
67. Ibid., p. 40.
68. Interview with Joschka Fischer.
69. Humphreys, "'Ein atomares Auschwitz': Die Lehren der Geschichte und der Streit um die Nachrüstung," p. 54. See also Volmer, pp. 213 ff. The key contributions by Fischer and others in the debate within the Greens about NATO are reproduced in Die Grünen im Bundestag, *Militärblock West. Die NATO-Broschüre der Grünen* (Bonn, 1988).
70. Interview with Jürgen Schnappertz. Schnappertz left the Greens in 1990 and joined the SPD. He later became an official in the German foreign ministry.
71. Humphreys, "'Ein atomares Auschwitz': Die Lehren der Geschichte und der Streit um die Nachrüstung," p. 56.
72. "Wir Kinder der Kapitulanten," *Die Zeit*, 10 May, 1985.

CHAPTER 9: NEW REPUBLIC

1. Thränhardt, p. 310.
2. Charles S. Maier, *Dissolution. The Crisis of Communism and the end of East Germany* (Princeton, 1997), p. 245.
3. See Timothy Garton Ash, *In Europe's Name. Germany and the Divided Continent* (London, 1993).
4. Volmer, p. 222.
5. Maier, *Dissolution*, p. 196.

6. Ibid., p. 196.
7. Gerhard Schröder, *Entscheidungen*, p. 52.
8. Müller, *Another Country*, p. 135. On the Greens' attitude towards the division of Germany, see Volmer, pp. 222 ff.
9. Jürgen Habermas, *Die nachholende Revolution* (Frankfurt am Main, 1990), p. 7.
10. Müller, *Another Country*, p. 102.
11. Maier, *Dissolution*, p. 167.
12. Ibid., p. 246.
13. Jürgen Habermas, "Der DM-Nationalismus," *Die Zeit*, 30 March, 1990.
14. Habermas, *Die nachholende Revolution*, p. 152.
15. Volmer, p. 63.
16. Ibid.
17. Peter Brandt/Herbert Ammon (hrsg.), *Die Linke und die nationale Frage* (Reinbek, 1981), p. 28.
18. Interview with Joschka Fischer.
19. Müller, *Another Country*, p. 135.
20. Joschka Fischer, "Jenseits von Mauer und Wiedervereinigung," *die tageszeitung*, 16 November, 1989. Quoted in: Geis/Ulrich, p. 126.
21. Joschka Fischer, "Zwischen Wiedervereinigungsillusionen und NATO-Austrittsfiktionen. Rede vor der Urania/Berlin vom 20.11.1988," in: Die Grünen im Bundestag, *Militärblock-West. Die NATO-Broschüre der Grünen* (Bonn, 1988). Quoted in Volmer, p. 217.
22. Volmer, p. 217.
23. Günter Grass, *Two States—One Nation? The case against German reunification* (London, 1990), p. 13.
24. Timothy Garton Ash, *We the People. The Revolution of '89 witnessed in Warsaw, Budapest, Berlin and Prague* (Cambridge, 1990).
25. Pulzer, p. 162.
26. Maier, *Dissolution*, p. 213.
27. On the debate, see *Berlin-Bonn. Die Debatte. Alle Bundestagsreden vom 20. Juni 1991* (Köln, 1991).
28. Markovits/Gorski, p. 136.
29. Ian Buruma, *The Wages of Guilt. Memories of War in Germany and Japan* (London, 1994), p. 15.
30. Markovits/Gorski, p. 136.
31. Diner, *Feindbild Amerika*, p. 150.
32. Markovits/Gorski, p. 138.
33. Ibid.
34. On the Greens' Middle East policy in the 1980s, see Volmer pp. 311 ff.
35. On the Greens campaigns against arms exports, see Volmer, pp. 193 ff.
36. Joschka Fischer, "Israel—ein Alptraum der deutschen Linken, *Pflasterstrand*, 9/1982, pp. 47–50.
37. "Raketenangriffe sind Konsequenz der Politik Israels", *Süddeutsche Zeitung*, 19 February, 1991. Quoted in Markovits/Gorski, p. 136.

38. Volmer, p. 454.
39. Thränhardt, p. 299.
40. Thränhardt, p. 305.
41. Daniel Cohn-Bendit/Thomas Schmid, *Heimat Babylon* (Hamburg, 1992), p. 10.
42. Cohn-Bendit/Schmid, *Heimat Babylon*, p. 261.
43. Anda/Kleine, p. 111.
44. Anda/Kleine, p. 147.
45. Anda/Kleine, p. 172.
46. Anda/Kleine, p. 186.
47. Geis/Ulrich, p. 136.
48. Geis/Ulrich, p. 136.
49. Geis/Ulrich, p. 149.
50. Bodo Hombach, *The Politics of the New Centre* (Cambridge, 2000), p. 105.
51. Hombach, p. xxxii.
52. Hombach, p. 24.
53. Schwelien, p. 291.
54. Schröder, *Entscheidungen*, p. 102.
55. Fischer, *Die rot-grüne Jahre*, p. 19 and p. 17.
56. Ibid., p. 39.

CHAPTER 10: POWER

1. Kraushaar, *1968 als Mythos, Chiffre und Zäsur*, pp 81 ff.
2. Kraushaar, *Fischer in Frankfurt*, p. 189.
3. Ibid.
4. Wolfgang Kraushaar, *1968 als Mythos, Chiffre und Zäsur* (Hamburg, 2000), p 81.
5. Interview with Thomas Schmid.
6. Auflösungserklärung der RAF, March 1998.
7. Ibid.
8. Ibid.
9. Speech given at the SPD party conference, Leipzig, April 1998.
10. Kraushaar, *1968 als Mythos, Chiffre und Zäsur*, p. 186.
11. Die Regierungserklärung von Bundeskanzler Gerhard Schröder, 10 November, 1998.
12. Kraushaar, *1968 als Mythos, Chiffre und Zäsur*, p. 186.
13. Martin Walser, "Die Banalität des Guten: Erfahrungen beim Verfassen einer Sonntagsrede aus Anlaß der Verleihung des Friedenspreis des Deutschen Buchhandels," in *Frankfurter Allgemeine Zeitung*, 12 October, 1998. Reprinted in Frank Schirrmacher (hrsg.), *Die Walser-Bubis Debatte. Eine Dokumentation* (Frankfurt am Main, 1999), pp. 7–17.
14. Ibid.
15. Ibid.

16. Ibid.
17. Ignatz Bubis, "Wer von der Schande spricht. Niemand darf die Erinnerung des Nationalsozialismus auslöschen. Eine Rede zum 9. November," *Frankfurter Allgemeine Zeitung*, 10 November, 1998. Reprinted in Schirrmacher (hrsg.), *Die Walser-Bubis Debatte*, pp. 106–113.
18. Werner A. Perger, "Wir Unbefangenen," *Die Zeit*, 12 November 1998.
19. See for example Andrei S. Markovits, "Die Zukunft als Ende der Vergangenheit," *die tageszeitung*, 12 November, 1998.
20. Hans Kundnani, "'Berlin Republic' gets down to business in reborn Reichstag," *The Observer*, 18 April, 1999.
21. Gordon A. Craig, "Berlin, the Hauptstadt," *Foreign Affairs*, July/August 1998, p. 169.
22. Richard Bernstein, "A Shrine to Power: Is Berlin Ready?" *New York Times*, 16 February, 2001.
23. On the history of the Reichsbank building, see Auswärtiges Amt, *Das Haus am werderschen Markt. Von der Reichsbank zum Auswärtigen Amt* (Berlin, 1999).
24. On Habermas's critique of the concept of "normality", see his essay "1989 im Schattten von 1945. Zur Normalität einer künftigen Berliner Republik," in: Jürgen Habermas, *Die Normalität einer Berliner Republik* (Frankfurt am Main, 1995), pp. 167–187.
25. Geis/Ulrich, pp. 153–155.
26. Interview with Wolfgang Ischinger.
27. *Die Zeit*, 12 November, 1998.
28. Geis/Ulrich, p. 166.
29. Horst Mahler, "Flugschrift an die Deutschen, die es noch sein wollen, über die Lage ihres Volkes," www.deutsches-kolleg.org.
30. Ibid.
31. Ibid. The Morgenthau Plan featured prominently in Nazi propaganda at the end of World War II. See Diner, *Feindbild Amerika*, pp. 119 ff.
32. Ibid.
33. Ibid.
34. Ibid.
35. Mahler/Schönhuber, *Schluss mit deutschem Selbsthass*, p. 5.
36. Interview with Ulrich K. Preuss.
37. Willi Winkler, "'Der Staat war das Böse'. Ein *Zeit*-Gespräch mit dem Ex-Terroristen Horst Mahler über die APO, den Weg in den Terror und die Versöhnung mit dem Grundgesetz," *Die Zeit*, 2 May, 1997.
38. Ibid.
39. Kraushaar, *1968 als Mythos, Chiffre und Zäsur*, p. 175.
40. Ibid.
41. Kraushaar, *1968 als Mythos, Chiffre und Zäsur*, p. 172.
42. Interview with Horst Mahler.
43. Ibid.
44. See Caspar von Schrenck-Notzing, *Charakterwäsche. Die Politik der amerikanischen Umerziehung* (München, 1965).

45. Interview with Horst Mahler.
46. Ibid.
47. Mahler, "Flugschrift an die Deutschen, die es noch sein wollen, über die Lage ihres Volkes."
48. Mahler/Schönhuber, p. 11.
49. Kraushaar, *1968 als Mythos, Chiffre und Zäsur*, p. 179.
50. Horst Mahler, "Die Zukunft der 68er Idee", www.deutsches-kolleg.org.
51. Horst Mahler, "Die Zukunft der 68er Idee".
52. Bernd Rabehl, "Ein Volk ohne Kultur kann zu allem verleitet werden", *Junge Freiheit*, 18 December, 1998.
53. Interview with Bernd Rabehl.
54. Ibid.
55. Ibid.
56. Ibid.
57. Ibid.
58. Kraushaar, *1968 als Mythos, Chiffre und Zäsur*, p. 179.
59. Ibid.
60. Ibid.
61. Ibid.
62. Interview with Tilman Fichter.
63. Ibid.
64. Interview with Hans-Christian Ströbele.
65. The foundation, entitled *Erinnerung, Verantwortung und Zukunft* (Memory, Responsibility and Future) was formally inaugurated in August 2000 with a fund of DM 10 billion. Otto Graf Lambsdorff, Schröder's chief negotiator, said it represented a "financial" but not a "moral" *Schlußstrich*. It began making one-time payments of between €2,500 and €8,000 to former slave labourers in June 2001.
66. Hans Kundnani, "Schröder faces poll test over passports," *The Observer*, 7 February, 1999.
67. Hans Kundnani, "Schröder felled by the right in Hesse state poll," *The Guardian*, 8 February, 1999.

CHAPTER 11: A WAR AGAINST THE PAST

1. On the re-emergence of Germany as Europe's "central power", see Hans-Peter Schwarz, *Die Zentralmacht Europas. Deutschlands Rückkehr auf die Weltbühne* (Berlin, 1994).
2. The term "civilian power", which originates in Norbert Elias's theory of the civilising process, was coined by Francois Duchêne in the early 1970s to describe the European Union. The term was subsequently applied by Hanns W. Maull to Germany. On Germany as a "civilian power", see Hanns W. Maull, "Zivilmacht Bundesrepublik Deutschland. Vierzehn Thesen für eine neue deutsche Außenpolitik," *Europa-Archiv* 47 (1992), pp. 269–278.

3. Sebastian Harnisch/Hanns W. Maull, *Germany as a civilian power? The foreign policy of the Berlin Republic* (Manchester, 2001), p. 2.

4. See Volmer, pp. 438 ff.

5. On the Greens' pacifism in the 1990s, see Volmer, pp. 493–496. Although the party was broadly pacifist, there were significant variations. Volmer distinguishes three kinds of pacifists among the Greens: "radical pacifists" who opposed all use of violence on principle; "political pacifists" who strove to eliminate the use of force in international politics in the long-term but accepted the need for military interventions in the interim; and "nuclear pacifists" who opposed only nuclear weapons.

6. NATO gave the first definition of its new, post-Cold War role in the Rome Declaration on Peace and Co-Operation in November 1991. http://www. nato.int/docu/comm/49–95/c911108a.htm.

7. Quoted in Geis/Ulrich, pp. 155–156.

8. Wolfgang Kraushaar, *Fischer in Frankfurt* (Hamburg, 2001), pp. 106–107.

9. See Fischer, *Die rot-grünen Jahre*, p. 212.

10. Daniel Cohn-Bendit, "Versager aller Länder, verteidigt Euch!" *die tagezeitung*, 24 June, 1993.

11. *Frankfurter Allgemeine Zeitung*, 11 September, 1993.

12. Interview with Joschka Fischer.

13. Geis/Ulrich, p. 169.

14. Koelbl, p. 28.

15. Interview with Joschka Fischer.

16. Ibid.

17. Interview with Hubert Kleinert.

18. Joschka Fischer, "Die Katastrophe in Bosnien und die Konsequenzen für unsere Partei Bündnis 90/Die Grünen. Ein Brief an die Bundestagsfraktion und an die Partei," 30 July, 1995.

19. On the debate sparked by the "Bosnia letter", see Volmer, pp. 514 ff. Volmer was a Green member of the Bundestag at the time and a critic of Fischer.

20. Interview with Ludger Volmer.

21. For Volmer's response to the "Bosnia letter", see Ludger Volmer, "Greif' zur Waffe, fahr' nach Sarajevo," *die tagezeitung*, 12 August, 1995.

22. Volmer, p. 521.

23. Richard Holbrooke, *To End a War* (New York, 1998), p. 360

24. Ivo H. Daalder/Michael E. O'Hanlon, *Winning Ugly. NATO's war to save Kosovo* (Washington, D.C., 2000), p. 12.

25. Fischer, *Die rot-grünen Jahre*, p. 103.

26. Fischer, *Die rot-grünen Jahre*, p. 104.

27. Schwelien, p. 109. See also Fischer, *Die rot-grünen Jahre*, p. 104.

28. Gunter Hofmann, "Wie Deutschland in den Krieg geriet," *Die Zeit*, 12 May 1999.

29. Hofmann, "Wie Deutschland in den Krieg geriet"; Geis/Ulrich, p. 169.

30. Daalder/O'Hanlon, p. 15.

31. Fischer, *Die rot-grünen Jahre*, p. 146.
32. Michael Walzer, *Just and Unjust Wars* (New York, 2000), p. xii.
33. Paul Berman, *Power and the Idealists. The passion of Joschka Fischer, and its aftermath* (New York, 2005), p. 91.
34. Tariq Ali, "Springtime for NATO," *New Left Review*, March/April 1999, p. 64.
35. Ali, "Springtime for NATO," p. 68.
36. Ibid., p. 64.
37. Roger Cohen, "Germany's Pragmatic Ex-Radical thinks globally," *New York Times*, 28 January, 1999.
38. Geis/Ulrich, p. 159. The comment was made at a press conference on 31 March. See also Fischer, *Die rot-grünen Jahre*, p. 185.
39. For example Klaus Meschkat, "Krieg in den Köpfen. Vietnam und Kosovo," http://www.soz.uni-hanover.de/isoz/veroeff/kmkrieg.htm.
40. Frank Schirrmacher, "Luftkampf. Deutschlands Anteil am Krieg," *Frankfurter Allgemeine Zeitung*, 17 April, 1999.
41. Interview with Angelika Beer.
42. Interview with Wolfgang Ischinger.
43. Interview with Gerhard Schröder.
44. Geis/Ulrich, p. 170.
45. Interview with Joschka Fischer.
46. Günter Joetze, *Der letzte Krieg in Europa? Das Kosovo und die deutsche Politk* (Stuttgart, 2001), p. 8.
47. Erklärung von Bundeskanzler Gerhard Schröder zur Lage in Kosovo, 24 May, 1999.
48. Fischer, *Die rot-grünen Jahre*, p. 175.
49. David Halberstam, *War in a time of peace. Bush, Clinton and the Generals* (New York, 2002), p. 423.
50. Schwelien, p. 126.
51. Ibid.
52. Jürgen Elsässer/Andrei S. Markovits (hrsg.) *Die Fratze der eigenen Geschichte. Von der Goldhagen-Debatte zum Jugoslavien-Krieg* (Berlin, 1999), p. 174.
53. Elsässer/ Markovits, p. 14.
54. Daniel Goldhagen, "German lessons," *The Guardian*, 29 April, 1999. (Published in Germany as "Eine 'deutsche Lösung' für den Balkan," *Süddeutsche Zeitung*, 30 April, 1999.)
55. Interview with Rezzo Schlauch.
56. Ibid.
57. Jochen Buchsteiner, "Das grüne Theater," *Die Zeit*, 12 May 1999.
58. Fischer, *Die rot-grünen Jahre*, p. 181.
59. Interview with Wolfgang Ischinger.
60. *Die Zeit*, 15 April, 1999.
61. Fischer, *Die rot-grünen Jahre*, p. 251.
62. *Die Zeit*, 17 June, 1999.

63. Geis/Ulrich, p. 174.
64. Interview with Wolfgang Ischinger.
65. Wesley K. Clark, *Waging Modern War* (New York, 2001), p. 417.
66. Gunter Hofmann, "Deutschland am Ende des Krieges. Der Schock setzt die Gedanken fre und bringt Europa voran," *Die Zeit*, 10 May 1999.
67. "From Confederacy to Federation—Thoughts on the finality of European integration." Speech by Joschka Fischer at the Humboldt University in Berlin, 12 May, 2000.
68. *Die Zeit*, 21 June, 2000.
69. Speech at the European Parliament, 12 January, 1999.
70. Schwelien, pp. 257–8.
71. Theo Sommer, quoted in Joetze, p. 7.
72. *Die Zeit*, 15 April, 1999.
73. Joetze, p. 8.
74. Quoted in Hanns W. Maull, "Germany's foreign policy, post-Kosovo: Still a 'Civilian Power'?" In: Sebastian Harnisch/Hanns W. Maull, *Germany as a civilian power? The foreign policy of the Berlin Republic* (Manchester, 2001), p. 106.
75. Hanns W. Maull, "Germany and the Use of Force, Still a 'Civilian Power?'" In: *Survival*, Vol. 42, No. 2 (Summer 2000), pp. 56–80.
76. Matthias Geyer/Dirk Kurbjuweit/Cordt Schnibben, *Operation Rot-Grün. Geschichte eines politischen Abenteuers* (München/Hamburg, 2005), p. 98.
77. Meschkat, "Krieg in den Köpfen."

CHAPTER 12: THE RETURN OF HISTORY

1. Geis/Ulrich, p. 208. See also Fischer, *Die rot-grünen Jahre*, p. 431.
2. Ibid.
3. Ibid.
4. Gerhard Schröder, *Entscheidungen*, p. 162.
5. Geis/Ulrich, p. 208.
6. Jason Burke, *Al-Qaeda* (Harmondsworth, 2004), p. 2.
7. Burke, *Al-Qaeda*, p. 36.
8. Ibid., p. 38.
9. The book was published as Hans-Joachim Klein, *Rückkehr in die Menschlichkeit. Appell eines ausgestiegenen Terroristen* (Reinbek, 1979).
10. "Ja, ich war militant", *Stern*, 3 January, 2001.
11. Ibid.
12. Ibid.
13. Ibid.
14. Ibid.
15. "Ein Segen für dieses Land," Der Spiegel, 29 January, 2001.
16. Christian Semler, "Verspätete Racheengel", *die tageszeitung*, 11 January, 2001.

17. Ibid.
18. Gerd Koenen, "Die Putzgruppe—Ein ABC der Gewalt," *Frankfurter Allgemeine Zeitung*, 13 January, 2001.
19. Thomas Schmid, "Ein Kollektiver *Sonderweg*," *Frankfurter Allgemeine Zeitung*, 8 January, 2001.
20. "Argumente von '68 können Militanz nicht verteidigen. Ein Gespräch mit Lord Dahrendorf," *Die Welt*, 18 January, 2001.
21. Fischer, *Die rot-grünen Jahre*, p. 378.
22. "Ein Segen für dieses Land".
23. Ibid.
24. Ibid.
25. Ibid.
26. Geyer/Kurbjuweit/Schnibben, *Operation Rot-Grün*, p. 136.
27. Interview on ABC's *This Week*, 23 January, 2000, quoted in Ivo H. Daalder/James M. Lindsay, *America Unbound. The Bush revolution in foreign policy* (Washington, 2003), p. 37.
28. Interview with Joschka Fischer.
29. Ibid.
30. Ibid.
31. Fischer, *Die rot-grünen Jahre*, p. 414.
32. On Fischer's June 2001 trip to Israel, see Fischer, *Die rot-grünen Jahre*, pp. 402–418. See also Geis/Ulrich, pp. 192–202.
33. Clyde Haberman, "New Middle East Peace Bid Brokered by German Envoy", *New York Times*, 22 August, 2001.
34. "'Israel darf keine Schwäche zeigen.' Außenminister Joschka Fischer über Terror, Antisemitismus und seinen neuen Friedensplan," *Die Zeit*, 11 April, 2002.
35. Fischer, *Die rot-grünen Jahre*, p. 423.
36. Ibid., p. 426.
37. Steven Erlanger, "German Seeks A New Force Led by NATO In Macedonia", *New York Times*, 9 September, 2001.
38. Gunther Hellman, "Germany's place in the sun: The rising ambition of a declining power", *International Herald Tribune*, 23 September, 2004. Germany first indicated that it wanted a permament seat on the Security Council under Helmut Kohl in 1992 but did not actively pursue the proposal.
39. Schröder, *Entscheidungen*, p. 164.
40. Ibid., p. 163.
41. Ibid., p. 164.
42. Ibid., p. 167.
43. Geyer/Kurbjuweit/Schnibben, *Operation Rot-Grün*, p. 155.
44. Interview with Ludger Volmer.
45. Interview with Joschka Fischer.
46. Ibid.
47. John Schmid, "Germany to assume NATO mission in Macedonia", *International Herald Tribune*, 28 September, 2001.

48. Schröder, *Entscheidungen*, p. 176.
49. Interview with Rezzo Schlauch.
50. Interview with Ludger Volmer.
51. "Meinen Sie, ich will in den Krieg ziehen?", *die tagezeitung*, 29 September, 2001.
52. Ibid.
53. Schröder, *Entscheidungen*, p. 180.
54. Regierungserklärung von Bundeskanzler Schröder zur aktuellen Lage nach Beginn der Operation gegen den internationalen Terrorismus in Afghanistan, 11 October, 2001.
55. Schröder, *Entscheidungen*, p. 171.
56. "Internationalen Terrorismus bekämpfen, in kritischer Solidarität handeln, die rot-grüne Koalition fortsetzen. Beschluß der 17. Ordentlichen Bundesdelegiertenkonferenz von Bündnis 90/Die Grünen am 24. November 2001 in Rostock.
57. Geis/Ulrich, p. 217.
58. Hanns W. Maull, "Germany's foreign policy, post-Kosovo: Still a 'Civilian Power'?" In: Sebastian Harnisch/Hanns W. Maull. *Germany as a civilian power? The foreign policy of the Berlin Republic* (Manchester, 2001), p. 117.
59. Lawrence Wright, *The Looming Tower. Al-Qaeda and the Road to 9/11* (New York, 2006), p. 306.
60. Heribert Prantl, "Otto Schilys Denkmal", *Süddeutsche Zeitung*, 3 August, 2001.
61. Jochen Bittner, "Die 'Otto'-Kataloge: verlockende Angebote für die Behörden," *Das Parlament*, 4 September, 2006.
62. Dirk Kurbjuweit, "Ganz links, ganz rechts, ganz oben," *Der Spiegel*, 9 February, 2002.
63. "Schily. Macht. Ordnung. Wie der Innenminister Staat macht," documentary broadcast on ARD German television, 27 May, 2002.
64. Ibid.
65. Ibid.
66. Horst Mahler, "Independence-Day Live", www.deutsches-kolleg.org.
67. Ibid.
68. Horst Mahler, "Den Völkern Freiheit. Den Globalisten ihr globales Vietnam", www.deutsches-kolleg.org.
69. Horst Mahler, "Der Untergang des judäo-amerikanischen Imperiums", www.deutsches-kolleg.org.
70. Ibid.
71. Bundesministerium des Innern, *Verfassungsschutzbericht 2001* (Berlin, 2001), p. 81.
72. Ibid., p. 84.
73. Interview with Horst Mahler.
74. Ibid.
75. Toralf Staud, "Wir sind ja so antifaschistisch," *Die Zeit*, 20 March, 2003.

76. Claus Leggewie/Horst Meier (hrsg.), *Verbot der NPD oder Mit Rechtsradikalen leben?* (Frankfurt am Main, 2002), p. 44.

77. Bundesministerium des Innern, p. 86.

78. Leggewie/Meier, p. 24.

79. Dirk Kurbjuweit, "Ganz links, ganz rechts, ganz oben," *Der Spiegel*, 9 February, 2002.

80. See Hans Kundnani, "After Westphalia," *Times Literary Supplement*, 23 December, 2005.

81. Joschka Fischer, *Die Rückkehr der Geschichte. Die Welt nach dem 11. September und die Erneuerung des Westens* (Köln, 2005), p. 194.

82. Fischer, *Die Rückkehr der Geschichte*, p. 194.

83. Ibid., p. 105.

84. Ibid., p. 119.

85. Ibid., p. 239.

86. Ibid., p. 60.

CHAPTER 13: A GERMAN WAY

1. Geyer/Kurbjuweit/Schnibben, *Operation Rot-Grün*, p. 191.

2. Ibid., p. 177.

3. Ibid.

4. Philip H. Gordon/Jeremy Shapiro, *Allies at war. America, Europe and the crisis over Iraq* (New York, 2004), p. 102.

5. Steven Erlanger, "Stance on Bush Policy Could Swing Election in Germany," *New York Times*, 9 September, 2002.

6. Gordon/Shapiro, *Allies at war*, p. 96.

7. Interview with Manfred Bissinger. Bissinger, a veteran journalist whose judgement Schröder trusted, was a key figure in these discussions, along with Schröder's chief of staff Frank-Walter Steinmeier and his spokesperson Uwe-Karsten Heye. As a young reporter for *Stern* in the 1968, Bissinger had delivered money from the magazine's owner to Rudi Dutschke for the planned hearing against the Springer press.

8. Interview with Gerhard Schröder.

9. The United States's claims about the existence of weapons of mass destruction in Iraq rested to a large extent on a source known as "Curveball" who was controlled by the German foreign intelligence service, the *Bundesnachrichtendienst* (BND). "Curveball", whose real name was Rafid Ahmed Alwan, was a Iraqi defector who had arrived in Germany in 1999 and claimed asylum. A chemical engineer, he falsely claimed he had worked at mobile biological weapons laboratories in Iraq. Although the BND passed on reports on Curveball's claims to the American Defence Intelligence Agency (DIA), it did not allow the DIA or other American intelligence agencies direct access to him.

10. Interview with Gerhard Schröder.

11. Geyer/Kurbjuweit/Schnibben, *Operation Rot-Grün*, p. 203.

12. Ibid.
13. Ibid.
14. Interview with Kajo Wasserhövel.
15. Geyer/Kurbjuweit/Schnibben, *Operation Rot-Grün*, p. 201.
16. Ibid. Also present at the meeting, apart from Müntefering and Wasserhövel, were SPD press spokesman Lars Kühn, and a pollster.
17. Geyer/Kurbjuweit/Schnibben, *Operation Rot-Grün*, p. 202.
18. Interview with Gerhard Schröder.
19. Ibid.
20. Interview with Kajo Wasserhövel.
21. Gordon/Shapiro, *Allies at war*, p. 64.
22. Ibid., p. 175.
23. Ibid., p. 107.
24. See Hanns W. Maull, "Zivilmacht Deutschland." In: Gunther Hellmann/Siegmar Schmidt/Reinhard Wolf (hrsg.), *Handwörterbuch zur deutschen Außenpolitik* (Opladen, 2006).
25. "Mr. Schröder Ducks," *Washington Post*, 17 September, 2002.
26. Geyer/Kurbjuweit/Schnibben, *Operation Rot-Grün*, p. 208.
27. Steven Erlanger, "German Leader's Warning: War Plan is a huge mistake," *New York Times*, 5 September, 2002.
28. Interview with Gerhard Schröder. See also Schröder, *Entscheidungen*, pp. 211–214.
29. Gordon/Shapiro, *Allies at war*, p. 99.
30. "Ja, es gab Fehler," *Der Spiegel*, 1 October, 2007.
31. "Ein unheimliches Gefühl," *Der Spiegel*, 18 May, 2002.
32. Ibid.
33. Author's notes from election rally, Berlin, September 20, 2002.
34. John Hooper, "Fischer rejects chancellor's 'German way'", *The Guardian*, 15 October, 2002.
35. Interview with Joschka Fischer.
36. Ibid.
37. "Das Comeback des Kanzlers," *Der Spiegel*, 16 September, 2002.
38. Ibid.
39. Steven Erlanger, "Stance on Bush Policy Could Swing election in Germany," *New York Times*, 9 September, 2002.
40. Ibid.; Geyer/Kurbjuweit/Schnibben, *Operation Rot-Grün*, p. 211.
41. Geyer/Kurbjuweit/Schnibben, *Operation Rot-Grün*, p. 212.
42. Ibid., p. 214.
43. Steven Erlanger, "Germans Vote in a Tight Election in Which Bush, Hitler and Israel Became Key Issues," *New York Times*, 22 September, 2002.
44. "Ja, es gab Fehler," *Der Spiegel*, 1 October, 2007.
45. Ibid.
46. Interview with Gerhard Schröder.
47. Transcript of US Department of Defence press conference, 22 January, 2003. http://www.defenselink.mil/transcripts/transcript.aspx?transcriptid=1330.

48. Richard Bernstein, "The German Question," *New York Times Magazine*, 2 May, 2004.
49. Schröder, *Entscheidungen*, p. 223.
50. Michael R. Gordon, "German intelligence gave U.S. Iraqi defense plan, report says," *New York Times*, 27 February, 2006.
51. Richard Bernstein and Michael R. Gordon, "Berlin file says Germany's spies aided U.S. in Iraq," *New York Times*, 2 March, 2006.
52. Christopher Rhoads, "Behind Iraq Stance in Germany: Flood of War Memories," *Wall Street Journal*, 25 February, 2003.
53. Ibid. On the discourse of German victimhood, see Bill Niven (ed.), *Germans as victims. Remembering the past in contemporary Germany* (London, 2006).
54. Jörg Friedrich, *Der Brand. Deutschland im Bombenkrieg 1940–1945* (München, 2002).
55. For a more detailed discussion of Friedrich's "historical decontextualisation" of the Allied bombing of German cities during World War II, see Niven (ed.), pp. 14–15.
56. See Ruth Wittlinger, "Taboo or Tradition? The 'Germans as victims' theme in the Federal Republic until the mid-1990s," in: Niven (ed.), pp. 62–75.
57. Meinhof, *Die Würde des Menschen ist antastbar*, p. 64.
58. See Andreas Huyssen, "Air War Legacies: From Dresden to Baghdad", in Niven (ed.), pp. 181–193.
59. Niven (ed.), p. 188.
60. Niven (ed.), p. 182; Richard Bernstein, "Germans Revisit War's Agony, Ending a Taboo", *New York Times*, 15 March, 2003.
61. Rhoads, "Behind Iraq Stance in Germany: Flood of War Memories."
62. Interview with Tilman Fichter.
63. Michael Kelly, "Germany's Mr. Tough Guy," *Washington Post*, 12 February, 2003. Kelly was killed in April 2003 while embedded with the 3rd Infrantry Division in Iraq.
64. Interview with Gerhard Scrhöder. See also Schröder, *Entscheidungen*, p. 209.
65. There were some on the left who did call Saddam Hussein's regime fascist such as Paul Berman, from whose long article in the *New Republic* Michael Kelly had drawn his information about Fischer's life. In a reply to Kelly's attack on Fischer, Berman wrote that Baathism and Islamism were both "branches of what ought to be regarded as Muslim fascism" and that "a war against Muslim fascism ought to be seen as a continuation of the long struggle against Nazism and fascism in Europe" (Paul Berman, "Why Germany isn't convinced," *Slate.com*, 14 February, 2003, http://www.slate.com/id/2078560/)
66. "Amerika hatte kein Verdun," *Der Spiegel*, 24 March, 2003.
67. See Hanns W. Maull, "Zivilmacht Deutschland." In: Gunther Hellmann/Siegmar Schmidt/Reinhard Wolf (hrsg.), *Handwörterbuch zur deutschen Außenpolitik* (Opladen, 2006).

68. Geyer/Kurbjuweit/Schnibben, *Operation Rot-Grün*, p. 316.
69. Schröder, *Entscheidungen*, p. 470.
70. Letter from Joschka Fischer to foreign ministry staff, 17 March, 2005, reprinted in *internAA. Mitarbeiterzeitung des Auswärtigen Amts*, Ausgabe 4, April 2005.
71. Interview with Joschka Fischer.
72. Charles Grant, "Germany's foreign policy: What lessons can be learned from the Schröder years?" Centre for European Reform essay, September 2005.
73. Matthias Küntzel in Elsaesser/Markovits, *Die Fratze der eigenen Geschichte*, p. 179.
74. "Ein unheimliches Gefühl," *Der Spiegel*, 18 May, 2002.
75. Fischer, *Die Rückkehr der Geschichte*, p. 154.
76. Ibid., p. 203.
77. Schröder, *Entscheidungen*, p. 246.
78. Ibid.
79. Schröder, *Entscheidungen*, p. 247.
80. Ibid.
81. Interview with Gerhard Schröder.
82. Ibid.
83. Schröder, *Entscheidungen*, p. 455.
84. Interview with Gerhard Schröder.
85. Schröder, *Entscheidungen*, p. 461.
86. "Gerhard Schröder's Sellout," *Washington Post*, 13 December, 2005.
87. "Ich war einer der letzten Rock n Roller der deutschen Politik," *die tageszeitung*, 23 September, 2005.
88. Ibid.
89. "Hurra, ich lebe noch!" *Stern*, 19 May, 1999.
90. Ibid.
91. Dieter Kunzelmann declined to be interviewed for this book.
92. On the debate about 1968 in 2008, see Oskar Negt, "Demokratie als Lebensform. Mein Achtundsechzig," *Aus Politik und Zeitgeschichte* 14–15/2008, 31 March, 2008. The most controversial book on 1968 to be published in 2008 was Götz Aly's *Unser Kampf*, which directly compared the *Achtundsechziger* to the *Dreiunddreissiger*—in other words the Nazis.

EPILOGUE: A NEW GENERATION

1. Yassin Musharbash, "Der Grünen-GAU von Göttingen," *Der Spiegel*, September 15, 2007.
2. "Kampf ums Erbe," *Der Spiegel*, 1 October, 2007.
3. Ibid.
4. "Ja, es gab Fehler," *Der Spiegel*, 1 October, 2007.

BIBLIOGRAPHY

AUTHOR INTERVIEWS

Tariq Ali
Neal Ascherson
Stefan Aust
Angelika Beer
Klaus-Uwe Benneter
Manfred Bissinger
Henryk M. Broder
Detlev Claussen
Gretchen Dutschke
Ulrich Enzensberger
Tilman Fichter
Joschka Fischer
Catherine Fried
Wolfgang Ischinger
Hubert Kleinert
Wolfgang Kraushaar
Alain Krivine
Klaus Lange
Rainer Langhans
Eckhard Lübkemeier
Horst Mahler

Hanns W. Maull
Klaus Meschkat
Bahman Nirumand
Reinhold Oberlercher
Ulrich K. Preuss
Horst Przytulla
Bernd Rabehl
Helke Sander
Ottmar Schreiner
Dagmar Seehuber
Rezzo Schlauch
Thomas Schmid
Jürgen Schnappertz
Gerhard Schröder
Christian Semler
Hans-Christian Ströbele
Ludger Volmer
Kajo Wasserhövel
Arno Widmann
Karl-Dietrich Wolff

NEWSPAPERS AND MAGAZINES

Financial Times
Frankfurter Allgemeine Zeitung
Frankfurter Rundschau
The Guardian
International Herald Tribune

New York Times
The Observer
Der Spiegel
Stern
Süddeutsche Zeitung

BIBLIOGRAPHY

die tageszeitung
Times Literary Supplement
Die Welt

Washington Post
Wall Street Journal
Die Zeit

BOOKS, JOURNAL ARTICLES AND UNPUBLISHED PAPERS

Adorno, Theodor. *Negative Dialektik*, (Frankfurt am Main, 1975). Translated as: *Negative Dialectics* (London, 1966).

——— "Was heißt: Aufarbeitung der Vergangenheit?" in: *Eingriffe. Neun kritische Modelle* (Frankfurt am Main, 1963).

Ali, Tariq. *Street Fighting Years. An Autobiography of the Sixties* (London, 2005).

——— "Springtime for NATO," *New Left Review*, March/April 1999.

Ali, Tariq/Watkins, Susan. *1968. Marching in the Streets* (London, 1998).

Aly, Götz. *Unser Kampf. 1968—ein irritierter Blick zurück* (Frankfurt, 2008).

Anda, Béla/Kleine, Rolf. *Gerhard Schröder. Eine Biographie* (München, 2002).

Arendt, Hannah. *Eichmann in Jersualem. A Report on the Banality of Evil* (Harmondsworth, 1977).

Ash, Timothy Garton, *We the People. The Revolution of '89 witnessed in Warsaw, Budapest, Berlin and Prague* (Cambridge, 1990).

Aust, Stefan. *Der Baader-Meinhof Komplex* (München, 1998).

Aust, Stefan/Schnibben, Cordt (hrsg.). *11. September. Geschichte eines Terrorangriffs* (München, 2003).

Baader, Andreas/Ensslin, Gudrun/Proll, Thorwald/Söhnlein, Horst. *Vor einer solchen Justiz verteidigen wir uns nicht. Schlußwort im Kaufhausbrandstiftungsprozeß* (Frankfurt, 1968).

Baring, Arnulf. *Machtwechsel. Die Ära Brandt-Scheel* (München, 1984).

——— "Unser Fundament bleiben die USA. Über den Dilettantismus rotgrüner Außenpolitik," *Merkur*, March 2005.

Bergmann, Uwe/Dutschke, Rudi/Lefèvre, Wolfgang/ Rabehl/Bernd, *Rebellion der Studenten oder die neue Opposition*, (Reinbek, 1968).

Baumann, Michael 'Bommi'. *Wie alles anfing* (München, 1988).

Berman, Paul. *A Tale of two Utopias. The Political Generation of 1968* (New York, 1997).

——— *Power and the Idealists The passion of Joschka Fischer, and its aftermath.* (New York, 2005).

——— "The Passion of Joschka Fischer," *The New Republic*, 27 August, 2001.

Bittner, Jochen. "Die "Otto"—Kataloge: verlockende Angebote für die Behörden," *Das Parlament*, 4 September, 2006.

Böckelmann, Frank/Nagel, Herbert (hrsg.). *Subversive Aktion. Der der Organisation ist ihr Scheitern* (Frankfurt am Main, 2002).

350

BIBLIOGRAPHY

Boock, Peter-Jürgen/Schneider, Peter. *Ratte—tot... Ein Briefwechsel* (Darmstadt und Neuwied, 1985).

Brandt, Peter/Ammon, Herbert (hrsg.). *Die Linke und die nationale Frage* (Reinbek, 1981).

Bude, Heinz. *Das Altern einer Generation. Die Jahrgänge 1938–1948* (Frankfurt am Main, 1997).

Buhmann, Inga. *Ich habe mir eine Geschichte geschrieben* (München, 1977).

Bundesministerium des Innern, *Verfassungsschutzbericht 2001* (Berlin, 2001).

Burke, Jason. *Al-Qaeda* (Harmondsworth, 2004).

Buruma, Ian. *The Wages of Guilt. Memories of War in Germany and Japan* (London, 1994).

Chaussy, Ulrich. *Die drei Leben des Rudi Dutschke. Eine Biographie* (Berlin, 1993).

Clark, Wesley K. *Waging Modern War* (New York, 2001).

Claussen, Detlev. *Theodor W. Adorno. Ein letztes Genie* (Frankfurt am Main, 2005).

—— "Der kurze Sommer der Theorie." (unpublished paper provided by author).

—— "Erinnern in eigener Sache." (unpublished paper provided by author).

Cohn-Bendit, Daniel. *Der grosse Basar* (München, 1975).

—— *Wir haben sie so geliebt, die Revolution* (Frankfurt am Main, 1987).

Cohn-Bendit, Daniel/Schmid, Thomas. *Heimat Babylon. Das Wagnis der multikulturellen Demokratie* (Hamburg, 1992).

Craig, Gordon A. "Berlin, the Hauptstadt," *Foreign Affairs*, July/August 1998.

Daalder, Ivo H./O'Hanlon, Michael E. *Winning Ugly. NATO's war to save Kosovo* (Washington, D.C., 2000).

Daalder, Ivo H./Lindsay, James M. *America Unbound. The Bush revolution in foreign policy* (Washington, D.C., 2003).

Deutscher, Isaac. *Der israelisch-arabische Konflikt. Mit einem Vorwort von Ulrike Marie Meinhof* (Frankfurt am Main, 1968). (Originally published in English as: "On the Israeli-Arab War," *New Left Review*, 1/44, July-August 1967.)

Diner, Dan. *Feindbild Amerika. Über die Beständigkeit eines Ressentiment* (München, 2002).

Ditfurth, Jitta. *Das waren die Grünen. Abschied von einer Hoffnung* (München, 2000).

Dubiel, Helmut. *Niemand ist frei von der Geschichte: Die nationalsozialistische Herrschaft in den Debatten des Deutschen Bundestages* (München, 1999).

Dutschke, Gretchen. *Wir hatten ein barbarisches, schönes, Leben. Rudi Dutschke. Eine Biographie* (Köln, 1996).

351

BIBLIOGRAPHY

Dutschke, Gretchen (hrsg.), *Rudi Dutschke. Jeder hat sein Leben ganz zu leben. Die Tagebücher 1963–1979* (Köln, 2003).

Dutschke-Klotz, Gretchen/Gollwitzer, Helmut/Miermeister, Jürgen. *Rudi Dutschke. Mein langer Marsch. Reden, Schriften und Tagebücher aus zwanzig Jahren* (Reinbek, 1980).

Dutschke, Rudi. *Aufrecht gehen. Eine fragmentarische Autobiographie* (Frankfurt am Main, 1981).

————. "Die Deutschen und der Sozialismus", in: *das da*, July 1977.

Dutschke, Rudi/Krahl, Hans-Jürgen. "Organisationsreferat," *diskus—Frankfurter Studentenzeitung*, February 1980.

Elias, Norbert. *Studien über die Deutschen. Machtkämpfe und Habitusentwicklung im 19. und 20. Jahrhundert* (Frankfurt am Main, 1989). (Translated as: *The Germans. Power Struggles and the Development of Habitus in Nineteenth and Twentieth Centuries* (Cambridge, 1996).)

Elsässer, Jürgen/Markovits, Andrei S. (hrsg.). *Die Fratze der eigenen Geschichte. Von der Goldhagen-Debatte zum Jugoslavien-Krieg* (Berlin, 1999).

Enzensberger, Hans Magnus (hrsg.). *Kursbuch 12. Der nicht erklärte Notstand. Dokumentation und Analyse eines Berliner Sommers* (Berlin, 1968).

———— *Kursbuch 14. Kritik der Zukunft* (Berlin, 1968).

Enzensberger, Ulrich. *Die Jahre der Kommune 1. Berlin 1967–1969* (München, 2006).

Fanon, Frantz. *The Wretched of the Earth* (Harmondsworth, 1967).

Fest, Joachim. *Begegnungen. Über nahe und ferne Freunde* (Reinbek, 2004).

Fichter, Tilman. "Die Achtundsechziger. Eine Replik auf Peter Glotz" (unpublished paper provided by author).

———— "Der Staat Israel und die neue Linke in Deutschland." In: Karlheinz Schneider/Nikolaus Simon, (hrsg.), *Solidarität und deutsche Geschichte. Die Linke zwischen Antisemitismus und Israelkritik. Dokumentation einer Arbeitstagung in der Evangelischen Akademie Arnoldshain, August 1984* (Berlin, 1987).

———— "Zur Vorgeschichte des Denkmals. Fünf Generationen nach Auschwitz." In: Lea Rosh (hrsg.), *"Die Juden, das sind doch die anderen". Der Streit um ein deutsches Denkmal* (Berlin, 1999).

Fichter, Tilman/Lönnendonker, Siegward. *Kleine Geschichte des SDS. Der Sozialistischer Deutsche Studentenbund von 1946 bis zur Selbstauflösung* (Berlin, 1977).

Finkielkraut, Alain. *The Imaginary Jew* (Lincoln, 1994).

Fischer, Joschka. *Die rot-grüne Jahre. Deutsche Außenpolitik vom Kosovo bis zum 11. September* (Köln, 2007).

———— *Die Rückkehr der Geschichte. Die Welt nach dem 11. September und die Erneuerung des Westens* (Köln, 2005).

———— *Regieren geht über Studieren. Ein politisches Tagebuch* (Frankfurt am Main, 1987).

BIBLIOGRAPHY

—— "Vortoß in 'primitivere' Zeiten—Befreiung und Militanz," in: *Autonomie. Materialien gegen die Fabrikgesellschaft*, Nr. 5, 2/77.

—— "Die Katastrophe in Bosnien und die Konsequenzen für unsere Partei Bündnis 90/Die Grünen. Ein Brief an die *Bundestags*fraktion und an die Partei," 30 July, 1995.

Frei, Norbert. *Vergangenheitspolitik* (München, 1997).

Garton Ash, Timothy. *In Europe's Name. Germany and the Divided Continent* (London, 1993).

—— *We the People. The Revolution of '89 witnessed in Warsaw, Budapest, Berlin and Prague* (Cambridge, 1990).

Geis, Matthias/Ulrich, Bernd. *Der Unvollendete. Das Leben des Joschka Fischer* (Berlin, 2002).

Geyer, Matthias/Kurbjuweit, Dirk/Schnibben, Cordt. *Operation Rot-Grün. Geschichte eines politischen Abenteuers* (München/Hamburg, 2005).

Gilcher-Holtey, Ingrid. *1968. Eine Zeitreise* (Frankfurt am Main, 2008).

—— *Die 68er Bewegung. Deutschland, Westeuropa, USA* (München, 2003).

—— *"Die Phantasie an der Macht". Mai 68 in Frankreich* (Frankfurt, 1995).

Gordon, Philip H./Shapiro, Jeremy. *Allies at war. America, Europe and the crisis over Iraq* (New York, 2004).

Grant, Charles. "Germany's foreign policy: What lessons can be learned from the Schröder years?" Centre for European Reform essay, September 2005.

Grass, Günter. *Two States—One Nation? The case against German reunification* (London, 1990).

Graw, Ansgar. *Gerhard Schröder. Der Weg nach oben* (Düsseldorf, 1998).

Die Grünen im Bundestag, *Militärblock West. Die NATO-Broschüre der Grünen* (Bonn, 1988).

Habermas, Jürgen. *Antworten auf Herbert Marcuse* (Frankfurt am Main, 1968).

—— *Die nachholende Revolution* (Frankfurt am Main, 1990).

—— *Die Normalität einer Berliner Republik* (Frankfurt am Main, 1995).

—— *Eine Art Schadensabwicklung* (Frankfurt am Main, 1987).

—— *Philosophisch-politische Profile* (Frankfurt am Main, 1971).

—— *Protestbewegung und Hochschulreform*, (Frankfurt am Main, 1969).

Hachmeister, Lutz. *Schleyer. Eine deutsche Geschichte* (München, 2007).

Halberstam, David. *War in a time of peace. Bush, Clinton and the Generals* (New York, 2002).

Harnisch, Sebastian/Maull, Hanns W. *Germany as a civilian power? The foreign policy of the Berlin Republic* (Manchester, 2001).

Hauser, Dorothea. *Baader und Herold. Beschreibung eines Kampfes* (Berlin, 1997).

BIBLIOGRAPHY

Hellmann, Gunther. "Der 'deutsche Weg'. Eine außenpolitische Gratwanderung," *Internationale Politik*, 9/2002.

Herf, Jeffrey. *Divided Memory. The Nazi Past in the two Germanys* (Cambridge, Mass., 1997).

"Historikerstreit." Die Dokumentation der Kontroverse um die Einzigartigkeit der nationalsozialistischen Judenvernichtung (München, 1987).

Hockenos, Paul. *Joschka Fischer and the Making of the Berlin Republic. An alternative history of post-war Germany* (New York, 2008).

Höhne, Heinz. *The Order of the Death's Head. The Story of Hitler's SS*, (Harmondsworth, 2000).

Holbrooke, Richard. *To End a War* (New York, 1998).

Hombach, Bodo. *Aufbruch. Die Politik der neuen Mitte* (München, 1998). Subsequently published in English as: *The Politics of the New Centre* (Cambridge, 2000).

Horkheimer, Max/Adorno, Theodor W. *Dialektik der Aufklärung. Philosophische Fragmente* (Frankfurt am Main, 1992).

Horlemann, Jürgen/Gäng, Peter. *Vietnam—Genesis eines Konflikts* (Frankfurt am Main, 1966).

Hughes, Michael. *Nationalism and Society. Germany, 1800–1945* (London, 1988).

Humphreys, Andrea. "'Ein atomares Auschwitz': Die Lehren der Geschichte und der Streit um die Nachrüstung," in *Jahrbuch Grünes Gedächtnis 2008* (Berlin, 2007).

Jay, Martin. *Adorno* (London, 1984).

—— *The Dialectical Imagination. A History of the Frankfurt School and the Institute of Social Research, 1923–1950* (London, 1973).

Joetze, Günter. *Der letzte Krieg in Europa? Das Kosovo und die deutsche Politik* (Stuttgart, 2001).

Jürgs, Michael. *Der Fall Axel Springer. Eine deutsche Biographie* (München, 1995).

Kapellen, Michael. *Doppelt leben. Berward Vesper und Gudrun Ensslin. Die Tübinger Jahre* (Tübingen, 2005).

Kelly, Petra. *Mit dem Herzen denken. Texte für eine glaubwürdige Politik.* (München, 1990).

Kelly, Petra (hrsg.). *Lasst uns die Kraniche suchen. Hiroshima—Analysen, Berichte, Gedanken* (München, 1983).

Klein, Hans-Joachim Klein. *Rückkehr in die Menschlichkeit. Appell eines ausgestiegenen Terroristen* (Reinbek, 1979).

Kleinert, Hubert. *Vom Protest zur Regierungspartei. Die Geschichte der Grünen* (Frankfurt am Main, 1992).

Knabe, Hubertus. *Die unterwanderte Republik. Stasi im Westen* (Berlin, 1999).

BIBLIOGRAPHY

——— "Der lange Arm der SED. Einflußnahmen des Ministerium für Staatssicherheit auf politische Protestbewegungen in Westdeutschland," *Aus Politik und Zeitgeschichte*, B38–99/1999.

Koenen, Gerd. *Das rote Jahrzehnt. Undere kleine deutsche Kulturrevolution 1967–1977* (Frankfurt am Main, 2002).

——— *Vesper, Ensslin, Baader. Urszenen des deutschen Terrorismus* (Frankfurt am Main, 2005).

——— "Mythen des 20. Jahrhunderts." In: Doron Rabinovici/Ulrich Speck/Natan Sznaider (hrsg.). *Neuer Antisemitismus? Eine globale Debatte* (Frankfurt am Main, 2004).

Koenen, Gerd/Veiel, Andres. *1968. Bildspur eines Jahres* (Köln, 2008).

Kloke, Martin. *Israel und die deutsche Linke: Zur Geschichte eines schwierigen Verhältnisses* (Frankfurt am Main, 1990).

——— "Antisemitismus in der deutschen Linken. Ein Blick in die Frühzeit der APO", *Tribüne*, March 2006, pp. 123–128.

——— "'Das zionistische Staatsgebilde als Brückenkopf des Imperialismus'. Vor vierzig Jahren wurde die neue deutsche Linke antiisraelisch", *Merkur*, June 2007.

Krahl, Hans-Jürgen. *Konstitution und Klassenkampf. Zur historischen Dialektik von bürgerlicher Emanzipation und proletarischer Revolution* (Frankfurt am Main, 1971).

Krause-Burger, Sibylle. *Joschka Fischer. Der lange March durch die Illusionen* (Stuttgart, 1997).

Kraushaar, Wolfgang. *1968 als Mythos, Chiffre und Zäsur* (Hamburg, 2000).

——— *1968. Das Jahr, das alles verändert hat* (München, 1998).

——— *Die Bombe im jüdischen Gemeindehaus* (Hamburg, 2005).

——— *Fischer in Frankfurt. Karriere eines Außenseiters* (Hamburg, 2001).

——— "Von der Totalitarismustheorie zur Faschmismustheorie—Zu einem Paradigmenwechsel der bundesdeutschen Studentenbewegung," in: Alfons Söllner/Ralf Walkenhaus/Karin Weiland (hrsg.), *Totalitarismus. Eine Ideengeschichte des 20. Jahrhunderts* (Berlin, 1997).

——— "Denkmodelle der 68er-Bewegung", in: *Aus Politik und Zeitgeschichte*, B22–23/2001.

——— "Hannah Arendt und die Studentenbewegung. Anmerkungen zum Briefwechsel zwischen Hans-Jürgen Benedict und Hannah Arendt", *Mittelweg 36*, 1/2008.

——— "Zur Dimension des Nationalen bei Rudi Dutschke" (unpublished paper provided by author).

Kraushaar, Wolfgang (hrsg.). *Frankfurter Schule und Studentenbewegung. Von der Flaschenpost zum Molotowcocktail 1946 bis 1995* (Frankfurt am Main, 1998).

——— *Die RAF und der linke Terrorismus* (Hamburg, 2006).

——— *Rudi Dutschke, Andreas Baader and die RAF* (Hamburg, 2005).

BIBLIOGRAPHY

Kunzelmann, Dieter. *Leisten Sie keinen Widerstand* (Berlin, 1998).

Kurnitzky, Horst/Kuhn, Hansmartin (hrsg.). *Das Ende der Utopie. Herbert Marcuse diskutiert mit Studenten und Professoren West-Berlins an der Freien Universität Berlin über Möglichkeiten einer politischen Opposition in den Metropolen im Zusammenhang mit den Befreiungsbewegungen in den Ländern der dritten Welt* (Berlin, 1967).

Langer, Günter. "Der Berliner 'Blues'. Tupamaros und umherschweifende Haschrebellen zwischen Wahnsinn und Verstand," in: Eckhard Siepmann u.a., *Che Schah Shit. Die sechziger Jahre zwischen Cocktail und Molotov* (West-Berlin, 1988).

Large, David Clay. *Berlin* (New York, 2000).

Lau, Jörg. *Hans Magnus Enzensberger. Ein öffentliches Leben* (Frankfurt, 2001).

Leggewie Claus/ Meier, Horst (hrsg.), *Verbot der NPD oder Mit Rechtsradikalen leben?* (Frankfurt, 2002).

Lönnendonker, Siegward/Rabehl, Bernd/Staadt, Jochen. *Die antiautoritäre Revolte. Der Sozialistische Deutsche Studentenbund nach der Trennung von der SPD. Band 1: 1960–1967* (Wiesbaden, 2002).

Maier, Charles S. *Dissolution. The Crisis of Communism and the end of East Germany* (Princeton, 1997).

————— *The Unmasterable Past. History, Holocaust and German National Identity* (Cambridge, Mass., 1997).

Mahler, Horst. "Ausbruch aus einem Mißverständnis", in: *Kursbuch* 48, 1977.

————— "Flugschrift an die Deutschen, die es noch sein wollen, über die Lage ihres Volkes," November 1998. www.deutsches-kolleg.org

————— "Independence-Day Live", www.deutsches-kolleg.org.

————— "Den Völkern Freiheit. Den Globalisten ihr globales Vietnam", www.deutsches-kolleg.org.

————— "Der Untergang des judäo-amerikanischen Imperiums", www.deutsches-kolleg.org.

Mahler, Horst/Preuss, Ulrich K., *Deserteur Kollektiv. BIG LIFT oder die Freiheit der Deserteure* (Frankfurt, 1969).

Mahler, Horst/Schönhuber, Franz. *Schluß mit deutschem Selbsthass. Plädoyers für ein anderes Deutschland* (Berg am Starnberger See, 2001).

Marcuse, Herbert. *One-Dimensional Man* (Boston, 1964).

————— *Versuch über die Befreiung* (Frankfurt am Main, 1969).

————— "Repressive Toleranz," in: Robert Paul Wolff/Barrington Moore/Herbert Marcuse, *Kritik der reinen Toleranz* (Frankfurt am Main, 1966). Originally published as: *A Critique of Pure Tolerance* (Boston, 1965).

Markovits, Andrei S. "On Anti-Americanism in West Germany," *New German Critique* #34, 1985.

————— "The Minister and the Terrorist," *Foreign Affairs*, November/December 2001.

BIBLIOGRAPHY

Markovits, Andrei S./Gorski, Philip S. *The German Left. Red, Green and Beyond* (Cambridge, 1993).

Marx, Karl, *Early Writings* (Harmondsworth, 1992).

Marx, Karl/Engels, Friedrich. *The Communist Manifesto* (Harmondsworth, 1985).

Maull, Hanns W. "Germany and Japan: The New Civilian Powers," *Foreign Affairs*, Winter 1990/91.

—— "Zivilmacht Bundesrepublik Deutschland. Vierzehn Thesen für eine neue deutsche Außenpolitik," *Europa-Archiv* 47 (1992), pp. 269–278.

—— "Germany and the Use of Force, Still a 'Civilian Power?'" In: *Survival*, Vol. 42, No. 2 (Summer 2000), pp. 56–80.

—— "Germany's foreign policy, post-Kosovo: Still a 'Civilian Power'?" In: Harnisch, Sebastian/Maull, Hanns W. *Germany as a civilian power? The foreign policy of the Berlin Republic* (Manchester, 2001).

—— "Zivilmacht Deutschland". In: Hellmann, Gunther/Schmidt, Siegmar, Wolf, Reinhard (hrsg.), *Handwörterbuch zur deutschen Außenpolitik* (Opladen, 2006).

Maull, Hanns/Harnisch, Sebastian/Grund, Constantin (hsrg.). *Deutschland im Abseits? Rot-grüne Außenpolitik, 1998–2003* (Baden-Baden, 2003).

May, Ernest R. "America's Berlin. Heart of the Cold War", *Foreign Affairs*, July/August 1998.

Meinhof, Ulrike. *Die Würde des Menschen ist antastbar* (Berlin, 1994).

Meschkat, Klaus. "Krieg in den Köpfen. Vietnam und Kosovo," http://www.soz.uni-hanover.de/isoz/veroeff/kmkrieg.htm.

Miermeister, Jürgen. *Rudi Dutschke* (Reinbek, 1986).

—— *Ernst Bloch, Rudi Dutschke* (Hamburg, 1996).

Mitscherlich, Alexander und Margarete. *Die Unfähigkeit zu trauern. Grundlagen kollektiven Verhaltens* (München, 1980).

Müller, Jan-Werner. *Another Country. German Intellectuals, Unification and National Identity* (New Haven/London, 2000).

—— *Constitutional Patriotism* (Princeton, 2007).

—— "1968 as event, milieu and ideology", *Journal of Political Ideologies*, Vol. 7, Nr. 1, February 2002.

—— "The End of Denial. Solidarity, Diversity and Constitutional Patriotism in Germany", *Dissent*, Summer 2006.

Müller, Jan-Werner (ed.). *Memory and Power in Post-War Europe: Studies in the Presence of the Past* (Cambridge, 2002).

Müller-Doohm, Stefan. *Adorno. A Biography* (Cambridge, 2005).

Negt, Oskar. *Achtundsechzig. Politische Intellektuelle und die Macht* (Göttingen, 1995).

Negt, Oskar (hrsg.). *Die Linke antwortet Jürgen Habermas* (Frankfurt am Main, 1968).

357

BIBLIOGRAPHY

Nevermann, Knut (hrsg.). *Der 2. Juni 1967. Studenten zwischen Notstand und Demokratie. Dokumente zu den Ereignissen anlässlich des Schah-Besuches* (Köln, 1967).

Nirumand, Bahman. *Persien. Modell eines Entwicklungslandes oder die Diktatur der Freien Welt*, (Reinbek, 1967).

—— *Mein Leben mit den Deutschen* (Reinbek, 1989).

Niven, Bill. *Facing the Nazi past. United Germany and the legacy of the Third Reich* (London, 2002).

Niven, Bill (ed.), *Germans as victims. Remembering the past in contemporary Germany* (London, 2006).

Novick, Peter. *The Holocaust and Collective Memory* (London, 1999).

Oren, Michael B. *Six Days of War. June 1967 and the Making of the Modern Middle East* (Harmondsworth, 2003).

Philippi, Nina. *Bundeswehr-Auslandeinätze als außen-und sicherheitspolitisches Problem des geeinten Deutschland* (Frankfurt am Main/Berlin/Bern/New York/Paris/Vienna, 1997).

Prantl, Heribert, *Rot-Grün. Eine erste Bilanz* (Hamburg, 1999).

Preuss, Ulrich K. *Das politische Mandat der Studentenschaft. Mit Gutachten von R. Havemann, W. Hofmann, und J. Habermas/A. Wellmer* (Frankfurt am Main, 1969).

Proll, Astrid (ed.). *Baader-Meinhof. Pictures on the Run 67–77* (Zurich/Berlin/New York, 1998).

Proll, Thorwald/Dubbe, Daniel. *Wir kamen vom anderen Stern. Über 1968, Andreas Baader und ein Kaufhaus* (Hamburg, 2003).

Pulzer, Peter. *German Politics, 1945–1995* (Oxford, 1995).

Raspe, Jan-Carl (hrsg.) *Kommune 2. Versuch einer Revolutionierung des bürgerlichen Individuums* (Berlin, 1969).

Rabehl, Bernd. *Am Ende der Utopie. Die politische Geschichte der Freien Universität Berlin* (Berlin, 1988).

—— *Rudi Dutschke. Revolutionär im geteilten Deutschland* (Dresden, 2002).

Reeve, Simon. *One Day in September* (London, 2000).

Reinecke, Stefan. *Otto Schily. Von RAF-Anwalt zum Innenminister* (Hamburg, 2003).

Reisner, Stefan (hrsg.). *Briefe an Rudi D.* (Berlin, 1968).

Revolutionärer Kampf, "Betriebsarbeit bei Opel-Rüsselsheim: Abbau gerwerkschaftlichter Herrschaftsinstrumente durch Massenagitation", in *diskus—Frankfurter Studentenzeitung*, December 1971.

Ruetz, Michael. *Ihr müsst diese Typen nur ins Gesicht sehen. APO Berlin 1966–69* (Frankfurt am Main, 1980).

Salvatore, Gaston/Dutschke, Rudi. "Einleitung zu: Che Guevara"; *Schaffen wir zwei, drei, viele Vietnams* (Berlin, 1967).

BIBLIOGRAPHY

Scharping, Rudolf. *Wir dürfen nicht wegsehen. Der Kosovo-Krieg und Europa* (München, 2001).

Schirrmacher, Frank (hrsg.). *Die Walser-Bubis Debatte. Eine Dokumentation* (Frankfurt am Main, 1999).

Schiller, Margrit. *Es war ein harter Kampf um meine Erinnerung. Ein Lebensbericht aus der RAF* (München, 2001).

Schily, Otto/Ströbele, Hans-Christian. *Plädoyer einer politischen Verteidigung. Reden und Mitschriften aus dem Mahler-Prozeß* (Berlin, 1973).

Schmidt, Christian. *Wir sind die Wahnsinnigen. Joschka Fischer und seiner Frankfurter Gang* (München, 1998).

Schneider, Peter. *Lenz* (Berlin, 1973).

——— *Rebellion und Wahn. Mein '68* (Köln, 2008).

Schrenck-Notzing, Caspar von. *Charakterwäsche. Die Politik der amerikanischen Umerziehung* (München, 1965).

Schröder, Gerhard. *Entscheidungen. Mein Leben in der Politik* (Hamburg, 2006).

Schwarz, Hans-Peter. *Die Zentralmacht Europas. Deutschlands Rückkehr auf die Weltbühne* (Berlin, 1994).

Schwelien, Michael. *Joschka Fischer. Eine Karriere* (Hamburg, 2000).

Siemens, Anne. *Für die RAF war er das System, für mich der Vater. Die andere Geschichte des deutschen Terrorismus* (München, 2007).

Siepmann, Eckhard (hrsg.). *Che Schah Shit: Die Sechziger Jahre zwischen Cocktail und Molotow* (Reinbek, 1988).

Sievers, Rudolf (hrsg.), *1968. Eine Enzyklopädie* (Frankfurt am Main, 2004).

Simms, Brendan. "From the Kohl to the Fischer Doctrine: Germany and the Wars of the Yugoslav Succession, 1991–1999." *German History*, Vol. 21, No. 3, 2003.

Thewelweit, Klaus, *Ghosts. Drei leicht inkorrekte Vorträge* (Frankfurt, 1998).

Thomas, Nick. *Protest Movements in 1960s West Germany. A Social History of Dissent and Democracy* (Oxford/New York, 2003).

Thränhardt, Dietrich. *Geschichte der Bundesrepublik Deutschland* (Frankfurt am Main, 1996).

Vesper, Bernward. *Die Reise. Romanessay. Ausgabe letzter Hand* (Reinbek, 1983).

Vesper, Bernward (hrsg.). *Bedingungen und Organisation des Widerstandes. Der Kongreß in Hanover* (Frankfurt am Main, 1967).

——— *Rudi Dutschke zu Protokoll. Fernsehinteview von Günter Gaus* (Frankfurt am Main, 1968).

Volmer, Ludger. *Die Grünen und die Außenpolitik—ein schwieriges Verhältnis. Eine Ideen-, Programm-und Ereignisgeschichte grüner Außenpolitik* (Münster, 1998).

BIBLIOGRAPHY

Walser, Martin. "Unser Auschwitz", in: Hans Magnus Enzensberger (hrsg.), *Kursbuch 1* (Berlin, 1965).

Walzer, Michael. *Just and Unjust Wars* (New York, 2000).

Wetzel, Dietrich (hrsg.). *Die Verlängerung von Geschichte. Deutsche, Juden und der Palästinakonflikt* (Frankfurt am Main, 1983).

Winkler, Willi. *Die Geschichte der RAF* (Berlin, 2007).

Wolff, Karl-Dietrich (hrsg.), *15 Jahre Almanach aufs Jahr 1968* (Basel/Frankfurt am Main, 1985).

Wolffsohn, Michael. *Ewige Schuld? 40 Jahre deutsche-jüdische-israelische Beziehungen* (München, 1988).

Wright, Lawrence. *The Looming Tower. Al-Qaeda and the Road to 9/11* (New York, 2006).

INDEX

INDEX

INDEX

Gorski, Philip S., 201
Grass, Günter, 48, 55, 79, 177, 198–200, 205, 217, 295
Grashof, Manfred, 100, 121
Greece, 17
Green Action Future (*Grüne Aktion Zukunft*), 162, 178
Greens, 1–5, 161–3, 165, 170–83, 189–90, 194, 196–200, 202, 205–9, 238–44, 246, 253–4, 269–71, 274, 292, 301–2, 306, 309–11
  attitude to Nazi past, 172–3, 183–4
  "fundamentalists", 175–6, 179, 206
  "realists", 175–6, 179, 189–90, 202, 205–6, 238–9
  response to fall of Berlin Wall, 196–200
  "pacifism debate", 238–40
  debate about Kosovo, 253–4
  debate about Afghanistan, 269–71
Gruhl, Herbert, 153, 162, 171, 178
GSG 9, 142
Guardian, The, 253, 290
Guevara, Ernesto "Che", 42, 60, 62, 64, 86, 163
Guillaume, Günter, 125
Gysi, Gregor, 310

Haag, Siegfried, 122, 139
Habermas, Jürgen, 44–6, 58, 79, 82, 138, 185–9, 195–6, 204, 220, 225–6
  and "left-wing fascism", 45–6, 185, 188
  and *Historikerstreit*, 185–6, 189–90
  and "constitutional patriotism", 186–7
  on German reunification, 195–6
Hamburg cell, 273–4
Hartz, Peter, 284, 299–300
Hauser, Dorothea, 66, 128

Hausner, Siegfried
Haußleiter, August, 153–4, 162, 171, 197
Heer, Hannes, 62
Hegel, 25, 27, 82, 138–9
Heidegger, Martin, 57
Heidenreich, Elisabeth, 262
Heinemann, Gustav, 21
Hendrix, Jimi, 97
Henze, Hans Werner, 73
Herder, 151
Herf, Jeffrey, 108, 184
Herold, Horst, 128, 144
Herzog, Roman, 44
Heye, Uwe-Karsten, 286
Himmler, Heinrich, 22
Hiroshima, 173, 190
Historikerstreit (Historians' Debate), 184–5, 189–90, 218, 220, 222, 264
Hitler, Adolf, 2, 13, 15, 21, 33, 65, 81, 101, 112, 116–7, 140, 154, 198, 219, 241, 248, 253, 292, 296, 300, 307
Hogefeld, Birgit, 127
Holbrooke, Richard, 244
Holocaust (*see also* Auschwitz), 4, 11–12, 14–15, 18, 21, 31, 36, 49, 150, 154, 173, 181–6, 199, 216–8, 222, 224, 226, 229–30, 238–9, 249–51, 281, 295–6, 298, 303, 305, 307
  student movement and, 18, 230
  Vietnam and, 31
  Dutschke and, 36, 150, 154, 230
  Israel and, 49
  environmental movement and, 154
  Greens and, 173
  as collective memory, 183–6, 296
  Historikerstreit and, 185
  Schröder and, 216, 250
  Mahler and, 222, 224, 229
Holocaust (television series), 183
Holocaust memorial, 217–8
Homann, Peter, 101, 140

INDEX

INDEX

INDEX

INDEX